MW00585785

HBR
AT
100

HBR AT 100

THE MOST INFLUENTIAL *and* INNOVATIVE ARTICLES *from* HARVARD BUSINESS REVIEW'S FIRST CENTURY

HARVARD BUSINESS REVIEW PRESS
BOSTON, MASSACHUSETTS

Library of Congress Cataloging-in-Publication Data

Title: HBR at 100 : the most influential and innovative articles from
    Harvard Business Review's first century.
Other titles: Harvard business review at 100
Description: Boston, Massachusetts : Harvard Business Review Press, 2022. |
    Includes index.
Identifiers: LCCN 2021053177 (print) | LCCN 2021053178 (ebook) | ISBN
    9781647823412 (paperback) | ISBN 9781647823429 (epub)
Subjects: LCSH: Success in business. | Industrial management.
Classification: LCC HF5386 .H3483 2022 (print) | LCC HF5386 (ebook) | DDC
    650.1—dc23/eng/20220105
LC record available at https://lccn.loc.gov/2021053177
LC ebook record available at https://lccn.loc.gov/2021053178

ISBN: 978-1-64782-341-2
eISBN: 978-1-64782-342-9

CONTENTS

Introduction

by Adi Ignatius, editor in chief of *Harvard Business Review*

When *Harvard Business Review* first rolled off the presses a century ago, it became a welcome showcase of fresh ideas for the relatively new field of business management.

It was a heady time in the United States. The dust of World War I had just begun to settle, and American business was taking off. This was the dawn of the Roaring Twenties, a period of breakneck economic growth and social experimentation (which lasted until the Great Depression abruptly ended the fun, in 1929). Auto manufacturing and other consumer industries were booming, but the processes for effectively guiding these enterprises were only just beginning to emerge.

And so HBR came to be. The magazine, originally a quarterly, was the brainchild of Wallace Brett Donham, the longest-serving dean in Harvard Business School's history. Donham, the son of a traveling dentist, was convinced that a proper "theory of business," based on rigorous research into how companies handle their greatest challenges, could teach executives sound judgment. Without this, he wrote in HBR's inaugural issue, in 1922, business would be "unsystematic, haphazard, and for many men a pathetic gamble."

Many of HBR's earliest articles focused on improving operational efficiency. The most celebrated school of thought up to that moment had been "scientific management," an approach championed by Frederick Winslow Taylor. A mechanical-engineer-turned-consultant, Taylor believed he could quantify and measure virtually any industrial process and optimize it for efficiency and consistency.

But as industries and stakeholder relations became more complex, the business world needed other approaches and ideas. HBR became a critical source of this evolving thinking. Soon the publication was covering a broad array of topics, from how macroeconomic trends were impacting business, to dealing with labor unions, to adjusting to the new rules of finance.

Over time, HBR would move, along with society, to new areas of focus. Topics that once might have seemed "soft"—employee motivation, authentic leadership, work-life balance—began to be recognized as vital aspects of a healthy organization. HBR eventually would launch new platforms and products, disseminating ideas not just in the magazine but also on the web, in videos and podcasts, on social media, and even (starting in 2020) on TikTok. The long print articles that HBR is known for are still among our crown jewels, but we also now aim to generate significant value for our readers via shorter pieces, graphics, data analysis, and more.

HBR has published some of the most influential ideas in the history of modern business, and this collection highlights many of them. We tried to select pieces that have remained relevant over decades, even as the business landscape has evolved and even as other authors have subsequently added their own thinking and research to these concepts. Some of the articles use language that, by today's standards, may seem outdated or even objectionable. We've chosen to preserve the original wording, but we acknowledge that certain passages may seem jarring. This book isn't meant to be a history of HBR, nor a chronology of how it has transformed over time. Rather, it is a showcase of the articles that present some of our best and most enduring ideas over the past century.

There may be recency bias in the articles we've chosen to highlight. Only five of the 30 showcased articles date from HBR's first 60 years, while nine are from 2015 or later. This partly reflects just how much business has changed, meaning that many of those earlier articles were narrow in their focus or offered what turned out to be only ephemeral insight. We publish much more these days on strategy, business models, change management, technology—topics that are broadly relevant to our large audience. (At this writing we serve about 11 million unique visitors to the website each month.) We also infuse what we publish with a consistent commitment to values that we think are eternal and fundamental to long-term success: sustainability, diversity and inclusion, fact-based decision-making. Several of the newer articles in this collection touch on these themes.

The showcased authors and articles are often legendary. From Peter Drucker, widely known as the father of modern management, we present "Managing Oneself," his 1999 challenge to would-be leaders to confront their strengths and weaknesses in order to become better managers. From Michael Porter, the celebrated HBS professor, we offer the 1979 article "How Competitive Forces Shape Strategy," the first look at the author's much-studied *five forces* framework for understanding a company's competitive challenge. From Clay Christensen (writing with Joseph Bower) we have the 1995 piece "Disruptive Technologies: Catching the Wave," the article that introduced Christensen's signature concept, *disruptive innovation*. And from W. Chan Kim and Renée Mauborgne, we include the 2004 article "Blue Ocean Strategy," which coined a term and inspired countless innovators to create new markets.

The more recent articles in the collection tend to focus on topics and challenges that have moved to the forefront of what leaders tell us they need to master. These include articles on gender, race and diversity, technology and artificial intelligence, climate change, the pandemic, and the future of work. As the business world continues to evolve, HBR will adapt with it—a constant guide for tomorrow's leaders who aim for long-term success.

Finally, we include in this collection a piece by Theodore Levitt, a critical figure in HBR's storied history. Levitt, a German-American economist and HBS professor, served as HBR's top editor from 1985 to 1989 and is credited with expanding the publication's mission and approach. His 1960 classic article, "Marketing Myopia," argued (early and effectively) that to succeed, companies need to reorient themselves toward customer needs.

Levitt used to joke that HBR was "a magazine written by people who can't write for people who won't read." It was a charming bit of self-deprecation, but the fact is the articles in this collection are exquisite in the depth of their ideas and rank among the most widely read and admired pieces in the history of business thinking.

I hope you enjoy the articles, and that they continue to inspire.

HBR
AT
100

CHAPTER ONE

Managing Oneself

by Peter F. Drucker

History's great achievers—a Napoléon, a da Vinci, a Mozart—have always managed themselves. That, in large measure, is what makes them great achievers. But they are rare exceptions, so unusual both in their talents and their accomplishments as to be considered outside the boundaries of ordinary human existence. Now, most of us, even those of us with modest endowments, will have to learn to manage ourselves. We will have to learn to develop ourselves. We will have to place ourselves where we can make the greatest contribution. And we will have to stay mentally alert and engaged during a 50-year working life, which means knowing how and when to change the work we do.

What Are My Strengths?

Most people think they know what they are good at. They are usually wrong. More often, people know what they are not good at—and even then more people are wrong than right. And yet, a person can perform only from strength. One cannot build performance on weaknesses, let alone on something one cannot do at all.

Throughout history, people had little need to know their strengths. A person was born into a position and a line of work: The peasant's son would also be a peasant; the artisan's daughter, an artisan's wife; and so on. But now people have choices. We need to know our strengths in order to know where we belong.

The only way to discover your strengths is through feedback analysis. Whenever you make a key decision or take a key action, write down what you expect will happen. Nine or 12 months later, compare the actual results with your expectations. I have been practicing this method for 15 to 20 years now, and every time I do it, I am surprised. The feedback analysis showed me, for instance—and to my great surprise—that I have an intuitive understanding of technical people, whether they are engineers or accountants or market researchers. It also showed me that I don't really resonate with generalists.

Feedback analysis is by no means new. It was invented sometime in the fourteenth century by an otherwise totally obscure German theologian and picked up quite independently, some 150 years later, by John Calvin and Ignatius of Loyola, each of whom incorporated it into the practice of his followers. In fact, the steadfast focus on performance and results that this habit produces explains why the institutions these two men founded, the Calvinist church and the Jesuit order, came to dominate Europe within 30 years.

Practiced consistently, this simple method will show you within a fairly short period of time, maybe two or three years, where your strengths lie—and this is the most important thing to know. The method will show you what you are doing or failing to do that deprives you of the full benefits of your strengths. It will show you where you are not particularly competent. And finally, it will show you where you have no strengths and cannot perform.

Several implications for action follow from feedback analysis. First and foremost, concentrate on your strengths. Put yourself where your strengths can produce results.

Second, work on improving your strengths. Analysis will rapidly show where you need to improve skills or acquire new ones. It will also show the gaps in your knowledge—and those can usually be filled. Mathematicians are born, but everyone can learn trigonometry.

Third, discover where your intellectual arrogance is causing disabling ignorance and overcome it. Far too many people—especially people with great expertise in one area—are contemptuous of knowledge in other areas or believe that being bright is a substitute for knowledge. First-rate engineers, for instance, tend to take pride in not knowing anything about people. Human beings, they believe, are much too disorderly for the good engineering mind. Human resources professionals, by contrast, often pride themselves on their ignorance of elementary accounting or of quantitative methods altogether. But taking pride in such ignorance is self-defeating. Go to work on acquiring the skills and knowledge you need to fully realize your strengths.

It is equally essential to remedy your bad habits—the things you do or fail to do that inhibit your effectiveness and performance. Such habits will quickly show up in the feedback. For example, a planner may find that his beautiful plans fail because he does not follow through on them. Like so many brilliant people, he believes that ideas move mountains. But bulldozers move mountains; ideas show where the bulldozers should go to work. This planner will have to learn that the work does not stop when the plan is completed. He must find people to carry out the plan and explain it to them. He must adapt and change it as he puts it into action. And finally, he must decide when to stop pushing the plan.

At the same time, feedback will also reveal when the problem is a lack of manners. Manners are the lubricating oil of an organization. It is a law of nature that two moving bodies in contact with each other create friction. This is as true for human beings as it is for inanimate objects. Manners—simple things like saying "please" and "thank you" and knowing a person's name or asking after her family—enable two people to work together whether they like each other or not. Bright people, especially bright young people, often do not understand this. If analysis shows that someone's brilliant work fails again and again as soon as cooperation from others is required, it probably indicates a lack of courtesy—that is, a lack of manners.

Comparing your expectations with your results also indicates what not to do. We all have a vast number of areas in which we have no talent or skill and little chance of becoming even mediocre. In those areas a person—and especially a knowledge worker—should not take on work, jobs, and assignments. One should waste as little effort as possible on improving areas of low competence. It takes far more energy and work to improve from incompetence to mediocrity than it takes to improve from first-rate performance to excellence. And yet most people—especially most teachers and most organizations—concentrate on making incompetent performers into mediocre ones. Energy, resources, and time should go instead to making a competent person into a star performer.

How Do I Perform?

Amazingly few people know how they get things done. Indeed, most of us do not even know that different people work and perform differently. Too many people work in ways that are not their ways, and that almost guarantees nonperformance. For knowledge workers, How do I perform? may be an even more important question than What are my strengths?

Like one's strengths, how one performs is unique. It is a matter of personality. Whether personality be a matter of nature or nurture, it surely is formed long before a person goes to work. And how a person performs is a given, just as *what* a person is good at or not good at is a given. A person's way of performing can be slightly modified, but it is unlikely to be completely changed—and certainly not easily. Just as people achieve results by doing what they are good at, they also achieve results by working in ways that they best perform. A few common personality traits usually determine how a person performs.

Am I a reader or a listener?

The first thing to know is whether you are a reader or a listener. Far too few people even know that there are readers and listeners and that people are rarely both. Even fewer know which of the two they themselves are. But some examples will show how damaging such ignorance can be.

When Dwight Eisenhower was Supreme Commander of the Allied forces in Europe, he was the darling of the press. His press conferences were famous for their style—General Eisenhower showed total command of whatever question he was asked, and he was able to describe a situation and explain a policy in two or three beautifully polished and elegant sentences. Ten years later, the same journalists who had been his admirers held President Eisenhower in open contempt. He never addressed the questions, they complained, but rambled on endlessly about something else. And they constantly ridiculed him for butchering the King's English in incoherent and ungrammatical answers.

Eisenhower apparently did not know that he was a reader, not a listener. When he was Supreme Commander in Europe, his aides made sure that every question from the press was presented in writing at least half an hour before a conference was to begin. And then Eisenhower was in total command. When he became president, he succeeded two listeners, Franklin D. Roosevelt and Harry Truman. Both men knew themselves to be listeners and both enjoyed free-for-all press conferences. Eisenhower may have felt that he had to do what his two predecessors had done. As a result, he never even heard the questions journalists asked. And Eisenhower is not even an extreme case of a nonlistener.

A few years later, Lyndon Johnson destroyed his presidency, in large measure, by not knowing that he was a listener. His predecessor, John Kennedy, was a reader who had assembled a brilliant group of writers as his assistants, making sure that they wrote to him before discussing their memos in person. Johnson kept these people on his staff—and they kept on writing. He never, apparently, understood one word of what they wrote. Yet as a senator, Johnson had been superb; for parliamentarians have to be, above all, listeners.

Few listeners can be made, or can make themselves, into competent readers—and vice versa. The listener who tries to be a reader will, therefore, suffer the fate of Lyndon Johnson, whereas the reader who tries to be a listener will suffer the fate of Dwight Eisenhower. They will not perform or achieve.

How do I learn?

The second thing to know about how one performs is to know how one learns. Many first-class writers—Winston Churchill is but one example—do poorly in school. They tend to remember their schooling as pure torture. Yet few of their classmates remember it the same way. They may not have enjoyed the school very much, but the worst they suffered was boredom. The explanation is that writers do not, as a rule, learn by listening and reading. They learn by writing. Because schools do not allow them to learn this way, they get poor grades.

Schools everywhere are organized on the assumption that there is only one right way to learn and that it is the same way for everybody. But to be forced to learn the way a school teaches is sheer hell for students who learn differently. Indeed, there are probably half a dozen different ways to learn.

There are people, like Churchill, who learn by writing. Some people learn by taking copious notes. Beethoven, for example, left behind an enormous number of sketchbooks, yet he said he never actually looked at them when he composed. Asked why he kept them, he is reported to have replied, "If I don't write it down immediately, I forget it right away. If I put it into a sketchbook, I never forget it and I never have to look it up again." Some people learn by doing. Others learn by hearing themselves talk.

A chief executive I know who converted a small and mediocre family business into the leading company in its industry was one of those people who learn by talking. He was in the habit of calling his entire senior staff into his office once a week and then talking at them for two or three hours. He would raise policy issues and argue three different positions on each one. He rarely asked his associates for comments or questions; he simply needed an audience to hear himself talk. That's how he learned. And although he is a fairly extreme case, learning through talking is by no means an unusual method. Successful trial lawyers learn the same way, as do many medical diagnosticians (and so do I).

Of all the important pieces of self-knowledge, understanding how you learn is the easiest to acquire. When I ask people, "How do you learn?" most of them know the answer. But when I ask, "Do you act on this knowledge?" few answer yes. And yet, acting on this knowledge is the key to performance; or rather, *not* acting on this knowledge condemns one to nonperformance.

Am I a reader or a listener? and How do I learn? are the first questions to ask. But they are by no means the only ones. To manage yourself effectively, you also have to ask, Do I work well with people, or am I a loner? And if you do work well with people, you then must ask, In what relationship?

Some people work best as subordinates. General George Patton, the great American military hero of World War II, is a prime example. Patton was America's top troop commander. Yet when he was proposed for an independent command, General George Marshall, the U.S. chief of staff—and probably the most successful picker of men in U.S. history—said, "Patton is the best subordinate the American army has ever produced, but he would be the worst commander."

Some people work best as team members. Others work best alone. Some are exceptionally talented as coaches and mentors; others are simply incompetent as mentors.

Another crucial question is, Do I produce results as a decision maker or as an adviser? A great many people perform best as advisers but cannot take the burden and pressure of making the decision. A good many other people, by contrast, need an adviser to force themselves to think; then they can make decisions and act on them with speed, self-confidence, and courage.

This is a reason, by the way, that the number two person in an organization often fails when promoted to the number one position. The top spot requires a decision maker. Strong decision makers often put somebody they trust into the number two spot as their adviser—and in that position the person is outstanding. But in the number one spot, the same person fails. He or she knows what the decision should be but cannot accept the responsibility of actually making it.

Other important questions to ask include, Do I perform well under stress, or do I need a highly structured and predictable environment? Do I work best in a big organization or a small one? Few people work well in all kinds of environments. Again and again, I have seen people who were very successful in large organizations flounder miserably when they moved into smaller ones. And the reverse is equally true.

The conclusion bears repeating: Do not try to change yourself—you are unlikely to succeed. But work hard to improve the way you perform. And try not to take on work you cannot perform or will only perform poorly.

What Are My Values?

To be able to manage yourself, you finally have to ask, What are my values? This is not a question of ethics. With respect to ethics, the rules are the same for everybody, and the test is a simple one. I call it the "mirror test."

In the early years of this century, the most highly respected diplomat of all the great powers was the German ambassador in London. He was clearly destined for great things—to become his country's foreign minister, at least, if not its federal chancellor. Yet in 1906 he abruptly resigned rather than preside over a dinner given by the diplomatic corps for Edward VII. The king was a notorious womanizer and made it clear what kind of dinner he wanted. The ambassador is reported to have said, "I refuse to see a pimp in the mirror in the morning when I shave."

That is the mirror test. Ethics requires that you ask yourself, What kind of person do I want to see in the mirror in the morning? What is ethical behavior in one kind of organization or situation is ethical behavior in another. But ethics is only part of a value system—especially of an organization's value system.

To work in an organization whose value system is unacceptable or incompatible with one's own condemns a person both to frustration and to nonperformance.

Consider the experience of a highly successful human resources executive whose company was acquired by a bigger organization.

After the acquisition, she was promoted to do the kind of work she did best, which included selecting people for important positions. The executive deeply believed that a company should hire people for such positions from the outside only after exhausting all the inside possibilities. But her new company believed in first looking outside "to bring in fresh blood." There is something to be said for both approaches—in my experience, the proper one is to do some of both. They are, however, fundamentally incompatible—not as policies but as values. They bespeak different views of the relationship between organizations and people; different views of the responsibility of an organization to its people and their development; and different views of a person's most important contribution to an enterprise. After several years of frustration, the executive quit—at considerable financial loss. Her values and the values of the organization simply were not compatible.

Similarly, whether a pharmaceutical company tries to obtain results by making constant, small improvements or by achieving occasional, highly expensive, and risky "breakthroughs" is not primarily an economic question. The results of either strategy may be pretty much the same. At bottom, there is a conflict between a value system that sees the company's contribution in terms of helping physicians do better what they already do and a value system that is oriented toward making scientific discoveries.

Whether a business should be run for short-term results or with a focus on the long term is likewise a question of values. Financial analysts believe that businesses can be run for both simultaneously. Successful businesspeople know better. To be sure, every company has to produce short-term results. But in any conflict between short-term results and long-term growth, each company will determine its own priority. This is not primarily a disagreement about economics. It is fundamentally a value conflict regarding the function of a business and the responsibility of management.

Value conflicts are not limited to business organizations. One of the fastest-growing pastoral churches in the United States measures success by the number of new parishioners. Its leadership believes that what matters is how many newcomers join the congregation.

The Good Lord will then minister to their spiritual needs or at least to the needs of a sufficient percentage. Another pastoral, evangelical church believes that what matters is people's spiritual growth. The church eases out newcomers who join but do not enter into its spiritual life.

Again, this is not a matter of numbers. At first glance, it appears that the second church grows more slowly. But it retains a far larger proportion of newcomers than the first one does. Its growth, in other words, is more solid. This is also not a theological problem, or only secondarily so. It is a problem about values. In a public debate, one pastor argued, "Unless you first come to church, you will never find the gate to the Kingdom of Heaven."

"No," answered the other. "Until you first look for the gate to the Kingdom of Heaven, you don't belong in church."

Organizations, like people, have values. To be effective in an organization, a person's values must be compatible with the organization's values. They do not need to be the same, but they must be close enough to coexist. Otherwise, the person will not only be frustrated but also will not produce results.

A person's strengths and the way that person performs rarely conflict; the two are complementary. But there is sometimes a conflict between a person's values and his or her strengths. What one does well—even very well and successfully—may not fit with one's value system. In that case, the work may not appear to be worth devoting one's life to (or even a substantial portion thereof).

If I may, allow me to interject a personal note. Many years ago, I too had to decide between my values and what I was doing successfully. I was doing very well as a young investment banker in London in the mid-1930s, and the work clearly fit my strengths. Yet I did not see myself making a contribution as an asset manager. People, I realized, were what I valued, and I saw no point in being the richest man in the cemetery. I had no money and no other job prospects. Despite the continuing Depression, I quit—and it was the right thing to do. Values, in other words, are and should be the ultimate test.

Where Do I Belong?

A small number of people know very early where they belong. Mathematicians, musicians, and cooks, for instance, are usually mathematicians, musicians, and cooks by the time they are four or five years old. Physicians usually decide on their careers in their teens, if not earlier. But most people, especially highly gifted people, do not really know where they belong until they are well past their mid-twenties. By that time, however, they should know the answers to the three questions: What are my strengths? How do I perform? and What are my values? And then they can and should decide where they belong.

Or rather, they should be able to decide where they do *not* belong. The person who has learned that he or she does not perform well in a big organization should have learned to say no to a position in one. The person who has learned that he or she is not a decision maker should have learned to say no to a decision-making assignment. A General Patton (who probably never learned this himself) should have learned to say no to an independent command.

Equally important, knowing the answer to these questions enables a person to say to an opportunity, an offer, or an assignment, "Yes, I will do that. But this is the way I should be doing it. This is the way it should be structured. This is the way the relationships should be. These are the kind of results you should expect from me, and in this time frame, because this is who I am."

Successful careers are not planned. They develop when people are prepared for opportunities because they know their strengths, their method of work, and their values. Knowing where one belongs can transform an ordinary person—hardworking and competent but otherwise mediocre—into an outstanding performer.

What Should I Contribute?

Throughout history, the great majority of people never had to ask the question, What should I contribute? They were told what to contribute, and their tasks were dictated either by the work itself—as it was for the peasant or artisan—or by a master or a mistress—as it was for domestic servants. And until very recently, it was taken for granted that most people were subordinates who did as they were told. Even in the 1950s and 1960s, the new knowledge workers (the so-called organization men) looked to their company's personnel department to plan their careers.

Then in the late 1960s, no one wanted to be told what to do any longer. Young men and women began to ask, What do I want to do? And what they heard was that the way to contribute was to "do your own thing." But this solution was as wrong as the organization men's had been. Very few of the people who believed that doing one's own thing would lead to contribution, self-fulfillment, and success achieved any of the three.

But still, there is no return to the old answer of doing what you are told or assigned to do. Knowledge workers in particular have to learn to ask a question that has not been asked before: What *should* my contribution be? To answer it, they must address three distinct elements: What does the situation require? Given my strengths, my way of performing, and my values, how can I make the greatest contribution to what needs to be done? And finally, What results have to be achieved to make a difference?

Consider the experience of a newly appointed hospital administrator. The hospital was big and prestigious, but it had been coasting on its reputation for 30 years. The new administrator decided that his contribution should be to establish a standard of excellence in one important area within two years. He chose to focus on the emergency room, which was big, visible, and sloppy. He decided that every patient who came into the ER had to be seen by a qualified nurse within 60 seconds. Within 12 months, the hospital's emergency room had become a model for all hospitals in the United States, and within another two years, the whole hospital had been transformed.

As this example suggests, it is rarely possible—or even particularly fruitful—to look too far ahead. A plan can usually cover no more than 18 months and still be reasonably clear and specific. So the question in most cases should be, Where and how can I achieve results that will make a difference within the next year and a half? The answer must balance several things. First, the results should be hard to achieve—they should require "stretching," to use the current buzzword. But also, they should be within reach. To aim at results that cannot be achieved—or that can be only under the most unlikely circumstances—is not being ambitious; it is being foolish. Second, the results should be meaningful. They should make a difference. Finally, results should be visible and, if at all possible, measurable. From this will come a course of action: what to do, where and how to start, and what goals and deadlines to set.

Responsibility for Relationships

Very few people work by themselves and achieve results by themselves—a few great artists, a few great scientists, a few great athletes. Most people work with others and are effective with other people. That is true whether they are members of an organization or independently employed. Managing yourself requires taking responsibility for relationships. This has two parts.

The first is to accept the fact that other people are as much individuals as you yourself are. They perversely insist on behaving like human beings. This means that they too have their strengths; they too have their ways of getting things done; they too have their values. To be effective, therefore, you have to know the strengths, the performance modes, and the values of your coworkers.

That sounds obvious, but few people pay attention to it. Typical is the person who was trained to write reports in his or her first assignment because that boss was a reader. Even if the next boss is a listener, the person goes on writing reports that, invariably, produce no results. Invariably the boss will think the employee is stupid, incompetent, and lazy, and he or she will fail. But that could have been avoided if the employee had only looked at the new boss and analyzed how *this* boss performs.

Bosses are neither a title on the organization chart nor a "function." They are individuals and are entitled to do their work in the way they do it best. It is incumbent on the people who work with them to observe them, to find out how they work, and to adapt themselves to what makes their bosses most effective. This, in fact, is the secret of "managing" the boss.

The same holds true for all your coworkers. Each works his or her way, not your way. And each is entitled to work in his or her way. What matters is whether they perform and what their values are. As for how they perform—each is likely to do it differently. The first secret of effectiveness is to understand the people you work with and depend on so that you can make use of their strengths, their ways of working, and their values. Working relationships are as much based on the people as they are on the work.

The second part of relationship responsibility is taking responsibility for communication. Whenever I, or any other consultant, start to work with an organization, the first thing I hear about are all the personality conflicts. Most of these arise from the fact that people do not know what other people are doing and how they do their work, or what contribution the other people are concentrating on and what results they expect. And the reason they do not know is that they have not asked and therefore have not been told.

This failure to ask reflects human stupidity less than it reflects human history. Until recently, it was unnecessary to tell any of these things to anybody. In the medieval city, everyone in a district plied the same trade. In the countryside, everyone in a valley planted the same crop as soon as the frost was out of the ground. Even those few people who did things that were not "common" worked alone, so they did not have to tell anyone what they were doing.

Today the great majority of people work with others who have different tasks and responsibilities. The marketing vice president may have come out of sales and know everything about sales, but she knows nothing about the things she has never done—pricing, advertising, packaging, and the like. So the people who do these things must make sure that the marketing vice president understands what they are trying to do, why they are trying to do it, how they are going to do it, and what results to expect.

If the marketing vice president does not understand what these high-grade knowledge specialists are doing, it is primarily their fault, not hers. They have not educated her. Conversely, it is the marketing vice president's responsibility to make sure that all of her coworkers understand how she looks at marketing: what her goals are, how she works, and what she expects of herself and of each one of them.

Even people who understand the importance of taking responsibility for relationships often do not communicate sufficiently with their associates. They are afraid of being thought presumptuous or inquisitive or stupid. They are wrong. Whenever someone goes to his or her associates and says, "This is what I am good at. This is how I work. These are my values. This is the contribution I plan to concentrate on and the results I should be expected to deliver," the response is always, "This is most helpful. But why didn't you tell me earlier?"

And one gets the same reaction—without exception, in my experience—if one continues by asking, "And what do I need to know about your strengths, how you perform, your values, and your proposed contribution?" In fact, knowledge workers should request this of everyone with whom they work, whether as subordinate, superior, colleague, or team member. And again, whenever this is done, the reaction is always, "Thanks for asking me. But why didn't you ask me earlier?"

Organizations are no longer built on force but on trust. The existence of trust between people does not necessarily mean that they like one another. It means that they understand one another. Taking responsibility for relationships is therefore an absolute necessity. It is a duty. Whether one is a member of the organization, a consultant to it, a supplier, or a distributor, one owes that responsibility to all one's coworkers: those whose work one depends on as well as those who depend on one's own work.

The Second Half of Your Life

When work for most people meant manual labor, there was no need to worry about the second half of your life. You simply kept on doing what you had always done. And if you were lucky enough to survive

40 years of hard work in the mill or on the railroad, you were quite happy to spend the rest of your life doing nothing. Today, however, most work is knowledge work, and knowledge workers are not "finished" after 40 years on the job—they are merely bored.

We hear a great deal of talk about the midlife crisis of the executive. It is mostly boredom. At 45, most executives have reached the peak of their business careers, and they know it. After 20 years of doing very much the same kind of work, they are very good at their jobs. But they are not learning or contributing or deriving challenge and satisfaction from the job. And yet they are still likely to face another 20 if not 25 years of work. That is why managing oneself increasingly leads one to begin a second career.

There are three ways to develop a second career. The first is actually to start one. Often this takes nothing more than moving from one kind of organization to another: the divisional controller in a large corporation, for instance, becomes the controller of a medium-sized hospital. But there are also growing numbers of people who move into different lines of work altogether: the business executive or government official who enters the ministry at 45, for instance; or the midlevel manager who leaves corporate life after 20 years to attend law school and become a small-town attorney.

We will see many more second careers undertaken by people who have achieved modest success in their first jobs. Such people have substantial skills, and they know how to work. They need a community—the house is empty with the children gone—and they need income as well. But above all, they need challenge.

The second way to prepare for the second half of your life is to develop a parallel career. Many people who are very successful in their first careers stay in the work they have been doing, either on a full-time or part-time or consulting basis. But in addition, they create a parallel job, usually in a nonprofit organization, that takes another ten hours of work a week. They might take over the administration of their church, for instance, or the presidency of the local Girl Scouts council. They might run the battered women's shelter, work as a children's librarian for the local public library, sit on the school board, and so on.

Finally, there are the social entrepreneurs. These are usually people who have been very successful in their first careers. They love their work, but it no longer challenges them. In many cases they keep on doing what they have been doing all along but spend less and less of their time on it. They also start another activity, usually a nonprofit. My friend Bob Buford, for example, built a very successful television company that he still runs. But he has also founded and built a successful nonprofit organization that works with Protestant churches, and he is building another to teach social entrepreneurs how to manage their own nonprofit ventures while still running their original businesses.

People who manage the second half of their lives may always be a minority. The majority may "retire on the job" and count the years until their actual retirement. But it is this minority, the men and women who see a long working-life expectancy as an opportunity both for themselves and for society, who will become leaders and models.

There is one prerequisite for managing the second half of your life: You must begin long before you enter it. When it first became clear 30 years ago that working-life expectancies were lengthening very fast, many observers (including myself) believed that retired people would increasingly become volunteers for nonprofit institutions. That has not happened. If one does not begin to volunteer before one is 40 or so, one will not volunteer once past 60.

Similarly, all the social entrepreneurs I know began to work in their chosen second enterprise long before they reached their peak in their original business. Consider the example of a successful lawyer, the legal counsel to a large corporation, who has started a venture to establish model schools in his state. He began to do volunteer legal work for the schools when he was around 35. He was elected to the school board at age 40. At age 50, when he had amassed a fortune, he started his own enterprise to build and to run model schools. He is, however, still working nearly full-time as the lead counsel in the company he helped found as a young lawyer.

There is another reason to develop a second major interest, and to develop it early. No one can expect to live very long without experiencing a serious setback in his or her life or work. There is the competent engineer who is passed over for promotion at age 45. There is the competent college professor who realizes at age 42 that she will never get a professorship at a big university, even though she may be fully qualified for it. There are tragedies in one's family life: the breakup of one's marriage or the loss of a child. At such times, a second major interest—not just a hobby—may make all the difference. The engineer, for example, now knows that he has not been very successful in his job. But in his outside activity—as church treasurer, for example—he is a success. One's family may break up, but in that outside activity there is still a community.

In a society in which success has become so terribly important, having options will become increasingly vital. Historically, there was no such thing as "success." The overwhelming majority of people did not expect anything but to stay in their "proper station," as an old English prayer has it. The only mobility was downward mobility.

In a knowledge society, however, we expect everyone to be a success. This is clearly an impossibility. For a great many people, there is at best an absence of failure. Wherever there is success, there has to be failure. And then it is vitally important for the individual, and equally for the individual's family, to have an area in which he or she can contribute, make a difference, and be *somebody*. That means finding a second area—whether in a second career, a parallel career, or a social venture—that offers an opportunity for being a leader, for being respected, for being a success.

The challenges of managing oneself may seem obvious, if not elementary. And the answers may seem self-evident to the point of appearing naive. But managing oneself requires new and unprecedented things from the individual, and especially from the knowledge worker. In effect, managing oneself demands that each knowledge worker think and behave like a chief executive officer. Further, the shift from manual workers who do as they are told to knowledge workers who have to manage themselves profoundly challenges social structure. Every existing society, even the most individualistic one, takes two things for granted, if only subconsciously: that organizations outlive workers, and that most people stay put.

But today the opposite is true. Knowledge workers outlive organizations, and they are mobile. The need to manage oneself is therefore creating a revolution in human affairs.

Reprinted from *Harvard Business Review*,
January 2005 (product #R0501K). Originally published March–April 1999.

CHAPTER TWO

What Makes a Leader?

by Daniel Goleman

Every businessperson knows a story about a highly intelligent, highly skilled executive who was promoted into a leadership position only to fail at the job. And they also know a story about someone with solid—but not extraordinary—intellectual abilities and technical skills who was promoted into a similar position and then soared.

Such anecdotes support the widespread belief that identifying individuals with the "right stuff" to be leaders is more art than science. After all, the personal styles of superb leaders vary: Some leaders are subdued and analytical; others shout their manifestos from the mountaintops. And just as important, different situations call for different types of leadership. Most mergers need a sensitive negotiator at the helm, whereas many turnarounds require a more forceful authority.

I have found, however, that the most effective leaders are alike in one crucial way: They all have a high degree of what has come to be known as *emotional intelligence.* It's not that IQ and technical skills are irrelevant. They do matter, but mainly as "threshold capabilities"; that is, they are the entry-level requirements for executive positions. But my research, along with other recent studies, clearly shows that emotional intelligence is the sine qua non of leadership. Without it, a person can have the best training in the world, an incisive, analytical mind, and an endless supply of smart ideas, but he still won't make a great leader.

The five components of emotional intelligence at work

	Definition	Hallmarks
Self-awareness	The ability to recognize and understand your moods, emotions, and drives, as well as their effect on others	Self-confidence Realistic self-assessment Self-deprecating sense of humor
Self-regulation	The ability to control or redirect disruptive impulses and moods The propensity to suspend judgment—to think before acting	Trustworthiness and integrity Comfort with ambiguity Openness to change
Motivation	A passion to work for reasons that go beyond money or status A propensity to pursue goals with energy and persistence	Strong drive to achieve Optimism, even in the face of failure Organizational commitment
Empathy	The ability to understand the emotional makeup of other people Skill in treating people according to their emotional reactions	Expertise in building and retaining talent Cross-cultural sensitivity Service to clients and customers
Social skill	Proficiency in managing relationships and building networks An ability to find common ground and build rapport	Effectiveness in leading change Persuasiveness Expertise in building and leading teams

In the course of the past year, my colleagues and I have focused on how emotional intelligence operates at work. We have examined the relationship between emotional intelligence and effective performance, especially in leaders. And we have observed how emotional intelligence shows itself on the job. How can you tell if someone has high emotional intelligence, for example, and how can you recognize it in yourself? In the following pages, we'll explore these questions, taking each of the components of emotional intelligence—self-awareness, self-regulation, motivation, empathy, and social skill—in turn.

Evaluating Emotional Intelligence

Most large companies today have employed trained psychologists to develop what are known as "competency models" to aid them in identifying, training, and promoting likely stars in the leadership firmament. The psychologists have also developed such models for lower-level positions. And in recent years, I have analyzed competency models from 188 companies, most of which were large and global and included the likes of Lucent Technologies, British Airways, and Credit Suisse.

In carrying out this work, my objective was to determine which personal capabilities drove outstanding performance within these organizations, and to what degree they did so. I grouped capabilities into three categories: purely technical skills like accounting and business planning; cognitive abilities like analytical reasoning; and competencies demonstrating emotional intelligence, such as the ability to work with others and effectiveness in leading change.

To create some of the competency models, psychologists asked senior managers at the companies to identify the capabilities that typified the organization's most outstanding leaders. To create other models, the psychologists used objective criteria, such as a division's profitability, to differentiate the star performers at senior levels within their organizations from the average ones. Those individuals were then extensively interviewed and tested, and their capabilities were compared. This process resulted in the creation of lists of ingredients for highly effective leaders. The lists ranged in length from seven to 15 items and included such ingredients as initiative and strategic vision.

When I analyzed all this data, I found dramatic results. To be sure, intellect was a driver of outstanding performance. Cognitive skills such as big-picture thinking and long-term vision were particularly important. But when I calculated the ratio of technical skills, IQ, and emotional intelligence as ingredients of excellent performance, emotional intelligence proved to be twice as important as the others for jobs at all levels.

Moreover, my analysis showed that emotional intelligence played an increasingly important role at the highest levels of the company, where differences in technical skills are of negligible importance. In other words, the higher the rank of a person considered to be a star performer, the more emotional intelligence capabilities showed up as the reason for his or her effectiveness. When I compared star performers with average ones in senior leadership positions, nearly 90% of the difference in their profiles was attributable to emotional intelligence factors rather than cognitive abilities.

Other researchers have confirmed that emotional intelligence not only distinguishes outstanding leaders but can also be linked to strong performance. The findings of the late David McClelland, the renowned researcher in human and organizational behavior, are a good example. In a 1996 study of a global food and beverage company, McClelland found that when senior managers had a critical mass of emotional intelligence capabilities, their divisions outperformed yearly earnings goals by 20%. Meanwhile, division leaders without that critical mass underperformed by almost the same amount. McClelland's findings, interestingly, held as true in the company's U.S. divisions as in its divisions in Asia and Europe.

In short, the numbers are beginning to tell us a persuasive story about the link between a company's success and the emotional intelligence of its leaders. And just as important, research is also demonstrating that people can, if they take the right approach, develop their emotional intelligence. (See the sidebar "Can Emotional Intelligence Be Learned?")

Can Emotional Intelligence Be Learned?

For ages, people have debated if leaders are born or made. So too goes the debate about emotional intelligence. Are people born with certain levels of empathy, for example, or do they acquire empathy as a result of life's experiences? The answer is both. Scientific inquiry strongly suggests that there is a genetic component to emotional intelligence. Psychological and developmental research indicates that nurture plays a role as well. How much of each perhaps will never be known, but research and practice clearly demonstrate that emotional intelligence can be learned.

One thing is certain: Emotional intelligence increases with age. There is an old-fashioned word for the phenomenon: maturity. Yet even with maturity, some people still need training to enhance their emotional intelligence. Unfortunately, far too many training programs that intend to build leadership skills—including emotional intelligence—are a waste of time and money. The problem is simple: They focus on the wrong part of the brain.

Emotional intelligence is born largely in the neurotransmitters of the brain's limbic system, which governs feelings, impulses, and drives. Research indicates that the limbic system learns best through motivation, extended practice, and feedback. Compare this with the kind of learning that goes on in the neocortex, which governs analytical and technical ability. The neocortex grasps concepts and logic. It is the part of the brain that figures out how to use a computer or make a sales call by reading a book. Not surprisingly—but mistakenly—it is also the part of the brain targeted by most training programs aimed at enhancing emotional intelligence. When such programs take, in effect, a neocortical approach, my research with the Consortium for Research on Emotional Intelligence in Organizations has shown they can even have a *negative* impact on people's job performance.

To enhance emotional intelligence, organizations must refocus their training to include the limbic system. They must help people break old behavioral habits and establish new ones. That not only takes much more time than conventional training programs, it also requires an individualized approach.

Imagine an executive who is thought to be low on empathy by her colleagues. Part of that deficit shows itself as an inability to listen; she interrupts people and doesn't pay close attention to what they're saying. To fix the problem, the executive needs to be motivated to change, and then she needs practice and feedback from others in the company. A colleague or coach could be tapped to let the executive know when she has been observed failing to listen. She would then have to replay the incident and give a better response; that is, demonstrate her ability to absorb what others are saying. And the executive could be directed to observe certain executives who listen well and to mimic their behavior.

(continued)

Can Emotional Intelligence Be Learned? *(continued)*

With persistence and practice, such a process can lead to lasting results. I know one Wall Street executive who sought to improve his empathy—specifically his ability to read people's reactions and see their perspectives. Before beginning his quest, the executive's subordinates were terrified of working with him. People even went so far as to hide bad news from him. Naturally, he was shocked when finally confronted with these facts. He went home and told his family—but they only confirmed what he had heard at work. When their opinions on any given subject did not mesh with his, they, too, were frightened of him.

Enlisting the help of a coach, the executive went to work to heighten his empathy through practice and feedback. His first step was to take a vacation to a foreign country where he did not speak the language. While there, he monitored his reactions to the unfamiliar and his openness to people who were different from him. When he returned home, humbled by his week abroad, the executive asked his coach to shadow him for parts of the day, several times a week, to critique how he treated people with new or different perspectives. At the same time, he consciously used on-the-job interactions as opportunities to practice "hearing" ideas that differed from his. Finally, the executive had himself video-taped in meetings and asked those who worked for and with him to critique his ability to acknowledge and understand the feelings of others. It took several months, but the executive's emotional intelligence did ultimately rise, and the improvement was reflected in his overall performance on the job.

It's important to emphasize that building one's emotional intelligence cannot—will not—happen without sincere desire and concerted effort. A brief seminar won't help; nor can one buy a how-to manual. It is much harder to learn to empathize—to internalize empathy as a natural response to people—than it is to become adept at regression analysis. But it can be done. "Nothing great was ever achieved without enthusiasm," wrote Ralph Waldo Emerson. If your goal is to become a real leader, these words can serve as a guidepost in your efforts to develop high emotional intelligence.

Self-Awareness

Self-awareness is the first component of emotional intelligence—which makes sense when one considers that the Delphic oracle gave the advice to "know thyself" thousands of years ago. Self-awareness means having a deep understanding of one's emotions, strengths, weaknesses, needs, and drives. People with strong self-awareness are neither overly critical nor unrealistically hopeful. Rather, they are honest—with themselves and with others.

People who have a high degree of self-awareness recognize how their feelings affect them, other people, and their job performance. Thus, a self-aware person who knows that tight deadlines bring out the worst in him plans his time carefully and gets his work done well in advance. Another person with high self-awareness will be able to work with a demanding client. She will understand the client's impact on her moods and the deeper reasons for her frustration. "Their trivial demands take us away from the real work that needs to be done," she might explain. And she will go one step further and turn her anger into something constructive.

Self-awareness extends to a person's understanding of his or her values and goals. Someone who is highly self-aware knows where he is headed and why; so, for example, he will be able to be firm in turning down a job offer that is tempting financially but does not fit with his principles or long-term goals. A person who lacks self-awareness is apt to make decisions that bring on inner turmoil by treading on buried values. "The money looked good, so I signed on," someone might say two years into a job, "but the work means so little to me that I'm constantly bored." The decisions of self-aware people mesh with their values; consequently, they often find work to be energizing.

How can one recognize self-awareness? First and foremost, it shows itself as candor and an ability to assess oneself realistically. People with high self-awareness are able to speak accurately and openly—although not necessarily effusively or confessionally— about their emotions and the impact they have on their work. For instance, one manager I know of was skeptical about a new personal-shopper service that her company, a major department-store chain, was about to introduce. Without prompting from her team or her boss, she offered them an explanation: "It's hard for me to get behind the rollout of this service," she admitted, "because I really wanted to run the project, but I wasn't selected. Bear with me while I deal with that." The manager did indeed examine her feelings; a week later, she was supporting the project fully.

— 2016 —

Three Ways to Better Understand Your Emotions

by Susan David

Dealing effectively with emotions is a key leadership skill. And naming our emotions—what psychologists call *labeling*—is an important first step in dealing with them effectively. But it's harder than it sounds; many of us struggle to identify exactly what we are feeling, and oftentimes the most obvious label isn't actually the most accurate.

For instance, anger and stress are two of the emotions we see most in the workplace—or at least those are the terms we use for them most frequently. Yet these terms are often masks for deeper feelings that we could and should describe in more nuanced and precise ways so that we develop greater levels of *emotional agility*, a critical capability that enables us to interact more successfully with ourselves and the world.

Yes, an employee may be mad, but what if they are also sad? Or anxious? We need a more nuanced vocabulary for emotions, not just for the sake of being more precise but because incorrectly diagnosing our emotions makes us respond incorrectly. If we think we need to attend to anger, we'll take a different approach than if we're handling disappointment or anxiety—or we might not address it at all.

Here are three ways to get a more accurate and precise sense of your emotions:

Broaden Your Emotional Vocabulary

Words matter. If you're experiencing a strong emotion, take a moment to consider what to call it. But don't stop there: Once you've identified it, try to come up with two more words that describe how you are feeling. You might be surprised at the breadth of your emotions—or that you've unearthed a deeper emotion buried beneath the more obvious one.

The table provides a sample vocabulary list of emotion terms; you can find many more by searching Google for any one of these.

It's equally important to do this with "positive" emotions as well as "negative" ones. Being able to say that you are excited about a new job (not just "nervous") or trusting of a colleague (not just "he's nice"), for example, will help you set your intentions for the role or the relationship in a way that is more likely to lead to success down the road.

A list of emotions

Go beyond the obvious to identify exactly what you're feeling.

Angry	Sad	Anxious	Hurt	Embarrassed	Happy
Grumpy	Disappointed	Afraid	Jealous	Isolated	Thankful
Frustrated	Mournful	Stressed	Betrayed	Self-conscious	Trusting
Annoyed	Regretful	Vulnerable	Isolated	Lonely	Comfortable
Defensive	Depressed	Confused	Shocked	Inferior	Content
Spiteful	Paralyzed	Bewildered	Deprived	Guilty	Excited
Impatient	Pessimistic	Skeptical	Victimized	Ashamed	Relaxed
Disgusted	Tearful	Worried	Aggrieved	Repugnant	Relieved
Offended	Dismayed	Cautious	Tormented	Pathetic	Elated
Irritated	Disillusioned	Nervous	Abandoned	Confused	Confident

Consider the Intensity of the Emotion

We're apt to leap to basic descriptors like "angry" or "stressed" even when our feelings are far less extreme. I had a client who was struggling in his marriage; he frequently described his wife as "angry" and often got angry in return. But as the table suggests, every emotion comes in a variety of flavors. When we talked about other words for his wife's emotions, my client saw that there were times when she was perhaps just annoyed or impatient. This insight transformed their relationship because he could suddenly see that she wasn't just angry all the time. This meant he could actually respond to her specific emotion and concern without getting angry himself. Similarly, it matters in your own self-assessment whether you are angry or just grumpy, mournful or just dismayed, elated or just pleased.

As you label your emotions, also rate them on a scale of 1–10. How deeply are you feeling the emotion? How urgent is it, or how strong? Does that make you choose a different set of words?

Write It Out

Experiments by James Pennebaker, a professor at the University of Texas who has done 40 years of research into the links between writing and emotional processing, revealed that people who write about emotionally charged episodes

(continued)

Three Ways to Better Understand
Your Emotions (*continued*)

experience a marked increase in their physical and mental well-being. In a study of recently laid-off workers, he found that those who delved into their feelings of humiliation, anger, anxiety, and relationship difficulties were three times more likely to have been reemployed than those in control groups.[1]

These experiments also revealed that over time those who wrote about their feelings began to develop insights into what those feelings meant (or didn't mean), using phrases such as "I have learned," "It struck me that," "The reason that," "I now realize," and "I understand." The process of writing allowed them to gain a new perspective on their emotions and to understand them and their implications more clearly.

Try this exercise: Set a timer for 20 minutes and write about your emotional experiences from the past week, month, or year. Don't worry about making it perfect or readable: Go where your mind takes you. At the end, you don't have to save the document; the point is that those thoughts are now out of you and on the page. You can do this exercise every day, but it's particularly useful when you're going through a tough time or a big transition, if you're feeling emotional turmoil, or if you've had a difficult experience that you think you haven't quite processed.

Once you understand *what* you are feeling, then you can better address and learn from those more accurately described emotions.

1. Stefanie P. Spera, Eric D. Buhrfeind, and James W. Pennebaker, "Expressive Writing and Coping with Job Loss," *Academy of Management Journal*, November 30, 2017, https://journals.aom.org/doi/abs/10.5465/256708.

Adapted from content on hbr.org, November 10, 2016 (product #H038KF).

Such self-knowledge often shows itself in the hiring process. Ask a candidate to describe a time he got carried away by his feelings and did something he later regretted. Self-aware candidates will be frank in admitting to failure—and will often tell their tales with a smile. One of the hallmarks of self-awareness is a self-deprecating sense of humor.

Self-awareness can also be identified during performance reviews. Self-aware people know—and are comfortable talking about—their limitations and strengths, and they often demonstrate a thirst for constructive criticism. By contrast, people with low self-awareness interpret the message that they need to improve as a threat or a sign of failure.

Self-aware people can also be recognized by their self-confidence. They have a firm grasp of their capabilities and are less likely to set themselves up to fail by, for example, overstretching on assignments. They know, too, when to ask for help. And the risks they take on the job are calculated. They won't ask for a challenge that they know they can't handle alone. They'll play to their strengths.

Consider the actions of a midlevel employee who was invited to sit in on a strategy meeting with her company's top executives. Although she was the most junior person in the room, she did not sit there quietly, listening in awestruck or fearful silence. She knew she had a head for clear logic and the skill to present ideas persuasively, and she offered cogent suggestions about the company's strategy. At the same time, her self-awareness stopped her from wandering into territory where she knew she was weak.

Despite the value of having self-aware people in the workplace, my research indicates that senior executives don't often give self-awareness the credit it deserves when they look for potential leaders. Many executives mistake candor about feelings for "wimpiness" and fail to give due respect to employees who openly acknowledge their shortcomings. Such people are too readily dismissed as "not tough enough" to lead others.

In fact, the opposite is true. In the first place, people generally admire and respect candor. Furthermore, leaders are constantly required to make judgment calls that require a candid assessment of capabilities—their own and those of others. Do we have the management expertise to acquire a competitor? Can we launch a new product within six months? People who assess themselves honestly—that is, self-aware people—are well suited to do the same for the organizations they run.

Self-Regulation

Biological impulses drive our emotions. We cannot do away with them—but we can do much to manage them. Self-regulation, which is like an ongoing inner conversation, is the component of emotional intelligence that frees us from being prisoners of our feelings.

People engaged in such a conversation feel bad moods and emotional impulses just as everyone else does, but they find ways to control them and even to channel them in useful ways.

Imagine an executive who has just watched a team of his employees present a botched analysis to the company's board of directors. In the gloom that follows, the executive might find himself tempted to pound on the table in anger or kick over a chair. He could leap up and scream at the group. Or he might maintain a grim silence, glaring at everyone before stalking off.

But if he had a gift for self-regulation, he would choose a different approach. He would pick his words carefully, acknowledging the team's poor performance without rushing to any hasty judgment. He would then step back to consider the reasons for the failure. Are they personal—a lack of effort? Are there any mitigating factors? What was his role in the debacle? After considering these questions, he would call the team together, lay out the incident's consequences, and offer his feelings about it. He would then present his analysis of the problem and a well-considered solution.

Why does self-regulation matter so much for leaders? First of all, people who are in control of their feelings and impulses—that is, people who are reasonable—are able to create an environment of trust and fairness. In such an environment, politics and infighting are sharply reduced and productivity is high. Talented people flock to the organization and aren't tempted to leave. And self-regulation has a trickle-down effect. No one wants to be known as a hothead when the boss is known for her calm approach. Fewer bad moods at the top mean fewer throughout the organization.

Second, self-regulation is important for competitive reasons. Everyone knows that business today is rife with ambiguity and change. Companies merge and break apart regularly. Technology transforms work at a dizzying pace. People who have mastered their emotions are able to roll with the changes. When a new program is announced, they don't panic; instead, they are able to suspend judgment, seek out information, and listen to the executives as they explain the new program. As the initiative moves forward, these people are able to move with it.

Sometimes they even lead the way. Consider the case of a manager at a large manufacturing company. Like her colleagues, she had used a certain software program for five years. The program drove how she collected and reported data and how she thought about the company's strategy. One day, senior executives announced that a new program was to be installed that would radically change how information was gathered and assessed within the organization. While many people in the company complained bitterly about how disruptive the change would be, the manager mulled over the reasons for the new program and was convinced of its potential to improve performance. She eagerly attended training sessions—some of her colleagues refused to do so—and was eventually promoted to run several divisions, in part because she used the new technology so effectively.

I want to push the importance of self-regulation to leadership even further and make the case that it enhances integrity, which is not only a personal virtue but also an organizational strength. Many of the bad things that happen in companies are a function of impulsive behavior. People rarely plan to exaggerate profits, pad expense accounts, dip into the till, or abuse power for selfish ends. Instead, an opportunity presents itself, and people with low impulse control just say yes.

By contrast, consider the behavior of the senior executive at a large food company. The executive was scrupulously honest in his negotiations with local distributors. He would routinely lay out his cost structure in detail, thereby giving the distributors a realistic understanding of the company's pricing. This approach meant the executive couldn't always drive a hard bargain. Now, on occasion, he felt the urge to increase profits by withholding information about the company's costs. But he challenged that impulse—he saw that it made more sense in the long run to counteract it. His emotional self-regulation paid off in strong, lasting relationships with distributors that benefited the company more than any short-term financial gains would have.

The signs of emotional self-regulation, therefore, are easy to see: a propensity for reflection and thoughtfulness; comfort with ambiguity and change; and integrity—an ability to say no to impulsive urges.

Like self-awareness, self-regulation often does not get its due. People who can master their emotions are sometimes seen as cold fish—their considered responses are taken as a lack of passion. People with fiery temperaments are frequently thought of as "classic" leaders—their outbursts are considered hallmarks of charisma and power. But when such people make it to the top, their impulsiveness often works against them. In my research, extreme displays of negative emotion have never emerged as a driver of good leadership.

Motivation

If there is one trait that virtually all effective leaders have, it is motivation. They are driven to achieve beyond expectations—their own and everyone else's. The key word here is *achieve*. Plenty of people are motivated by external factors, such as a big salary or the status that comes from having an impressive title or being part of a prestigious company. By contrast, those with leadership potential are motivated by a deeply embedded desire to achieve for the sake of achievement.

If you are looking for leaders, how can you identify people who are motivated by the drive to achieve rather than by external rewards? The first sign is a passion for the work itself—such people seek out creative challenges, love to learn, and take great pride in a job well done. They also display an unflagging energy to do things better. People with such energy often seem restless with the status quo. They are persistent with their questions about why things are done one way rather than another; they are eager to explore new approaches to their work.

A cosmetics company manager, for example, was frustrated that he had to wait two weeks to get sales results from people in the field. He finally tracked down an automated phone system that would beep each of his salespeople at 5 p.m. every day. An automated message then prompted them to punch in their numbers—how many calls and sales they had made that day. The system shortened the feedback time on sales results from weeks to hours.

That story illustrates two other common traits of people who are driven to achieve. They are forever raising the performance bar, and they like to keep score. Take the performance bar first. During performance reviews, people with high levels of motivation might ask to be "stretched" by their superiors. Of course, an employee who combines self-awareness with internal motivation will recognize her limits—but she won't settle for objectives that seem too easy to fulfill.

And it follows naturally that people who are driven to do better also want a way of tracking progress—their own, their team's, and their company's. Whereas people with low achievement motivation are often fuzzy about results, those with high achievement motivation often keep score by tracking such hard measures as profitability or market share. I know of a money manager who starts and ends his day on the Internet, gauging the performance of his stock fund against four industry-set benchmarks.

Interestingly, people with high motivation remain optimistic even when the score is against them. In such cases, self-regulation combines with achievement motivation to overcome the frustration and depression that come after a setback or failure. Take the case of another portfolio manager at a large investment company. After several successful years, her fund tumbled for three consecutive quarters, leading three large institutional clients to shift their business elsewhere.

Some executives would have blamed the nosedive on circumstances outside their control; others might have seen the setback as evidence of personal failure. This portfolio manager, however, saw an opportunity to prove she could lead a turnaround. Two years later, when she was promoted to a very senior level in the company, she described the experience as "the best thing that ever happened to me; I learned so much from it."

Executives trying to recognize high levels of achievement motivation in their people can look for one last piece of evidence:

commitment to the organization. When people love their jobs for the work itself, they often feel committed to the organizations that make that work possible. Committed employees are likely to stay with an organization even when they are pursued by headhunters waving money.

It's not difficult to understand how and why a motivation to achieve translates into strong leadership. If you set the performance bar high for yourself, you will do the same for the organization when you are in a position to do so. Likewise, a drive to surpass goals and an interest in keeping score can be contagious. Leaders with these traits can often build a team of managers around them with the same traits. And of course, optimism and organizational commitment are fundamental to leadership—just try to imagine running a company without them.

Empathy

Of all the dimensions of emotional intelligence, empathy is the most easily recognized. We have all felt the empathy of a sensitive teacher or friend; we have all been struck by its absence in an unfeeling coach or boss. But when it comes to business, we rarely hear people praised, let alone rewarded, for their empathy. The very word seems unbusinesslike, out of place amid the tough realities of the marketplace.

But empathy doesn't mean a kind of "I'm OK, you're OK" mushiness. For a leader, that is, it doesn't mean adopting other people's emotions as one's own and trying to please everybody. That would be a nightmare—it would make action impossible. Rather, empathy means thoughtfully considering employees' feelings—along with other factors—in the process of making intelligent decisions.

For an example of empathy in action, consider what happened when two giant brokerage companies merged, creating redundant jobs in all their divisions. One division manager called his people together and gave a gloomy speech that emphasized the number of people who would soon be fired. The manager of another division gave his people a different kind of speech. He was up-front about his own worry and confusion, and he promised to keep people informed and to treat everyone fairly.

The difference between these two managers was empathy. The first manager was too worried about his own fate to consider the feelings of his anxiety-stricken colleagues. The second knew intuitively what his people were feeling, and he acknowledged their fears with his words. Is it any surprise that the first manager saw his division sink as many demoralized people, especially the most talented, departed? By contrast, the second manager continued to be a strong leader, his best people stayed, and his division remained as productive as ever.

Empathy is particularly important today as a component of leadership for at least three reasons: the increasing use of teams; the rapid pace of globalization; and the growing need to retain talent.

Consider the challenge of leading a team. As anyone who has ever been a part of one can attest, teams are cauldrons of bubbling emotions. They are often charged with reaching a consensus—which is hard enough with two people and much more difficult as the numbers increase. Even in groups with as few as four or five members, alliances form and clashing agendas get set. A team's leader must be able to sense and understand the viewpoints of everyone around the table.

That's exactly what a marketing manager at a large information technology company was able to do when she was appointed to lead a troubled team. The group was in turmoil, overloaded by work and missing deadlines. Tensions were high among the members. Tinkering with procedures was not enough to bring the group together and make it an effective part of the company.

So the manager took several steps. In a series of one-on-one sessions, she took the time to listen to everyone in the group—what was frustrating them, how they rated their colleagues, whether they felt they had been ignored. And then she directed the team in a way that brought it together: She encouraged people to speak more openly about their frustrations, and she helped people raise constructive complaints during meetings. In short, her empathy allowed her to understand her team's emotional makeup. The result was not just heightened collaboration among members but also added business, as the team was called on for help by a wider range of internal clients.

Globalization is another reason for the rising importance of empathy for business leaders. Cross-cultural dialogue can easily lead to miscues and misunderstandings. Empathy is an antidote. People who have it are attuned to subtleties in body language; they can hear the message beneath the words being spoken. Beyond that, they have a deep understanding of both the existence and the importance of cultural and ethnic differences.

Consider the case of an American consultant whose team had just pitched a project to a potential Japanese client. In its dealings with Americans, the team was accustomed to being bombarded with questions after such a proposal, but this time it was greeted with a long silence. Other members of the team, taking the silence as disapproval, were ready to pack and leave. The lead consultant gestured them to stop. Although he was not particularly familiar with Japanese culture, he read the client's face and posture and sensed not rejection but interest—even deep consideration. He was right: When the client finally spoke, it was to give the consulting firm the job.

Finally, empathy plays a key role in the retention of talent, particularly in today's information economy. Leaders have always needed empathy to develop and keep good people, but today the stakes are higher. When good people leave, they take the company's knowledge with them.

That's where coaching and mentoring come in. It has repeatedly been shown that coaching and mentoring pay off not just in better performance but also in increased job satisfaction and decreased turnover. But what makes coaching and mentoring work best is the nature of the relationship. Outstanding coaches and mentors get inside the heads of the people they are helping. They sense how to give effective feedback. They know when to push for better performance and when to hold back. In the way they motivate their protégés, they demonstrate empathy in action.

In what is probably sounding like a refrain, let me repeat that empathy doesn't get much respect in business. People wonder how leaders can make hard decisions if they are "feeling" for all the people who will be affected. But leaders with empathy do more than sympathize with people around them: They use their knowledge to improve their companies in subtle but important ways.

Social Skill

The first three components of emotional intelligence are self-management skills. The last two, empathy and social skill, concern a person's ability to manage relationships with others. As a component of emotional intelligence, social skill is not as simple as it sounds. It's not just a matter of friendliness, although people with high levels of social skill are rarely mean-spirited. Social skill, rather, is friendliness with a purpose: moving people in the direction you desire, whether that's agreement on a new marketing strategy or enthusiasm about a new product.

Socially skilled people tend to have a wide circle of acquaintances, and they have a knack for finding common ground with people of all kinds—a knack for building rapport. That doesn't mean they socialize continually; it means they work according to the assumption that nothing important gets done alone. Such people have a network in place when the time for action comes.

Social skill is the culmination of the other dimensions of emotional intelligence. People tend to be very effective at managing relationships when they can understand and control their own emotions and can empathize with the feelings of others. Even motivation contributes to social skill. Remember that people who are driven to achieve tend to be optimistic, even in the face of setbacks or failure. When people are upbeat, their "glow" is cast upon conversations and other social encounters. They are popular, and for good reason.

Because it is the outcome of the other dimensions of emotional intelligence, social skill is recognizable on the job in many ways that will by now sound familiar. Socially skilled people, for instance, are adept at managing teams—that's their empathy at work. Likewise, they are expert persuaders—a manifestation of self-awareness, self-regulation, and empathy combined. Given those skills, good persuaders know when to make an emotional plea, for instance, and when an appeal to reason will work better. And motivation, when publicly visible, makes such people excellent collaborators; their passion for the work spreads to others, and they are driven to find solutions.

But sometimes social skill shows itself in ways the other emotional intelligence components do not. For instance, socially skilled people may at times appear not to be working while at work. They seem to be idly schmoozing—chatting in the hallways with colleagues or joking around with people who are not even connected to their "real" jobs. Socially skilled people, however, don't think it makes sense to arbitrarily limit the scope of their relationships. They build bonds widely because they know that in these fluid times, they may need help someday from people they are just getting to know today.

For example, consider the case of an executive in the strategy department of a global computer manufacturer. By 1993, he was convinced that the company's future lay with the Internet. Over the course of the next year, he found kindred spirits and used his social skill to stitch together a virtual community that cut across levels, divisions, and nations. He then used this de facto team to put up a corporate Web site, among the first by a major company. And, on his own initiative, with no budget or formal status, he signed up the company to participate in an annual Internet industry convention. Calling on his allies and persuading various divisions to donate funds, he recruited more than 50 people from a dozen different units to represent the company at the convention.

Management took notice: Within a year of the conference, the executive's team formed the basis for the company's first Internet division, and he was formally put in charge of it. To get there, the executive had ignored conventional boundaries, forging and maintaining connections with people in every corner of the organization.

Is social skill considered a key leadership capability in most companies? The answer is yes, especially when compared with the other components of emotional intelligence. People seem to know intuitively that leaders need to manage relationships effectively; no leader is an island. After all, the leader's task is to get work done through other people, and social skill makes that possible. A leader who cannot express her empathy may as well not have it at all. And a leader's motivation will be useless if he cannot communicate his passion to the organization. Social skill allows leaders to put their emotional intelligence to work.

It would be foolish to assert that good old-fashioned IQ and technical ability are not important ingredients in strong leadership. But the recipe would not be complete without emotional intelligence. It was once thought that the components of emotional intelligence were "nice to have" in business leaders. But now we know that, for the sake of performance, these are ingredients that leaders "need to have."

It is fortunate, then, that emotional intelligence can be learned. The process is not easy. It takes time and, most of all, commitment. But the benefits that come from having a well-developed emotional intelligence, both for the individual and for the organization, make it worth the effort.

Reprinted from *Harvard Business Review*,
January 2004 (product #R0401H).
Originally published November–December 1998.

—— 2018 ——

CHAPTER THREE

Lead with Authenticity

An interview with Tina Opie by Amy Bernstein,
Sarah Green Carmichael, and Nicole Torres

Authenticity is what it feels like when you can bring your whole self to work—when your behavior matches your intentions. But there's a challenge for women who want to be authentic at work. They are daughters, mothers, sisters, and bosses, and all these different roles can be tough to reconcile. So while authentic leadership is often viewed as geared toward a single norm, women live in a multipolar world. How can they be true to themselves when there are so many competing selves?

Tina Opie is an associate professor at Babson College. She sat down with *Women at Work* cohosts Amy Bernstein, Sarah Green Carmichael, and Nicole Torres to talk about what feels authentic to women at work and what doesn't.

SARAH GREEN CARMICHAEL: *I worked with a woman once whose boss told her, "You have a lot of potential—I can see you moving into management. But if you want to do that, you need to dress differently and you should start wearing makeup." Everyone in this case was a woman, but my peer was furious. Is it sexist to give someone that kind of advice?*

TINA OPIE: We have to differentiate between how we want the world to be and how the world actually is. Would I like that advice to never be heard or uttered? Would I like it if the way you want to go to work was completely fine as long as you're doing an amazing job? That's the kind of world I want to live in, and the kind of world that I've dedicated my research and teaching toward building. But unfortunately, that is not the world in which we live.

We live in a world where impressions matter, and where appearance is highly connected to impressions. The way that humans categorize other people is instantaneous. And because of those types of connections, we automatically think, "*This* kind of person is going to be more professional. *This* kind of person is not going to be." If you happen to fall into the latter category, you may have some additional work to do to demonstrate that you are, in fact, fierce, professional, or amazing. But that may come after that initial impression.

AMY BERNSTEIN: *I graduated from college with a wardrobe that consisted of two pairs of blue jeans and three button-down shirts, so my brilliant and wise mother, who was an advertising executive, took me shopping before I started my first job. She made me buy a straight skirt, nice jacket, and nice blouse. If you had dressed me in a Superman outfit, I could not have felt more uncomfortable and less authentic. Her advice to me was if you want to be the vice president one day, dress like the vice president. It was excellent advice to someone who didn't understand what being authentic in the new context would be. What do you think of that?*

TO: What your mother did was provide you with a uniform. We don't like to think of ourselves as professionals having to wear uniforms. In our minds, we feel above that—we're more professional.

But the business suit is in fact a uniform. I have done some research that talks about the origins of the suit, which is very Eurocentric. It came from royal court and was very masculine. It was actually designed as a way to differentiate the classes from each other and show a certain level of modesty. Initially, while the suits were brilliant colors—reds, purples, etc.—they eventually toned down to what we now have—navies, blacks, grays; very subdued, subtle colors—because that conveyed and communicated a certain level of professionalism and trustworthiness.

Your mother was extending to you the same kind of advice. She was offering to you to wear a uniform and was introducing you, or hoping to socialize you into, a new world. The corporate world and the workforce were new for you. If you had shown up with those jeans and a button-down shirt, you probably would've been flabbergasted and embarrassed when you got there because no one else would've been attired in that way.

Now, I'm wearing jeggings, a nice floral top, and some cute earrings, and my hair is up in a puff right now. One of my goals is to run a corporation where I can be the CEO and be dressed exactly this way. And I dare anybody to come in there and tell me I'm unprofessional. But I also want to have a corporation where if someone is more comfortable in a business suit, they can feel comfortable wearing that.

AB: *Your students come to you for advice all the time. Can you walk us through a conversation when a student has asked for advice about how to dress for a job interview?*

TO: I have a former student who has now graduated named Nadia. I had been running a workshop on authenticity in the workplace at Babson, and she said, "I see that you wear your hair natural; do you think it's OK if I wear my hair natural to the workplace?" I walked her through the decision: "Do you like your natural hair?" "Yes, I feel good about it. It makes me feel good as a Black, Latina woman. That's what I'd like to do." Great, we're establishing the fact that her natural hair is connected to her authenticity and her identity.

Then I said, "Where are you interested in going?" "I want to go into law." "Describe for me the kind of context or environment you think you're going to confront in the legal profession." "They're very conservative and wear tailored suits." And when she said "they," she was describing the men. We quickly went into the women, and it was very similar. I don't think we can escape the fact that initially, women's business attire was very much created to replicate or duplicate men's business attire. Women's uniforms in the workplace were designed to cover up their femininity and their differences.

So the first thing I established with Nadia was what her authentic identity was. Then we established the legal context. Here comes the difficult part. There's not a clear-cut answer. I told her that she has to weigh the consequences. If your hair is authentic to you, and if changing it makes you feel like you're giving up, selling yourself out, or conforming to a point where it just makes you uncomfortable, then perhaps that's not the best decision. But understand that if you walk into this particular context, it may mean that you don't get the job.

The alternative is that you conform and straighten your hair. Because for many people of African descent, when we say "conform" in terms of their hair, we mean cover it—straighten it, get rid of any visible evidence of your African-ness or of your Blackness. You can do that, but if that is going to make you feel bad about yourself, then maybe that's not the best place for you to be.

This is a very privileged comment to make, because if you have to pay your bills, you're going to straighten your hair. You're going to cover up the tattoo and get rid of the piercings. Now, there are some things people might say, like, "We would like her more if she was a little whiter." I can't do anything with my skin color—or if I can, I'm not willing to. The cost of doing that is so high that most people are not willing to do it. But we do have instances of people who are willing to change their names, specifically in the Asian community. I have many students who will say, "Just call me Amy." I want to call them by the name that's on their birth certificate, but for them that is uncomfortable because it calls out their Asian-ness. I want to get to a place where we are all able to bring who we authentically identify and describe ourselves as to the workforce, and our colleagues and classmates embrace that, rather than trying to get us to conform.

NICOLE TORRES: *Aside from appearance, how else do we think about authenticity in the workplace?*

TO: It could be the way that you communicate. I was once told that I was too ethnic because I speak with my hands. But the clients loved me. They said, "You're such a great storyteller." So the way that you communicate, your accent, or the way that you articulate anger, disagreement, and conflict all matter for authenticity. Some people will avoid anger at all costs; others will dive right in. For me, it is authentic to convey anger, but that's considered unprofessional in some settings.

Imagine a setting where you're direct with your supervisor, subordinate, or colleague and say, "Listen, that was my idea in the meeting. We talked about it. Explain to me why you took credit for it."

NT: *I could never imagine saying that.*

TO: But ask yourself why. Some of it is about personality, but in many professional contexts you're going to be considered bad if you advocate for yourself, especially if you do that in front of the group.

SGC: *When we talk about leaders being authentic, a lot of what we talk about is that we want to invite in happy feelings to the work-place. We say we want people to bring their whole selves to work, but we really mean those parts of themselves that are shiny and happy. We don't usually mean anger, especially for women.*

TO: You're absolutely right. Women experience significant backlash when they express anger in the workplace—Tori Brescoll at the Yale School of Management has done some work on that. But then Ash-leigh Shelby Rosette at Duke's Fuqua School of Business, Robert Livingston at the Harvard Kennedy School, and some other folks have done some additional research that shows that this may have to do with intersectionality, because Black women don't receive as much backlash as white women do when expressing anger in the workforce.

I have never understood the visceral negative reaction to anger in the workplace. Now, I'm not talking about someone going up and down the aisles and yelling at people, cursing people out, phys-ical violence, or throwing things around. Anger means displeasure, annoyance. It's a signal that something is awry or unjust. Why is it bad to express that?

Of course, we have to think about the way that we channel that emotion and the way that we communicate those ideas at work. Women in particular have to be mindful of that. Women who can figure out how to use their anger in a productive way may find themselves at an advantage.

Have you all been angry in the workplace? What have you done? Have you gone to your cube or office? Have you called a friend? Gone into the bathroom and cried? I'd be curious to know if you all have seen examples of when anger has been successfully used.

AB: *You just made me think about the instances when I've been angry and when I've cried. There are two kinds of anger as I've experienced them. One is the hurt anger:* I can't believe you just did that to me. That is really difficult for me. *I always question whether or not this is justified and how much of it is my fault. I go through that checklist of reasons not to deal with it, and when I have dealt with it, it's brought change that I needed.*

But there's another kind of anger that I have had more frequently, which is when things aren't done the way I've asked for them to be done. I run a team and an operation; if I believe that my requests have been countermanded, I get angry and I will say so. I'll call people out for it, but I'll do it privately, usually. If it is impeding progress for the organization, that will make me quite angry, and I can be articulate about it. The other one, holy cow, I just go up in flames.

TO: What's interesting is that when it's about you in that way, we give ourselves permission to be mad: *This is about the work, so I have permission to be angry because if I don't say something, the organization suffers.* Here we are as women who want to save the organization. So we're willing to go to bat for that kind of anger.

I would also say that we as women may be more willing to articulate our anger if someone has been unjust to someone *else* or we see someone treating one of our subordinates unfairly—Here I am, angry woman, hands on hips, head to the side, *what are you doing?*

But if they had done the same thing to us, we don't give ourselves permission to articulate that anger and to address the injustices that are personal.

SGC: *I've spent most of my career in HBR, and my experience of our company culture is that visible displays of anger are not welcome. On the whole, this anti-anger culture works for me because I'm a conflict-avoidant person. That said, there have been times when I have felt angry at work. The older I have gotten, the more I have been willing to call it anger and the more I've been able to decide what to do with it as opposed to just feeling it.*

NT: *It seems related to women being expected not to show too much emotion at work. Even being passionate about something can be misinterpreted as being too emotional. That line gets put on women much more often than on men.*

AB: *I also think it's connected to our fear of directness. I get called out on that occasionally. In a polite culture, like ours, being direct can be misinterpreted as being angry or rude when all you're trying to do is be clear, because a lack of clarity in my view leads to all kinds of problems. Plus, I'm a New Yorker; it's in my DNA. Tina, what are your thoughts?*

TO: I absolutely agree. You're still getting at the idea that there are organizational cultural notions of what is and isn't professional. How you express yourself in the workplace is connected to authenticity.

I come from a very direct family. We're from the South, and people often think about Southern gentility. But we're a Black Southern family, and let me tell you—if somebody comes to the house and they're rude, we might not say it in front of them, but we will talk about it for days. The interesting thing is that as I grew older, I was known as the one who was direct, who was forthright. My mother would say, "Go get 'em, Tina. Go tell 'em what the deal is." Because that was my personality.

I absolutely think as a woman in the workplace, I have been slapped on the wrist for being too direct. But I've also tried to figure out how to work around that. I will say to someone when they come to me and ask a question, "Do you want to hear the truth? Do you want to hear what I really think? Or do you want me to just say something to appease the situation?" If you tell me you really want to hear what I think, I'm going to be direct. People know that about me, and for some reason people like that. I actually think we could adjust our cultures and workplaces so that being direct with kindness would be valued, as opposed to being indirect, which doesn't necessarily have a kind intention behind it. Someone may not want to hurt your feelings, but they also may not want to give you the direct critical feedback that would help you evolve into a better employee.

SGC: *My background is a white Anglo-Saxon Protestant New Englander, and my family is not direct. In the workplace, I have always struggled with how I can be indirect but clear and nice, versus what feels to me like being direct and clear but mean. Nicole, what about you?*

NT: *Background? Very indirect. We're suppressors of emotion. We seethe if we're sad or angry. It was not a very emotional household, and I am not a very emotional person. When I come into work, I don't consider myself very indirect, but I think I'm very polite in my emails, though asking for things can be kind of a challenge: This will be a great idea; this is great for both of us—*

SGC: *You may be the most polite person in our office.*

NT: *I'm very polite. I love exclamation points! I want people to feel my positive energy going to them. I think that's internalized from growing up and not really getting to be angry or getting to show anger or even ask for things directly.*

TO: I'm putting you on the spot, Nicole. Do you identify as Asian?

NT: *Uh-huh.*

TO: From what country?

NT: *Philippines.*

TO: I asked because there are stereotypes. In the workplace, Asian people are known as model minorities. Really polite, they will get the work done and focus on the task, but they're not leaders. Have you heard that stereotype before?

NT: *Oh, yeah. We've published research on that.*

TO: I've read that research and have counseled some of my students of Asian descent because that's something that they encounter. My question is, when you said you're not very emotional, is it that you don't feel the emotions? Or that you don't want to express the emotion?

NT: *I feel these emotions. Not knowing how to express them or what's appropriate to express is probably a big question that I think about subconsciously. I think it is cultural, and that norms of my household growing up and the trajectory that was laid out for me is very different than the expectations and path that I envision for myself now. Trying to advance in the workplace, trying to lead and be heard— that's very different than the role I was expected to play growing up: Do really well in school, don't talk back, get good grades, get a good job, don't cause a fuss.*

TO: We all have our cultural upbringing. We go into a workplace context and have to figure out where we as authentic individuals reside and how we navigate those spaces. Because if you want to express your emotion but you feel like you don't know how to, that's one thing. But if you feel like you have to express emotion because the workplace is forcing you to do that, then that's still inauthentic.

AB: *Herminia Ibarra of London Business School wrote this great HBR article, "The Authenticity Paradox." One of the points she made that really resonated for me was that when you think about authenticity, particularly someone who's closer to the beginning of her career, you have to try on different personas to see which one feels comfortable. Because the person who graduated from college a few years ago probably isn't going to be the one who thrives in any workplace, right? You learn, you grow, you bump into a few things, you find the right way forward for yourself. Does that resonate for you, Nicole?*

NT: *Yeah. She said in that piece that you don't want to have too rigid a definition of authenticity. What I would love to know is what's the difference between being inauthentic and just being pushed out of your comfort zone. With the latter, you do need to evolve in the workplace and as a leader.*

TO: For me, authenticity is about being your best self. There's some research that has said: *Keep your authentic self at home. Nobody wants to see your authentic self—it's nasty.* Well, that's not the authentic self that I'm talking about. It's one thing to be driving, see someone do something that makes you angry, and give them the finger. Some people would say that's being authentic. But I would say it's not. That is being under stress or duress. If I had time to stop and reflect and didn't allow my emotions to carry me away, I wouldn't do that. Because that's not what I value; that doesn't align with the values that I authentically hold.

SGC: *A work example is how women can adjust their communication style to be heard more in meetings. Rather than phrasing something as a question, such as, "How about we do this?" instead saying, "My strong recommendation is this." Does it feel inauthentic when you are consciously trying to change the way that you talk to be heard?*

TO: It's difficult to know because some of that may come from career counseling and career advice that will help women, men—

everyone. But some of it is subtle cues to conform; to speak louder; to use more declarative statements; to be more emphatic; to stand up, spread yourself out, and possess the room; to get in there and command the space. Are we talking about a football field or a conference room? What if you have someone who has a softer voice, who is brilliant but can argue and present both sides? Don't we have room at the table or in the workplace for that kind of voice as well?

I think we can quickly go down a road where we're advising women in ways like, "Speak in a deeper voice." Is that really necessary? If they're communicating the ideas, do they need to communicate in a particular way?

AB: *How is that different from how you dress?*

TO: That's the question. I don't know. Because we're trying to figure out the boundary lines, right? We're trying to figure out how this person can be authentic and excel in the workplace.

I do not have much of a Southern accent unless I'm angry or really tired. And that is because my parents raised us to not have a Southern accent, because they recognized that it might be inhibiting to our academic and career success. Would I be more authentic if I still had my Southern accent? I don't know. I was willing to give that up. I'm not willing to relax my hair though. That's the line for me.

SGC: *How are authenticity and the expectations of authenticity different for women of different races?*

TO: I have done some research with Katherine Phillips on hair in the workplace—hair penalties in particular. The reason why I studied hair is because it's a mutable trait that you can alter, and it's very relevant to identity. As a Black woman in corporate America, I had been advised not to wear my hair in specific styles because the clients might not like it. And when we conducted our experimental research, what we found was that people with Afros or dreadlocks in their hair were rated as less professional than the same images of women when they were portrayed as having straight, relaxed hair.

That was across the board, by both Black and white people. What was interesting was that we found that while Afrocentric hair—meaning textured hair (and I want to note, not all women of African descent have the same textured hair)—was denigrated across the board, it was most denigrated by people of African descent. There was an in-group bias.

We still have to do follow-up research to examine that, because some people immediately said, "That's because Black people hate themselves." That's not necessarily the case. There could be some kind of internalized racism, but it could also be that Black people are keenly aware of the impression-management techniques that are necessary to successfully navigate the workplace. So when we asked questions like, "What advice would you give to this candidate?" they didn't mention hair at all to the people with straight hair. But when Black people were rating these Black images with Afros or dreadlocks, they would say things like, "She might need to change her hairstyle," "She might need to straighten her hair," or "She might need to relax her hair."

I think the reason they were emphasizing that is because that's probably advice that they received both in and outside of the workplace. People have no idea how much time it takes to groom your hair if it is naturally textured and you're having to straighten it every day. That's a lot of uncompensated shadow work that you're doing outside of the workplace, and there's a lot of thinking that goes into it. Wouldn't we rather have employees who are focused on their work? This is not to say that people of African descent are distracted. It's just that they're having to put in extra for the same thing. And really, is it even related to the work? What does it have to do with the job?

It is simply a cultural understanding of what is and is not professional, and that's what I want the takeaway to be. Organizations really and truly need to check themselves. There have been lawsuits by people being hired and then having job offers reneged upon because they wouldn't cut off their dreadlocks. You're telling me that as an organization, you're so concerned that your clientele is going to be offended by this hairstyle that you would fire someone that you thought was highly qualified to perform this role?

Or maybe you have rules like "you need to be clean." Believe it or not, even that can be debatable. In certain cultures, people might shower only once a week. They come to a meeting in a place where people are accustomed to showering once or twice a day, and they may have an odor. Are they clean? According to their culture they are. But according to our culture they might not be. What do we expect from that individual? What's the kind of conversation that we would have around that example?

I don't know what the answer is. But we need to wrestle with our cultural understanding of what is professional. It is no longer OK to just keep these things on the books without questioning them and thinking about how they affect employees.

NT: *When I got my nose pierced, my mom almost fainted: "You're never going to get a job with that." My thinking was, well, I don't want to work anywhere where that's not OK. Is that a millennial attitude? I know it's a privilege attitude—I can pick where I'm going to go. But I wonder if that is a different mentality associated with younger generations.*

TO: Every generation has had the desire to rebel. It might have been, *well, I have on this pinstriped suit, but I have on yellow socks.* Or *I have on this tailored suit, but I have tattoos on my arm that they'll never see.* Or *my hair is in a bun, but really it's dreadlocks.* Who knows? It is human nature to rebel against conformity. Every generation thinks that they're the most rebellious; I will agree with that.

I do wonder, though, if you were a Black woman with dreadlocks, a pierced nose, and pink hair, would that be acceptable? Because it's sort of like, *maybe we can venture out in one or two ways but don't come in here totally nonconformist.* That's not going to be accepted.

SGC: *Do you think that it is possible for a woman to be a truly authentic leader?*

TO: I do think it's possible for a woman to be an authentic leader—a person who is expressing themselves, who is reflected in the values that they want to bring to the workplace, who is willing to share the pros and cons with the people who are following them.

What I'm struggling with is *authentic leadership*. The definition of it can shift depending on what you're talking about. Do we mean someone who's honest and transparent? Or do we mean someone who is pursuing their best self, who is working to take the perspectives of the people who follow them so that they can take that into consideration when they're making decisions? I think it's possible for women to be authentic and to be leaders in that way.

I do not think it's necessarily limited to certain kinds of women, but I do think it's harder for women. The less power you have, the more challenging it can be to be authentic, period. If you're an hourly worker who is dependent upon your employer and they tell you to wear an apron and straighten your hair, you may be more inclined to do that than if you are the CEO of an organization. We have to be sensitive to the fact that it's not as easy for everyone, and power rears its head and impacts women's and men's ability to be authentic in the workplace and to be authentic leaders.

Adapted from "Lead with Authenticity" on
Women at Work (podcast), February 9, 2018.

CHAPTER FOUR

How Competitive Forces Shape Strategy

by Michael E. Porter

The essence of strategy formulation is coping with competition. Yet it is easy to view competition too narrowly and too pessimistically. While one sometimes hears executives complaining to the contrary, intense competition in an industry is neither coincidence nor bad luck.

Moreover, in the fight for market share, competition is not manifested only in the other players. Rather, competition in an industry is rooted in its underlying economics, and competitive forces exist that go well beyond the established combatants in a particular industry. Customers, suppliers, potential entrants, and substitute products are all competitors that may be more or less prominent or active depending on the industry.

The state of competition in an industry depends on five basic forces, which are diagrammed in figure 4-1. The collective strength of these forces determines the ultimate profit potential of an industry. It ranges from *intense* in industries like tires, metal cans, and steel, where no company earns spectacular returns on investment, to *mild* in industries like oil field services and equipment, soft drinks, and toiletries, where there is room for quite high returns.

In the economists' "perfectly competitive" industry, jockeying for position is unbridled and entry to the industry very easy. This kind of industry structure, of course, offers the worst prospect for

FIGURE 4-1

Forces governing competition in an industry

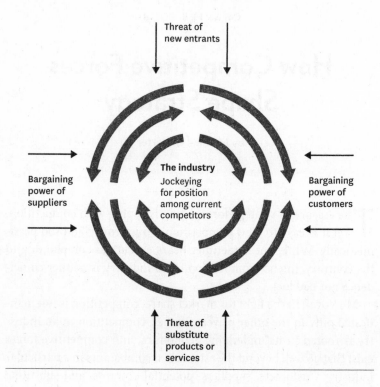

long-run profitability. The weaker the forces collectively, however, the greater the opportunity for superior performance.

Whatever their collective strength, the corporate strategist's goal is to find a position in the industry where his or her company can best defend itself against these forces or can influence them in its favor. The collective strength of the forces may be painfully apparent to all the antagonists; but to cope with them, the strategist must delve below the surface and analyze the sources of each. For example, what makes the industry vulnerable to entry? What determines the bargaining power of suppliers?

Knowledge of these underlying sources of competitive pressure provides the groundwork for a strategic agenda of action. They highlight the critical strengths and weaknesses of the company, animate the positioning of the company in its industry, clarify the areas where strategic changes may yield the greatest payoff, and highlight the places where industry trends promise to hold the greatest significance as either opportunities or threats. Understanding these sources also proves to be of help in considering areas for diversification.

Contending Forces

The strongest competitive force or forces determine the profitability of an industry and so are of greatest importance in strategy formulation. For example, even a company with a strong position in an industry unthreatened by potential entrants will earn low returns if it faces a superior or a lower-cost substitute product—as the leading manufacturers of vacuum tubes and coffee percolators have learned to their sorrow. In such a situation, coping with the substitute product becomes the number one strategic priority.

Different forces take on prominence, of course, in shaping competition in each industry. In the oceangoing tanker industry the key force is probably the buyers (the major oil companies), while in tires it is powerful OEM buyers coupled with tough competitors. In the steel industry the key forces are foreign competitors and substitute materials.

Every industry has an underlying structure, or a set of fundamental economic and technical characteristics, that gives rise to these competitive forces. The strategist, wanting to position his or her company to cope best with its industry environment or to influence that environment in the company's favor, must learn what makes the environment tick.

This view of competition pertains equally to industries dealing in services and to those selling products. To avoid monotony in this article, I refer to both products and services as "products." The same general principles apply to all types of business.

A few characteristics are critical to the strength of each competitive force. I shall discuss them in this section.

Threat of entry

New entrants to an industry bring new capacity, the desire to gain market share, and often substantial resources. Companies diversifying through acquisition into the industry from other markets often leverage their resources to cause a shake-up, as Philip Morris did with Miller beer.

The seriousness of the threat of entry depends on the barriers present and on the reaction from existing competitors that entrants can expect. If barriers to entry are high and newcomers can expect sharp retaliation from the entrenched competitors, obviously the newcomers will not pose a serious threat of entering.

There are six major sources of barriers to entry:

1. **Economies of scale.** These economies deter entry by forcing the aspirant either to come in on a large scale or to accept a cost disadvantage. Scale economies in production, research, marketing, and service are probably the key barriers to entry in the mainframe computer industry, as Xerox and GE sadly discovered. Economies of scale can also act as hurdles in distribution, utilization of the sales force, financing, and nearly any other part of a business.

2. **Product differentiation.** Brand identification creates a barrier by forcing entrants to spend heavily to overcome customer loyalty. Advertising, customer service, being first in the industry, and product differences are among the factors fostering brand identification. It is perhaps the most important entry barrier in soft drinks, over-the-counter drugs, cosmetics, investment banking, and public accounting. To create high fences around their businesses, brewers couple brand identification with economies of scale in production, distribution, and marketing.

3. **Capital requirements.** The need to invest large financial resources in order to compete creates a barrier to entry, particularly if the capital is required for unrecoverable ex-

penditures in up-front advertising or R&D. Capital is necessary not only for fixed facilities but also for customer credit, inventories, and absorbing start-up losses. While major corporations have the financial resources to invade almost any industry, the huge capital requirements in certain fields, such as computer manufacturing and mineral extraction, limit the pool of likely entrants.

4. **Cost disadvantages independent of size.** Entrenched companies may have cost advantages not available to potential rivals, no matter what their size and attainable economies of scale. These advantages can stem from the effects of the learning curve (and of its first cousin, the experience curve), proprietary technology, access to the best raw materials sources, assets purchased at preinflation prices, government subsidies, or favorable locations. Sometimes cost advantages are legally enforceable, as they are through patents. (For an analysis of the much-discussed experience curve as a barrier to entry, see the sidebar "The Experience Curve as an Entry Barrier.")

5. **Access to distribution channels.** The newcomer on the block must, of course, secure distribution of its product or service. A new food product, for example, must displace others from the supermarket shelf via price breaks, promotions, intense selling efforts, or some other means. The more limited the wholesale or retail channels are and the more that existing competitors have these tied up, obviously the tougher that entry into the industry will be. Sometimes this barrier is so high that, to surmount it, a new contestant must create its own distribution channels, as Timex did in the watch industry in the 1950s.

6. **Government policy.** The government can limit or even foreclose entry to industries with such controls as license requirements and limits on access to raw materials. Regulated industries like trucking, liquor retailing, and freight

The Experience Curve as an Entry Barrier

In recent years, the experience curve has become widely discussed as a key element of industry structure. According to this concept, unit costs in many manufacturing industries (some dogmatic adherents say in *all* manufacturing industries) as well as in some service industries decline with "experience," or a particular company's cumulative volume of production. (The experience curve, which encompasses many factors, is a broader concept than the better known learning curve, which refers to the efficiency achieved over a period of time by workers through much repetition.)

The causes of the decline in unit costs are a combination of elements, including economies of scale, the learning curve for labor, and capital-labor substitution. The cost decline creates a barrier to entry because new competitors with no "experience" face higher costs than established ones, particularly the producer with the largest market share, and have difficulty catching up with the entrenched competitors.

Adherents of the experience curve concept stress the importance of achieving market leadership to maximize this barrier to entry, and they recommend aggressive action to achieve it, such as price cutting in anticipation of falling costs in order to build volume. For the combatant that cannot achieve a healthy market share, the prescription is usually, "Get out."

Is the experience curve an entry barrier on which strategies should be built? The answer is: not in every industry. In fact, in some industries, building a strategy on the experience curve can be potentially disastrous. That costs decline with experience in some industries is not news to corporate executives. The significance of the experience curve for strategy depends on what factors are causing the decline.

If costs are falling because a growing company can reap economies of scale through more efficient, automated facilities and vertical integration, then the cumulative volume of production is unimportant to its relative cost position. Here the lowest-cost producer is the one with the largest, most efficient facilities.

A new entrant may well be more efficient than the more experienced competitors; if it has built the newest plant, it will face no disadvantage in having to catch up. The strategic prescription, "You must have the largest, most efficient plant," is a lot different from, "You must produce the greatest cumulative output of the item to get your costs down."

Whether a drop in costs with cumulative (not absolute) volume erects an entry barrier also depends on the sources of the decline. If costs go down because of technical advances known generally in the industry or because of the development of improved equipment that can be copied or purchased from equipment suppliers, the experience curve is no entry barrier at all—in fact, new or less experienced competitors may actually enjoy a cost *advantage* over the leaders. Free of the legacy of heavy past investments, the newcomer or less experienced competitor can purchase or copy the newest and lowest-cost equipment and technology.

If, however, experience can be kept proprietary, the leaders will maintain a cost advantage. But new entrants may require less experience to reduce their costs than the leaders needed. All this suggests that the experience curve can be a shaky entry barrier on which to build a strategy.

While space does not permit a complete treatment here, I want to mention a few other crucial elements in determining the appropriateness of a strategy built on the entry barrier provided by the experience curve:

- The height of the barrier depends on how important costs are to competition compared with other areas like marketing, selling, and innovation.

- The barrier can be nullified by product or process innovations leading to a substantially new technology and thereby creating an entirely new experience curve.* New entrants can leapfrog the industry leaders and alight on the new experience curve, to which those leaders may be poorly positioned to jump.

- If more than one strong company is building its strategy on the experience curve, the consequences can be nearly fatal. By the time only one rival is left pursuing such a strategy, industry growth may have stopped and the prospects of reaping the spoils of victory long since evaporated.

*For an example drawn from the history of the automobile industry, see William J. Abernathy and Kenneth Wayne, "The Limits of the Learning Curve," *Harvard Business Review*, September–October 1974, p. 109.

forwarding are noticeable examples; more subtle government restrictions operate in fields like ski-area development and coal mining. The government also can play a major indirect role by affecting entry barriers through controls such as air and water pollution standards and safety regulations.

The potential rival's expectations about the reaction of existing competitors also will influence its decision on whether to enter. The company is likely to have second thoughts if incumbents have previously lashed out at new entrants or if:

- The incumbents possess substantial resources to fight back, including excess cash and unused borrowing power, productive capacity, or clout with distribution channels and customers.

- The incumbents seem likely to cut prices because of a desire to keep market shares or because of industrywide excess capacity.

- Industry growth is slow, affecting its ability to absorb the new arrival and probably causing the financial performance of all the parties involved to decline.

Changing conditions

From a strategic standpoint there are two important additional points to note about the threat of entry.

First, it changes, of course, as these conditions change. The expiration of Polaroid's basic patents on instant photography, for instance, greatly reduced its absolute cost entry barrier built by proprietary technology. It is not surprising that Kodak plunged into the market. Product differentiation in printing has all but disappeared. Conversely, in the auto industry economies of scale increased enormously with post–World War II automation and vertical integration—virtually stopping successful new entry.

Second, strategic decisions involving a large segment of an industry can have a major impact on the conditions determining the threat of entry. For example, the actions of many U.S. wine producers in the 1960s to step up product introductions, raise advertising levels, and expand distribution nationally surely strengthened the entry roadblocks by raising economies of scale and making access to distribution channels more difficult. Similarly, decisions by members of the recreational vehicle industry to vertically integrate in order to lower costs have greatly increased the economies of scale and raised the capital cost barriers.

Powerful suppliers and buyers

Suppliers can exert bargaining power on participants in an industry by raising prices or reducing the quality of purchased goods and services. Powerful suppliers can thereby squeeze profitability out of an industry unable to recover cost increases in its own prices. By raising their prices, soft drink concentrate producers have contributed to the erosion of profitability of bottling companies because the bottlers, facing intense competition from powdered mixes, fruit drinks, and other beverages, have limited freedom to raise their prices accordingly. Customers likewise can force down prices, demand higher quality or more service, and play competitors off against each other—all at the expense of industry profits.

The power of each important supplier or buyer group depends on a number of characteristics of its market situation and on the relative importance of its sales or purchases to the industry compared with its overall business.

A *supplier* group is powerful if:

- It is dominated by a few companies and is more concentrated than the industry it sells to.

- Its product is unique or at least differentiated, or if it has built up switching costs. Switching costs are fixed costs buyers face in changing suppliers. These arise because, among other things, a buyer's product specifications tie it to particular suppliers, it has invested heavily in specialized ancillary equipment or in learning how to operate a supplier's equipment (as in computer software), or its production lines are connected to the supplier's manufacturing facilities (as in some manufacture of beverage containers).

- It is not obliged to contend with other products for sale to the industry. For instance, the competition between the steel companies and the aluminum companies to sell to the can industry checks the power of each supplier.

- It poses a credible threat of integrating forward into the industry's business. This provides a check against the industry's ability to improve the terms on which it purchases.

- The industry is not an important customer of the supplier group. If the industry is an important customer, suppliers' fortunes will be closely tied to the industry, and they will want to protect the industry through reasonable pricing and assistance in activities like R&D and lobbying.

A *buyer* group is powerful if:

- It is concentrated or purchases in large volumes. Large volume buyers are particularly potent forces if heavy fixed costs characterize the industry—as they do in metal containers, corn refining, and bulk chemicals, for example—which raise the stakes to keep capacity filled.

- The products it purchases from the industry are standard or undifferentiated. The buyers, sure that they can always find alternative suppliers, may play one company against another, as they do in aluminum extrusion.

- The products it purchases from the industry form a component of its product and represent a significant fraction of its cost. The buyers are likely to shop for a favorable price and purchase selectively. Where the product sold by the industry in question is a small fraction of buyers' costs, buyers are usually much less price sensitive.

- It earns low profits, which create great incentive to lower its purchasing costs. Highly profitable buyers, however, are generally less price sensitive (that is, of course, if the item does not represent a large fraction of their costs).

- The industry's product is unimportant to the quality of the buyers' products or services. Where the quality of the buyers' products is very much affected by the industry's product, buyers are generally less price sensitive. Industries in which this situation obtains include oil field equipment, where a malfunction can lead to large losses, and enclosures for electronic medical and test instruments, where the quality of the enclosure can influence the user's impression about the quality of the equipment inside.

- The industry's product does not save the buyer money. Where the industry's product or service can pay for itself many times over, the buyer is rarely price sensitive; rather, he is interested in quality. This is true in services like investment banking and public accounting, where errors in judgment can be costly and embarrassing, and in businesses like the logging of oil wells, where an accurate survey can save thousands of dollars in drilling costs.

- The buyers pose a credible threat of integrating backward to make the industry's product. The Big Three auto producers and major buyers of cars have often used the threat of self-manufacture as a bargaining lever. But sometimes an industry engenders a threat to buyers that its members may integrate forward.

Most of these sources of buyer power can be attributed to consumers as a group as well as to industrial and commercial buyers; only a modification of the frame of reference is necessary. Consumers tend to be more price sensitive if they are purchasing products that are undifferentiated, expensive relative to their incomes, and of a sort where quality is not particularly important.

The buying power of retailers is determined by the same rules, with one important addition. Retailers can gain significant bargaining power over manufacturers when they can influence consumers' purchasing decisions, as they do in audio components, jewelry, appliances, sporting goods, and other goods.

Strategic action

A company's choice of suppliers to buy from or buyer groups to sell to should be viewed as a crucial strategic decision. A company can improve its strategic posture by finding suppliers or buyers who possess the least power to influence it adversely.

Most common is the situation of a company being able to choose whom it will sell to—in other words, buyer selection. Rarely do all the buyer groups a company sells to enjoy equal power. Even if a company sells to a single industry, segments usually exist within that industry that exercise less power (and that are therefore less price sensitive) than others. For example, the replacement market for most products is less price sensitive than the overall market.

As a rule, a company can sell to powerful buyers and still come away with above-average profitability only if it is a low-cost producer in its industry or if its product enjoys some unusual, if not unique, features. In supplying large customers with electric motors, Emerson Electric earns high returns because its low cost position permits the company to meet or undercut competitors' prices.

If the company lacks a low cost position or a unique product, selling to everyone is self-defeating because the more sales it achieves, the more vulnerable it becomes. The company may have to muster the courage to turn away business and sell only to less potent customers.

Buyer selection has been a key to the success of National Can and Crown Cork & Seal. They focus on the segments of the can industry where they can create product differentiation, minimize the threat of backward integration, and otherwise mitigate the awesome power of their customers. Of course, some industries do not enjoy the luxury of selecting "good" buyers.

As the factors creating supplier and buyer power change with time or as a result of a company's strategic decisions, naturally the power of these groups rises or declines. In the ready-to-wear clothing industry, as the buyers (department stores and clothing stores) have become more concentrated and control has passed to large chains, the industry has come under increasing pressure and suffered falling margins. The industry has been unable to differentiate its product or engender switching costs that lock in its buyers enough to neutralize these trends.

Substitute products

By placing a ceiling on prices it can charge, substitute products or services limit the potential of an industry. Unless it can upgrade the quality of the product or differentiate it somehow (as via marketing), the industry will suffer in earnings and possibly in growth.

Manifestly, the more attractive the price-performance trade-off offered by substitute products, the firmer the lid placed on the industry's profit potential. Sugar producers confronted with the large-scale commercialization of high-fructose corn syrup, a sugar substitute, are learning this lesson today.

Substitutes not only limit profits in normal times; they also reduce the bonanza an industry can reap in boom times. In 1978 the producers of fiberglass insulation enjoyed unprecedented demand as a result of high energy costs and severe winter weather. But the industry's ability to raise prices was tempered by the plethora of insulation substitutes, including cellulose, rock wool, and styrofoam. These substitutes are bound to become an even stronger force once the current round of plant additions by fiberglass insulation producers has boosted capacity enough to meet demand (and then some).

Substitute products that deserve the most attention strategically are those that (a) are subject to trends improving their price-performance trade-off with the industry's product, or (b) are produced by industries earning high profits. Substitutes often come rapidly into play if some development increases competition in their industries and causes price reduction or performance improvement.

Jockeying for position

Rivalry among existing competitors takes the familiar form of jockeying for position—using tactics like price competition, product introduction, and advertising slugfests. Intense rivalry is related to the presence of a number of factors:

- Competitors are numerous or are roughly equal in size and power. In many U.S. industries in recent years foreign contenders, of course, have become part of the competitive picture.

- Industry growth is slow, precipitating fights for market share that involve expansion-minded members.

- The product or service lacks differentiation or switching costs, which lock in buyers and protect one combatant from raids on its customers by another.

- Fixed costs are high or the product is perishable, creating strong temptation to cut prices. Many basic materials businesses, like paper and aluminum, suffer from this problem when demand slackens.

- Capacity is normally augmented in large increments. Such additions, as in the chlorine and vinyl chloride businesses, disrupt the industry's supply–demand balance and often lead to periods of overcapacity and price cutting.

- Exit barriers are high. Exit barriers, like very specialized assets or management's loyalty to a particular business, keep companies competing even though they may be earning low or even negative returns on investment. Excess capacity remains functioning, and the profitability of the healthy competitors suffers as the sick ones hang on.[1] If the entire industry suffers from overcapacity, it may seek government help—particularly if foreign competition is present.

- The rivals are diverse in strategies, origins, and "personalities." They have different ideas about how to compete and continually run head-on into each other in the process.

As an industry matures, its growth rate changes, resulting in declining profits and (often) a shakeout. In the booming recreational vehicle industry of the early 1970s, nearly every producer did well; but slow growth since then has eliminated the high returns, except for the strongest members, not to mention many of the weaker companies. The same profit story has been played out in industry after industry—snowmobiles, aerosol packaging, and sports equipment are just a few examples.

An acquisition can introduce a very different personality to an industry, as has been the case with Black & Decker's takeover of McCullough, the producer of chain saws. Technological innovation can boost the level of fixed costs in the production process, as it did in the shift from batch to continuous-line photo finishing in the 1960s.

While a company must live with many of these factors—because they are built into industry economics—it may have some latitude for improving matters through strategic shifts. For example, it may try to raise buyers' switching costs or increase product differentiation. A focus on selling efforts in the fastest-growing segments of the industry or on market areas with the lowest fixed costs can reduce the impact of industry rivalry. If it is feasible, a company can try to avoid confrontation with competitors having high exit barriers and can thus sidestep involvement in bitter price cutting.

Formulation of Strategy

Once having assessed the forces affecting competition in an industry and their underlying causes, the corporate strategist can identify the company's strengths and weaknesses. The crucial strengths and weaknesses from a strategic standpoint are the company's posture vis-à-vis the underlying causes of each force. Where does it stand against substitutes? Against the sources of energy barriers?

Then the strategist can devise a plan of action that may include (1) positioning the company so that its capabilities provide the best defense against the competitive force; and/or (2) influencing the balance of the forces through strategic moves, thereby improving the company's position; and/or (3) anticipating shifts in the factors underlying the forces and responding to them, with the hope of exploiting change by choosing a strategy appropriate for the new competitive balance before opponents recognize it. I shall consider each strategic approach in turn.

Positioning the company

The first approach takes the structure of the industry as given and matches the company's strengths and weaknesses to it. Strategy can be viewed as building defenses against the competitive forces or as finding positions in the industry where the forces are weakest.

Knowledge of the company's capabilities and of the causes of the competitive forces will highlight the areas where the company should confront competition and where to avoid it. If the company is a low-cost producer, it may choose to confront powerful buyers while it takes care to sell them only products not vulnerable to competition from substitutes.

The success of Dr Pepper in the soft drink industry illustrates the coupling of realistic knowledge of corporate strengths with sound industry analysis to yield a superior strategy. Coca-Cola and PepsiCola dominate Dr Pepper's industry, where many small concentrate producers compete for a piece of the action. Dr Pepper chose a strategy of avoiding the largest-selling drink segment, maintaining a narrow flavor line, forgoing the development of a captive bottler network, and marketing heavily. The company positioned itself so as to be least vulnerable to its competitive forces while it exploited its small size.

In the $11.5 billion soft drink industry, barriers to entry in the form of brand identification, large-scale marketing, and access to a bottler network are enormous. Rather than accept the formidable costs and scale economies in having its own bottler network—that is, following the lead of the Big Two and of Seven-Up—Dr Pepper took advantage of the different flavor of its drink to "piggyback" on Coke and Pepsi bottlers who wanted a full line to sell to customers. Dr Pepper coped with the power of these buyers through extraordinary service and other efforts to distinguish its treatment of them from that of Coke and Pepsi.

Many small companies in the soft drink business offer cola drinks that thrust them into head-to-head competition against the majors. Dr Pepper, however, maximized product differentiation by maintaining a narrow line of beverages built around an unusual flavor.

Finally, Dr Pepper met Coke and Pepsi with an advertising on-slaught emphasizing the alleged uniqueness of its single flavor. This campaign built strong brand identification and great customer loyalty. Helping its efforts was the fact that Dr Pepper's formula involved lower raw materials cost, which gave the company an ab-solute cost advantage over its major competitors.

There are no economies of scale in soft drink concentrate pro-duction, so Dr Pepper could prosper despite its small share of the business (6%). Thus Dr Pepper confronted competition in market-ing but avoided it in product line and in distribution. This artful positioning combined with good implementation has led to an enviable record in earnings and in the stock market.

Influencing the balance

When dealing with the forces that drive industry competition, a company can devise a strategy that takes the offensive. This posture is designed to do more than merely cope with the forces themselves; it is meant to alter their causes.

Innovations in marketing can raise brand identification or oth-erwise differentiate the product. Capital investments in large-scale facilities or vertical integration affect entry barriers. The balance of forces is partly a result of external factors and partly in the compa-ny's control.

Exploiting industry change

Industry evolution is important strategically because evolution, of course, brings with it changes in the sources of competition I have identified. In the familiar product life-cycle pattern, for example, growth rates change, product differentiation is said to decline as the business becomes more mature, and the companies tend to in-tegrate vertically.

These trends are not so important in themselves; what is critical is whether they affect the sources of competition. Consider verti-cal integration. In the maturing minicomputer industry, extensive

— 2015 —

What Is Strategy, Again?

by Andrea Ovans

If you read what Peter Drucker had to say about competition back in the late '50s and early '60s, he really only talked about one thing: competition on price. He was hardly alone—that was evidently how most economists thought about competition, too.

It was this received opinion Michael Porter was questioning when, in 1979, he mapped out four additional competitive forces in "How Competitive Forces Shape Strategy." "Price competition can't be all there is to it," he explained to me, when during the course of updating that seminal piece in 2008, I asked him about the origins of the five forces framework.

And so, he famously argued, in addition to the fierceness of price competition among industry rivals, the degree of competitiveness in an industry (that is, the degree to which players are free to set their own prices) depends on the bargaining power of buyers and of suppliers, as well as how threatening substitute products and new entrants are. When these forces are weak, as in software and soft drinks, many companies are profitable. When they are strong, as in the airline and hotel industries, almost no company earns an attractive return on investment. Strategy, it follows for Porter, is a matter of working out your company's best position relative not just to pricing pressures from rivals but to all the forces in your competitive environment.

And for many, it seemed, that was pretty much the last word on the subject. In March 2015, for instance, Rebecca Homkes and Don and Charles Sull said in their *Harvard Business Review* article "Why Strategy Execution Unravels—and What to Do About It": "Since Michael Porter's seminal work in the 1980s we have had a clear and widely accepted definition of what strategy is."

But that wasn't exactly so.

Interestingly, Porter's thinking on the definition of strategy wasn't published until November 1996, which means that 17 years after he burst on the scene with his original five forces article he still felt the need to address the question explicitly.

In his article "What Is Strategy?" Porter argues against a bevy of alternate views, both old and then new, that were circulating in the intervening years. In particular he takes issue with the views that strategy is a matter of:

- Seeking a single ideal competitive position in an industry (as the dot-com wannabes were apparently doing at the time he was writing)

- Benchmarking and adopting best practices (a veiled reference to everyone's favorite punching bag, *In Search of Excellence*)

- Aggressive outsourcing and partnering to improve efficiencies (perhaps a reference to "The Origin of Strategy," published in 1989 by the granddaddy of strategy consulting, BCG founder Bruce Henderson)

- Focusing on a few key success factors, critical resources, and core competencies (maybe a reference to C.K. Prahalad and Gary Hamel's 1990 article, "The Core Competence of the Corporation")

- Rapidly responding to ever-evolving competitive and market changes (perhaps a reference to Rita McGrath and Ian MacMillan's 1995 article on innovation strategy, "Discovery-Driven Planning")

At a fundamental level, all strategies for Porter boil down to two very broad options: Do what everyone else is doing (but spend less money doing it), or do something no one else can do. While either approach can be successful, the two are for him not economically (or, I think, morally) equivalent. Competing by doing what everyone else is doing means, he says, competing on price (that is, learning to be more efficient than your rivals). But that just shrinks the pie as, in the rush to the bottom, profitability declines for the entire industry.

Alternatively, you could expand the pie by staking out some sustainable position based on a unique advantage you create with a clever, preferably complicated and interdependent, set of activities (which some thinkers also call a value chain or a business model). This choice is easy to see in the airline industry, where most airlines "compete to be the best," as Porter puts it, fighting over a very stingy pie indeed, while Southwest, among a handful of other airlines, built far more profitable businesses with a completely different approach, which targeted a different customer (people who might otherwise drive, for example) with a cleverly efficient set of interdependent activities, thereby expanding the entire market.

A tour de force by any measure, "What Is Strategy?" is certainly required reading for all strategists. But it was far from the final word on the subject.

Adapted from content posted on hbr.org, May 12, 2015 (product #H0224M).

vertical integration, both in manufacturing and in software development, is taking place. This very significant trend is greatly raising
economies of scale as well as the amount of capital necessary to
compete in the industry. This in turn is raising barriers to entry
and may drive some smaller competitors out of the industry once
growth levels off.

Obviously, the trends carrying the highest priority from a strategic
standpoint are those that affect the most important sources of competition in the industry and those that elevate new causes to the forefront. In contract aerosol packaging, for example, the trend toward
less product differentiation is now dominant. It has increased buyers'
power, lowered the barriers to entry, and intensified competition.

The framework for analyzing competition that I have described
can also be used to predict the eventual profitability of an industry. In long-range planning the task is to examine each competitive
force, forecast the magnitude of each underlying cause, and then
construct a composite picture of the likely profit potential of the
industry.

The outcome of such an exercise may differ a great deal from the
existing industry structure. Today, for example, the solar heating
business is populated by dozens and perhaps hundreds of companies, none with a major market position. Entry is easy, and competitors are battling to establish solar heating as a superior substitute
for conventional methods.

The potential of this industry will depend largely on the shape of
future barriers to entry, the improvement of the industry's position
relative to substitutes, the ultimate intensity of competition, and the
power captured by buyers and suppliers. These characteristics will
in turn be influenced by such factors as the establishment of brand
identities, significant economies of scale or experience curves in
equipment manufacture wrought by technological change, the ultimate capital costs to compete, and the extent of overhead in production facilities.

The framework for analyzing industry competition has direct
benefits in setting diversification strategy. It provides a road map
for answering the extremely difficult question inherent in diversi-

fication decisions: "What is the potential of this business?" Combining the framework with judgment in its application, a company may be able to spot an industry with a good future before this good future is reflected in the prices of acquisition candidates.

Multifaceted Rivalry

Corporate managers have directed a great deal of attention to defining their businesses as a crucial step in strategy formulation. Theodore Levitt, in his classic 1960 article in HBR, argued strongly for avoiding the myopia of narrow, product-oriented industry definition.[2] Numerous other authorities have also stressed the need to look beyond product to function in defining a business, beyond national boundaries to potential international competition, and beyond the ranks of one's competitors today to those that may become competitors tomorrow. As a result of these urgings, the proper definition of a company's industry or industries has become an endlessly debated subject.

One motive behind this debate is the desire to exploit new markets. Another, perhaps more important motive is the fear of overlooking latent sources of competition that someday may threaten the industry. Many managers concentrate so single-mindedly on their direct antagonists in the fight for market share that they fail to realize that they are also competing with their customers and their suppliers for bargaining power. Meanwhile, they also neglect to keep a wary eye out for new entrants to the contest or fail to recognize the subtle threat of substitute products.

The key to growth—even survival—is to stake out a position that is less vulnerable to attack from head-to-head opponents, whether established or new, and less vulnerable to erosion from the direction of buyers, suppliers, and substitute goods. Establishing such a position can take many forms—solidifying relationships with favorable customers, differentiating the product either substantively or psychologically through marketing, integrating forward or backward, establishing technological leadership.

NOTES

1. For a more complete discussion of exit barriers and their implications for strategy, see my article, "Please Note Location of Nearest Exit," *California Management Review*, Winter 1976, p. 21.

2. Theodore Levitt, "Marketing Myopia," reprinted as an HBR Classic, September–October 1975, p. 26.

Reprinted from *Harvard Business Review*,
March–April 1979 (product #79208).

CHAPTER FIVE

Blue Ocean Strategy

by W. Chan Kim and Renée Mauborgne

A onetime accordion player, stilt walker, and fire-eater, Guy Laliberté is now CEO of one of Canada's largest cultural exports, Cirque du Soleil. Founded in 1984 by a group of street performers, Cirque has staged dozens of productions seen by some 40 million people in 90 cities around the world. In 20 years, Cirque has achieved revenues that Ringling Bros. and Barnum & Bailey— the world's leading circus—took more than a century to attain.

Cirque's rapid growth occurred in an unlikely setting. The circus business was (and still is) in long-term decline. Alternative forms of entertainment—sporting events, TV, and video games—were casting a growing shadow. Children, the mainstay of the circus audience, preferred PlayStations to circus acts. There was also rising sentiment, fueled by animal rights groups, against the use of animals, traditionally an integral part of the circus. On the supply side, the star performers that Ringling and the other circuses relied on to draw in the crowds could often name their own terms. As a result, the industry was hit by steadily decreasing audiences and increasing costs. What's more, any new entrant to this business would be competing against a formidable incumbent that for most of the last century had set the industry standard.

How did Cirque profitably increase revenues by a factor of 22 over the last ten years in such an unattractive environment? The tagline for one of the first Cirque productions is revealing: "We reinvent the circus." Cirque did not make its money by competing within the confines of the existing industry or by stealing customers from Ringling and the others. Instead it created uncontested market space that made the competition irrelevant. It pulled in a whole new group of customers who were traditionally noncustomers of the industry—adults and corporate clients who had turned to theater, opera, or ballet and were, therefore, prepared to pay several times more than the price of a conventional circus ticket for an unprecedented entertainment experience.

To understand the nature of Cirque's achievement, you have to realize that the business universe consists of two distinct kinds of space, which we think of as red and blue oceans. Red oceans represent all the industries in existence today—the known market space. In red oceans, industry boundaries are defined and accepted, and the competitive rules of the game are well understood. Here, companies try to outperform their rivals in order to grab a greater share of existing demand. As the space gets more and more crowded, prospects for profits and growth are reduced. Products turn into commodities, and increasing competition turns the water bloody.

Blue oceans denote all the industries *not* in existence today—the unknown market space, untainted by competition. In blue oceans, demand is created rather than fought over. There is ample opportunity for growth that is both profitable and rapid. There are two ways to create blue oceans. In a few cases, companies can give rise to completely new industries, as eBay did with the online auction industry. But in most cases, a blue ocean is created from within a red ocean when a company alters the boundaries of an existing industry. As will become evident later, this is what Cirque did. In breaking through the boundary traditionally separating circus and theater, it made a new and profitable blue ocean from within the red ocean of the circus industry.

Cirque is just one of more than 150 blue ocean creations that we have studied in over 30 industries, using data stretching back more than 100 years. We analyzed companies that created those blue oceans and their less successful competitors, which were caught in red oceans. In studying these data, we have observed a consistent pattern of strategic thinking behind the creation of new markets and industries, what we call blue ocean strategy. The logic behind blue ocean strategy parts with traditional models focused on competing in existing market space. Indeed, it can be argued that managers' failure to realize the differences between red and blue ocean strategy lies behind the difficulties many companies encounter as they try to break from the competition.

In this article, we present the concept of blue ocean strategy and describe its defining characteristics. We assess the profit and growth consequences of blue oceans and discuss why their creation is a rising imperative for companies in the future. We believe that an understanding of blue ocean strategy will help today's companies as they struggle to thrive in an accelerating and expanding business universe.

Blue and Red Oceans

Although the term may be new, blue oceans have always been with us. Look back 100 years and ask yourself which industries known today were then unknown. The answer: Industries as basic as automobiles, music recording, aviation, petrochemicals, pharmaceuticals, and management consulting were unheard-of or had just begun to emerge. Now turn the clock back only 30 years and ask yourself the same question. Again, a plethora of multibillion-dollar industries jump out: mutual funds, cellular telephones, biotechnology, discount retailing, express package delivery, snowboards, coffee bars, and home videos, to name a few. Just three decades ago, none of these industries existed in a meaningful way.

This time, put the clock forward 20 years. Ask yourself: How many industries that are unknown today will exist then? If history is any predictor of the future, the answer is many. Companies have a huge capacity to create new industries and re-create existing ones, a fact that is reflected in the deep changes that have been necessary in the way industries are classified. The half-century-old Standard Industrial Classification (SIC) system was replaced in 1997 by the North American Industry Classification System (NAICS). The new system expanded the ten SIC industry sectors into 20 to reflect the emerging realities of new industry territories—blue oceans. The services sector under the old system, for example, is now seven sectors ranging from information to health care and social assistance. Given that these classification systems are designed for standardization and continuity, such a replacement shows how significant a source of economic growth the creation of blue oceans has been.

Looking forward, it seems clear to us that blue oceans will remain the engine of growth. Prospects in most established market spaces—red oceans—are shrinking steadily. Technological advances have substantially improved industrial productivity, permitting suppliers to produce an unprecedented array of products and services. And as trade barriers between nations and regions fall and information on products and prices becomes instantly and globally available, niche markets and monopoly havens are continuing to disappear. At the same time, there is little evidence of any increase in demand, at least in the developed markets, where recent United Nations statistics even point to declining populations. The result is that in more and more industries, supply is overtaking demand.

This situation has inevitably hastened the commoditization of products and services, stoked price wars, and shrunk profit margins. According to recent studies, major American brands in a variety of product and service categories have become more and more alike. And as brands become more similar, people increasingly base purchase choices on price. People no longer insist, as in the past, that their laundry detergent be Tide. Nor do they necessarily stick to Colgate when there is a special promotion for Crest, and vice versa. In overcrowded industries, differentiating brands becomes harder both in economic upturns and in downturns.

The Paradox of Strategy

Unfortunately, most companies seem becalmed in their red oceans. In a study of business launches in 108 companies, we found that 86% of those new ventures were line extensions—incremental improvements to existing industry offerings—and a mere 14% were aimed at creating new markets or industries. While line extensions did account for 62% of the total revenues, they delivered only 39% of the total profits. By contrast, the 14% invested in creating new markets and industries delivered 38% of total revenues and a startling 61% of total profits.

So why the dramatic imbalance in favor of red oceans? Part of the explanation is that corporate strategy is heavily influenced by its roots in military strategy. The very language of strategy is deeply imbued with military references—chief executive "officers" in "headquarters" "troops" on the "front lines." Described this way, strategy is all about red ocean competition. It is about confronting an opponent and driving him off a battlefield of limited territory. Blue ocean strategy, by contrast, is about doing business where there is no competitor. It is about creating new land, not dividing up existing land. Focusing on the red ocean therefore means accepting the key constraining factors of war—limited terrain and the need to beat an enemy to succeed. And it means denying the distinctive strength of the business world—the capacity to create new market space that is uncontested.

The tendency of corporate strategy to focus on winning against rivals was exacerbated by the meteoric rise of Japanese companies in the 1970s and 1980s. For the first time in corporate history, customers were deserting Western companies in droves. As competition mounted in the global marketplace, a slew of red ocean strategies emerged, all arguing that competition was at the core of corporate success and failure. Today, one hardly talks about strategy without using the language of competition. The term that best symbolizes this is "competitive advantage." In the competitive-advantage worldview, companies are often driven to outperform rivals and capture greater shares of existing market space.

Of course competition matters. But by focusing on competition, scholars, companies, and consultants have ignored two very important—and, we would argue, far more lucrative—aspects of strategy: One is to find and develop markets where there is little or no competition—blue oceans—and the other is to exploit and protect blue oceans. These challenges are very different from those to which strategists have devoted most of their attention.

Toward Blue Ocean Strategy

What kind of strategic logic is needed to guide the creation of blue oceans? To answer that question, we looked back over 100 years of data on blue ocean creation to see what patterns could be discerned. Some of our data are presented in table 5-1. It shows an overview of key blue ocean creations in three industries that closely touch people's lives: autos—how people get to work; computers—what people use at work; and movie theaters—where people go after work for enjoyment. We found that:

Blue oceans are not about technology innovation

Leading-edge technology is sometimes involved in the creation of blue oceans, but it is not a defining feature of them. This is often true even in industries that are technology intensive. As the table reveals, across all three representative industries, blue oceans were seldom the result of technological innovation per se; the underlying technology was often already in existence. Even Ford's revolutionary assembly line can be traced to the meatpacking industry in America. Like those within the auto industry, the blue oceans within the computer industry did not come about through technology innovations alone but by linking technology to what buyers valued. As with the IBM 650 and the Compaq PC server, this often involved simplifying the technology.

Incumbents often create blue oceans—and usually within their core businesses

GM, the Japanese automakers, and Chrysler were established players when they created blue oceans in the auto industry. So were CTR and its later incarnation, IBM, and Compaq in the computer

TABLE 5-1

A snapshot of blue ocean creation

This table identifies the strategic elements that were common to blue ocean creations in three different industries in different eras. It is not intended to be comprehensive in coverage or exhaustive in content. We chose to show American industries because they represented the largest and least-regulated market during our study period. The pattern of blue ocean creations exemplified by these three industries is consistent with what we observed in the other industries in our study.

Key blue ocean creations	Was the blue ocean created by a new entrant or an incumbent?	Was it driven by technology pioneering or value pioneering?	At the time of the blue ocean creation, was the industry attractive or unattractive?
AUTOMOBILES			
Ford Model T Unveiled in 1908, the Model T was the first mass-produced car, priced so that many Americans could afford it.	New entrant	Value pioneering* (mostly existing technologies)	Unattractive
GM's "car for every purse and purpose" GM created a blue ocean in 1924 by injecting fun and fashion into the car.	Incumbent	Value pioneering (some new technologies)	Attractive
Japanese fuel-efficient autos Japanese automakers created a blue ocean in the mid-1970s with small, reliable lines of cars.	Incumbent	Value pioneering (some new technologies)	Unattractive
Chrysler minivan With its 1984 minivan, Chrysler created a new class of automobile that was as easy to use as a car but had the passenger space of a van.	Incumbent	Value pioneering (mostly existing technologies)	Unattractive

*Driven by value pioneering does not mean that technologies were not involved. Rather, it means that the defining technologies used had largely been in existence, whether in that industry or elsewhere.

(continued)

TABLE 5-1 (*continued*)

Key blue ocean creations	Was the blue ocean created by a new entrant or an incumbent?	Was it driven by technology pioneering or value pioneering?	At the time of the blue ocean creation, was the industry attractive or unattractive?
COMPUTERS			
CTR's tabulating machine In 1914, CTR created the business machine industry by simplifying, modularizing, and leasing tabulating machines. CTR later changed its name to IBM.	Incumbent	Value pioneering (some new technologies)	Unattractive
IBM 650 electronic computer and System/360 In 1952, IBM created the business computer industry by simplifying and reducing the power and price of existing technology. And in 1964, it exploded the blue ocean created by the 650, when it unveiled the System/360, the first modularized computer system.	Incumbent	Value pioneering (650: mostly existing technologies) Value and technology pioneering (System/360: new and existing technologies)	Nonexistent
Apple personal computer Although it was not the first home computer, the all-in-one, simple-to-use Apple II was a blue ocean creation when it appeared in 1978.	New entrant	Value pioneering (mostly existing technologies)	Unattractive
Compaq PC servers Compaq created a blue ocean in 1992 with its ProSignia server, which gave buyers twice the file and print capability of the minicomputer at one-third the price.	Incumbent	Value pioneering (mostly existing technologies)	Nonexistent

industry. And in the cinema industry, the same can be said of palace theaters and AMC. Of the companies listed here, only Ford, Apple, Dell, and Nickelodeon were new entrants in their industries; the first three were start-ups, and the fourth was an estab-

Key blue ocean creations	Was the blue ocean created by a new entrant or an incumbent?	Was it driven by technology pioneering or value pioneering?	At the time of the blue ocean creation, was the industry attractive or unattractive?
Dell built-to-order computers In the mid-1990s, Dell created a blue ocean in a highly competitive industry by creating a new purchase and delivery experience for buyers.	New entrant	Value pioneering (mostly existing technologies)	Unattractive
MOVIE THEATERS			
Nickelodeon The first Nickelodeon opened its doors in 1905, showing short films around the clock to working-class audiences for five cents.	New entrant	Value pioneering (mostly existing technologies)	Nonexistent
Palace theaters Created by Roxy Rothapfel in 1914, these theaters provided an operalike environment for cinema viewing at an affordable price.	Incumbent	Value pioneering (mostly existing technologies)	Attractive
AMC multiplex In the 1960s, the number of multiplexes in America's suburban shopping malls mushroomed. The multiplex gave viewers greater choice while reducing owners' costs.	Incumbent	Value pioneering (mostly existing technologies)	Unattractive
AMC megaplex Megaplexes, introduced in 1995, offered every current blockbuster and provided spectacular viewing experiences in theater complexes as big as stadiums at a lower cost to theater owners.	Incumbent	Value pioneering (mostly existing technologies)	Unattractive

lished player entering an industry that was new to it. This suggests that incumbents are not at a disadvantage in creating new market spaces. Moreover, the blue oceans made by incumbents were usually within their core businesses. In fact, as the table shows, most blue oceans are created from within, not beyond, red oceans of existing industries. This challenges the view that new markets are in distant waters. Blue oceans are right next to you in every industry.

Company and industry are the wrong units of analysis

The traditional units of strategic analysis—company and industry— have little explanatory power when it comes to analyzing how and why blue oceans are created. There is no consistently excellent company; the same company can be brilliant at one time and wrong-headed at another. Every company rises and falls over time. Likewise, there is no perpetually excellent industry; relative attractiveness is driven largely by the creation of blue oceans from within them.

The most appropriate unit of analysis for explaining the creation of blue oceans is the strategic move—the set of managerial actions and decisions involved in making a major market-creating business offering. Compaq, for example, is considered by many people to be "unsuccessful" because it was acquired by Hewlett-Packard in 2001 and ceased to be a company. But the firm's ultimate fate does not invalidate the smart strategic move Compaq made that led to the creation of the multibillion-dollar market in PC servers, a move that was a key cause of the company's powerful comeback in the 1990s.

Creating blue oceans builds brands

So powerful is blue ocean strategy that a blue ocean strategic move can create brand equity that lasts for decades. Almost all of the companies listed in the table are remembered in no small part for the blue oceans they created long ago. Very few people alive today were around when the first Model T rolled off Henry Ford's assembly line in 1908, but the company's brand still benefits from that blue ocean move. IBM, too, is often regarded as an "American institution" largely for the blue oceans it created in computing; the 360 series was its equivalent of the Model T.

Our findings are encouraging for executives at the large, established corporations that are traditionally seen as the victims of new market space creation. For what they reveal is that large R&D budgets are not the key to creating new market space. The key is making the right strategic moves. What's more, companies that understand what drives a good strategic move will be well placed to create multiple blue oceans over time, thereby continuing to deliver high growth and profits over a sustained period. The creation of blue oceans, in other words, is a product of strategy and as such is very much a product of managerial action.

The Defining Characteristics

Our research shows several common characteristics across strategic moves that create blue oceans. We found that the creators of blue oceans, in sharp contrast to companies playing by traditional rules, never use the competition as a benchmark. Instead they make it irrelevant by creating a leap in value for both buyers and the company itself. (Table 5-2 compares the chief characteristics of these two strategy models.)

Perhaps the most important feature of blue ocean strategy is that it rejects the fundamental tenet of conventional strategy: that a trade-off exists between value and cost. According to this thesis, companies can either create greater value for customers at

TABLE 5-2

Red ocean versus blue ocean strategy

The imperatives for red ocean and blue ocean strategies are starkly different.

Red ocean strategy	Blue ocean strategy
Compete in existing market space.	Create uncontested market space.
Beat the competition.	Make the competition irrelevant.
Exploit existing demand.	Create and capture new demand.
Make the value/cost trade-off.	Break the value/cost trade-off.
Align the whole system of a company's activities with its strategic choice of differentiation *or* low cost.	Align the whole system of a company's activities in pursuit of differentiation *and* low cost.

a higher cost or create reasonable value at a lower cost. In other words, strategy is essentially a choice between differentiation and low cost. But when it comes to creating blue oceans, the evidence shows that successful companies pursue differentiation and low cost simultaneously.

To see how this is done, let us go back to Cirque du Soleil. At the time of Cirque's debut, circuses focused on benchmarking one another and maximizing their shares of shrinking demand by tweaking traditional circus acts. This included trying to secure more and better-known clowns and lion tamers, efforts that raised circuses' cost structure without substantially altering the circus experience. The result was rising costs without rising revenues and a downward spiral in overall circus demand. Enter Cirque. Instead of following the conventional logic of outpacing the competition by offering a better solution to the given problem—creating a circus with even greater fun and thrills—it redefined the problem itself by offering people the fun and thrill of the circus *and* the intellectual sophistication and artistic richness of the theater.

In designing performances that landed both these punches, Cirque had to reevaluate the components of the traditional circus offering. What the company found was that many of the elements considered essential to the fun and thrill of the circus were unnecessary and in many cases costly. For instance, most circuses offer animal acts. These are a heavy economic burden, because circuses have to shell out not only for the animals but also for their training, medical care, housing, insurance, and transportation. Yet Cirque found that the appetite for animal shows was rapidly diminishing because of rising public concern about the treatment of circus animals and the ethics of exhibiting them.

Similarly, although traditional circuses promoted their performers as stars, Cirque realized that the public no longer thought of circus artists as stars, at least not in the movie star sense. Cirque did away with traditional three-ring shows, too. Not only did these create confusion among spectators forced to switch their attention from one ring to another, they also increased the number of performers needed, with obvious cost implications. And while aisle concession sales appeared to be a good way to generate revenue, the high prices discouraged parents from making purchases and made them feel they were being taken for a ride.

Cirque found that the lasting allure of the traditional circus came down to just three factors: the clowns, the tent, and the classic acrobatic acts. So Cirque kept the clowns, while shifting their humor away from slapstick to a more enchanting, sophisticated style. It glamorized the tent, which many circuses had abandoned in favor of rented venues. Realizing that the tent, more than anything else, captured the magic of the circus, Cirque designed this classic symbol with a glorious external finish and a high level of audience comfort. Gone were the sawdust and hard benches. Acrobats and other thrilling performers were retained, but Cirque reduced their roles and made their acts more elegant by adding artistic flair.

Even as Cirque stripped away some of the traditional circus offerings, it injected new elements drawn from the world of theater. For instance, unlike traditional circuses featuring a series of unrelated acts, each Cirque creation resembles a theater performance in that it has a theme and story line. Although the themes are intentionally vague, they bring harmony and an intellectual element to the acts. Cirque also borrows ideas from Broadway. For example, rather than putting on the traditional "once and for all" show, Cirque mounts multiple productions based on different themes and story lines. As with Broadway productions, too, each Cirque show has an original musical score, which drives the performance, lighting, and timing of the acts, rather than the other way around. The productions feature abstract and spiritual dance, an idea derived from theater and ballet. By introducing these factors, Cirque has created highly sophisticated entertainments. And by staging multiple productions, Cirque gives people reason to come to the circus more often, thereby increasing revenues.

Cirque offers the best of both circus and theater. And by eliminating many of the most expensive elements of the circus, it has been able to dramatically reduce its cost structure, achieving both differentiation and low cost. (For a depiction of the economics underpinning blue ocean strategy, see figure 5-1.)

FIGURE 5-1

The simultaneous pursuit of differentiation and low cost

A blue ocean is created in the region where a company's actions favorably affect both its cost structure and its value proposition to buyers. Cost savings are made from eliminating and reducing the factors an industry competes on. Buyer value is lifted by raising and creating elements the industry has never offered. Over time, costs are reduced further as scale economies kick in, due to the high sales volumes that superior value generates.

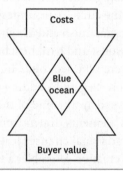

By driving down costs while simultaneously driving up value for buyers, a company can achieve a leap in value for both itself and its customers. Since buyer value comes from the utility and price a company offers, and a company generates value for itself through cost structure and price, blue ocean strategy is achieved only when the whole system of a company's utility, price, and cost activities is properly aligned. It is this whole-system approach that makes the creation of blue oceans a sustainable strategy. Blue ocean strategy integrates the range of a firm's functional and operational activities.

A rejection of the trade-off between low cost and differentiation implies a fundamental change in strategic mindset—we cannot emphasize enough how fundamental a shift it is. The red ocean assumption that industry structural conditions are a given and firms are forced to compete within them is based on an intellectual worldview that academics call the *structuralist* view, or *environmental determinism*. According to this view, companies and managers are largely at the mercy of economic forces greater than themselves. Blue ocean strategies, by contrast, are based on a worldview in which market boundaries and industries can be reconstructed by the actions and beliefs of industry players. We call this the *reconstructionist* view.

The founders of Cirque du Soleil clearly did not feel constrained to act within the confines of their industry. Indeed, is Cirque really a circus with all that it has eliminated, reduced, raised, and created? Or is it theater? If it is theater, then what genre—Broadway show, opera, ballet? The magic of Cirque was created through a reconstruction of elements drawn from all of these alternatives. In the end, Cirque is none of them and a little of all of them. From within the red oceans of theater and circus, Cirque has created a blue ocean of uncontested market space that has, as yet, no name.

Barriers to Imitation

Companies that create blue oceans usually reap the benefits without credible challenges for ten to 15 years, as was the case with Cirque du Soleil, Home Depot, Federal Express, Southwest Airlines, and CNN, to name just a few. The reason is that blue ocean strategy creates considerable economic and cognitive barriers to imitation.

For a start, adopting a blue ocean creator's business model is easier to imagine than to do. Because blue ocean creators immediately attract customers in large volumes, they are able to generate scale economies very rapidly, putting would-be imitators at an immediate and continuing cost disadvantage. The huge economies of scale in purchasing that Wal-Mart enjoys, for example, have significantly discouraged other companies from imitating its business model. The immediate attraction of large numbers of customers can also create network externalities. The more customers eBay has online, the more attractive the auction site becomes for both sellers and buyers of wares, giving users few incentives to go elsewhere.

When imitation requires companies to make changes to their whole system of activities, organizational politics may impede a would-be competitor's ability to switch to the divergent business model of a blue ocean strategy. For instance, airlines trying to follow Southwest's example of offering the speed of air travel with the flexibility and cost of driving would have faced major revisions in routing, training, marketing, and pricing, not to mention culture. Few established airlines had the flexibility to make such extensive organizational and operating changes overnight. Imitating a whole-system approach is not an easy feat.

The cognitive barriers can be just as effective. When a company offers a leap in value, it rapidly earns brand buzz and a loyal following in the marketplace. Experience shows that even the most expensive marketing campaigns struggle to unseat a blue ocean creator. Microsoft, for example, has been trying for more than ten years to occupy the center of the blue ocean that Intuit created with its financial software product Quicken. Despite all of its efforts and all of its investment, Microsoft has not been able to unseat Intuit as the industry leader.

In other situations, attempts to imitate a blue ocean creator conflict with the imitator's existing brand image. The Body Shop, for example, shuns top models and makes no promises of eternal youth and beauty. For the established cosmetic brands like Estée Lauder and L'Oréal, imitation was very difficult, because it would have signaled a complete invalidation of their current images, which are based on promises of eternal youth and beauty.

A Consistent Pattern

While our conceptual articulation of the pattern may be new, blue ocean strategy has always existed, whether or not companies have been conscious of the fact. Just consider the striking parallels between the Cirque du Soleil theater-circus experience and Ford's creation of the Model T.

At the end of the nineteenth century, the automobile industry was small and unattractive. More than 500 automakers in America competed in turning out handmade luxury cars that cost around $1,500 and were enormously *un*popular with all but the very rich. Anticar activists tore up roads, ringed parked cars with barbed wire, and organized boycotts of car-driving businessmen and politicians. Woodrow Wilson caught the spirit of the times when he said in 1906 that "nothing has spread socialistic feeling more than the automobile." He called it "a picture of the arrogance of wealth."

Instead of trying to beat the competition and steal a share of existing demand from other automakers, Ford reconstructed the industry boundaries of cars and horse-drawn carriages to create a blue ocean. At the time, horse-drawn carriages were the primary means of local transportation across America. The carriage had two distinct advantages over cars. Horses could easily negotiate the bumps and mud that stymied cars—especially in rain and snow—on the nation's ubiquitous dirt roads. And horses and carriages were much easier to maintain than the luxurious autos of the time, which frequently broke down, requiring expert repairmen who were expensive and in short supply. It was Henry Ford's understanding of these advantages that showed him how he could break away from the competition and unlock enormous untapped demand.

Ford called the Model T the car "for the great multitude, constructed of the best materials." Like Cirque, the Ford Motor Company made the competition irrelevant. Instead of creating fashionable, customized cars for weekends in the countryside, a luxury few could justify, Ford built a car that, like the horse-drawn carriage, was for everyday use. The Model T came in just one color, black, and there were few optional extras. It was reliable and durable, designed to travel effortlessly over dirt roads in rain, snow, or sunshine. It was easy to use and fix. People could learn to drive it in a day. And like Cirque, Ford went outside the industry for a price point, looking at horse-drawn carriages ($400), not other autos. In 1908, the first Model T cost $850; in 1909, the price dropped to $609, and by 1924 it was down to $290. In this way, Ford converted buyers of horse-drawn carriages into car buyers—just as Cirque turned theatergoers into circusgoers. Sales of the Model T boomed. Ford's market share surged from 9% in 1908 to 61% in 1921, and by 1923, a majority of American households had a car.

Even as Ford offered the mass of buyers a leap in value, the company also achieved the lowest cost structure in the industry, much as Cirque did later. By keeping the cars highly standardized with limited options and interchangeable parts, Ford was able to scrap the prevailing manufacturing system in which cars were constructed by skilled craftsmen who swarmed around one work-station and built a car piece by piece from start to finish. Ford's revolutionary assembly line replaced craftsmen with unskilled la-borers, each of whom worked quickly and efficiently on one small task. This allowed Ford to make a car in just four days—21 days was the industry norm—creating huge cost savings.

Blue and red oceans have always coexisted and always will. Prac-tical reality, therefore, demands that companies understand the strategic logic of both types of oceans. At present, competing in red oceans dominates the field of strategy in theory and in practice, even as businesses' need to create blue oceans intensifies. It is time to even the scales in the field of strategy with a better balance of efforts across both oceans. For although blue ocean strategists have always existed, for the most part their strategies have been largely unconscious. But once corporations realize that the strategies for creating and capturing blue oceans have a different underlying logic from red ocean strategies, they will be able to create many more blue oceans in the future.

Reprinted from *Harvard Business Review*,
October 2004 (product #R0410D).

CHAPTER SIX

Disruptive Technologies

Catching the Wave

by Joseph L. Bower and Clayton M. Christensen

One of the most consistent patterns in business is the failure of leading companies to stay at the top of their industries when technologies or markets change. Goodyear and Firestone entered the radial-tire market quite late. Xerox let Canon create the small-copier market. Bucyrus-Erie allowed Caterpillar and Deere to take over the mechanical excavator market. Sears gave way to Wal-Mart.

The pattern of failure has been especially striking in the computer industry. IBM dominated the mainframe market but missed by years the emergence of minicomputers, which were technologically much simpler than mainframes. Digital Equipment dominated the minicomputer market with innovations like its VAX architecture but missed the personal-computer market almost completely. Apple Computer led the world of personal computing and established the standard for user-friendly computing but lagged five years behind the leaders in bringing its portable computer to market.

Why is it that companies like these invest aggressively—and successfully—in the technologies necessary to retain their current customers but then fail to make certain other technological investments that customers of the future will demand? Undoubtedly, bureaucracy, arrogance, tired executive blood, poor planning, and short-term investment horizons have all played a role. But a more fundamental reason lies at the heart of the paradox: leading companies succumb to one of the most popular, and valuable, management dogmas. They stay close to their customers.

Although most managers like to think they are in control, customers wield extraordinary power in directing a company's investments. Before managers decide to launch a technology, develop a product, build a plant, or establish new channels of distribution, they must look to their customers first: Do their customers want it? How big will the market be? Will the investment be profitable? The more astutely managers ask and answer these questions, the more completely their investments will be aligned with the needs of their customers.

This is the way a well-managed company should operate. Right? But what happens when customers reject a new technology, product concept, or way of doing business because it does *not* address their needs as effectively as a company's current approach? The large photocopying centers that represented the core of Xerox's customer base at first had no use for small, slow tabletop copiers. The excavation contractors that had relied on Bucyrus-Erie's big-bucket steam- and diesel-powered cable shovels didn't want hydraulic excavators because initially they were small and weak. IBM's large commercial, government, and industrial customers saw no immediate use for minicomputers. In each instance, companies listened to their customers, gave them the product performance they were looking for, and, in the end, were hurt by the very technologies their customers led them to ignore.

We have seen this pattern repeatedly in an ongoing study of leading companies in a variety of industries that have confronted technological change. The research shows that most well-managed, established companies are consistently ahead of their industries in developing and commercializing new technologies—from incremental improvements to radically new approaches—as long as those technologies address the next-generation performance needs of their customers. However, these same companies are rarely in the forefront of commercializing new technologies that don't initially meet the needs of mainstream customers and appeal only to small or emerging markets.

Using the rational, analytical investment processes that most well-managed companies have developed, it is nearly impossible to build a cogent case for diverting resources from known customer needs in established markets to markets and customers that seem insignificant or do not yet exist. After all, meeting the needs of established customers and fending off competitors takes all the resources a company has, and then some. In well-managed companies, the processes used to identify customers' needs, forecast technological trends, assess profitability, allocate resources across competing proposals for investment, and take new products to market are focused—for all the right reasons—on current customers and markets. These processes are designed to weed out proposed products and technologies that do *not* address customers' needs.

In fact, the processes and incentives that companies use to keep focused on their main customers work so well that they blind those companies to important new technologies in emerging markets. Many companies have learned the hard way the perils of ignoring new technologies that do not initially meet the needs of mainstream customers. For example, although personal computers did not meet the requirements of mainstream minicomputer users in the early 1980s, the computing power of the desktop machines improved at a much faster rate than minicomputer users' *demands* for computing power did. As a result, personal computers caught up with the computing needs of many of the customers of Wang, Prime, Nixdorf, Data General, and Digital Equipment. Today they are performance-competitive with minicomputers in many applications. For the minicomputer makers, keeping close to mainstream customers and ignoring what were initially low-performance desktop technologies used by seemingly insignificant customers in emerging markets was a rational decision—but one that proved disastrous.

The technological changes that damage established companies are usually not radically new or difficult from a *technological* point of view. They do, however, have two important characteristics: First, they typically present a different package of performance attributes—ones that, at least at the outset, are not valued by existing customers. Second, the performance attributes that existing customers do value improve at such a rapid rate that the new technology can later invade those established markets. Only at this point will mainstream customers want the technology. Unfortunately for the established suppliers, by then it is often too late: The pioneers of the new technology dominate the market.

It follows, then, that senior executives must first be able to spot the technologies that seem to fall into this category. Next, to commercialize and develop the new technologies, managers must protect them from the processes and incentives that are geared to serving established customers. And the only way to protect them is to create organizations that are completely independent from the mainstream business.

No industry demonstrates the danger of staying too close to customers more dramatically than the hard-disk-drive industry. Between 1976 and 1992, disk-drive performance improved at a stunning rate: The physical size of a 100-megabyte (MB) system shrank from 5,400 to 8 cubic inches, and the cost per MB fell from $560 to $5. Technological change, of course, drove these breathtaking achievements. About half of the improvement came from a host of radical advances that were critical to continued improvements in disk-drive performance; the other half came from incremental advances.

The pattern in the disk-drive industry has been repeated in many other industries: The leading, established companies have consistently led the industry in developing and adopting new technologies that their customers demanded—even when those technologies required completely different technological competencies and manufacturing capabilities from the ones the companies had. In spite of this aggressive technological posture, no single disk-drive manufacturer has been able to dominate the industry for more than a few years. A series of companies have entered the business and risen to prominence, only to be toppled by newcomers who pursued technologies that at first did not meet the needs of mainstream customers. As a result, not one of the independent disk-drive companies that existed in 1976 survives today.

To explain the differences in the impact of certain kinds of technological innovations on a given industry, the concept of *performance trajectories*—the rate at which the performance of a product has improved, and is expected to improve, over time—can be helpful. Almost every industry has a critical performance trajectory. In mechanical excavators, the critical trajectory is the annual improvement in cubic yards of earth moved per minute. In photocopiers, an important performance trajectory is improvement in number of copies per minute. In disk drives, one crucial measure of performance is storage capacity, which has advanced 50% each year on average for a given size of drive.

Different types of technological innovations affect performance trajectories in different ways. On the one hand, *sustaining* technologies tend to maintain a rate of improvement; that is, they give customers something more or better in the attributes they already value. For example, thin-film components in disk drives, which replaced conventional ferrite heads and oxide disks between 1982 and 1990, enabled information to be recorded more densely on disks. Engineers had been pushing the limits of the performance they could wring from ferrite heads and oxide disks, but the drives employing these technologies seemed to have reached the natural limits of an *S* curve. At that point, new thin-film technologies emerged that restored—or sustained—the historical trajectory of performance improvement.

On the other hand, *disruptive* technologies introduce a very different package of attributes from the one mainstream customers historically value, and they often perform far worse along one or two dimensions that are particularly important to those customers. As a rule, mainstream customers are unwilling to use a disruptive product in applications they know and understand. At first, then, disruptive technologies tend to be used and valued only in new markets or new applications; in fact, they generally make possible the emergence of new markets. For example, Sony's early transistor radios sacrificed sound fidelity but created a market for portable radios by offering a new and different package of attributes—small size, light weight, and portability.

In the history of the hard-disk-drive industry, the leaders stumbled at each point of disruptive technological change: when the diameter of disk drives shrank from the original 14 inches to 8 inches, then to 5.25 inches, and finally to 3.5 inches. Each of these new architectures initially offered the market substantially less storage capacity than the typical user in the established market required. For example, the 8-inch drive offered 20 MB when it was introduced, while the primary market for disk drives at that time— mainframes—required 200 MB on average. Not surprisingly, the leading computer manufacturers rejected the 8-inch architecture at first. As a result, their suppliers, whose mainstream products consisted of 14-inch drives with more than 200 MB of capacity, did not pursue the disruptive products aggressively. The pattern was repeated when the 5.25-inch and 3.5-inch drives emerged: Established computer makers rejected the drives as inadequate, and, in turn, their disk-drive suppliers ignored them as well.

But while they offered less storage capacity, the disruptive architectures created other important attributes—internal power supplies and smaller size (8-inch drives); still smaller size and low-cost stepper motors (5.25-inch drives); and ruggedness, light weight, and low-power consumption (3.5-inch drives). From the late 1970s to the mid-1980s, the availability of the three drives made possible the development of new markets for minicomputers, desktop PCs, and portable computers, respectively.

Although the smaller drives represented disruptive technological change, each was technologically straightforward. In fact, there were engineers at many leading companies who championed the new technologies and built working prototypes with bootlegged resources before management gave a formal go-ahead. Still, the leading companies could not move the products through their organizations and into the market in a timely way. Each time a disruptive technology emerged, between one-half and two-thirds of the established manufacturers failed to introduce models employing the new architecture—in stark contrast to their timely launches of critical sustaining technologies. Those companies that finally did launch new models typically lagged behind entrant companies by two years—eons in an industry whose products' life cycles are often two years. Three waves of entrant companies led these revolutions; they first captured the new markets and then dethroned the leading companies in the mainstream markets.

How could technologies that were initially inferior and useful only to new markets eventually threaten leading companies in established markets? Once the disruptive architectures became established in their new markets, sustaining innovations raised each architecture's performance along steep trajectories—so steep that the performance available from each architecture soon satisfied the needs of customers in the established markets. For example, the 5.25-inch drive, whose initial 5 MB of capacity in 1980 was only a fraction of the capacity that the minicomputer market needed, became fully performance-competitive in the minicomputer market by 1986 and in the mainframe market by 1991. (See figure 6-1.)

A company's revenue and cost structures play a critical role in the way it evaluates proposed technological innovations. Generally, disruptive technologies look financially unattractive to established companies. The potential revenues from the discernible markets are small, and it is often difficult to project how big the markets for the technology will be over the long term. As a result, managers typically conclude that the technology cannot make a meaningful contribution to corporate growth and, therefore, that it is not worth the management effort required to develop it. In addition, established companies have often installed higher cost structures to serve sustaining technologies than those required by disruptive technologies. As a result, managers typically see themselves as having two choices when deciding whether to pursue disruptive technologies. One is to go *downmarket* and accept the lower profit margins of the emerging markets that the disruptive technologies will initially serve. The other is to go *upmarket* with sustaining technologies and enter market segments whose profit margins are alluringly high. (For example, the margins of IBM's mainframes are still higher than those of PCs.) Any rational resource-allocation process in companies serving established markets will choose going upmarket rather than going down.

FIGURE 6-1

How disk-drive performance met market needs

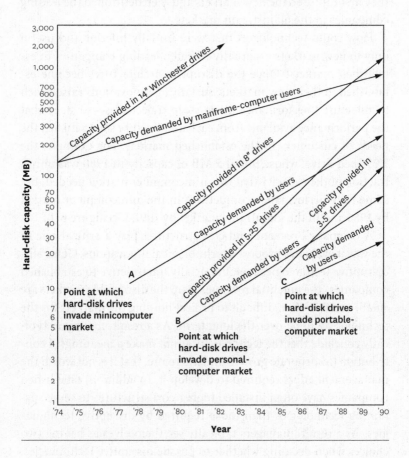

Managers of companies that have championed disruptive technologies in emerging markets look at the world quite differently. Without the high cost structures of their established counterparts, these companies find the emerging markets appealing. Once the companies have secured a foothold in the markets and improved the performance of their technologies, the established markets above them, served by high-cost suppliers, look appetizing. When they do attack, the entrant companies find the established players to be easy and unprepared opponents because the opponents have been looking upmarket themselves, discounting the threat from below.

It is tempting to stop at this point and conclude that a valuable lesson has been learned: Managers can avoid missing the next wave by paying careful attention to potentially disruptive technologies that do *not* meet current customers' needs. But recognizing the pattern and figuring out how to break it are two different things. Although entrants invaded established markets with new technologies three times in succession, none of the established leaders in the disk-drive industry seemed to learn from the experiences of those that fell before them. Management myopia or lack of foresight cannot explain these failures. The problem is that managers keep doing what has worked in the past: serving the rapidly growing needs of their current customers. The processes that successful, well-managed companies have developed to allocate resources among proposed investments are *incapable* of funneling resources into programs that current customers explicitly don't want and whose profit margins seem unattractive.

Managing the development of new technology is tightly linked to a company's investment processes. Most strategic proposals—to add capacity or to develop new products or processes—take shape at the lower levels of organizations in engineering groups or project teams. Companies then use analytical planning and budgeting systems to select from among the candidates competing for funds. Proposals to create new businesses in emerging markets are particularly challenging to assess because they depend on notoriously unreliable estimates of market size. Because managers are evaluated on their ability to place the right bets, it is not surprising that in well-managed companies, mid- and top-level managers back projects in which the market seems assured. By staying close to lead customers, as they have been trained to do, managers focus resources on fulfilling the requirements of those reliable customers that can be served profitably. Risk is reduced—and careers are safeguarded—by giving known customers what they want.

Seagate Technology's experience illustrates the consequences of relying on such resource-allocation processes to evaluate disruptive technologies. By almost any measure, Seagate, based in Scotts Valley, California, was one of the most successful and aggressively managed companies in the history of the microelectronics industry: From its inception in 1980, Seagate's revenues had grown to more than $700 million by 1986. It had pioneered 5.25-inch hard-disk drives and was the main supplier of them to IBM and IBM-compatible personal-computer manufacturers. The company was the leading manufacturer of 5.25-inch drives at the time the disruptive 3.5-inch drives emerged in the mid-1980s.

Engineers at Seagate were the second in the industry to develop working prototypes of 3.5-inch drives. By early 1985, they had made more than 80 such models with a low level of company funding. The engineers forwarded the new models to key marketing executives, and the trade press reported that Seagate was actively developing 3.5-inch drives. But Seagate's principal customers—IBM and other manufacturers of AT-class personal computers—showed no interest in the new drives. They wanted to incorporate 40-MB and 60-MB drives in their next-generation models, and Seagate's early 3.5-inch prototypes packed only 10 MB. In response, Seagate's marketing executives lowered their sales forecasts for the new disk drives.

Manufacturing and financial executives at the company pointed out another drawback to the 3.5-inch drives. According to their analysis, the new drives would never be competitive with the 5.25-inch architecture on a cost-per-megabyte basis—an important metric that Seagate's customers used to evaluate disk drives. Given Seagate's cost structure, margins on the higher-capacity 5.25-inch models therefore promised to be much higher than those on the smaller products.

Senior managers quite rationally decided that the 3.5-inch drive would not provide the sales volume and profit margins that Seagate needed from a new product. A former Seagate marketing executive recalled, "We needed a new model that could become the next ST412 [a 5.25-inch drive generating more than $300 million in annual sales, which was nearing the end of its life cycle]. At the time, the entire market for 3.5-inch drives was less than $50 million. The 3.5-inch drive just didn't fit the bill—for sales or profits."

The shelving of the 3.5-inch drive was *not* a signal that Seagate was complacent about innovation. Seagate subsequently introduced new models of 5.25-inch drives at an accelerated rate and, in so doing, introduced an impressive array of sustaining technological improvements, even though introducing them rendered a significant portion of its manufacturing capacity obsolete.

While Seagate's attention was glued to the personal-computer market, former employees of Seagate and other 5.25-inch drive makers, who had become frustrated by their employers' delays in launching 3.5-inch drives, founded a new company, Conner Peripherals. Conner focused on selling its 3.5-inch drives to companies in emerging markets for portable computers and small-footprint desktop products (PCs that take up a smaller amount of space on a desk). Conner's primary customer was Compaq Computer, a customer that Seagate had never served. Seagate's own prosperity, coupled with Conner's focus on customers who valued different disk-drive attributes (ruggedness, physical volume, and weight), minimized the threat Seagate saw in Conner and its 3.5-inch drives.

From its beachhead in the emerging market for portable computers, however, Conner improved the storage capacity of its drives by 50% per year. By the end of 1987, 3.5-inch drives packed the capacity demanded in the mainstream personal-computer market. At this point, Seagate executives took their company's 3.5-inch drive off the shelf, introducing it to the market as a *defensive* response to the attack of entrant companies like Conner and Quantum Corporation, the other pioneer of 3.5-inch drives. But it was too late.

By then, Seagate faced strong competition. For a while, the company was able to defend its existing market by selling 3.5-inch drives to its established customer base—manufacturers and resellers of full-size personal computers. In fact, a large proportion of its 3.5-inch products continued to be shipped in frames that enabled its customers to mount the drives in computers designed to accommodate 5.25-inch drives. But, in the end, Seagate could only struggle to become a second-tier supplier in the new portable-computer market.

In contrast, Conner and Quantum built a dominant position in the new portable-computer market and then used their scale and experience base in designing and manufacturing 3.5-inch products to drive Seagate from the personal-computer market. In their 1994 fiscal years, the combined revenues of Conner and Quantum exceeded $5 billion.

Seagate's poor timing typifies the responses of many established companies to the emergence of disruptive technologies. Seagate was willing to enter the market for 3.5-inch drives only when it had become large enough to satisfy the company's financial requirements—that is, only when existing customers wanted the new technology. Seagate has survived through its savvy acquisition of Control Data Corporation's disk-drive business in 1990. With CDC's technology base and Seagate's volume-manufacturing expertise, the company has become a powerful player in the business of supplying large-capacity drives for high-end computers. Nonetheless, Seagate has been reduced to a shadow of its former self in the personal-computer market.

It should come as no surprise that few companies, when confronted with disruptive technologies, have been able to overcome the handicaps of size or success. But it can be done. There is a method to spotting and cultivating disruptive technologies.

Determine whether the technology is disruptive or sustaining

The first step is to decide which of the myriad technologies on the horizon are disruptive and, of those, which are real threats. Most companies have well-conceived processes for identifying and tracking the progress of potentially sustaining technologies, because they are important to serving and protecting current customers. But few have systematic processes in place to identify and track potentially disruptive technologies.

One approach to identifying disruptive technologies is to examine internal disagreements over the development of new products or technologies. Who supports the project and who doesn't? Marketing and financial managers, because of their managerial and financial incentives, will rarely support a disruptive technology. On the other hand, technical personnel with outstanding track records will often persist in arguing that a new market for the technology will emerge—even in the face of opposition from key customers and marketing and financial staff. Disagreement between the two groups often signals a disruptive technology that top-level managers should explore.

Define the strategic significance of the disruptive technology

The next step is to ask the right people the right questions about the strategic importance of the disruptive technology. Disruptive technologies tend to stall early in strategic reviews because managers either ask the wrong questions or ask the wrong people the right questions. For example, established companies have regular procedures for asking mainstream customers—especially the important accounts where new ideas are actually tested—to assess the value of innovative products. Generally, these customers are selected because they are the ones striving the hardest to stay ahead of *their* competitors in pushing the performance of *their* products. Hence these customers are most likely to demand the highest performance from their suppliers. For this reason, lead customers are reliably accurate when it comes to assessing the potential of sustaining technologies, but they are reliably *in*accurate when it comes to assessing the potential of disruptive technologies. They are the wrong people to ask.

A simple graph plotting product performance as it is defined in mainstream markets on the vertical axis and time on the horizontal axis can help managers identify both the right questions and the right people to ask. First, draw a line depicting the level of performance and the trajectory of performance improvement that customers have historically enjoyed and are likely to expect in the future. Then locate the estimated initial performance level of the new technology. If the technology is disruptive, the point will lie far below the performance demanded by current customers. (See figure 6-2.)

What is the likely slope of performance improvement of the disruptive technology compared with the slope of performance improvement demanded by existing markets? If knowledgeable technologists believe the new technology might progress faster than the market's demand for performance improvement, then that technology, which does not meet customers' needs today, may very well address them tomorrow. The new technology, therefore, is strategically critical.

Instead of taking this approach, most managers ask the wrong questions. They compare the anticipated rate of performance improvement of the new technology with that of the established technology. If the new technology has the potential to surpass the established one, the reasoning goes, they should get busy developing it.

Pretty simple. But this sort of comparison, while valid for sustaining technologies, misses the central strategic issue in assess-

FIGURE 6-2

How to assess disruptive technologies

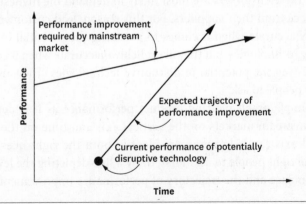

ing potentially disruptive technologies. Many of the disruptive technologies we studied *never* surpassed the capability of the old technology. It is the trajectory of the disruptive technology compared with that of the *market* that is significant. For example, the reason the mainframe-computer market is shrinking is not that personal computers outperform mainframes but because personal computers networked with a file server meet the computing and data-storage needs of many organizations effectively. Mainframe-computer makers are reeling not because the performance of personal-computing technology surpassed the performance of mainframe *technology* but because it intersected with the performance demanded by the established *market*.

Consider the graph again. If technologists believe that the new technology will progress at the same rate as the market's demand for performance improvement, the disruptive technology may be slower to invade established markets. Recall that Seagate had targeted personal computing, where demand for hard-disk capacity per computer was growing at 30% per year. Because the capacity of 3.5-inch drives improved at a much faster rate, leading 3.5-inch-drive makers were able to force Seagate out of the market. However, two other 5.25-inch-drive makers, Maxtor and Micropolis, had targeted the engineering-workstation market, in which demand for hard-disk capacity was insatiable. In that market, the trajectory of capacity demanded was essentially parallel to the trajectory of capacity improvement that technologists could supply in the 3.5-inch architecture. As a result, entering the 3.5-inch-drive business was strategically less critical for those companies than it was for Seagate.

Locate the initial market for the disruptive technology

Once managers have determined that a new technology is disruptive and strategically critical, the next step is to locate the initial markets for that technology. Market research, the tool that managers have traditionally relied on, is seldom helpful: At the point a company needs to make a strategic commitment to a disruptive technology, no concrete market exists. When Edwin Land asked

— 2009 —

Is Reverse Innovation Like Disruptive Innovation?

by Vijay Govindarajan and Chris Trimble

In the October 2009 issue of *Harvard Business Review*, we published the article "How GE Is Disrupting Itself," coauthored with Jeff Immelt, then chairman and CEO of General Electric. The article introduces the phenomenon of reverse innovation. Since that introduction, several people have asked us about the relationship between *reverse* innovation and *disruptive* innovation, as defined by Clay Christensen.

There is an overlap between reverse innovation and disruptive innovation but not a one-to-one relationship. In other words, some, but not all, illustrations of reverse innovation are also illustrations of disruptive innovation.

A *reverse innovation*, very simply, is any innovation likely to be adopted first in the developing world. It is so called because historically nearly all innovations have been adopted first in rich countries. In our article, we argued that reverse innovation will become more and more common, and that it presents a formidable organizational challenge for incumbent multinationals headquartered in the rich world. We also explained an organizational model for overcoming that challenge.

A *disruptive innovation* has a particular dynamic that endangers incumbents. The incumbent's product has two primary dimensions of merit, A and B. (For example, A could be quality and B could be speed of delivery.) Mainstream customers are mostly interested in A, but there is a minority customer set that values B more than A. The disruptive innovation, at launch, is weak on A but strong on B. As such, it attracts only the minority. Because mainstream customers don't want it, incumbents tend to ignore the new entrant and the new technology. But over time, technology improves, and the innovation gets better and better at A. Eventually it meets the needs of mainstream customers on dimension A, and, since they also place at least some value on B, they start choosing the new product. The incumbent is suddenly disrupted; they have ignored the new technology all along.

In Christensen's famous study of the disk-drive industry, A was the capacity of the disk drive and B was the size of the disk drive. Christensen showed that new entrants repeatedly disrupted incumbents by introducing smaller disk drives with lower capacity. Initially, mainstream customers were uninterested. They needed more memory, not less. But, over time, the capacity of the smaller drives went up and up until mainstream customers were interested.

So, what is the relationship between reverse innovation and disruptive innovation?

We see three primary situations that create the possibility of reverse innovation. Only the first is also an illustration of disruptive innovation.

The first situation is created by the *income gap* between rich countries and developing ones. Because per-capita incomes are so low in the developing world, conditions are ripe for innovations that offer decent quality at an ultralow price—that is, a 50% solution at a 5% price. At first, the 50% solution is unattractive in the rich world, but eventually, performance rises to the point that it *is* attractive in the rich world. This is clearly also a disruptive innovation story, where A is performance or quality and B is price.

The second is created by the *infrastructure gap* between rich countries and developing ones. Most of the infrastructure (energy, transportation, telecom, and so forth) in the developing world has yet to be built. As such, demand for new infrastructure technologies is much higher in the developing world than it is in the rich world, where demand for infrastructure is created primarily by the need to replace existing infrastructure. This is not an illustration of disruptive innovation.

The third situation is created by the *sustainability gap* between rich countries and developing ones. Many developing nations are confronted with environmental constraints far sooner in their path of economic development than rich nations were. Desalination technologies, for example, are likely to be adopted in places like Northern Africa before the desert southwest in the United States needs them. This is also not an illustration of disruptive innovation.

Whether an innovation is reverse, disruptive, or both, it is difficult for an established organization to execute. For reverse innovations, companies must overcome resistance to shifting power and control away from headquarters, and they must be willing to reshape the organizational models and expectations of in-country teams. For disruptive innovations, companies must overcome the initial resistance to prioritizing an investment that does not interest mainstream customers. And, even if they do invest, they must overcome the fear that the new product will eventually cannibalize the existing business.

Adapted from content on hbr.org, September 30, 2009 (product #H003V5).

Polaroid's market researchers to assess the potential sales of his new camera, they concluded that Polaroid would sell a mere 100,000 cameras over the product's lifetime; few people they interviewed could imagine the uses of instant photography.

Because disruptive technologies frequently signal the emergence of new markets or market segments, managers must *create* information about such markets—who the customers will be, which dimensions of product performance will matter most to which customers, what the right price points will be. Managers can create this kind of information only by experimenting rapidly, iteratively, and inexpensively with both the product and the market.

For established companies to undertake such experiments is very difficult. The resource-allocation processes that are critical to profitability and competitiveness will not—and should not—direct resources to markets in which sales will be relatively small. How, then, can an established company probe a market for a disruptive technology? Let start-ups—either ones the company funds or others with no connection to the company—conduct the experiments. Small, hungry organizations are good at placing economical bets, rolling with the punches, and agilely changing product and market strategies in response to feedback from initial forays into the market.

Consider Apple Computer in its start-up days. The company's original product, the Apple I, was a flop when it was launched in 1977. But Apple had not placed a huge bet on the product and had gotten at least *something* into the hands of early users quickly. The company learned a lot from the Apple I about the new technology and about what customers wanted and did not want. Just as important, a group of *customers* learned about what they did and did not want from personal computers. Armed with this information, Apple launched the Apple II quite successfully.

Many companies could have learned the same valuable lessons by watching Apple closely. In fact, some companies pursue an explicit strategy of being *second to invent*—allowing small pioneers to lead the way into uncharted market territory. For instance, IBM let Apple, Commodore, and Tandy define the personal computer. It then aggressively entered the market and built a considerable personal-computer business.

But IBM's relative success in entering a new market late is the exception, not the rule. All too often, successful companies hold the performance of small-market pioneers to the financial standards they apply to their own performance. In an attempt to ensure that they are using their resources well, companies explicitly or implicitly set relatively high thresholds for the size of the markets they should consider entering. This approach sentences them to making late entries into markets already filled with powerful players.

For example, when the 3.5-inch drive emerged, Seagate needed a $300-million-a-year product to replace its mature flagship 5.25-inch model, the ST412, and the 3.5-inch market wasn't large enough. Over the next two years, when the trade press asked when Seagate would introduce its 3.5-inch drive, company executives consistently responded that there was no market yet. There actually *was* a market, and it was growing rapidly. The signals that Seagate was picking up about the market, influenced as they were by customers who didn't want 3.5-inch drives, were misleading. When Seagate finally introduced its 3.5-inch drive in 1987, more than $750 million in 3.5-inch drives had already been sold. Information about the market's size had been widely available throughout the industry. But it wasn't compelling enough to shift the focus of Seagate's managers. They continued to look at the new market through the eyes of their current customers and in the context of their current financial structure.

The posture of today's leading disk-drive makers toward the newest disruptive technology, 1.8-inch drives, is eerily familiar. Each of the industry leaders has designed one or more models of the tiny drives, and the models are sitting on shelves. Their capacity is too low to be used in notebook computers, and no one yet knows where the initial market for 1.8-inch drives will be. Fax machines, printers, and automobile dashboard mapping systems are all candidates. "There just isn't a market," complained one industry executive. "We've got the product, and the sales force can take orders for it. But there are no orders because nobody needs it. It just sits there." This executive has not considered the fact that his sales force has no incentive to sell the 1.8-inch drives instead of the higher-margin products it sells to higher-volume customers. And while the 1.8-inch drive is sitting on the shelf at his company and others, last year more than $50 million worth of 1.8-inch drives were sold, almost all by startups. This year, the market will be an estimated $150 million.

To avoid allowing small, pioneering companies to dominate new markets, executives must personally monitor the available intelligence on the progress of pioneering companies through monthly meetings with technologists, academics, venture capitalists, and other nontraditional sources of information. They *cannot* rely on the company's traditional channels for gauging markets because those channels were not designed for that purpose.

Place responsibility for building a disruptive-technology business in an independent organization

The strategy of forming small teams into skunkworks projects to isolate them from the stifling demands of mainstream organizations is widely known but poorly understood. For example, isolating a team of engineers so that it can develop a radically new sustaining technology just because that technology is radically different is a fundamental misapplication of the skunkworks approach. Managing out of context is also unnecessary in the unusual event that a disruptive technology is more financially attractive than existing products. Consider Intel's transition from dynamic random access memory (DRAM) chips to microprocessors. Intel's early microprocessor business had a higher gross margin than that of its DRAM business; in other words, Intel's normal resource-allocation process naturally provided the new business with the resources it needed.[1]

Creating a separate organization is necessary only when the disruptive technology has a lower profit margin than the mainstream business and must serve the unique needs of a new set of customers. CDC, for example, successfully created a remote organization to commercialize its 5.25-inch drive. Through 1980, CDC was the dominant independent disk-drive supplier due to its expertise in making 14-inch drives for mainframe-computer makers. When the 8-inch drive emerged, CDC launched a late development effort, but its engineers were repeatedly pulled off the project to solve problems for the more profitable, higher-priority 14-inch projects targeted at the company's most important customers. As a result, CDC was three years late in launching its first 8-inch product and never captured more than 5% of that market.

When the 5.25-inch generation arrived, CDC decided that it would face the new challenge more strategically. The company assigned a small group of engineers and marketers in Oklahoma City, Oklahoma, far from the mainstream organization's customers, the task of developing and commercializing a competitive 5.25-inch product. "We needed to launch it in an environment in which everybody got excited about a $50,000 order," one executive recalled. "In Minneapolis, you needed a $1 million order to turn anyone's head." CDC never regained the 70% share it had once enjoyed in the market for mainframe disk drives, but its Oklahoma City operation secured a profitable 20% of the high-performance 5.25-inch market.

Had Apple created a similar organization to develop its Newton personal digital assistant (PDA), those who have pronounced it a flop might have deemed it a success. In launching the product, Apple made the mistake of acting as if it were dealing with an established market. Apple managers went into the PDA project assuming that it had to make a significant contribution to corporate growth. Accordingly, they researched customer desires exhaustively and then bet huge sums launching the Newton. Had Apple made a more modest technological and financial bet and entrusted the Newton to an organization the size that Apple itself was when it launched the Apple I, the outcome might have been different. The Newton might have been seen more broadly as a solid step forward in the quest to discover what customers really want. In fact, many more Newtons than Apple I models were sold within a year of their introduction.

Keep the disruptive organization independent

Established companies can only dominate emerging markets by creating small organizations of the sort CDC created in Oklahoma City. But what should they do when the emerging market becomes large and established?

Most managers assume that once a spin-off has become commercially viable in a new market, it should be integrated into the mainstream organization. They reason that the fixed costs associated with engineering, manufacturing, sales, and distribution activities can be shared across a broader group of customers and products.

This approach might work with sustaining technologies; however, with disruptive technologies, folding the spin-off into the mainstream organization can be disastrous. When the independent and mainstream organizations are folded together in order to share resources, debilitating arguments inevitably arise over which groups get what resources and whether or when to cannibalize established products. In the history of the disk-drive industry, every company that has tried to manage mainstream and disruptive businesses within a single organization failed.

No matter the industry, a corporation consists of business units with finite life spans: The technological and market bases of any business will eventually disappear. Disruptive technologies are part of that cycle. Companies that understand this process can create new businesses to replace the ones that must inevitably die. To do so, companies must give managers of disruptive innovation free rein to realize the technology's full potential—even if it means ultimately killing the mainstream business. For the corporation to live, it must be willing to see business units die. If the corporation doesn't kill them off itself, competitors will.

The key to prospering at points of disruptive change is not simply to take more risks, invest for the long term, or fight bureaucracy. The key is to manage strategically important disruptive technologies in an organizational context where small orders create energy, where fast low-cost forays into ill-defined markets are possible, and where overhead is low enough to permit profit even in emerging markets.

Managers of established companies can master disruptive technologies with extraordinary success. But when they seek to develop and launch a disruptive technology that is rejected by important customers within the context of the mainstream business's financial demands, they fail—not because they make the wrong decisions, but because they make the right decisions for circumstances that are about to become history.

NOTE

1. Robert A. Burgelman, "Fading Memories: A Process Theory of Strategic Business Exit in Dynamic Environments," *Administrative Science Quarterly* 39 (1994), pp. 24–56.

Reprinted from *Harvard Business Review*,
January–February 1995 (product #95103).

CHAPTER SEVEN

Leading Change

Why Transformation Efforts Fail

by John P. Kotter

Over the past decade, I have watched more than 100 companies try to remake themselves into significantly better competitors. They have included large organizations (Ford) and small ones (Landmark Communications), companies based in the United States (General Motors) and elsewhere (British Airways), corporations that were on their knees (Eastern Airlines), and companies that were earning good money (Bristol-Myers Squibb). These efforts have gone under many banners: total quality management, reengineering, rightsizing, restructuring, cultural change, and turnaround. But, in almost every case, the basic goal has been the same: to make fundamental changes in how business is conducted in order to help cope with a new, more challenging market environment.

A few of these corporate change efforts have been very successful. A few have been utter failures. Most fall somewhere in between, with a distinct tilt toward the lower end of the scale. The lessons that can be drawn are interesting and will probably be relevant to even more organizations in the increasingly competitive business environment of the coming decade.

The most general lesson to be learned from the more successful cases is that the change process goes through a series of phases that, in total, usually require a considerable length of time. Skipping steps creates only the illusion of speed and never produces a satisfying result. A second very general lesson is that critical mistakes in any of the phases can have a devastating impact, slowing momentum and negating hard-won gains. Perhaps because we have relatively little experience in renewing organizations, even very capable people often make at least one big error.

Error 1: Not Establishing a Great Enough Sense of Urgency

Most successful change efforts begin when some individuals or some groups start to look hard at a company's competitive situation, market position, technological trends, and financial performance. They focus on the potential revenue drop when an important patent expires, the five-year trend in declining margins in a core business, or an emerging market that everyone seems to be ignoring. They then find ways to communicate this information broadly and dramatically, especially with respect to crises, potential crises, or great opportunities that are very timely. This first step is essential because just getting a transformation program started requires the aggressive cooperation of many individuals. Without motivation, people won't help and the effort goes nowhere.

Compared with other steps in the change process, phase one can sound easy. It is not. Well over 50% of the companies I have watched fail in this first phase. What are the reasons for that failure? Sometimes executives underestimate how hard it can be to drive people out of their comfort zones. Sometimes they grossly overestimate how successful they have already been in increasing urgency. Sometimes they lack patience: "Enough with the preliminaries; let's get on with it." In many cases, executives become paralyzed by the downside possibilities. They worry that employees with seniority will become defensive, that morale will drop, that events will spin out of control, that short-term business results will be jeopardized, that the stock will sink, and that they will be blamed for creating a crisis.

Eight steps to transforming your organization

1. Establishing a sense of urgency
- Examining market and competitive realities
- Identifying and discussing crises, potential crises, or major opportunities

2. Forming a powerful guiding coalition
- Assembling a group with enough power to lead the change effort
- Encouraging the group to work together as a team

3. Creating a vision
- Creating a vision to help direct the change effort
- Developing strategies for achieving that vision

4. Communicating the vision
- Using every vehicle possible to communicate the new vision and strategies
- Teaching new behaviors by the example of the guiding coalition

5. Empowering others to act on the vision
- Getting rid of obstacles to change
- Changing systems or structures that seriously undermine the vision
- Encouraging risk taking and nontraditional ideas, activities, and actions

6. Planning for and creating short-term wins
- Planning for visible performance improvements
- Creating those improvements
- Recognizing and rewarding employees involved in the improvements

7. Consolidating improvements and producing still more change
- Using increased credibility to change systems, structures, and policies that don't fit the vision
- Hiring, promoting, and developing employees who can implement the vision
- Reinvigorating the process with new projects, themes, and change agents

8. Institutionalizing new approaches
- Articulating the connections between the new behaviors and corporate success
- Developing the means to ensure leadership development and succession

A paralyzed senior management often comes from having too many managers and not enough leaders. Management's mandate is to minimize risk and to keep the current system operating. Change, by definition, requires creating a new system, which in turn always demands leadership. Phase one in a renewal process typically goes nowhere until enough real leaders are promoted or hired into senior-level jobs.

Transformations often begin, and begin well, when an organization has a new head who is a good leader and who sees the need for a major change. If the renewal target is the entire company, the CEO is key. If change is needed in a division, the division general manager is key. When these individuals are not new leaders, great leaders, or change champions, phase one can be a huge challenge.

Bad business results are both a blessing and a curse in the first phase. On the positive side, losing money does catch people's attention. But it also gives less maneuvering room. With good business results, the opposite is true: Convincing people of the need for change is much harder, but you have more resources to help make changes.

But whether the starting point is good performance or bad, in the more successful cases I have witnessed, an individual or a group always facilitates a frank discussion of potentially unpleasant facts: about new competition, shrinking margins, decreasing market share, flat earnings, a lack of revenue growth, or other relevant indices of a declining competitive position. Because there seems to be an almost universal human tendency to shoot the bearer of bad news, especially if the head of the organization is not a change champion, executives in these companies often rely on outsiders to bring unwanted information. Wall Street analysts, customers, and consultants can all be helpful in this regard. The purpose of all this activity, in the words of one former CEO of a large European company, is "to make the status quo seem more dangerous than launching into the unknown."

In a few of the most successful cases, a group has manufactured a crisis. One CEO deliberately engineered the largest accounting loss in the company's history, creating huge pressures from Wall

Street in the process. One division president commissioned first-ever customer-satisfaction surveys, knowing full well that the results would be terrible. He then made these findings public. On the surface, such moves can look unduly risky. But there is also risk in playing it too safe: When the urgency rate is not pumped up enough, the transformation process cannot succeed and the long-term future of the organization is put in jeopardy.

When is the urgency rate high enough? From what I have seen, the answer is when about 75% of a company's management is honestly convinced that business-as-usual is totally unacceptable. Anything less can produce very serious problems later on in the process.

Error 2: Not Creating a Powerful Enough Guiding Coalition

Major renewal programs often start with just one or two people. In cases of successful transformation efforts, the leadership coalition grows and grows over time. But whenever some minimum mass is not achieved early in the effort, nothing much worthwhile happens.

It is often said that major change is impossible unless the head of the organization is an active supporter. What I am talking about goes far beyond that. In successful transformations, the chairman or president or division general manager, plus another 5 or 15 or 50 people, come together and develop a shared commitment to excellent performance through renewal. In my experience, this group never includes all of the company's most senior executives because some people just won't buy in, at least not at first. But in the most successful cases, the coalition is always pretty powerful—in terms of titles, information and expertise, reputations and relationships.

In both small and large organizations, a successful guiding team may consist of only three to five people during the first year of a renewal effort. But in big companies, the coalition needs to grow to the 20 to 50 range before much progress can be made in phase three and beyond. Senior managers always form the core of the group.

But sometimes you find board members, a representative from a key customer, or even a powerful union leader.

Because the guiding coalition includes members who are not part of senior management, it tends to operate outside of the normal hierarchy by definition. This can be awkward, but it is clearly necessary. If the existing hierarchy were working well, there would be no need for a major transformation. But since the current system is not working, reform generally demands activity outside of formal boundaries, expectations, and protocol.

A high sense of urgency within the managerial ranks helps enormously in putting a guiding coalition together. But more is usually required. Someone needs to get these people together, help them develop a shared assessment of their company's problems and opportunities, and create a minimum level of trust and communication. Off-site retreats, for two or three days, are one popular vehicle for accomplishing this task. I have seen many groups of 5 to 35 executives attend a series of these retreats over a period of months.

Companies that fail in phase two usually underestimate the difficulties of producing change and thus the importance of a powerful guiding coalition. Sometimes they have no history of teamwork at the top and therefore undervalue the importance of this type of coalition. Sometimes they expect the team to be led by a staff executive from human resources, quality, or strategic planning instead of a key line manager. No matter how capable or dedicated the staff head, groups without strong line leadership never achieve the power that is required.

Efforts that don't have a powerful enough guiding coalition can make apparent progress for a while. But, sooner or later, the opposition gathers itself together and stops the change.

Error 3: Lacking a Vision

In every successful transformation effort that I have seen, the guiding coalition develops a picture of the future that is relatively easy to communicate and appeals to customers, stockholders, and employees. A vision always goes beyond the numbers that are typically found in five-year plans. A vision says something that helps clarify the direction in which an organization needs to move. Sometimes the first draft comes mostly from a single individual. It is usually a bit blurry, at least initially. But after the coalition works at it for 3 or 5 or even 12 months, something much better emerges through their tough analytical thinking and a little dreaming. Eventually, a strategy for achieving that vision is also developed.

In one midsize European company, the first pass at a vision contained two-thirds of the basic ideas that were in the final product. The concept of global reach was in the initial version from the beginning. So was the idea of becoming preeminent in certain businesses. But one central idea in the final version—getting out of low value-added activities—came only after a series of discussions over a period of several months.

Without a sensible vision, a transformation effort can easily dissolve into a list of confusing and incompatible projects that can take the organization in the wrong direction or nowhere at all. Without a sound vision, the reengineering project in the accounting department, the new 360-degree performance appraisal from the human resources department, the plant's quality program, the cultural change project in the sales force will not add up in a meaningful way.

In failed transformations, you often find plenty of plans and directives and programs, but no vision. In one case, a company gave out four-inch-thick notebooks describing its change effort. In mind-numbing detail, the books spelled out procedures, goals, methods, and deadlines. But nowhere was there a clear and compelling statement of where all this was leading. Not surprisingly, most of the employees with whom I talked were either confused or alienated. The big, thick books did not rally them together or inspire change. In fact, they probably had just the opposite effect.

In a few of the less successful cases that I have seen, management had a sense of direction, but it was too complicated or blurry to be useful. Recently, I asked an executive in a midsize company to describe his vision and received in return a barely comprehensible

30-minute lecture. Buried in his answer were the basic elements of a sound vision. But they were buried—deeply.

A useful rule of thumb: if you can't communicate the vision to someone in five minutes or less and get a reaction that signifies both understanding and interest, you are not yet done with this phase of the transformation process.

Error 4: Undercommunicating the Vision by a Factor of Ten

I've seen three patterns with respect to communication, all very common. In the first, a group actually does develop a pretty good transformation vision and then proceeds to communicate it by holding a single meeting or sending out a single communication. Having used about 0.0001% of the yearly intracompany communication, the group is startled that few people seem to understand the new approach. In the second pattern, the head of the organization spends a considerable amount of time making speeches to employee groups, but most people still don't get it (not surprising, since vision captures only 0.0005% of the total yearly communication). In the third pattern, much more effort goes into newsletters and speeches, but some very visible senior executives still behave in ways that are antithetical to the vision. The net result is that cynicism among the troops goes up, while belief in the communication goes down.

Transformation is impossible unless hundreds or thousands of people are willing to help, often to the point of making short-term sacrifices. Employees will not make sacrifices, even if they are unhappy with the status quo, unless they believe that useful change is possible. Without credible communication, and a lot of it, the hearts and minds of the troops are never captured.

This fourth phase is particularly challenging if the short-term sacrifices include job losses. Gaining understanding and support is tough when downsizing is a part of the vision. For this reason, successful visions usually include new growth possibilities and the commitment to treat fairly anyone who is laid off.

Executives who communicate well incorporate messages into their hour-by-hour activities. In a routine discussion about a business problem, they talk about how proposed solutions fit (or don't fit) into the bigger picture. In a regular performance appraisal, they talk about how the employee's behavior helps or undermines the vision. In a review of a division's quarterly performance, they talk not only about the numbers but also about how the division's executives are contributing to the transformation. In a routine Q&A with employees at a company facility, they tie their answers back to renewal goals.

In more successful transformation efforts, executives use all existing communication channels to broadcast the vision. They turn boring and unread company newsletters into lively articles about the vision. They take ritualistic and tedious quarterly management meetings and turn them into exciting discussions of the transformation. They throw out much of the company's generic management education and replace it with courses that focus on business problems and the new vision. The guiding principle is simple: use every possible channel, especially those that are being wasted on nonessential information.

Perhaps even more important, most of the executives I have known in successful cases of major change learn to "walk the talk." They consciously attempt to become a living symbol of the new corporate culture. This is often not easy. A 60-year-old plant manager who has spent precious little time over 40 years thinking about customers will not suddenly behave in a customer-oriented way. But I have witnessed just such a person change, and change a great deal. In that case, a high level of urgency helped. The fact that the man was a part of the guiding coalition and the vision-creation team also helped. So did all the communication, which kept reminding him of the desired behavior, and all the feedback from his peers and subordinates, which helped him see when he was not engaging in that behavior.

Communication comes in both words and deeds, and the latter are often the most powerful form. Nothing undermines change more than behavior by important individuals that is inconsistent with their words.

Error 5: Not Removing Obstacles
to the New Vision

Successful transformations begin to involve large numbers of people as the process progresses. Employees are emboldened to try new approaches, to develop new ideas, and to provide leadership. The only constraint is that the actions fit within the broad parameters of the overall vision. The more people involved, the better the outcome.

To some degree, a guiding coalition empowers others to take action simply by successfully communicating the new direction. But communication is never sufficient by itself. Renewal also requires the removal of obstacles. Too often, an employee understands the new vision and wants to help make it happen. But an elephant appears to be blocking the path. In some cases, the elephant is in the person's head, and the challenge is to convince the individual that no external obstacle exists. But in most cases, the blockers are very real.

Sometimes the obstacle is the organizational structure: narrow job categories can seriously undermine efforts to increase productivity or make it very difficult even to think about customers. Sometimes compensation or performance-appraisal systems make people choose between the new vision and their own self-interest. Perhaps worst of all are bosses who refuse to change and who make demands that are inconsistent with the overall effort.

One company began its transformation process with much publicity and actually made good progress through the fourth phase. Then the change effort ground to a halt because the officer in charge of the company's largest division was allowed to undermine most of the new initiatives. He paid lip service to the process but did not change his behavior or encourage his managers to change. He did not reward the unconventional ideas called for in the vision. He allowed human resource systems to remain intact even when they were clearly inconsistent with the new ideals. I think the officer's motives were complex. To some degree, he did not believe the company needed major change. To some degree, he felt personally threatened by all the change. To some degree, he was afraid that he could not produce both change and the expected operating profit. But despite the fact that they backed the renewal effort, the other officers did virtually nothing to stop the one blocker. Again, the reasons were complex. The company had no history of confronting problems like this. Some people were afraid of the officer. The CEO was concerned that he might lose a talented executive. The net result was disastrous. Lower-level managers concluded that senior management had lied to them about their commitment to renewal, cynicism grew, and the whole effort collapsed.

In the first half of a transformation, no organization has the momentum, power, or time to get rid of all obstacles. But the big ones must be confronted and removed. If the blocker is a person, it is important that he or she be treated fairly and in a way that is consistent with the new vision. But action is essential, both to empower others and to maintain the credibility of the change effort as a whole.

Error 6: Not Systematically Planning for and Creating Short-Term Wins

Real transformation takes time, and a renewal effort risks losing momentum if there are no short-term goals to meet and celebrate. Most people won't go on the long march unless they see compelling evidence within 12 to 24 months that the journey is producing expected results. Without short-term wins, too many people give up or actively join the ranks of those people who have been resisting change.

One to two years into a successful transformation effort, you find quality beginning to go up on certain indices or the decline in net income stopping. You find some successful new product introductions or an upward shift in market share. You find an impressive productivity improvement or a statistically higher customer-satisfaction rating. But whatever the case, the win is unambiguous. The result is not just a judgment call that can be discounted by those opposing change.

Creating short-term wins is different from hoping for short-term wins. The latter is passive, the former active. In a successful transformation, managers actively look for ways to obtain clear performance improvements, establish goals in the yearly planning system, achieve the objectives, and reward the people involved with recognition, promotions, and even money. For example, the guiding coalition at a U.S. manufacturing company produced a highly visible and successful new product introduction about 20 months after the start of its renewal effort. The new product was selected about six months into the effort because it met multiple criteria: It could be designed and launched in a relatively short period; it could be handled by a small team of people who were devoted to the new vision; it had upside potential; and the new product-development team could operate outside the established departmental structure without practical problems. Little was left to chance, and the win boosted the credibility of the renewal process.

Managers often complain about being forced to produce short-term wins, but I've found that pressure can be a useful element in a change effort. When it becomes clear to people that major change will take a long time, urgency levels can drop. Commitments to produce short-term wins help keep the urgency level up and force detailed analytical thinking that can clarify or revise visions.

Error 7: Declaring Victory Too Soon

After a few years of hard work, managers may be tempted to declare victory with the first clear performance improvement. While celebrating a win is fine, declaring the war won can be catastrophic. Until changes sink deeply into a company's culture, a process that can take five to ten years, new approaches are fragile and subject to regression.

In the recent past, I have watched a dozen change efforts operate under the reengineering theme. In all but two cases, victory was declared and the expensive consultants were paid and thanked when the first major project was completed after two to three years. Within two more years, the useful changes that had been introduced slowly disappeared. In two of the ten cases, it's hard to find any trace of the reengineering work today.

Over the past 20 years, I've seen the same sort of thing happen to huge quality projects, organizational development efforts, and more. Typically, the problems start early in the process: the urgency level is not intense enough, the guiding coalition is not powerful enough, and the vision is not clear enough. But it is the premature victory celebration that kills momentum. And then the powerful forces associated with tradition take over.

Ironically, it is often a combination of change initiators and change resistors that creates the premature victory celebration. In their enthusiasm over a clear sign of progress, the initiators go overboard. They are then joined by resistors, who are quick to spot any opportunity to stop change. After the celebration is over, the resistors point to the victory as a sign that the war has been won and the troops should be sent home. Weary troops allow themselves to be convinced that they won. Once home, the foot soldiers are reluctant to climb back on the ships. Soon thereafter, change comes to a halt, and tradition creeps back in.

Instead of declaring victory, leaders of successful efforts use the credibility afforded by short-term wins to tackle even bigger problems. They go after systems and structures that are not consistent with the transformation vision and have not been confronted before. They pay great attention to who is promoted, who is hired, and how people are developed. They include new reengineering projects that are even bigger in scope than the initial ones. They understand that renewal efforts take not months but years. In fact, in one of the most successful transformations that I have ever seen, we quantified the amount of change that occurred each year over a seven-year period. On a scale of 1 (low) to 10 (high), year one received a 2, year two a 4, year three a 3, year four a 7, year five an 8, year six a 4, and year seven a 2. The peak came in year five, fully 36 months after the first set of visible wins.

Error 8: Not Anchoring Changes in the Corporation's Culture

In the final analysis, change sticks when it becomes "the way we do things around here," when it seeps into the bloodstream of the corporate body. Until new behaviors are rooted in social norms and shared values, they are subject to degradation as soon as the pressure for change is removed.

Two factors are particularly important in institutionalizing change in corporate culture. The first is a conscious attempt to show people how the new approaches, behaviors, and attitudes have helped improve performance. When people are left on their own to make the connections, they sometimes create very inaccurate links. For example, because results improved while charismatic Harry was boss, the troops link his mostly idiosyncratic style with those results instead of seeing how their own improved customer service and productivity were instrumental. Helping people see the right connections requires communication. Indeed, one company was relentless, and it paid off enormously. Time was spent at every major management meeting to discuss why performance was increasing. The company newspaper ran article after article showing how changes had boosted earnings.

The second factor is taking sufficient time to make sure that the next generation of top management really does personify the new approach. If the requirements for promotion don't change, renewal rarely lasts. One bad succession decision at the top of an organization can undermine a decade of hard work. Poor succession decisions are possible when boards of directors are not an integral part of the renewal effort. In at least three instances I have seen, the champion for change was the retiring executive, and although his successor was not a resistor, he was not a change champion. Because the boards did not understand the transformations in any detail, they could not see that their choices were not good fits. The retiring executive in one case tried unsuccessfully to talk his board into a less seasoned candidate who better personified the transformation. In the other two cases, the CEOs did not resist the boards' choices, because they felt the transformation could not be undone by their successors. They were wrong. Within two years, signs of renewal began to disappear at both companies.

———————

There are still more mistakes that people make, but these eight are the big ones. I realize that in a short article everything is made to sound a bit too simplistic. In reality, even successful change efforts are messy and full of surprises. But just as a relatively simple vision is needed to guide people through a major change, so a vision of the change process can reduce the error rate. And fewer errors can spell the difference between success and failure.

———————

Reprinted from *Harvard Business Review*,
March–April 1995 (product #95204).

CHAPTER EIGHT

One More Time: How Do You Motivate Employees?

by Frederick Herzberg

How many articles, books, speeches, and workshops have pleaded plaintively, "How do I get an employee to do what I want?"

The psychology of motivation is tremendously complex, and what has been unraveled with any degree of assurance is small indeed. But the dismal ratio of knowledge to speculation has not dampened the enthusiasm for new forms of snake oil that are constantly coming on the market, many of them with academic testimonials. Doubtless this article will have no depressing impact on the market for snake oil, but since the ideas expressed in it have been tested in many corporations and other organizations, it will help—I hope—to redress the imbalance in the aforementioned ratio.

"Motivating" with KITA

In lectures to industry on the problem, I have found that the audiences are usually anxious for quick and practical answers, so I will begin with a straightforward, practical formula for moving people.

What is the simplest, surest, and most direct way of getting someone to do something? Ask? But if the person responds that he or she does not want to do it, then that calls for psychological consultation to determine the reason for such obstinacy. Tell the person? The response shows that he or she does not understand you, and now an expert in communication methods has to be brought in to show you how to get through. Give the person a monetary incentive? I do not need to remind the reader of the complexity and difficulty involved in setting up and administering an incentive system. Show the person? This means a costly training program. We need a simple way.

Every audience contains the "direct action" manager who shouts, "Kick the person!" And this type of manager is right. The surest and least circumlocuted way of getting someone to do something is to administer a kick in the pants—to give what might be called the KITA.

There are various forms of KITA, and here are some of them:

Negative physical KITA

This is a literal application of the term and was frequently used in the past. It has, however, three major drawbacks: (1) It is inelegant; (2) it contradicts the precious image of benevolence that most organizations cherish; and (3) since it is a physical attack, it directly stimulates the autonomic nervous system, and this often results in negative feedback—the employee may just kick you in return. These factors give rise to certain taboos against negative physical KITA.

In uncovering infinite sources of psychological vulnerabilities and the appropriate methods to play tunes on them, psychologists have come to the rescue of those who are no longer permitted to use negative physical KITA. "He took my rug away"; "I wonder what she meant by that"; "The boss is always going around me"—these symptomatic expressions of ego sores that have been rubbed raw are the result of application of:

Negative psychological KITA

This has several advantages over negative physical KITA. First, the cruelty is not visible; the bleeding is internal and comes much later. Second, since it affects the higher cortical centers of the brain with its inhibitory powers, it reduces the possibility of physical backlash.

Third, since the number of psychological pains that a person can feel is almost infinite, the direction and site possibilities of the KITA are increased many times. Fourth, the person administering the kick can manage to be above it all and let the system accomplish the dirty work. Fifth, those who practice it receive some ego satisfaction (one-upmanship), whereas they would find drawing blood abhorrent. Finally, if the employee does complain, he or she can always be accused of being paranoid; there is no tangible evidence of an actual attack.

Now, what does negative KITA accomplish? If I kick you in the rear (physically or psychologically), who is motivated? *I* am motivated; *you* move! Negative KITA does not lead to motivation, but to movement. So:

Positive KITA

Let us consider motivation. If I say to you, "Do this for me or the company, and in return I will give you a reward, an incentive, more status, a promotion, all the quid pro quos that exist in the industrial organization," am I motivating you? The overwhelming opinion I receive from management people is, "Yes, this is motivation."

I have a year-old schnauzer. When it was a small puppy and I wanted it to move, I kicked it in the rear and it moved. Now that I have finished its obedience training, I hold up a dog biscuit when I want the schnauzer to move. In this instance, who is motivated—I or the dog? The dog wants the biscuit, but it is I who want it to move. Again, I am the one who is motivated, and the dog is the one who moves. In this instance all I did was apply KITA frontally; I exerted a pull instead of a push. When industry wishes to use such positive KITAs, it has available an incredible number and variety of dog biscuits (jelly beans for humans) to wave in front of employees to get them to jump.

Myths About Motivation

Why is KITA not motivation? If I kick my dog (from the front or the back), he will move. And when I want him to move again, what must I do? I must kick him again. Similarly, I can charge a person's battery, and then recharge it, and recharge it again. But it is only when one has a generator of one's own that we can talk about motivation. One then needs no outside stimulation. One *wants* to do it.

With this in mind, we can review some positive KITA personnel practices that were developed as attempts to instill "motivation":

1. Reducing time spent at work

This represents a marvelous way of motivating people to work—getting them off the job! We have reduced (formally and informally) the time spent on the job over the last 50 or 60 years until we are finally on the way to the "six-day weekend." An interesting variant of this approach is the development of off-hour recreation programs. The philosophy here seems to be that those who play together, work together. The fact is that motivated people seek more hours of work, not fewer.

2. Spiraling wages

Have these motivated people? Yes, to seek the next wage increase. Some medievalists still can be heard to say that a good depression will get employees moving. They feel that if rising wages don't or won't do the job, reducing them will.

3. Fringe benefits

Industry has outdone the most welfare-minded of welfare states in dispensing cradle-to-the-grave succor. One company I know of had an informal "fringe benefit of the month club" going for a while. The cost of fringe benefits in this country has reached approximately 25% of the wage dollar, and we still cry for motivation.

People spend less time working for more money and more security than ever before, and the trend cannot be reversed. These benefits are no longer rewards; they are rights. A six-day week is inhuman, a 10-hour day is exploitation, extended medical coverage is a basic decency, and stock options are the salvation of American initiative. Unless the ante is continuously raised, the psychological reaction of employees is that the company is turning back the clock.

When industry began to realize that both the economic nerve and the lazy nerve of their employees had insatiable appetites, it started to listen to the behavioral scientists who, more out of a humanist tradition than from scientific study, criticized management for not knowing how to deal with people. The next KITA easily followed.

4. Human relations training

More than 30 years of teaching and, in many instances, of practicing psychological approaches to handling people have resulted in costly human relations programs and, in the end, the same question: How do you motivate workers? Here, too, escalations have taken place. Thirty years ago it was necessary to request, "Please don't spit on the floor." Today the same admonition requires three "pleases" before the employee feels that a superior has demonstrated the psychologically proper attitude.

The failure of human relations training to produce motivation led to the conclusion that supervisors or managers themselves were not psychologically true to themselves in their practice of interpersonal decency. So an advanced form of human relations KITA, sensitivity training, was unfolded.

5. Sensitivity training

Do you really, really understand yourself? Do you really, really, really trust other people? Do you really, really, really, really cooperate? The failure of sensitivity training is now being explained, by those who have become opportunistic exploiters of the technique, as a failure to really (five times) conduct proper sensitivity training courses.

With the realization that there are only temporary gains from comfort and economic and interpersonal KITA, personnel managers concluded that the fault lay not in what they were doing, but in the employee's failure to appreciate what they were doing. This opened up the field of communications, a new area of "scientifically" sanctioned KITA.

6. Communications

The professor of communications was invited to join the faculty of management training programs and help in making employees understand what management was doing for them. House organs, briefing sessions, supervisory instruction on the importance of communication, and all sorts of propaganda have proliferated until today there is even an International Council of Industrial Editors. But no motivation resulted, and the obvious thought occurred that perhaps management was not hearing what the employees were saying. That led to the next KITA.

7. Two-way communication

Management ordered morale surveys, suggestion plans, and group participation programs. Then both management and employees were communicating and listening to each other more than ever, but without much improvement in motivation.

The behavioral scientists began to take another look at their conceptions and their data, and they took human relations one step further. A glimmer of truth was beginning to show through in the writings of the so-called higher-order-need psychologists. People, so they said, want to actualize themselves. Unfortunately, the "actualizing" psychologists got mixed up with the human relations psychologists, and a new KITA emerged.

8. Job participation

Though it may not have been the theoretical intention, job participation often became a "give them the big picture" approach. For example, if a man is tightening 10,000 nuts a day on an assembly line with a torque wrench, tell him he is building a Chevrolet. Another approach had the goal of giving employees a "feeling" that they are determining, in some measure, what they do on the job. The goal was to provide a *sense* of achievement rather than a substantive achievement in the task. Real achievement, of course, requires a task that makes it possible.

But still there was no motivation. This led to the inevitable conclusion that the employees must be sick, and therefore to the next KITA.

9. Employee counseling

The initial use of this form of KITA in a systematic fashion can be credited to the Hawthorne experiment of the Western Electric Company during the early 1930s. At that time, it was found that the employees harbored irrational feelings that were interfering with the rational operation of the factory. Counseling in this instance was a means of letting the employees unburden themselves by talking to someone about their problems. Although the counseling techniques were primitive, the program was large indeed.

The counseling approach suffered as a result of experiences during World War II, when the programs themselves were found to be interfering with the operation of the organizations; the counselors had forgotten their role of benevolent listeners and were attempting to do something about the problems that they heard about. Psychological counseling, however, has managed to survive the negative impact of World War II experiences and today is beginning to flourish with renewed sophistication. But, alas, many of these programs, like all the others, do not seem to have lessened the pressure of demands to find out how to motivate workers.

Since KITA results only in short-term movement, it is safe to predict that the cost of these programs will increase steadily and new varieties will be developed as old positive KITAs reach their satiation points.

Hygiene vs. Motivators

Let me rephrase the perennial question this way: How do you in-
stall a generator in an employee? A brief review of my motivation-
hygiene theory of job attitudes is required before theoretical and
practical suggestions can be offered. The theory was first drawn
from an examination of events in the lives of engineers and accountants. At least 16 other investigations, using a wide variety of populations (including some in the Communist countries), have since
been completed, making the original research one of the most rep-
licated studies in the field of job attitudes.

The findings of these studies, along with corroboration from
many other investigations using different procedures, suggest
that the factors involved in producing job satisfaction (and motivation) are separate and distinct from the factors that lead to job
dissatisfaction. (See figure 8-1.) Since separate factors need to be
considered, depending on whether job satisfaction or job dissatisfaction is being examined, it follows that these two feelings are
not opposites of each other. The opposite of job satisfaction is not
job dissatisfaction but, rather, *no* job satisfaction; and similarly,
the opposite of job dissatisfaction is not job satisfaction, but *no* job
dissatisfaction.

Stating the concept presents a problem in semantics, for we normally think of satisfaction and dissatisfaction as opposites; that
is, what is not satisfying must be dissatisfying and vice versa. But
when it comes to understanding the behavior of people in their
jobs, more than a play on words is involved.

Two different needs of human beings are involved here. One set
of needs can be thought of as stemming from humankind's animal
nature—the built-in drive to avoid pain from the environment, plus
all the learned drives that become conditioned to the basic biological needs. For example, hunger, a basic biological drive, makes it
necessary to earn money, and then money becomes a specific drive.
The other set of needs relates to that unique human characteristic,
the ability to achieve and, through achievement, to experience psychological growth. The stimuli for the growth needs are tasks that

FIGURE 8-1

Factors affecting job attitudes as reported in 12 investigations

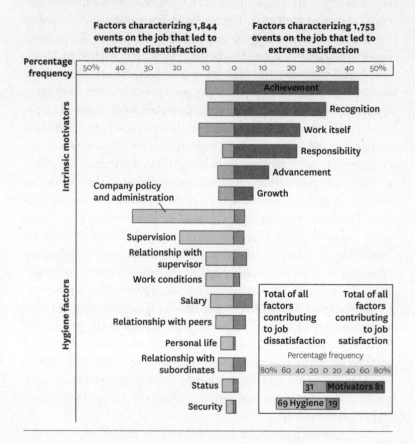

induce growth; in the industrial setting, they are the job content. Contrariwise, the stimuli inducing pain-avoidance behavior are found in the job environment.

The growth or *motivator* factors that are intrinsic to the job are: achievement, recognition for achievement, the work itself, responsibility, and growth or advancement. The dissatisfaction-avoidance or hygiene (KITA) factors that are extrinsic to the job include: company policy and administration, supervision, interpersonal relationships, working conditions, salary, status, and security.

A composite of the factors that are involved in causing job satisfaction and job dissatisfaction, drawn from samples of 1,685 employees, is shown in figure 8-1. The results indicate that motivators were the primary cause of satisfaction, and hygiene factors the primary cause of unhappiness on the job. The employees, studied in 12 different investigations, included lower level supervisors, professional women, agricultural administrators, men about to retire from management positions, hospital maintenance personnel, manufacturing supervisors, nurses, food handlers, military officers, engineers, scientists, housekeepers, teachers, technicians, female assemblers, accountants, Finnish foremen, and Hungarian engineers.

They were asked what job events had occurred in their work that had led to extreme satisfaction or extreme dissatisfaction on their part. Their responses are broken down into percentages of total "positive" job events and of total "negative" job events. (The figures total more than 100% on both the "hygiene" and "motivators" sides because often at least two factors can be attributed to a single event; advancement, for instance, often accompanies assumption of responsibility.)

To illustrate, a typical response involving achievement that had a negative effect for the employee was, "I was unhappy because I didn't do the job successfully." A typical response in the small number of positive job events in the company policy and administration grouping was, "I was happy because the company reorganized the section so that I didn't report any longer to the guy I didn't get along with."

As the lower right-hand part of the figure shows, of all the factors contributing to job satisfaction, 81% were motivators. And of all the factors contributing to the employees' dissatisfaction over their work, 69% involved hygiene elements.

Eternal triangle

There are three general philosophies of personnel management. The first is based on organizational theory, the second on industrial engineering, and the third on behavioral science.

Organizational theorists believe that human needs are either so irrational or so varied and adjustable to specific situations that the major function of personnel management is to be as pragmatic as the occasion demands. If jobs are organized in a proper manner, they reason, the result will be the most efficient job structure, and the most favorable job attitudes will follow as a matter of course.

Industrial engineers hold that humankind is mechanistically oriented and economically motivated and that human needs are best met by attuning the individual to the most efficient work process. The goal of personnel management therefore should be to concoct the most appropriate incentive system and to design the specific working conditions in a way that facilitates the most efficient use of the human machine. By structuring jobs in a manner that leads to the most efficient operation, engineers believe that they can obtain the optimal organization of work and the proper work attitudes.

Behavioral scientists focus on group sentiments, attitudes of individual employees, and the organization's social and psychological climate. This persuasion emphasizes one or more of the various hygiene and motivator needs. Its approach to personnel management is generally to emphasize some form of human relations education, in the hope of instilling healthy employee attitudes and an organizational climate that is considered to be felicitous to human values. The belief is that proper attitudes will lead to efficient job and organizational structure.

There is always a lively debate concerning the overall effectiveness of the approaches of organizational theorists and industrial engineers. Manifestly, both have achieved much. But the nagging question for behavioral scientists has been: What is the cost in human problems that eventually cause more expense to the organization—for instance, turnover, absenteeism, errors, violation of safety rules, strikes, restriction of output, higher wages, and greater fringe benefits? On the other hand, behavioral scientists are hard put to document much manifest improvement in personnel management, using their approach.

The motivation-hygiene theory suggests that work be *enriched* to bring about effective utilization of personnel. Such a systematic attempt to motivate employees by manipulating the motivator factors is just beginning. The term *job enrichment* describes this embryonic movement. An older term, *job enlargement*, should be avoided because it is associated with past failures stemming from a misunderstanding of the problem. Job enrichment provides the opportunity for the employee's psychological growth, while job enlargement merely makes a job structurally bigger. Since scientific job enrichment is very new, this article only suggests the principles and practical steps that have recently emerged from several successful experiments in industry.

Job loading

In attempting to enrich certain jobs, management often reduces the personal contribution of employees rather than giving them opportunities for growth in their accustomed jobs. Such endeavors, which I shall call horizontal job loading (as opposed to vertical loading, or providing motivator factors), have been the problem of earlier job enlargement programs. Job loading merely enlarges the meaninglessness of the job.

Some examples of this approach, and their effect, are:

- Challenging the employee by increasing the amount of production expected. If each tightens 10,000 bolts a day, see if each can tighten 20,000 bolts a day. The arithmetic involved shows that multiplying zero by zero still equals zero.

- Adding another meaningless task to the existing one, usually some routine clerical activity. The arithmetic here is adding zero to zero.

- Rotating the assignments of a number of jobs that need to be enriched. This means washing dishes for a while, then washing silverware. The arithmetic is substituting one zero for another zero.

- Removing the most difficult parts of the assignment in order to free the worker to accomplish more of the less challenging assignments. This traditional industrial engineering approach amounts to subtraction in the hope of accomplishing addition.

These are common forms of horizontal loading that frequently come up in preliminary brainstorming sessions of job enrichment. The principles of vertical loading have not all been worked out as yet, and they remain rather general, but I have furnished seven useful starting points for consideration in table 8-1.

A successful application

An example from a highly successful job enrichment experiment can illustrate the distinction between horizontal and vertical loading of a job. The subjects of this study were the stockholder correspondents employed by a very large corporation. Seemingly, the task required of these carefully selected and highly trained

TABLE 8-1

Principles of vertical job loading

Principle	Motivators involved
A. Removing some controls while retaining accountability	Responsibility and personal achievement
B. Increasing the accountability of individuals for their own work	Responsibility and recognition
C. Giving a person a complete natural unit of work (module, division, area, and so on)	Responsibility, achievement, and recognition
D. Granting additional authority to employees in their activity; job freedom	Responsibility, achievement, and recognition
E. Making periodic reports directly available to the workers themselves rather than to supervisors	Internal recognition
F. Introducing new and more difficult tasks not previously handled	Growth and learning
G. Assigning individuals specific or specialized tasks, enabling them to become experts	Responsibility, growth, and advancement

correspondents was quite complex and challenging. But almost all indexes of performance and job attitudes were low, and exit interviewing confirmed that the challenge of the job existed merely as words.

A job enrichment project was initiated in the form of an experiment with one group, designated as an achieving unit, having its job enriched by the principles described in table 8-1. A control group continued to do its job in the traditional way. (There were also two "uncommitted" groups of correspondents formed to measure the so-called Hawthorne effect—that is, to gauge whether productivity and attitudes toward the job changed artificially merely because employees sensed that the company was paying more attention to them in doing something different or novel. The results for these groups were substantially the same as for the control group, and for the sake of simplicity I do not deal with them in this summary.) No changes in hygiene were introduced for either group other than those that would have been made anyway, such as normal pay increases.

The changes for the achieving unit were introduced in the first two months, averaging one per week of the seven motivators listed in table 8-1. At the end of six months the members of the achieving unit were found to be outperforming their counterparts in the control group and, in addition, indicated a marked increase in their liking for their jobs. Other results showed that the achieving group had lower absenteeism and, subsequently, a much higher rate of promotion.

Figure 8-2 illustrates the changes in performance, measured in February and March, before the study period began, and at the end of each month of the study period. The shareholder service index represents quality of letters, including accuracy of information, and speed of response to stockholders' letters of inquiry. The index of a current month was averaged into the average of the two prior months, which means that improvement was harder to obtain if the indexes of the previous months were low. The "achievers" were performing less well before the six-month period started, and their performance service index continued to decline after the intro-

FIGURE 8-2

Employee performance in company experiment (three-month cumulative average)

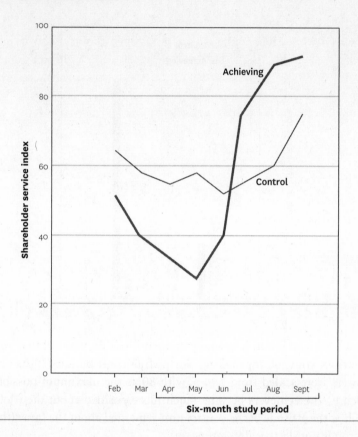

duction of the motivators, evidently because of uncertainty after their newly granted responsibilities. In the third month, however, performance improved, and soon the members of this group had reached a high level of accomplishment.

Figure 8-3 shows the two groups' attitudes toward their job, measured at the end of March, just before the first motivator was introduced, and again at the end of September. The correspondents were asked 16 questions, all involving motivation. A typical one

FIGURE 8-3

Change in attitudes toward tasks in company experiment (mean scores at beginning and end of six-month period)

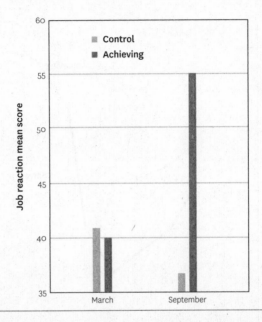

was, "As you see it, how many opportunities do you feel that you have in your job for making worthwhile contributions?" The answers were scaled from 1 to 5, with 80 as the maximum possible score. The achievers became much more positive about their job, while the attitude of the control unit remained about the same (the drop is not statistically significant).

How was the job of these correspondents restructured? Table 8-2 lists the suggestions made that were deemed to be horizontal loading, and the actual vertical loading changes that were incorporated in the job of the achieving unit. The capital letters under "Principle" after "Vertical loading" refer to the corresponding letters in table 8-1. The reader will note that the rejected forms of horizontal loading correspond closely to the list of common manifestations I mentioned earlier.

TABLE 8-2

Enlargement vs. enrichment of correspondents' tasks in company experiment

Horizontal loading suggestions rejected

Firm quotas could be set for letters to be answered each day, using a rate that would be hard to reach.

The secretaries could type the letters themselves, as well as compose them, or take on any other clerical functions.

All difficult or complex inquiries could be channeled to a few secretaries so that the remainder could achieve high rates of output. These jobs could be exchanged from time to time.

The secretaries could be rotated through units handling different customers and then sent back to their own units.

Vertical loading suggestions adopted	Principle
Subject matter experts were appointed within each unit for other members of the unit to consult before seeking supervisory help. (The supervisor had been answering all specialized and difficult questions.)	G
Correspondents signed their own names on letters. (The supervisor had been signing all letters.)	B
The work of the more experienced correspondents was proofread less frequently by supervisors and was done at the correspondents' desks, dropping verification from 100% to 10%. (Previously, all correspondents' letters had been checked by the supervisor.)	A
Production was discussed, but only in terms such as "a full day's work is expected." As time went on, this was no longer mentioned. (Before, the group had been constantly reminded of the number of letters that needed to be answered.)	D
Outgoing mail went directly to the mailroom without going over supervisors' desks. (The letters had always been routed through the supervisors.)	A
Correspondents were encouraged to answer letters in a more personalized way. (Reliance on the form-letter approach had been standard practice.)	C
Each correspondent was held personally responsible for the quality and accuracy of letters. (This responsibility had been the province of the supervisor and the verifier.)	B, E

Steps for Job Enrichment

Now that the motivator idea has been described in practice, here are the steps that managers should take in instituting the principle with their employees:

1. Select those jobs in which (a) the investment in industrial engineering does not make changes too costly, (b) attitudes are poor, (c) hygiene is becoming very costly, and (d) motivation will make a difference in performance.

2. Approach these jobs with the conviction that they can be changed. Years of tradition have led managers to believe that job content is sacrosanct and the only scope of action that they have is in ways of stimulating people.

3. Brainstorm a list of changes that may enrich the jobs, without concern for their practicality.

4. Screen the list to eliminate suggestions that involve hygiene, rather than actual motivation.

5. Screen the list for generalities, such as "give them more responsibility," that are rarely followed in practice. This might seem obvious, but the motivator words have never left industry; the substance has just been rationalized and organized out. Words like "responsibility," "growth," "achievement," and "challenge," for example, have been elevated to the lyrics of the patriotic anthem for all organizations. It is the old problem typified by the pledge of allegiance to the flag being more important than contributions to the country—of following the form, rather than the substance.

6. Screen the list to eliminate any *horizontal* loading suggestions.

7. Avoid direct participation by the employees whose jobs are to be enriched. Ideas they have expressed previously certainly constitute a valuable source for recommended

changes, but their direct involvement contaminates the process with human relations *hygiene* and, more specifically, gives them only a *sense* of making a contribution. The job is to be changed, and it is the content that will produce the motivation, not attitudes about being involved or the challenge inherent in setting up a job. That process will be over shortly, and it is what the employees will be doing from then on that will determine their motivation. A sense of participation will result only in short-term movement.

8. In the initial attempts at job enrichment, set up a controlled experiment. At least two equivalent groups should be chosen, one an experimental unit in which the motivators are systematically introduced over a period of time, and the other one a control group in which no changes are made. For both groups, hygiene should be allowed to follow its natural course for the duration of the experiment. Pre- and post-installation tests of performance and job attitudes are necessary to evaluate the effectiveness of the job enrichment program. The attitude test must be limited to motivator items in order to divorce employees' views of the jobs they are given from all the surrounding hygiene feelings that they might have.

9. Be prepared for a drop in performance in the experimental group the first few weeks. The changeover to a new job may lead to a temporary reduction in efficiency.

10. Expect your first-line supervisors to experience some anxiety and hostility over the changes you are making. The anxiety comes from their fear that the changes will result in poorer performance for their unit. Hostility will arise when the employees start assuming what the supervisors regard as their own responsibility for performance. The supervisor without checking duties to perform may then be left with little to do.

After successful experiment, however, the supervisors usually discover the supervisory and managerial functions they have neglected, or which were never theirs because all their time was given over to checking the work of their subordinates. For example, in the R&D division of one large chemical company I know of, the supervisors of the laboratory assistants were theoretically responsible for their training and evaluation. These functions, however, had come to be performed in a routine, unsubstantial fashion. After the job enrichment program, during which the supervisors were not merely passive observers of the assistants' performance, the supervisors actually were devoting their time to reviewing performance and administering thorough training.

What has been called an employee-centered style of supervision will come about not through education of supervisors, but by changing the jobs that they do.

Job enrichment will not be a one-time proposition, but a continuous management function. The initial changes should last for a very long period of time. There are a number of reasons for this:

- The changes should bring the job up to the level of challenge commensurate with the skill that was hired.

- Those who have still more ability eventually will be able to demonstrate it better and win promotion to higher level jobs.

- The very nature of motivators, as opposed to hygiene factors, is that they have a much longer-term effect on employees' attitudes. It is possible that the job will have to be enriched again, but this will not occur as frequently as the need for hygiene.

Not all jobs can be enriched, nor do all jobs need to be enriched. If only a small percentage of the time and money that is now devoted to hygiene, however, were given to job enrichment efforts, the return in human satisfaction and economic gain would be one of the largest dividends that industry and society have ever reaped through their efforts at better personnel management.

The argument for job enrichment can be summed up quite simply: If you have employees on a job, use them. If you can't use them on the job, get rid of them, either via automation or by selecting someone with lesser ability. If you can't use them and you can't get rid of them, you will have a motivation problem.

Reprinted from *Harvard Business Review*,
January 2003 (product #R0301F).
Originally published January–February 1968.

CHAPTER NINE

The Power of Small Wins

by Teresa M. Amabile and Steven J. Kramer

What is the best way to drive innovative work inside organizations? Important clues hide in the stories of world-renowned creators. It turns out that ordinary scientists, marketers, programmers, and other unsung knowledge workers, whose jobs require creative productivity every day, have more in common with famous innovators than most managers realize. The workday events that ignite their emotions, fuel their motivation, and trigger their perceptions are fundamentally the same.

The Double Helix, James Watson's 1968 memoir about discovering the structure of DNA, describes the roller coaster of emotions he and Francis Crick experienced through the progress and setbacks of the work that eventually earned them the Nobel Prize. After the excitement of their first attempt to build a DNA model, Watson and Crick noticed some serious flaws. According to Watson, "Our first minutes with the models . . . were not joyous." Later that evening, "a shape began to emerge which brought back our spirits." But when they showed their "breakthrough" to colleagues, they found that their model would not work. Dark days of doubt and ebbing motivation followed. When the duo finally had their bona fide breakthrough, and their colleagues found no fault with it, Watson wrote, "My morale skyrocketed, for I suspected that we now had the answer to the riddle." Watson and Crick were so driven by this success that they practically lived in the lab, trying to complete the work.

Throughout these episodes, Watson and Crick's progress—or lack thereof—ruled their reactions. In our recent research on creative work inside businesses, we stumbled upon a remarkably similar phenomenon. Through exhaustive analysis of diaries kept by knowledge workers, we discovered the *progress principle*: Of all the things that can boost emotions, motivation, and perceptions during a workday, the single most important is making progress in meaningful work. And the more frequently people experience that sense of progress, the more likely they are to be creatively productive in the long run. Whether they are trying to solve a major scientific mystery or simply produce a high-quality product or service, everyday progress—even a small win—can make all the difference in how they feel and perform.

The power of progress is fundamental to human nature, but few managers understand it or know how to leverage progress to boost motivation. In fact, work motivation has been a subject of long-standing debate. In a survey asking about the keys to motivating workers, we found that some managers ranked recognition for good work most important, while others put more stock in tangible incentives. Some focused on the value of interpersonal support, while still others thought clear goals were the answer. Interestingly, very few of our surveyed managers ranked progress first. (See the sidebar "A Surprise for Managers.")

If you are a manager, the progress principle holds clear implications for where to focus your efforts. It suggests that you have more influence than you may realize over employees' well-being, motivation, and creative output. Knowing what serves to catalyze and nourish progress—and what does the opposite—turns out to be the key to effectively managing people and their work.

In this article, we share what we have learned about the power of progress and how managers can leverage it. We spell out how a focus on progress translates into concrete managerial actions and provide a checklist to help make such behaviors habitual. But to clarify why those actions are so potent, we first describe our research and what the knowledge workers' diaries revealed about their *inner work lives*.

Inner Work Life and Performance

For nearly 15 years, we have been studying the psychological experiences and the performance of people doing complex work inside organizations. Early on, we realized that a central driver of creative, productive performance was the quality of a person's inner work life—the mix of emotions, motivations, and perceptions over the course of a workday. How happy workers feel; how motivated they are by an intrinsic interest in the work; how positively they view their organization, their management, their team, their work, and themselves—all these combine either to push them to higher levels of achievement or to drag them down.

To understand such interior dynamics better, we asked members of project teams to respond individually to an end-of-day e-mail survey during the course of the project—just over four months, on average. (For more on this research, see our article "Inner Work Life: Understanding the Subtext of Business Performance," HBR, May 2007.) The projects—inventing kitchen gadgets, managing product lines of cleaning tools, and solving complex IT problems for a hotel empire, for example—all involved creativity. The daily survey inquired about participants' emotions and moods, motivation levels, and perceptions of the work environment that day, as well as what work they did and what events stood out in their minds.

Twenty-six project teams from seven companies participated, comprising 238 individuals. This yielded nearly 12,000 diary entries. Naturally, every individual in our population experienced ups and downs. Our goal was to discover the states of inner work life and the workday events that correlated with the highest levels of creative output.

In a dramatic rebuttal to the commonplace claim that high pressure and fear spur achievement, we found that, at least in the realm of knowledge work, people are more creative and productive when their inner work lives are positive—when they feel happy, are intrinsically motivated by the work itself, and have positive perceptions of their colleagues and the organization. Moreover, in those

A Surprise for Managers

In a 1968 issue of HBR, Frederick Herzberg published a now-classic article titled "One More Time: How Do You Motivate Employees?" (See chapter 8.) Our findings are consistent with his message: People are most satisfied with their jobs (and therefore most motivated) when those jobs give them the opportunity to experience achievement.

The diary research we describe in this article—in which we microscopically examined the events of thousands of workdays, in real time—uncovered the mechanism underlying the sense of achievement: making consistent, meaningful progress.

But managers seem not to have taken Herzberg's lesson to heart. To assess contemporary awareness of the importance of daily work progress, we recently administered a survey to 669 managers of varying levels from dozens of companies around the world. We asked about the managerial tools that can affect employees' motivation and emotions. The respondents ranked five tools—support for making progress in the work, recognition for good work, incentives, interpersonal support, and clear goals—in order of importance.

Fully 95% of the managers who took our survey would probably be surprised to learn that supporting progress is the primary way to elevate motivation—because that's the percentage that failed to rank progress number one. In fact, only 35 managers ranked progress as the number one motivator—a mere 5%. The vast majority of respondents ranked support for making progress dead last as a motivator and third as an influence on emotion. They ranked "recognition for good work (either public or private)" as the most important factor in motivating workers and making them happy. In our diary study, recognition certainly did boost inner work life. But it wasn't nearly as prominent as progress. Besides, without work achievements, there is little to recognize.

---

positive states, people are more committed to the work and more collegial toward those around them. Inner work life, we saw, can fluctuate from one day to the next—sometimes wildly—and performance along with it. A person's inner work life on a given day fuels his or her performance for the day and can even affect performance the *next* day.

Once this *inner work life effect* became clear, our inquiry turned to whether and how managerial action could set it in motion. What events could evoke positive or negative emotions, motivations, and perceptions? The answers were tucked within our research participants' diary entries. There are predictable triggers that inflate or deflate inner work life, and, even accounting for variation among individuals, they are pretty much the same for everyone.

The Power of Progress

Our hunt for inner work life triggers led us to the progress principle. When we compared our research participants' best and worst days (based on their overall mood, specific emotions, and motivation levels), we found that the most common event triggering a "best day" was any progress in the work by the individual or the team. The most common event triggering a "worst day" was a setback.

Consider, for example, how progress relates to one component of inner work life: overall mood ratings. Steps forward occurred on 76% of people's best-mood days. By contrast, setbacks occurred on only 13% of those days. (See "Good Days" in the figure "What happens on good days and bad days?")

Two other types of inner work life triggers also occur frequently on best days: *catalysts,* actions that directly support work, including help from a person or group, and *nourishers,* events such as shows of respect and words of encouragement. Each has an opposite: *inhibitors,* actions that fail to support or actively hinder work, and *toxins*, discouraging or undermining events. Whereas catalysts and inhibitors are directed at the project, nourishers and toxins are directed at the person. Like setbacks, inhibitors and toxins are rare on days of great inner work life.

Events on worst-mood days are nearly the mirror image of those on best-mood days (see "Bad Days" in the figure "What happens on good days and bad days?"). Here, setbacks predominated, occurring on 67% of those days; progress occurred on only 25% of them. Inhibitors and toxins also marked many worst-mood days, and catalysts and nourishers were rare.

This is the progress principle made visible: If a person is motivated and happy at the end of the workday, it's a good bet that he or

What happens on good days and bad days?

Progress—even a small step forward—occurs on many of the days people report being in a good mood. Events on bad days—setbacks and other hindrances—are nearly the mirror image of those on good days.

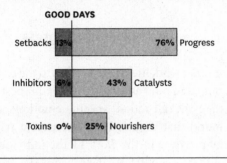

GOOD DAYS

Setbacks 13%	76% Progress
Inhibitors 6%	43% Catalysts
Toxins 0%	25% Nourishers

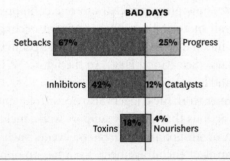

BAD DAYS

Setbacks 67%	25% Progress
Inhibitors 42%	12% Catalysts
Toxins 18%	4% Nourishers

she made some progress. If the person drags out of the office disengaged and joyless, a setback is most likely to blame.

When we analyzed all 12,000 daily surveys filled out by our participants, we discovered that progress and setbacks influence all three aspects of inner work life. On days when they made progress, our participants reported more positive *emotions*. They not only were in a more upbeat mood in general but also expressed more joy, warmth, and pride. When they suffered setbacks, they experienced more frustration, fear, and sadness.

Motivations were also affected: On progress days, people were more intrinsically motivated—by interest in and enjoyment of the work itself. On setback days, they were not only less intrinsically motivated but also less extrinsically motivated by recognition. Apparently, setbacks can lead a person to feel generally apathetic and disinclined to do the work at all.

Perceptions differed in many ways, too. On progress days, people perceived significantly more positive challenge in their work. They saw their teams as more mutually supportive and reported more positive interactions between the teams and their supervisors. On a number of dimensions, perceptions suffered when people encountered setbacks. They found less positive challenge in the work, felt that they had less freedom in carrying it out, and reported that they had insufficient resources. On setback days, participants perceived both their teams and their supervisors as less supportive.

To be sure, our analyses establish correlations but do not prove causality. Were these changes in inner work life the result of progress and setbacks, or was the effect the other way around? The numbers alone cannot answer that. However, we do know, from reading thousands of diary entries, that more-positive perceptions, a sense of accomplishment, satisfaction, happiness, and even elation often followed progress. Here's a typical post-progress entry, from a programmer: "I smashed that bug that's been frustrating me for almost a calendar week. That may not be an event to you, but I live a very drab life, so I'm all hyped."

Likewise, we saw that deteriorating perceptions, frustration, sadness, and even disgust often followed setbacks. As another participant, a product marketer, wrote, "We spent a lot of time updating the Cost Reduction project list, and after tallying all the numbers, we are still coming up short of our goal. It is discouraging to not be able to hit it after all the time spent and hard work."

Almost certainly, the causality goes both ways, and managers can use this feedback loop between progress and inner work life to support both.

Minor Milestones

When we think about progress, we often imagine how good it feels to achieve a long-term goal or experience a major breakthrough. These big wins are great—but they are relatively rare. The good news is that even small wins can boost inner work life tremendously. Many of the progress events our research participants reported represented only minor steps forward. Yet they often evoked outsize positive reactions. Consider this diary entry from a programmer in a high-tech company, which was accompanied by very positive self-ratings of her emotions, motivations, and perceptions that day: "I figured out why something was not working correctly. I felt relieved and happy because this was a minor milestone for me."

Even ordinary, incremental progress can increase people's engagement in the work and their happiness during the workday. Across all types of events our participants reported, a notable proportion (28%) of incidents that had a minor impact on the project had a major impact on people's feelings about it. Because inner work life has such a potent effect on creativity and productivity, and because small but consistent steps forward, shared by many people, can accumulate into excellent execution, progress events that often go unnoticed are critical to the overall performance of organizations.

Unfortunately, there is a flip side. Small losses or setbacks can have an extremely negative effect on inner work life. In fact, our study and research by others show that negative events can have a more powerful impact than positive ones. Consequently, it is especially important for managers to minimize daily hassles.

Progress in Meaningful Work

We've shown how gratifying it is for workers when they are able to chip away at a goal, but recall what we said earlier: The key to motivating performance is supporting progress in *meaningful* work. Making headway boosts your inner work life, but only if the work matters to you.

Think of the most boring job you've ever had. Many people nominate their first job as a teenager—washing pots and pans in a restaurant kitchen, for example, or checking coats at a museum. In jobs like those, the power of progress seems elusive. No matter how hard you work, there are always more pots to wash and coats to check;

only punching the time clock at the end of the day or getting the paycheck at the end of the week yields a sense of accomplishment.

In jobs with much more challenge and room for creativity, like the ones our research participants had, simply "making progress"—getting tasks done—doesn't guarantee a good inner work life, either. You may have experienced this rude fact in your own job, on days (or in projects) when you felt demotivated, devalued, and frustrated, even though you worked hard and got things done. The likely cause is your perception of the completed tasks as peripheral or irrelevant. For the progress principle to operate, the work must be meaningful to the person doing it.

In 1983, Steve Jobs was trying to entice John Sculley to leave a wildly successful career at PepsiCo to become Apple's new CEO. Jobs reportedly asked him, "Do you want to spend the rest of your life selling sugared water or do you want a chance to change the world?" In making his pitch, Jobs leveraged a potent psychological force: the deep-seated human desire to do meaningful work.

Fortunately, to feel meaningful, work doesn't have to involve putting the first personal computers in the hands of ordinary people, or alleviating poverty, or helping to cure cancer. Work with less profound importance to society can matter if it contributes value to something or someone important to the worker. Meaning can be as simple as making a useful and high-quality product for a customer or providing a genuine service for a community. It can be supporting a colleague or boosting an organization's profits by reducing inefficiencies in a production process. Whether the goals are lofty or modest, as long as they are meaningful to the worker and it is clear how his or her efforts contribute to them, progress toward them can galvanize inner work life.

In principle, managers shouldn't have to go to extraordinary lengths to infuse jobs with meaning. Most jobs in modern organizations are potentially meaningful for the people doing them. However, managers can make sure that employees know just how their work is contributing. And, most important, they can avoid actions that negate its value. (See the sidebar "How Work Gets Stripped of Its Meaning.") All the participants in our research were doing

How Work Gets Stripped of Its Meaning

Diary entries from 238 knowledge workers who were members of creative project teams revealed four primary ways in which managers unwittingly drain work of its meaning.

- **Managers may dismiss the importance of employees' work or ideas.** Consider the case of Richard, a senior lab technician at a chemical company, who found meaning in helping his new-product development team solve complex technical problems. However, in team meetings over the course of a three-week period, Richard perceived that his team leader was ignoring his suggestions and those of his teammates. As a result, he felt that his contributions were not meaningful, and his spirits flagged. When at last he believed that he was again making a substantive contribution to the success of the project, his mood improved dramatically:

  > I felt much better at today's team meeting. I felt that my opinions and information were important to the project and that we have made some progress.

- **They may destroy employees' sense of ownership of their work.** Frequent and abrupt reassignments often have this effect. This happened repeatedly to the members of a product development team in a giant consumer products company, as described by team member Bruce:

  > As I've been handing over some projects, I do realize that I don't like to give them up. Especially when you have been with them from the start and are nearly to the end. You lose ownership. This happens to us way too often.

work that should have been meaningful; no one was washing pots or checking coats. Shockingly often, however, we saw potentially important, challenging work losing its power to inspire.

Supporting Progress: Catalysts and Nourishers

What can managers do to ensure that people are motivated, committed, and happy? How can they support workers' daily progress? They can use catalysts and nourishers, the other kinds of frequent "best day" events we discovered.

- **Managers may send the message that the work employees are doing will never see the light of day.** They can signal this—unintentionally—by shifting their priorities or changing their minds about how something should be done. We saw the latter in an internet technology company after user-interface developer Burt had spent weeks designing seamless transitions for non-English-speaking users. Not surprisingly, Burt's mood was seriously marred on the day he reported this incident:

  > Other options for the international [interfaces] were [given] to the team during a team meeting, which could render the work I am doing useless.

- **They may neglect to inform employees about unexpected changes in a customer's priorities.** Often, this arises from poor customer management or inadequate communication within the company. For example, Stuart, a data transformation expert at an IT company, reported deep frustration and low motivation on the day he learned that weeks of the team's hard work might have been for naught:

  > Found out that there is a strong possibility that the project may not be going forward, due to a shift in the client's agenda. There-fore, there is a strong possibility that all the time and effort put into the project was a waste of our time.

Catalysts are actions that support work. They include setting clear goals, allowing autonomy, providing sufficient resources and time, helping with the work, openly learning from problems and successes, and allowing a free exchange of ideas. Their opposites, in-hibitors, include failing to provide support and actively interfering with the work. Because of their impact on progress, catalysts and inhibitors ultimately affect inner work life. But they also have a more immediate impact: When people realize that they have clear and meaningful goals, sufficient resources, helpful colleagues, and so on, they get an instant boost to their emotions, their motivation to do a great job, and their perceptions of the work and the organization.

Nourishers are acts of interpersonal support, such as re-spect and recognition, encouragement, emotional comfort, and opportunities for affiliation. Toxins, their opposites, include disre-spect, discouragement, disregard for emotions, and interpersonal conflict. For good and for ill, nourishers and toxins affect inner work life directly and immediately.

Catalysts and nourishers—and their opposites—can alter the meaningfulness of work by shifting people's perceptions of their jobs and even themselves. For instance, when a manager makes sure that people have the resources they need, it signals to them that what they are doing is important and valuable. When managers recognize people for the work they do, it signals that they are important to the organization. In this way, catalysts and nourishers can lend greater meaning to the work—and amplify the operation of the progress principle.

The managerial actions that constitute catalysts and nourishers are not particularly mysterious; they may sound like Management 101, if not just common sense and common decency. But our diary study reminded us how often they are ignored or forgotten. Even some of the more attentive managers in the companies we studied did not consistently provide catalysts and nourishers. For example, a supply-chain specialist named Michael was, in many ways and on most days, an excellent subteam manager. But he was occasionally so overwhelmed that he became toxic toward his people. When a supplier failed to complete a "hot" order on time and Michael's team had to resort to air shipping to meet the customer's deadline, he realized that the profit margin on the sale would be blown. In irritation, he lashed out at his subordinates, demeaning the solid work they had done and disregarding their own frustration with the supplier. In his diary, he admitted as much:

> As of Friday, we have spent $28,000 in air freight to send 1,500
> $30 spray jet mops to our number two customer. Another
> 2,800 remain on this order, and there is a good probability
> that they too will gain wings. I have turned from the kindly
> Supply Chain Manager into the black-masked executioner. All
> similarity to civility is gone, our backs are against the wall,
> flight is not possible, therefore fight is probable.

Even when managers don't have their backs against the wall, developing long-term strategy and launching new initiatives can often seem more important—and perhaps sexier—than making sure that subordinates have what they need to make steady progress and feel supported as human beings. But as we saw repeatedly in our research, even the best strategy will fail if managers ignore the people working in the trenches to execute it.

A Model Manager—and a Tool for Emulating Him

We could explain the many (and largely unsurprising) moves that can catalyze progress and nourish spirits, but it may be more useful to give an example of a manager who consistently used those moves—and then to provide a simple tool that can help any manager do so.

Our model manager is Graham, whom we observed leading a small team of chemical engineers within a multinational European firm we'll call Kruger-Bern. The mission of the team's NewPoly project was clear and meaningful enough: develop a safe, biodegradable polymer to replace petrochemicals in cosmetics and, eventually, in a wide range of consumer products. As in many large firms, however, the project was nested in a confusing and sometimes threatening corporate setting of shifting top-management priorities, conflicting signals, and wavering commitments. Resources were uncomfortably tight, and uncertainty loomed over the project's future—and every team member's career. Even worse, an incident early in the project, in which an important customer reacted angrily to a sample, left the team reeling. Yet Graham was able to sustain team members' inner work lives by repeatedly and visibly removing obstacles, materially supporting progress, and emotionally supporting the team.

Graham's management approach excelled in four ways. First, he established a positive climate, one event at a time, which set behavioral norms for the entire team. When the customer complaint stopped the project in its tracks, for example, he engaged immediately with the team to analyze the problem, without recriminations, and develop a plan for repairing the relationship.

In doing so, he modeled how to respond to crises in the work: not by panicking or pointing fingers but by identifying problems and their causes, and developing a coordinated action plan. This is both a practical approach and a great way to give subordinates a sense of forward movement even in the face of the missteps and failures inherent in any complex project.

Second, Graham stayed attuned to his team's everyday activities and progress. In fact, the nonjudgmental climate he had established made this happen naturally. Team members updated him frequently—without being asked—on their setbacks, progress, and plans. At one point, one of his hardest-working colleagues, Brady, had to abort a trial of a new material because he couldn't get the parameters right on the equipment. It was bad news, because the NewPoly team had access to the equipment only one day a week, but Brady immediately informed Graham. In his diary entry that evening, Brady noted, "He didn't like the lost week but seemed to understand." That understanding assured Graham's place in the stream of information that would allow him to give his people just what they needed to make progress.

Third, Graham targeted his support according to recent events in the team and the project. Each day, he could anticipate what type of intervention—a catalyst or the removal of an inhibitor; a nourisher or some antidote to a toxin—would have the most impact on team members' inner work lives and progress. And if he could not make that judgment, he asked. Most days it was not hard to figure out, as on the day he received some uplifting news about his bosses' commitment to the project. He knew the team was jittery about a rumored corporate reorganization and could use the encouragement. Even though the clarification came during a well-earned vacation day, he immediately got on the phone to relay the good news to the team.

Finally, Graham established himself as a resource for team members, rather than a micromanager; he was sure to *check in* while never seeming to *check up* on them. Superficially, checking in and checking up seem quite similar, but micromanagers make four kinds of mistakes. First, they fail to allow autonomy in carrying out the work. Unlike Graham, who gave the NewPoly team a clear strategic goal but respected members' ideas about how to meet it, micromanagers dictate every move. Second, they frequently ask subordinates about their work without providing any real help. By contrast, when one of Graham's team members reported problems, Graham helped analyze them—remaining open to alternative interpretations—and often ended up helping to get things back on track. Third, micromanagers are quick to affix personal blame when problems arise, leading subordinates to hide problems rather than honestly discuss how to surmount them, as Graham did with Brady. And fourth, micromanagers tend to hoard information to use as a secret weapon. Few realize how damaging this is to inner work life. When subordinates perceive that a manager is withholding potentially useful information, they feel infantilized, their motivation wanes, and their work is handicapped. Graham was quick to communicate upper management's views of the project, customers' opinions and needs, and possible sources of assistance or resistance within and outside the organization.

In all those ways, Graham sustained his team's positive emotions, intrinsic motivation, and favorable perceptions. His actions serve as a powerful example of how managers at any level can approach each day determined to foster progress.

We know that many managers, however well-intentioned, will find it hard to establish the habits that seemed to come so naturally to Graham. Awareness, of course, is the first step. However, turning an awareness of the importance of inner work life into routine action takes discipline. With that in mind, we developed a checklist for managers to consult on a daily basis (see the sidebar "The Daily Progress Checklist"). The aim of the checklist is managing for meaningful progress, one day at a time.

The Progress Loop

Inner work life drives performance; in turn, good performance, which depends on consistent progress, enhances inner work life. We call this the *progress loop;* it reveals the potential for self-reinforcing benefits.

The Daily Progress Checklist

Near the end of each workday, use this checklist to review the day and plan your managerial actions for the next day. After a few days, you will be able to identify issues by scanning the boldface words. First, focus on progress and setbacks and think about specific events (catalysts, nourishers, inhibitors, and toxins) that contributed to them. Next, consider any clear inner-work-life clues and what further information they provide about progress and other events. Finally, prioritize for action. The action plan for the next day is the most important part of your daily review: What is the one thing you can do to best facilitate progress?

Progress

Which one or two events today indicated either a small win or a possible breakthrough? (Describe briefly.)

Setbacks

Which one or two events today indicated either a small setback or a possible crisis? (Describe briefly.)

Catalysts

- ☐ Did the team have clear short- and long-term **goals** for meaningful work?

- ☐ Did team members have sufficient **autonomy** to solve problems and take ownership of the project?

- ☐ Did they have all the **resources** they needed to move forward efficiently?

- ☐ Did they have sufficient **time** to focus on meaningful work?

- ☐ Did I give or get them **help** when they needed or requested it? Did I encourage team members to help one another?

- ☐ Did I discuss **lessons** from today's successes and problems with my team?

- ☐ Did I help **ideas** flow freely within the group?

Inhibitors

- ☐ Was there any confusion regarding long- or short-term **goals** for meaningful work?

- ☐ Were team members overly **constrained** in their ability to solve problems and feel ownership of the project?

- ☐ Did they lack any of the **resources** they needed to move forward effectively?

- ☐ Did they lack sufficient **time** to focus on meaningful work?

- ☐ Did I or others fail to provide needed or requested **help**?

- ☐ Did I "punish" failure or neglect to find **lessons** and/or opportunities in problems and successes?

- ☐ Did I or others cut off the presentation or debate of **ideas** prematurely?

Nourishers

□ Did I show **respect** to team members by recognizing their contributions to progress, attending to their ideas, and treating them as trusted professionals?

□ Did I **support** team members who had a personal or professional problem?

□ Is there a sense of personal and professional **affiliation** and camaraderie within the team?

□ Did I **encourage** team members who faced difficult challenges?

Toxins

□ Did I **disrespect** any team members by failing to recognize their contributions to progress, not attending to their ideas, or not treating them as trusted professionals?

□ Did I **discourage** a member of the team in any way?

□ Did I **neglect** a team member who had a personal or professional problem?

□ Is there tension or **antagonism** among members of the team or between team members and me?

Inner work life

Did I see any indications of the quality of my subordinates' inner work lives today?

Perceptions of the work, team, management, firm _____

Emotions _____

Motivation _____

What specific events might have affected inner work life today? _____

Action plan

What can I do tomorrow to strengthen the catalysts and nourishers identified and provide the ones that are lacking?

What can I do tomorrow to start eliminating the inhibitors and toxins identified?

_____

_____

_____

So, the most important implication of the progress principle is this: By supporting people and their daily progress in meaningful work, managers improve not only the inner work lives of their employees but also the organization's long-term performance, which enhances inner work life even more. Of course, there is a dark side—the possibility of negative feedback loops. If managers fail to support progress and the people trying to make it, inner work life suffers and so does performance; and degraded performance further undermines inner work life.

A second implication of the progress principle is that managers needn't fret about trying to read the psyches of their workers, or manipulate complicated incentive schemes, to ensure that employees are motivated and happy. As long as they show basic respect and consideration, they can focus on supporting the work itself.

To become an effective manager, you must learn to set this positive feedback loop in motion. That may require a significant shift. Business schools, business books, and managers themselves usually focus on managing organizations or people. But if you focus on managing progress, the management of people—and even of entire organizations—becomes much more feasible. You won't have to figure out how to x-ray the inner work lives of subordinates; if you facilitate their steady progress in meaningful work, make that progress salient to them, and treat them well, they will experience the emotions, motivations, and perceptions necessary for great performance. Their superior work will contribute to organizational success. And here's the beauty of it: They will love their jobs.

Reprinted from *Harvard Business Review*,
May 2011 (product #R1105C).

CHAPTER TEN

Why You Should Have (at Least) Two Careers

by Kabir Sehgal

It's not uncommon to meet a lawyer who'd like to work in renewable energy, or an app developer who'd like to write a novel, or an editor who fantasizes about becoming a landscape designer. Maybe you also dream about switching to a career that's drastically different from your current job. But in my experience, it's rare for such people to actually make the leap. The costs of switching seem too high, and the possibility of success seems too remote.

But the answer isn't to plug away in your current job, unfulfilled and slowly burning out. I think the answer is to *do both*. Two careers are better than one. And by committing to two careers, you will produce benefits for both.

In my case, I have four vocations: I'm a corporate strategist at a *Fortune* 500 company, U.S. Navy Reserve officer, author of several books, and record producer. The two questions that people ask me most frequently are "How much do you sleep?" and "How do you find time to do it all?" (My answers: "plenty" and "I make the time.") Yet these "process" questions don't get to the heart of my reasons and motivations. Instead, a more revealing query would be, "Why do you have multiple careers?" Quite simply, working many jobs makes me happier and leaves me more fulfilled. It also helps me perform better at each job. Here's how.

Subsidize Your Skill Development

My corporate job paycheck subsidizes my record-producing career. With no track record as a producer, nobody was going to pay me to produce their music, and it wasn't money that motivated me to become a producer in the first place—it was my passion for jazz and classical music. Therefore, I volunteered so that I could gain experience in this new industry. My day job not only afforded me the capital to make albums, it taught me the skills to succeed as a producer. A good producer should be someone who knows how to create a vision, recruit personnel, establish a time line, raise money, and deliver products. After producing over a dozen albums and winning a few Grammys, record labels and musicians have started to reach out to see if they can hire me as a producer. I still refuse payment, because making music—something that is everlasting—is reward enough for me.

At the same time, I typically invite my corporate clients to recording sessions. For someone who works at an office all day, it's exciting to go "behind the scenes" and interact with singers, musicians, and other creative professionals. While I was in Cuba making an album, one of my clients observed about the dancing musicians, "I've never been around people who have so much fun at work." That my clients have a phenomenal experience only helps me drive revenue at work, so my corporate and recording careers are mutually beneficial.

Make Friends in Different Circles

When I worked on Wall Street, my professional circle was initially limited to other folks in the financial services sector: bankers, traders, analysts, economists. Taken together, all of us establish a "consensus" view on the markets. And most of my asset manager clients were looking for something different: "Give me a contrarian perspective." In other words, they didn't want to hear the groupthink. I took this as marching orders to tap my Rolodex for people who could provide my clients a differentiated perspective.

—— **2021** ——

Flirt with Your Future Self

by Amantha Imber

It's normal to get urges to try out different roles or career paths. But instead of doing something dramatic like jumping ship or enrolling in a two- or three-year degree, Scott D. Anthony, a global innovation thought leader, senior partner at Innosight, and author of the book *Eat, Sleep, Innovate*, is a fan of London Business School professor Herminia Ibarra's suggestion to "flirt with your future self."[a]

"The idea is that you consciously experiment and 'try on' different roles, and indeed leadership styles, to see what fits the best," Anthony said on my *How I Work* podcast. "For example, I think that a natural next act for me someday would be to become a teacher. But will I actually like teaching? There are small experiments I can do in my current role that help me understand that better, which includes talking to people who have made similar transitions to see what surprised them."

Try to get out of work mode and get into play mode more often. As Anthony suggests, treat it as a little experiment. Feeling inclined to make a new career move? Make a list of five people you can speak to who can provide insight into this career. For example, if you want to pivot into travel blogging, ask colleagues who they think the best travel bloggers are and reach out to them on LinkedIn or other social media channels for a chat. Turn up your curiosity, and make a list of things you want to know and questions you might ask. For example: How do they make money? How did they get their start? How many hours do they work?

As you think about switching jobs or careers, don't do so blindly. Connecting with those who've "been there, done that" to learn about their experiences and listening to any advice they have can come in handy before making the leap.

a. Amantha Imber, "Global Innovation Thought Leader Scott D. Anthony on His Daily Creativity Ritual," October 21, 2020, in *How I Work* (podcast), produced by Amantha Imber, https://www.amantha.com/podcasts/global-innovation-thought-leader-scott-d-anthony-on-his-daily-creativity-ritual; and Herminia Ibarra, "The Most Productive Way to Develop as a Leader," hbr.org, March 27, 2015, https://hbr.org/2015/03/the-most-productive-way-to-develop-as-a-leader.

Adapted from "Career Advice from Wildly Successful People,"
Ascend, on hbr.org, June 30, 2021.

For example, one of my clients wanted to understand what Chinese citizens were saying to each other. Because I am an author, I have gotten to know other writers, so I reached out to my friend who was a journalist at a periodical that monitors chatter in China. Not restricted by the compliance department of a bank, he was able to give an unbridled perspective to my client, who was most appreciative. My client got a new idea. I got a trade. My friend got a new subscriber. By being in different circles, you can selectively introduce people who would typically never meet and unlock value for everyone.

Discover Real Innovations

When you work different jobs, you can identify where ideas interact—and more significantly, where they *should* interact. "It's technology married with liberal arts, married with the humanities, that yields us the result that makes our heart sing," said Steve Jobs, who was the embodiment of interdisciplinary thinking.

Because of Hurricane Katrina, many musicians left New Orleans. In order to generate funds to help musicians in the city, I could have created a typical nonprofit organization that solicits people for money. Instead, I helped create a more sustainable solution: a brokerage for musicians that I described as "Wall Street meets Bourbon Street." People wanting to book a musician for a party in New York could find a band on my organization's website, which would then ask the booker to add a "tip" to be allocated to a New Orleans–based charity. The booker (who in some cases were my corporate clients) easily found a band for the party, the New York City–based musician got a gig, and the charity in New Orleans got a small donation. Because of my time working at a bank, I was able to create a different type of organization, one that has since merged with an even larger charitable organization.

When you follow your curiosities, you will bring passion to your new careers, which will leave you more fulfilled. And by doing more than one job, you may end up doing all of them better.

Adapted from content posted on hbr.org,
April 25, 2017 (product #H03M9A).

— 2007 —

CHAPTER ELEVEN

Becoming the Boss

by Linda A. Hill

Even for the most gifted individuals, the process of becoming a leader is an arduous, albeit rewarding, journey of continuous learning and self-development. The initial test along the path is so fundamental that we often overlook it: becoming a boss for the first time. That's a shame, because the trials involved in this rite of passage have serious consequences for both the individual and the organization.

Executives are shaped irrevocably by their first management positions. Decades later, they recall those first months as transformational experiences that forged their leadership philosophies and styles in ways that may continue to haunt and hobble them throughout their careers. Organizations suffer considerable human and financial costs when a person who has been promoted because of strong individual performance and qualifications fails to adjust successfully to management responsibilities.

The failures aren't surprising, given the difficulty of the transition. Ask any new manager about the early days of being a boss—indeed, ask any senior executive to recall how he or she felt as a new manager. If you get an honest answer, you'll hear a tale of disorientation and, for some, overwhelming confusion. The new role didn't feel anything like it was supposed to. It felt too big for any one person to handle. And whatever its scope, it sure didn't seem to have anything to do with leadership.

In the words of one new branch manager at a securities firm: "Do you know how hard it is to be the boss when you are so out of control? It's hard to verbalize. It's the feeling you get when you have a child. On day X minus 1, you still don't have a child. On day X, all of a sudden you're a mother or a father and you're supposed to know everything there is to know about taking care of a kid."

Given the significance and difficulty of this first leadership test, it's surprising how little attention has been paid to the experiences of new managers and the challenges they face. The shelves are lined with books describing effective and successful leaders. But very few address the challenges of learning to lead, especially for the first-time manager.

For the past 15 years or so, I've studied people making major career transitions to management, focusing in particular on the star performer who is promoted to manager. My original ambition was to provide a forum for new managers to speak in their own words about what it means to learn to manage. I initially followed 19 new managers over the course of their first year in an effort to get a rare glimpse into their subjective experience: What did they find most difficult? What did they need to learn? How did they go about learning it? What resources did they rely upon to ease the transition and master their new assignments?

Since my original research, which I described in the first edition of *Becoming a Manager,* published in 1992, I've continued to study the personal transformation involved when someone becomes a boss. I've written case studies about new managers in a variety of functions and industries and have designed and led new-manager leadership programs for companies and not-for-profit organizations. As firms have become leaner and more dynamic—with different units working together to offer integrated products and services and with companies working with suppliers, customers, and competitors in an array of strategic alliances—new managers have described a transition that gets harder all the time.

Let me emphasize that the struggles these new managers face represent the norm, not the exception. These aren't impaired managers operating in dysfunctional organizations. They're ordinary people facing ordinary adjustment problems. The vast majority of them survive the transition and learn to function in their new role. But imagine how much more effective they would be if the transition were less traumatic.

To help new managers pass this first leadership test, we need to help them understand the essential nature of their role—what it truly means to be in charge. Most see themselves as managers and leaders; they use the rhetoric of leadership; they certainly feel the burdens of leadership. But they just don't get it.

Why Learning to Manage Is So Hard

One of the first things new managers discover is that their role, by definition a stretch assignment, is even more demanding than they'd anticipated. They are surprised to learn that the skills and methods required for success as an individual contributor and those required for success as a manager are starkly different—and that there is a gap between their current capabilities and the requirements of the new position.

In their prior jobs, success depended primarily on their personal expertise and actions. As managers, they are responsible for setting and implementing an agenda for a whole group, something for which their careers as individual performers haven't prepared them.

Take the case of Michael Jones, the new securities-firm branch manager I just mentioned. (The identities of individuals cited in this article have been disguised.) Michael had been a broker for 13 years and was a stellar producer, one of the most aggressive and innovative professionals in his region. At his company, new branch managers were generally promoted from the ranks on the basis of individual competence and achievements, so no one was surprised when the regional director asked him to consider a management career. Michael was confident he understood what it took to be an effective manager. In fact, on numerous occasions he had commented that if he had been in charge, he would have been willing and able to fix things and make life better in the branch. After a month in his new role, however, he was feeling moments of intense panic; it was harder than he had imagined to get his ideas implemented. He realized he had given up his "security blanket" and there was no turning back.

Michael's reaction, although a shock to him, isn't unusual. Learning to lead is a process of learning by doing. It can't be taught in a classroom. It is a craft primarily acquired through on-the-job experiences—especially adverse experiences in which the new manager, working beyond his current capabilities, proceeds by trial and error. Most star individual performers haven't made many mistakes, so this is new for them. Furthermore, few managers are aware, in the stressful, mistake-making moments, that they are learning. The learning occurs incrementally and gradually.

As this process slowly progresses—as the new manager unlearns a mindset and habits that have served him over a highly successful early career—a new professional identity emerges. He internalizes new ways of thinking and being and discovers new ways of measuring success and deriving satisfaction from work. Not surprisingly, this kind of psychological adjustment is taxing. As one new manager notes, "I never knew a promotion could be so painful."

Painful—and stressful. New managers inevitably ponder two questions: "Will I like management?" and "Will I be good at management?" Of course, there are no immediate answers; they come only with experience. And these two questions are often accompanied by an even more unsettling one: "Who am I becoming?"

A New Manager's Misconceptions

Becoming a boss is difficult, but I don't want to paint an unrelentingly bleak picture. What I have found in my research is that the transition is often harder than it need be because of new managers' misconceptions about their role. Their ideas about what it means to be a manager hold some truth. But, because these notions are simplistic and incomplete, they create false expectations that individuals struggle to reconcile with the reality of managerial life. By acknowledging the following misconceptions—some of which rise

TABLE 11-1

Why new managers don't get it

Beginning managers often fail in their new role, at least initially, because they come to it with misconceptions or myths about what it means to be a boss. These myths, because they are simplistic and incomplete, lead new managers to neglect key leadership responsibilities.

	Myth	Reality
Defining characteristic of the new role	**Authority** "Now I will have the freedom to implement my ideas."	**Interdependency** "It's humbling that someone who works for me could get me fired."
Source of power	**Formal authority** "I will finally be at the top of the ladder."	**"Everything but"** "Folks were wary, and you really had to earn it."
Desired outcome	**Control** "I must get compliance from my subordinates."	**Commitment** "Compliance does not equal commitment."
Managerial focus	**Managing one-on-one** "My role is to build relationships with individual subordinates."	**Leading the team** "I need to create a culture that will allow the group to fulfill its potential."
Key challenge	**Keeping the operation in working order** "My job is to make sure the operation runs smoothly."	**Making changes that will make the team perform better** "I am responsible for initiating changes to enhance the group's performance."

almost to the level of myth in their near-universal acceptance—new managers have a far greater chance of success. (For a comparison of the misconceptions and the reality, see table 11-1.)

Managers wield significant authority

When asked to describe their role, new managers typically focus on the rights and privileges that come with being the boss. They assume the position will give them more authority and, with that, more freedom and autonomy to do what they think is best for the organization. No longer, in the words of one, will they be "burdened by the unreasonable demands of others."

New managers nursing this assumption face a rude awakening. Instead of gaining new authority, those I have studied describe finding themselves hemmed in by interdependencies. Instead of feeling free, they feel constrained, especially if they were accustomed to the relative independence of a star performer. They are enmeshed in a web of relationships—not only with subordinates but also with bosses, peers, and others inside and outside the organization, all of whom make relentless and often conflicting demands on them. The resulting daily routine is pressured, hectic, and fragmented.

"The fact is that you really are not in control of anything," says one new manager. "The only time I am in control is when I shut my door, and then I feel I am not doing the job I'm supposed to be doing, which is being with the people." Another new manager observes: "It's humbling that someone who works for me could get me fired."

The people most likely to make a new manager's life miserable are those who don't fall under her formal authority: outside suppliers, for example, or managers in another division. Sally McDonald, a rising star at a chemical company, stepped into a product development position with high hopes, impeccable credentials as an individual performer, a deep appreciation for the company's culture—and even the supposed wisdom gained in a leadership development course. Three weeks later, she observed grimly: "Becoming a manager is not about becoming a boss. It's about becoming a hostage. There are many terrorists in this organization that want to kidnap me."

Until they give up the myth of authority for the reality of negotiating interdependencies, new managers will not be able to lead effectively. As we have seen, this goes beyond managing the team of direct reports and requires managing the context within which the team operates. Unless they identify and build effective relationships with the key people the team depends upon, the team will lack the resources necessary to do its job.

Even if new managers appreciate the importance of these relationships, they often ignore or neglect them and focus instead on what seems like the more immediate task of leading those closest to them: their subordinates. When they finally do accept their network-builder role, they often feel overwhelmed by its demands. Besides, negotiating with these other parties from a position of relative weakness—for that's often the plight of new managers at the bottom of the hierarchy—gets tiresome.

But the dividends of managing the interdependencies are great. While working in business development at a large U.S. media concern, Winona Finch developed a business plan for launching a Latin American edition of the company's U.S. teen magazine. When the project got tentative approval, Finch asked to manage it. She and her team faced a number of obstacles. International projects were not favored by top management, and before getting final funding, Finch would need to secure agreements with regional distributors representing 20% of the Latin American market—not an easy task for an untested publication competing for scarce newsstand space. To control costs, her venture would have to rely on the sales staff of the Spanish-language edition of the company's flagship women's magazine, people who were used to selling a very different kind of product.

Winona had served a stint as an acting manager two years before, so despite the morass of detail she had to deal with in setting up the new venture, she understood the importance of devoting time and attention to managing relationships with her superiors and peers. For example, she compiled biweekly executive notes from her department heads that she circulated to executives at headquarters. To enhance communication with the women's magazine, she initiated regular Latin American board meetings at which top worldwide executives from both the teen and women's publications could discuss regional strategy.

Her prior experience notwithstanding, she faced the typical stresses of a new manager: "It's like you are in final exams 365 days a year," she says. Still, the new edition was launched on schedule and exceeded its business plan forecasts.

Authority flows from the manager's position

Don't get me wrong: Despite the interdependencies that constrain them, new managers do wield some power. The problem is that most of them mistakenly believe their power is based on the formal authority that comes with their now lofty—well, relatively speaking—position in the hierarchy. This operating assumption leads many to adopt a hands-on, autocratic approach, not because they are eager to exercise their new power over people but because they believe it is the most effective way to produce results.

New managers soon learn, however, that when direct reports are told to do something, they don't necessarily respond. In fact, the more talented the subordinate, the less likely she is to simply follow orders. (Some new managers, when pressed, admit that they didn't always listen to their bosses either.)

After a few painful experiences, new managers come to the unsettling realization that the source of their power is, according to one, "everything but" formal authority. That is, authority emerges only as the manager establishes credibility with subordinates, peers, and superiors. "It took me three months to realize I had no effect on many of my people," recalls one manager I followed. "It was like I was talking to myself."

Many new managers are surprised by how difficult it is to earn people's respect and trust. They are shocked, and even insulted, that their expertise and track record don't speak for themselves. My research shows that many also aren't aware of the qualities that contribute to credibility.

They need to demonstrate their *character*—the intention to do the right thing. This is of particular importance to subordinates, who tend to analyze every statement and nonverbal gesture for signs of the new boss's motives. Such scrutiny can be unnerving. "I knew I was a good guy, and I kind of expected people to accept me immediately for what I was," says one new manager. "But folks were wary, and you really had to earn it."

They need to demonstrate their *competence*—knowing how to do the right thing. This can be problematic, because new managers initially feel the need to prove their technical knowledge and prowess, the foundations of their success as individual performers. But while evidence of technical competence is important in gaining subordinates' respect, it isn't ultimately the primary area of competence that direct reports are looking for.

When Peter Isenberg took over the management of a trading desk in a global investment bank, he oversaw a group of seasoned, senior traders. To establish his credibility, he adopted a hands-on approach, advising traders to close down particular positions or try different trading strategies. The traders pushed back, demanding to know the rationale for each directive. Things got uncomfortable. The traders' responses to their new boss's comments became prickly and terse. One day, Isenberg, who recognized his lack of knowledge about foreign markets, asked one of the senior people a simple question about pricing. The trader stopped what he was doing for several minutes to explain the issue and offered to discuss the matter further at the end of the day. "Once I stopped talking all the time and began to listen, people on the desk started to educate me about the job and, significantly, seemed to question my calls far less," Isenberg says.

The new manager's eagerness to show off his technical competence had undermined his credibility as a manager and leader. His eagerness to jump in and try to solve problems raised implicit questions about his managerial competence. In the traders' eyes, he was becoming a micromanager and a "control freak" who didn't deserve their respect.

Finally, new managers need to demonstrate their *influence*— the ability to deliver and execute the right thing. There is "nothing worse than working for a powerless boss," says a direct report of one new manager I studied. Gaining and wielding influence within the organization is particularly difficult because, as I have noted, new managers are the "little bosses" of the organization. "I was on top of world when I knew I was finally getting promoted," one new manager says. "I felt like I would be on the top of the ladder I had been climbing for years. But then I suddenly felt like I was at the bottom again—except this time it's not even clear what the rungs are and where I am climbing to."

Once again, we see a new manager fall into the trap of relying too heavily on his formal authority as his source of influence. Instead, he needs to build his influence by creating a web of strong, interdependent relationships, based on credibility and trust, throughout his team and the entire organization—one strand at a time.

Managers must control their direct reports

Most new managers, in part because of insecurity in an unfamiliar role, yearn for compliance from their subordinates. They fear that if they don't establish this early on, their direct reports will walk all over them. As a means of gaining this control, they often rely too much on their formal authority—a technique whose effectiveness is, as we have seen, questionable at best.

But even if they are able to achieve some measure of control, whether through formal authority or authority earned over time, they have achieved a false victory. Compliance does not equal commitment. If people aren't committed, they won't take the initiative. And if subordinates aren't taking the initiative, the manager can't delegate effectively. The direct reports won't take the calculated risks that lead to the continuous change and improvement required by today's turbulent business environment.

Winona Finch, who led the launch of the teen magazine in Latin America, knew she faced a business challenge that would require her team's total support. She had in fact been awarded the job in part because of her personal style, which her superiors hoped would compensate for her lack of experience in the Latin American market and in managing profit-and-loss responsibilities. In addition to being known as a clear thinker, she had a warm and personable way with people. During the project, she successfully leveraged these natural abilities in developing her leadership philosophy and style.

Instead of relying on formal authority to get what she wanted from her team, she exercised influence by creating a culture of inquiry. The result was an organization in which people felt empowered, committed, and accountable for fulfilling the company's vision. "Winona was easygoing and fun," a subordinate says. "But she would ask and ask and ask to get to the bottom of something.

You would say something to her, she would say it back to you, and that way everyone was 100% clear on what we were talking about. Once she got the information and knew what you were doing, you had to be consistent. She would say, 'You told me X; why are you doing Y? I'm confused.'" Although she was demanding, she didn't demand that people do things her way. Her subordinates were committed to the team's goals because they were empowered, not ordered, to achieve them.

The more power managers are willing to share with subordinates in this way, the more influence they tend to command. When they lead in a manner that allows their people to take the initiative, they build their own credibility as managers.

Managers must focus on forging good individual relationships

Managing interdependencies and exercising informal authority derived from personal credibility require new managers to build trust, influence, and mutual expectations with a wide array of people. This is often achieved by establishing productive personal relationships. Ultimately, however, the new manager must figure out how to harness the power of a team. Simply focusing on one-on-one relationships with members of the team can undermine that process.

During their first year on the job, many new managers fail to recognize, much less address, their team-building responsibilities. Instead, they conceive of their people-management role as building the most effective relationships they can with each individual subordinate, erroneously equating the management of their team with managing the individuals on the team.

They attend primarily to individual performance and pay little or no attention to team culture and performance. They hardly ever rely on group forums for identifying and solving problems. Some spend too much time with a small number of trusted subordinates, often those who seem most supportive. New managers tend to handle issues, even those with teamwide implications, one-on-one. This leads them to make decisions based on unnecessarily limited information.

In his first week as a sales manager at a Texas software company, Roger Collins was asked by a subordinate for an assigned parking spot that had just become available. The salesman had been at the company for years, and Collins, wanting to get off to a good start with this veteran, said, "Sure, why not?" Within the hour, another salesman, a big moneymaker, stormed into Collins's office threatening to quit. It seems the shaded parking spot was coveted for pragmatic and symbolic reasons, and the beneficiary of Collins's casual gesture was widely viewed as incompetent. The manager's decision was unfathomable to the star.

Collins eventually solved what he regarded as a trivial management problem—"This is not the sort of thing I'm supposed to be worrying about," he said—but he began to recognize that every decision about individuals affected the team. He had been working on the assumption that if he could establish a good relationship with each person who reported to him, his whole team would function smoothly. What he learned was that supervising each individual was not the same as leading the team. In my research, I repeatedly hear new managers describe situations in which they made an exception for one subordinate—usually with the aim of creating a positive relationship with that person—but ended up regretting the action's unexpected negative consequences for the team. Grasping this notion can be especially difficult for up-and-comers who have been able to accomplish a great deal on their own.

When new managers focus solely on one-on-one relationships, they neglect a fundamental aspect of effective leadership: harnessing the collective power of the group to improve individual performance and commitment. By shaping team culture—the group's norms and values—a leader can unleash the problem-solving prowess of the diverse talents that make up the team.

Managers must ensure that things run smoothly

Like many managerial myths, this one is partly true but is misleading because it tells only some of the story. Making sure an operation is operating smoothly is an incredibly difficult task, requiring

Oh, One More Thing: Create the Conditions for Your Success

New managers often discover, belatedly, that they are expected to do more than just make sure their groups function smoothly today. They must also recommend and initiate changes that will help their groups do even better in the future.

A new marketing manager at a telecommunications company whom I'll call John Delhorne discovered that his predecessor had failed to make critical investments, so he tried on numerous occasions to convince his immediate superior to increase the marketing budget. He also presented a proposal to acquire a new information system that could allow his team to optimize its marketing initiatives. When he could not persuade his boss to release more money, he hunkered down and focused on changes within his team that would make it as productive as possible under the circumstances. This course seemed prudent, especially because his relationship with his boss, who was taking longer and longer to answer Delhorne's e-mails, was becoming strained.

When the service failed to meet certain targets, the CEO unceremoniously fired Delhorne because, Delhorne was told, he hadn't been proactive. The CEO chastised Delhorne for "sitting back and not asking for his help" in securing the funds needed to succeed in a critical new market. Delhorne, shocked and hurt, thought the CEO was being grossly unfair. Delhorne contended it wasn't his fault that the company's strategic-planning and budgeting procedures were flawed. The CEO's response: It was Delhorne's responsibility to create the conditions for his success.

---

a manager to keep countless balls in the air at all times. Indeed, the complexity of maintaining the status quo can absorb all of a junior manager's time and energy.

But new managers also need to realize they are responsible for recommending and initiating changes that will enhance their groups' performance. Often—and it comes as a surprise to most—this means challenging organizational processes or structures that exist above and beyond their area of formal authority. Only when they understand this part of the job will they begin to address seriously their leadership responsibilities. (See the sidebar "Oh, One More Thing: Create the Conditions for Your Success.")

In fact, most new managers see themselves as targets of organizational change initiatives, implementing with their groups the changes ordered from above. They don't see themselves as change agents. Hierarchical thinking and their fixation on the authority that comes with being the boss lead them to define their responsibilities too narrowly. Consequently, they tend to blame flawed systems, and the superiors directly responsible for those systems, for their teams' setbacks—and they tend to wait for other people to fix the problems.

But this represents a fundamental misunderstanding of their role within the organization. New managers need to generate changes, both within *and outside* their areas of responsibility, to ensure that their teams can succeed. They need to work to change the context in which their teams operate, ignoring their lack of formal authority.

This broader view benefits the organization as well as the new manager. Organizations must continually revitalize and transform themselves. They can meet these challenges only if they have cadres of effective leaders capable of both managing the complexity of the status quo and initiating change.

New Managers Aren't Alone

As they go through the daunting process of becoming a boss, new managers can gain a tremendous advantage by learning to recognize the misconceptions I've just outlined. But given the multilayered nature of their new responsibilities, they are still going to make mistakes as they try to put together the managerial puzzle—and making mistakes, no matter how important to the learning process, is no fun. They are going to feel pain as their professional identities are stretched and reshaped. As they struggle to learn a new role, they will often feel isolated.

Unfortunately, my research has shown that few new managers ask for help. This is in part the outcome of yet another misconception: The boss is supposed to have all the answers, so seeking help is a sure sign that a new manager is a "promotion mistake." Of course, seasoned managers know that no one has all the answers. The insights a manager does possess come over time, through experience.

And, as countless studies show, it is easier to learn on the job if you can draw on the support and assistance of peers and superiors.

Another reason new managers don't seek help is that they perceive the dangers (sometimes more imagined than real) of forging developmental relationships. When you share your anxieties, mistakes, and shortcomings with peers in your part of the organization, there's a risk that the individuals will use that information against you. The same goes for sharing your problems with your superior. The inherent conflict between the roles of evaluator and developer is an age-old dilemma. So new managers need to be creative in finding support. For instance, they might seek out peers who are outside their region or function or in another organization altogether. The problem with bosses, while difficult to solve neatly, can be alleviated. And herein lies a lesson not only for new managers but for experienced bosses, as well.

The new manager avoids turning to her immediate superior for advice because she sees that person as a threat to, rather than an ally in, her development. Because she fears punishment for missteps and failures, she resists seeking the help that might prevent such mistakes, even when she's desperate for it. As one new manager reports:

"I know on one level that I should deal more with my manager because that is what he is there for. He's got the experience, and I probably owe it to him to go to him and tell him what's up. He would probably have some good advice. But it's not safe to share with him. He's an unknown quantity. If you ask too many questions, he may lose confidence in you and think things aren't going very well. He may see that you are a little bit out of control, and then you really have a tough job. Because he'll be down there lickety-split, asking lots of questions about what you are doing, and before you know it, he'll be involved right in the middle of it. That's a really uncomfortable situation. He's the last place I'd go for help."

Such fears are often justified. Many a new manager has regretted trying to establish a mentoring relationship with his boss. "I don't dare even ask a question that could be perceived as naive or stupid," says one. "Once I asked him a question and he made me feel like I was a kindergartner in the business. It was as if he had said, 'That was the dumbest thing I've ever seen. What on earth did you have in mind?'"

This is a tragically lost opportunity for the new manager, the boss, and the organization as a whole. It means that the new manager's boss loses a chance to influence the manager's initial conceptions and misconceptions of her new position and how she should approach it. The new manager loses the chance to draw on organizational assets—from financial resources to information about senior management's priorities—that the superior could best provide.

When a new manager can develop a good relationship with his boss, it can make all the difference in the world—though not necessarily in ways the new manager expects. My research suggests that eventually about half of new managers turn to their bosses for assistance, often because of a looming crisis. Many are relieved to find their superiors more tolerant of their questions and mistakes than they had expected. "He recognized that I was still in the learning mode and was more than willing to help in any way he could," recalls one new manager.

Sometimes, the most expert mentors can seem deceptively hands-off. One manager reports how she learned from an immediate superior: "She is demanding, but she enjoys a reputation for growing people and helping them, not throwing them to the wolves. I wasn't sure after the first 60 days, though. Everything was so hard and I was so frustrated, but she didn't offer to help. It was driving me nuts. When I asked her a question, she asked me a question. I got no answers. Then I saw what she wanted. I had to come in with some ideas about how I would handle the situation, and then she would talk about them with me. She would spend all the time in the world with me."

His experience vividly highlights why it's important for the bosses of new managers to understand—or simply recall—how difficult it is to step into a management role for the first time. Helping a new manager succeed doesn't benefit only that individual. Ensuring the new manager's success is also crucially important to the success of the entire organization.

Reprinted from *Harvard Business Review*,
January 2007 (product #R0701D).

CHAPTER TWELVE

The Memo Every Woman Keeps in Her Desk

by Kathleen Reardon

AUTHOR'S NOTE: *When I wrote "The Memo Every Woman Keeps in Her Desk" in 1993 it was generally thought that men rising in the workforce at that time would be far more comfortable working beside women than their fathers had been.*

I wrote the case study to reflect what I saw at the time—that women directly competing with men for jobs was easier to accept in theory than in reality, especially at senior levels. And while it wasn't acceptable in most organizations to overtly voice objections to women's promotions simply because of gender, that did not mean such feelings no longer existed. With regard to gender equity, the job was far from done in 1993 and remains far from done now.

Of course, there have been many positive changes in the last 25 years. The overall pay gap has narrowed somewhat. Increasingly, there are efforts to recruit women to the fields of science, math, and engineering. Women are seeking graduate degrees in higher numbers than ever before and are very well represented among successful entrepreneurs.

But despite these and other positive changes, the memo case has stayed surprisingly relevant. It did not focus on sexual harassment or assault but rather on a young woman's intention to inform her CEO of an atmosphere in their workplace that slowly eroded a "woman's sense of worth and place." The case posed several questions still faced today. Should a woman tell her CEO about issues creating a hostile work culture for her and other female employees? Should she do so alone? What is the right way to word and convey such a message? What are the risks? Is it likely that a male CEO will listen and appreciate such unsolicited input?

In the light of the #MeToo movement, a woman's decision to speak up may seem less risky now, especially about issues relatively low on the spectrum of gender-based offenses. But is that the case? Or do we still have a long way to go before women can share their experiences with confidence that their observations and courage will not only be welcomed but lead to significant change?

—Kathleen Reardon, January 2018

EDITOR'S NOTE: The following is a fictionalized case study that appeared in *Harvard Business Review* along with commentary from experts.

What kind of advice was I going to give Liz Ames, my pal from the good old days when we worked together in market development at Vision Software? Liz and I had been through a lot together, from working for an egomaniac who was finally fired to laying the groundwork for the biggest product launch in the company's history. We always seemed to understand each other's thoughts, and those Friday nights unwinding at the tavern made it possible for both of us to face work again Monday morning. We both had come a long way at Vision, and we were genuinely glad to see the other succeed. When I got the marketing director position in Germany, Liz was the first to congratulate me.

When we met for dinner the first night of the annual marketing retreat, I was ready to tell Liz all about my first six months on the new job, but she made it clear from the start that she had something urgent to discuss. She needed me to help her out of a dilemma, and she said my perspective as a man would be helpful. She had written a memo to John Clark, Vision's CEO, complaining about sexism at the company. Now she was agonizing over whether to send it. Liz seldom raised the subject of sexism, but she had written the memo because she thought it was time that someone at the top knew what was really going on at the company—in the trenches, as she put it.

She had no doubt that the message was important. But she did have doubts about how it would be received and about the fate of the messenger. She wanted me, her most trusted friend at Vision and a man, to help her decide what to do.

"In an ideal world," she said, "I wouldn't have any second thoughts about sending it. But you know what can happen to messengers. If Clark likes what I have to say, there's no problem. But then, there are the other possibilities."

"You've never been afraid to speak your mind. What's the worst that could happen?" I asked.

"Clark isn't going to fire me, if that's what you mean. But I can think of several ways this thing could backfire. What if Clark doesn't believe me, or he just can't relate to what I'm saying? He'll dismiss me as a radical feminist or a chronic complainer. Word will get around, and my career at Vision will be over. Or maybe he won't respond at all. It'll be one more example of not being heard. I don't know if I have the mental energy for that."

At first I thought Liz was being melodramatic, but as we talked I could see that to her, the decision was a turning point. She knew that ultimately she had to take responsibility for whatever decision she made, but she wanted my perspective. Reluctantly, I promised to use the memo as bedtime reading and get back to her in the morning. So there I sat with the memo in my lap, the hotel lamp glaring off the neatly typed pages.

Liz's memo seemed reasonable and compelling. Wouldn't Clark be grateful to hear from someone in the trenches? He liked to boast about the company's progressive policies toward diversity, and this would give him a chance to renew the crusade. He'd respect Liz for taking his commitment seriously.

But then again, Clark had an ego. Maybe he'd resent the implication that the company is not what he professes it to be. And, of

To: Mr. John Clark, CEO
From: Elizabeth C. Ames,
Director of Consumer Marketing
Date: March 8, 1993

I've been working in the marketing department at Vision Software for more than ten years, where I've had my share of challenges and successes. I've enjoyed being part of an interesting and exciting company. Despite my general enthusiasm about the company and my job, however, I was taken aback when I received your memo announcing the resignations of Mariam Blackwell and Susan French, Vision's two most senior women. This is not the first time Vision has lost its highest-ranking women. Just nine months ago, Kathryn Hobbs resigned, and a year before that, it was Suzanne LaHaise. The reasons are surprisingly similar: They wanted to "spend more time with their families" or "explore new career directions."

I can't help but detect a disturbing pattern. Why do such capable, conscientious women who have demonstrated intense commitment to their careers suddenly want to change course or spend more time at home? It's a question I've thought long and hard about.

Despite Vision's policies to hire and promote women and your own efforts to recognize and reward women's contributions, the overall atmosphere in this company is one that slowly erodes a woman's sense of worth and place. I believe that top-level women are leaving Vision Software not because they are drawn to other pursuits but because they are tired of struggling against a climate of female failure. Little things that happen daily—things many men don't even notice and women can't help but notice—send subtle messages that women are less important, less talented, less likely to make a difference than their male peers.

Let me try to describe what I mean. I'll start with meetings, which are a way of life at Vision and one of the most devaluing experiences for women. Women are often talked over and interrupted; their ideas never seem to be heard. Last week, I attended a meeting with ten men and one other woman. As soon as the woman started her presentation, several side conversations began. Her presentation skills were excellent, but she couldn't seem to get people's attention. When it was

course, it wasn't John Clark whom Liz had to face every day. Not all of Liz's male colleagues would give her criticisms any credence. And if they heard that she was writing to the boss complaining about them, they would shut her out. I had to admit, I could imagine that happening.

time to take questions, one man said dismissively, "We did something like this a couple of years ago, and it didn't work." She explained how her ideas differed, but the explanation fell on deaf ears. When I tried to give her support by expressing interest, I was interrupted.

But it's not just meetings. There are many things that make women feel unwelcome or unimportant. One department holds its biannual retreats at a country club with a "men only" bar. At the end of the sessions, the men typically hang around at the bar and talk, while the women quietly disappear. Needless to say, important information is often shared during those casual conversations.

Almost every formal meeting is followed by a series of informal ones behind closed doors. Women are rarely invited. Nor are they privy to the discussions before the formal meetings. As a result, they are often less likely to know what the boss has on his mind and therefore less prepared to react.

My female colleagues and I are also subjected to a daily barrage of seemingly innocent comments that belittle women. A coworker of mine recently boasted about how much he respects women by saying, "My wife is the wind beneath my wings. In fact, some people call me Mr. Karen Snyder." The men chuckled; the women didn't. And just last week, a male colleague stood up at 5:30 and jokingly informed a group of us that he would be leaving early: "I have to play mom tonight." Women play mom every night, and it never gets a laugh. In fact, most women try to appear devoid of concern about their families.

Any one of these incidents on its own is a small thing. But together and in repetition, they are quite powerful. The women at Vision fight to get their ideas heard and to crack the informal channels of information. Their energy goes into keeping up, not getting ahead, until they just don't have any more to give.

I can assure you that my observations are shared by many women in the company. I can only speculate that they were shared by Mariam Blackwell and Susan French.

Vision needs men and women if it is to become the preeminent educational software company. We need to send stronger, clearer signals that men are not the only people who matter. And this kind of change can work only if it starts with strong commitment at the top. That's why I'm writing to you. If I can be of help, please let me know.

Did the consequences of sending the memo really matter? Wasn't there a principle involved? I knew that the stonewalling Liz had referred to was real. I'd witnessed it myself over the years. Liz was one of the most positive and energetic people I knew, but I remember several times when she was so strung out from having to prove herself to men who constantly challenged her authority that she was ready to quit. That would have been a serious loss of experience. She knew how to work with educators better than anyone I knew, and her impeccable follow-up was largely responsible for the success of the Vision II product line that now represents 20% of Vision's revenues.

But men were under pressure too. Maybe it just took a different form. Vision was a tough place, and marketing was the toughest department. Many times, I was tempted to pack it in myself. I'd seen a lot of men fail and a lot of women succeed at Vision. Take Mariam Blackwell. She fit Vision's corporate culture like a glove. If she wasn't heard the first time, she'd say it again. I think she left because she ran out of challenges, not because her psychic energy had been depleted. Susan French left because they gave her a VP title but removed the decision-making authority of her male predecessors—something Liz had not mentioned in her memo.

As I wrestled with the issues Liz raised, I realized that her dilemma had become a dilemma for me. If I advised Liz to send the memo, was I being naive about the consequences she might suffer? If I told her not to send it, was I somehow condoning the behavior she described? If I suggested that women were not the only ones who were sometimes run aground by Vision's demanding environment, was I being insensitive? If I don't buy into it, does that mean that I just don't get it?

What would I tell Liz?

Should Liz Send the Memo?

Richard D. Glovsky is the former chief of the Civil Division of the United States Attorney's Office in Boston. He is the founder of Boston-based Glovsky & Associates, a law firm that specializes in employment law.

I would advise Liz not to send the memo at this time. A vigilant CEO would not have permitted this kind of discriminatory work environment to evolve in the first place. In short, the issues with which Liz is concerned would not exist at Vision unless Clark tacitly allowed them to develop. Clark cannot be trusted with Liz's message.

Instead of sending it, Liz should marshal her resources. She should speak with Mariam Blackwell, Susan French, Kathryn Hobbs, and Suzanne LaHaise to ascertain whether they have similar observations and would support her publicly. Liz also should talk to other women at Vision who can be trusted to maintain her confidence.

She should not "go it alone," especially when addressing a man more likely to be unreceptive than sympathetic. If Liz can get support (and statements) from other women who will corroborate her claims, she may be able to force Clark to do what is proper: review the employment environment at Vision and address Liz's issues on a companywide basis.

Finally, if Liz decides to take her message to Clark, she should either see him in person with as many other credible colleagues she can collect or send a memo signed by several Vision employees.

At a meeting, she should not be the only person to speak. Liz and her colleagues should divide the presentation so that no one person is the messenger. Clark will have a tendency to be vengeful and will focus on the leader of the group.

Unfortunately, because Clark may not react positively to the memo, Liz must use a more calculated and broad-based approach.

Philip A. Marineau is executive vice president and chief operating officer at the Quaker Oats Company, Chicago, Illinois.

My advice is to send the memo. Sure, it's a risk. But not sending it will lead only to greater frustration—and eventually Liz will resign anyway. Chances are the CEO is already alarmed about the loss of his top two women executives and is wondering what he can do to prevent others from leaving. If he's smart, he'll not only listen to Liz's concerns but also make her a part of the search for solutions.

It's been my experience that listening to bright, committed employees throughout the company—regardless of gender, race, or level of experience—is one of the most important aspects of my job. It's the best way for me to identify situations that need more resources or attention from management.

Working with Quaker's Diversity Council, which includes staff members from a variety of demographic backgrounds and represents all divisions and levels, I have come to realize that pursuing traditional methods of developing future managers will not itself increase diversity significantly at the highest levels.

I am convinced that in order to ensure a better future, changes must begin with those at the top of the corporation. We've created a task force whose charge is to develop specific recommendations for ways in which Quaker can identify, nurture, retain, and advance women and minority executives. To make this work, we will have to set measurable goals, carefully and continuously monitor our progress, reward those managers who successfully carry out this mandate, and penalize those who don't. As a consumer products company, our guiding marketing principle is to stay close to our customers. To be successful, our internal policies and the makeup of our top management must reflect this principle as well. In the best interests of their company's future, Vision Software's senior executives should follow suit.

———

Jay M. Jackman, MD, is a private-practice psychiatrist in Stanford, California, and a consultant for organizational change, with a particular interest in the "glass ceiling." Myra H. Strober is a labor economist at the School of Education at Stanford University and a consultant on issues of employment of women and minorities.

As any good mountaineer will tell you, a successful ascent requires a good deal of preparation: choosing fellow climbers, ensuring team conditioning, assembling first-rate equipment, and hiring experienced guides. Raising issues of sexism with the CEO of a cor-

If the Dinosaur Won't Change...

Over the last 20 years, the percentage of women business owners has grown from 5% to over 30% and is still rising. By the end of 1992, more people will work in companies owned by women than will work in the *Fortune* 500. Liz helps us see why. If the dinosaur won't change, it will become extinct.

After years of banging heads against glass ceilings, huge numbers of women are realizing that learning how to dress, getting the right degrees, and struggling to fit in are essentially fruitless exercises. Of a certain age and self-awareness, women who are weary of trying to adapt to environments in which they are not welcome are leaving to create companies that fit them. The woman who feels strongly enough to write a memo is in the process of breaking with an unfriendly culture. Whether she sends it or not is unimportant—the process of alienation has begun. And if she chooses not to spend another calorie of energy teaching lessons that companies have had over two decades to learn—and are in their own best interests—that is her prerogative.

In fact, the Harvard Business School itself has documented the case of a woman whose ideas were rejected as "not workable" in a corporation. She eventually left that company and went on to start not one, but two highly successful companies ("Ruth M. Owades," HBS 9-383-051, revised Feb. 1985). Tired of sending memos and sounding alarms, women are taking charge of their lives. What the leadership of the company does to address its workforce challenges will spell the survival or extinction of the company, regardless of whether Liz's memo is ever sent.

Joline Godfrey is the founder and director of An Income of Her Own, a company that specializes in entrepreneurial education for teenage women, and author of *Our Wildest Dreams: Women Making Money, Having Fun, Doing Good* (Harper Business, New York).

poration requires similar preparation. Liz definitely should discuss the issues of gender stonewalling at Vision Software with Clark but not alone, not yet, and not by memo.

Liz should not underestimate the difficulty of the mountain she has set out to climb. The undermining of women in the workplace is both common and difficult to change. It stems from a complicated interaction of men's beliefs and behaviors, women's beliefs and behaviors, the structures and procedures set up by companies, and the ways in which we organize and run our families. That the behaviors Liz cites have gone on for at least ten years without the

CEO's notice (hardly an uncommon situation) underscores the difficulty of change. At the moment, the CEO is part of the problem; Liz's task is to make him part of the solution—no mean feat.

Liz needs to assemble allies: other women in the company, perhaps even some who have left, possibly certain members of the board, or men in the company. Single-handedly attempting to change Clark's views is as foolhardy as attempting a solo alpine ascent. Also, Liz needs to strengthen the case to be presented to Clark. She needs more than the "anecdotes" she cites in her memo and must give Clark concrete reasons why women are leaving the company, not just speculation.

Liz also must talk with experts. There are many academics and consultants who help women and companies understand the dynamics behind sexist practices and work with them toward change. Successfully approaching a CEO about alleviating sexism—a process that ultimately will require major changes in corporate culture and structure—needs expert guidance.

Finally, we would urge Liz, with one or two people from the group she assembles, to talk to Clark in person rather than sending a memo. At the moment, she has no idea where he stands on the subject of sexism. In a meeting, she can observe when he gets defensive, test his willingness to cooperate, and suggest incremental changes that he is likely to back. Women with ten years of experience in a corporation are precious assets; as they move to improve the system for women in general, they should not sacrifice themselves.

———————

Gloria Steinem is a founder and consulting editor of Ms. *magazine. She also travels widely as a feminist speaker and organizer. She is the author of* Revolution from Within *(Little, Brown).*

Unless Liz is in imminent danger of hunger or homelessness, I would advise her to send the memo. If she doesn't, she is not only acting against her own and other women's long-term interest but also failing to give her company her best advice.

Overcoming the Culture of Exclusion

Liz Ames's dilemma raises a larger issue that permeates corporate life: How is it that we have created institutions in which people are afraid to express the truth as they see it? Bhopal, Three Mile Island, and the Ford Pinto all were preceded by memos unsent or unread.

Vision Software is losing out because it operates in a culture of exclusion. The company has suffered and will continue to suffer, both internally and in the marketplace, because it refuses to look clearly at itself. If it cannot intelligently reveal its own inner workings in a way that is collaborative and supportive of its members, then it defies its own mission to produce educational software. The company's mission, and Liz's challenge, is to absorb information from the environment and incorporate that information into an evolving system, whether it be a human being or a corporation—that is what learning is all about.

If we are to re-create our corporate organizations so that they become more socially and environmentally responsible, business will have to learn from nature. All living systems depend on constant feedback loops that recalibrate the organism's relationship to life around it. Vision's corporate culture appears to accept only feedback loops that reinforce maladaptive behavior such as sexist or exclusionary practices.

For that reason Liz has to send her memo. Her career, after all, does depend on it. Maybe not her career within the context of Vision Software—particularly if it is read in an unsympathetic light—but her life goal. Liz has to remember that she set out not only to bring home a paycheck but also to express her own values and qualities in the commercial arena.

If she doesn't file the memo, Liz will be left with the new dilemma of subordinating her own wisdom and sense of self to a system that is not fully functional. She will have an aborted sense of her own value, an acute loss in a world that is crying out for more value to be added to it. If business is about adding value, then what better place to find it than within ourselves.

Paul Hawken is the author of *The Ecology of Commerce* (HarperCollins, September 1993). He is the founder of Smith & Hawken, a catalog company known for its environmental initiatives, but is no longer affiliated with the company.

With that in mind, I would also change the memo's tone. Right now, it has a tone of apology and includes no reference at all to the company's goals. Liz should make a case for Vision Software to choose a self-interested path toward inclusiveness for the long-term benefit of the company's employees—and its bottom line.

I would advise her to write the memo with the same enthusiasm she would express if she were telling her boss about a new technology that could put Vision ahead of its competitors. Because that is exactly what she's doing: discovering a new technology. Just because it's a "soft" technology of human resources rather than one relating to inanimate objects doesn't mean her discoveries are less important. Indeed, they may be further-reaching and more important. Liz can underscore this by using such "hard" facts as company and industrywide statistics on the cost of losing a trained executive. The goal here is to help the boss see his female employees' problems as his own and thus their solution as his victory. Empathy is the most revolutionary emotion.

What's interesting about this case study, however, is that Liz's male colleague never raises the question of whether he should co-sign the memo. Or whether he should offer to support it with one of his own. Or whether he might join her in asking one or more supportive colleagues—male or female—to become part of this process.

These unaddressed options are symbolic of the ways in which sexism is regarded as the problem of women—just as racism is regarded as the problem of people of color—when in fact, those problems limit everyone. Until the more powerful own the responsibility for prejudice, it will continue to cripple us all.

Reprinted from *Harvard Business Review*,
March–April 1993 (product #93209).

CHAPTER THIRTEEN

Why Do So Many Incompetent Men Become Leaders?

by Tomas Chamorro-Premuzic

There are three popular explanations for the clear underrepresentation of women in management: They are not capable; they are not interested; or they are both interested and capable, but they are unable to break the glass ceiling, an invisible career barrier based on prejudiced stereotypes that prevents women from accessing the ranks of power. Conservatives and chauvinists tend to endorse the first; liberals and feminists prefer the third; and those somewhere in the middle are usually drawn to the second. But what if they have all missed the big picture?

In my view, the main reason for the unbalanced gender ratio in management is our inability to discern between confidence and competence. That is, because we (people in general) commonly misinterpret displays of confidence as a sign of competence, we are fooled into believing that men are better leaders than women. In other words, when it comes to leadership, the only advantage that men have over women (from Argentina to Norway and the USA to Japan) is the fact that manifestations of hubris—often masked as charisma or charm—are commonly mistaken for leadership potential and that these occur much more frequently in men than in women.[1]

This is consistent with the finding that leaderless groups have a natural tendency to elect self-centered, overconfident, and narcissistic individuals as leaders and that these personality characteristics are not equally common in men and women.[2] In line, Freud argued that the psychological process of leadership occurs because a group of people—the followers—have replaced their own narcissistic tendencies with those of the leader, such that their love for the leader is a disguised form of self-love or a substitute for their inability to love themselves. "Another person's narcissism," he said, "has a great attraction for those who have renounced part of their own . . . as if we envied them for maintaining a blissful state of mind."

The truth of the matter is that pretty much anywhere in the world, men tend to *think* that they are much smarter than women.[3] Yet arrogance and overconfidence are inversely related to leadership talent—the ability to build and maintain high-performing teams and to inspire followers to set aside their selfish agendas in order to work for the common interest of the group. Indeed, whether in sports, politics, or business, the best leaders are usually humble—and whether through nature or nurture, humility is a much more common feature in women than men. For example, women outperform men on emotional intelligence, which is a strong driver of modest behaviors.[4] Furthermore, a quantitative review of gender differences in personality involving more than 23,000 participants in 26 cultures indicated that women are more sensitive, considerate, and humble than men, which is arguably one of the least counterintuitive findings in the social sciences.[5] An even clearer picture emerges when one examines the dark side of personality: For instance, our normative data, which includes thousands of managers from across all industry sectors and 40 countries, shows that men are consistently more arrogant, manipulative, and risk-prone than women.[6]

The paradoxical implication is that the same psychological characteristics that enable male managers to rise to the top of the corporate or political ladder are actually responsible for their downfall. In other words, what it takes to *get* the job is not just different from, but also the reverse of, what it takes to *do the job well*. As a result, too many incompetent people are promoted to management jobs, and promoted over more competent people.

Unsurprisingly, the mythical image of a "leader" embodies many of the characteristics commonly found in personality disorders, such as narcissism (Steve Jobs or Vladimir Putin), psychopathy (fill in the name of your favorite despot here), histrionic tendencies (Richard Branson or Steve Ballmer), or a Machiavellian personality (nearly any federal-level politician). The sad thing is not that these mythical figures are unrepresentative of the average manager, but that the average manager will fail precisely for having these characteristics.

In fact, most leaders—whether in politics or business—fail. That has always been the case: The majority of nations, companies, societies, and organizations are poorly managed, as indicated by their longevity, revenues, and approval ratings, or by the effects they have on their citizens, employees, subordinates, or members. Good leadership has always been the exception, not the norm.

So it struck me as a little odd that so much of the recent debate over getting women to "lean in" has focused on getting them to adopt more of these dysfunctional leadership traits. Yes, these are the people we often choose as our leaders—but should they be?

Most of the character traits that are truly advantageous for effective leadership are predominantly found in those who fail to impress others with their talent for management. This is especially true for women. There is now compelling scientific evidence supporting the notion that women are more likely to adopt more-effective leadership strategies than are men. Most notably, in a comprehensive review of studies, Alice Eagly and colleagues showed that female managers are more likely to elicit respect and pride from their followers, communicate their vision effectively, empower and mentor subordinates, and approach problem solving in a more flexible and creative way (all characteristics of "transformational leadership"), as well as fairly reward direct reports.[7] In contrast, male managers are statistically less likely to bond or connect with their subordinates, and they are relatively less adept at rewarding them for their actual performance. Although these findings may reflect a sampling bias that requires women to be more qualified and competent than men in order to be chosen as leaders, there is no way of really knowing until this bias is eliminated.

In sum, there is no denying that women's path to leadership positions is paved with many barriers, including a very thick glass ceiling. But a much bigger problem is the lack of career obstacles for incompetent men, and the fact that we tend to equate leadership with the very psychological features that make the average man a more inept leader than the average woman.[8] The result is a pathological system that rewards men for their incompetence while punishing women for their competence, to everybody's detriment.

NOTES

1. Adrian Furnham et al., "Male Hubris and Female Humility? A Cross-Cultural Study of Ratings of Self, Parental, and Sibling Multiple Intelligence in America, Britain, and Japan," *Intelligence* 30, no. 1 (January–February 2001): 101–115; Amanda S. Shipman and Michael D. Mumford, "When Confidence Is Detrimental: Influence of Overconfidence on Leadership Effectiveness," *The Leadership Quarterly* 22, no. 4 (2011): 649–655; and Ernesto Reuben et al., "The Emergence of Male Leadership in Competitive Environments," *Journal of Economic Behavior & Organization* 83, no. 1 (June 2012): 111–117.

2. The Ohio State University, "Narcissistic People Most Likely to Emerge as Leaders," Newswise, October 7, 2008, https://newswise.com/articles/view/545089/.

3. Sophie von Stumm et al., "Decomposing Self-Estimates of Intelligence: Structure and Sex Differences Across 12 Nations," *British Journal of Psychology* 100, no. 2 (May 2009): 429–442.

4. S. Y. H. Hur et al., "Transformational Leadership as a Mediator Between Emotional Intelligence and Team Outcomes," *The Leadership Quarterly* 22, no. 4 (August 2011): 591–603.

5. Paul T. Costa, Jr., et al., "Gender Differences in Personality Traits Across Cultures: Robust and Surprising Findings," *Journal of Personality and Social Psychology* 81, no. 2 (2001): 322–331.

6. Blaine H. Gladdis and Jeff L. Foster, "Meta-Analysis of Dark Side Personality Characteristics and Critical Work Behaviors among Leaders across the Globe: Findings and Implications for Leadership Development and Executive Coaching," *Applied Psychology* 64, no. 1 (August 27, 2013).

7. Alice H. Eagly and Blair T. Johnson, "Gender and Leadership Style: A Meta-Analysis," *Psychological Bulletin* 108, no. 2 (1990): 233–256.

8. A. M. Koenig et al., "Are Leader Stereotypes Masculine? A Meta-Analysis of Three Research Paradigms," *Psychological Bulletin* 137, no. 4 (July 2011): 616–642.

Adapted from content posted on hbr.org,
August 22, 2013 (product #H00B50).

CHAPTER FOURTEEN

How to Promote Racial Equity in the Workplace

by Robert Livingston

Intractable as it seems, the problem of racism in the workplace can be effectively addressed with the right information, incentives, and investment. Corporate leaders may not be able to change the world, but they can certainly change *their* world.

Organizations are relatively small, autonomous entities that afford leaders a high level of control over cultural norms and procedural rules, making them ideal places to develop policies and practices that promote racial equity. In this article, I'll offer a practical road map for making profound and sustainable progress toward that goal.

I've devoted much of my academic career to the study of diversity, leadership, and social justice, and over the years I've consulted on these topics with scores of *Fortune* 500 companies, federal agencies, nonprofits, and municipalities. Often, these organizations have called me in because they are in crisis and suffering—they just want a quick fix to stop the pain. But that's akin to asking a physician to write a prescription without first understanding the patient's underlying health condition. Enduring, long-term solutions usually require more than just a pill. Organizations and societies alike must resist the impulse to seek immediate relief for the symptoms, and instead focus on the disease. Otherwise they run the risk of a recurring ailment.

To effectively address racism in your organization, it's important to first build consensus around whether there is a problem (most likely, there is) and, if so, what it is and where it comes from. If many of your employees do not believe that racism against people of color exists in the organization, or if feedback is rising through various communication channels showing that Whites feel that they are the real victims of discrimination, then diversity initiatives will be perceived as the problem, not the solution. This is one of the reasons such initiatives are frequently met with resentment and resistance, often by mid-level managers. Beliefs, not reality, are what determine how employees respond to efforts taken to increase equity. So, the first step is getting everyone on the same page as to what the reality is and why it is a problem for the organization.

FIGURE 14-1

A road map for racial equity

Organizations move through these stages sequentially, first establishing an understanding of the underlying condition, then developing genuine concern, and finally focusing on correcting the problem.

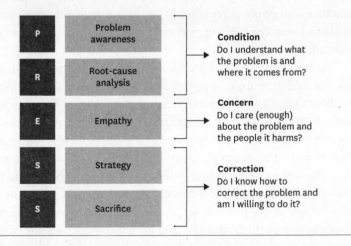

But there's much more to the job than just raising awareness. Effective interventions involve many stages, which I've incorporated into a model I call PRESS. The stages, which organizations must move through sequentially, are: (1) Problem awareness, (2) Root-cause analysis, (3) Empathy, or level of concern about the problem and the people it afflicts, (4) Strategies for addressing the problem, and (5) Sacrifice, or willingness to invest the time, energy, and resources necessary for strategy implementation (see figure 14-1). Organizations going through these stages move from understanding the underlying condition, to developing genuine concern, to focusing on correction.

Let's now have a closer look at these stages and examine how each informs, at a practical level, the process of working toward racial equity.

Problem Awareness

To a lot of people, it may seem obvious that racism continues to oppress people of color. Yet research consistently reveals that many Whites don't see it that way. For example, a 2011 study by Michael Norton and Sam Sommers found that on the whole, Whites in the United States believe that systemic anti-Black racism has steadily decreased over the past 50 years—and that systemic anti-White racism (an implausibility in the United States) has steadily increased over the same time frame. The result: As a group, Whites believe that there is more racism against them than against Blacks. Other recent surveys echo Sommers and Norton's findings, one revealing, for example, that 57% of all Whites and 66% of working-class Whites consider discrimination against Whites to be as big a problem as discrimination against Blacks and other people of color. These beliefs are important, because they can undermine an organization's efforts to address racism by weakening support for diversity policies. (Interestingly, surveys taken since the George

Floyd murder indicate an increase in perceptions of systemic racism among Whites. But it's too soon to tell whether those surveys reflect a permanent shift or a temporary uptick in awareness.)

Even managers who recognize racism in society often fail to see it in their own organizations. For example, one senior executive told me, "We don't have any discriminatory policies in our company." However, it is important to recognize that even seemingly "race neutral" policies can enable discrimination. Other executives point to their organizations' commitment to diversity as evidence for the absence of racial discrimination. "Our firm really values diversity and making this a welcoming and inclusive place for everybody to work," another leader remarked.

Despite these beliefs, many studies in the 21st century have documented that racial discrimination is prevalent in the workplace, and that organizations with strong commitments to diversity are no less likely to discriminate. In fact, research by Cheryl Kaiser and colleagues has demonstrated that the presence of diversity values and structures can actually make matters worse, by lulling an organization into complacency and making Blacks and ethnic minorities more likely to be ignored or harshly treated when they raise valid concerns about racism.

Many White people deny the existence of racism against people of color because they assume that racism is defined by deliberate actions motivated by malice and hatred. However, racism can occur without conscious awareness or intent. When defined simply as differential evaluation or treatment based solely on race, regardless of intent, racism occurs far more frequently than most White people suspect. Let's look at a few examples.

In a well-publicized résumé study by the economists Marianne Bertrand and Sendhil Mullainathan, applicants with White-sounding names (such as Emily Walsh) received, on average, 50% more callbacks for interviews than equally qualified applicants with Black-sounding names (such as Lakisha Washington). The researchers estimated that just being White conferred the same benefit as an additional eight years of work experience—a dramatic head start over equally qualified Black candidates.

Research shows that people of color are well-aware of these discriminatory tendencies and sometimes try to counteract them by masking their race. A 2016 study by Sonia Kang and colleagues found that 31% of the Black professionals and 40% of the Asian professionals they interviewed admitted to "Whitening" their résumés, by either adopting a less "ethnic" name or omitting extracurricular experiences (a college club membership, for instance) that might reveal their racial identities.

These findings raise another question: Does Whitening a résumé actually benefit Black and Asian applicants, or does it disadvantage them when applying to organizations seeking to increase diversity? In a follow-up experiment, Kang and her colleagues sent Whitened and non-Whitened résumés of Black or Asian applicants to 1,600 real-world job postings across various industries and geographical areas in the United States. Half of these job postings were from companies that expressed a strong desire to seek diverse candidates. They found that Whitening résumés by altering names and extracurricular experiences increased the callback rate from 10% to nearly 26% for Blacks, and from about 12% to 21% for Asians. What's particularly unsettling is that a company's stated commitment to diversity failed to diminish this preference for Whitened résumés.

This is a very small sample of the many studies that have confirmed the prevalence of racism in the workplace, all of which underscore the fact that people's beliefs and biases must be recognized and addressed as the first step toward progress. Although some leaders acknowledge systemic racism in their organizations and can skip step one, many may need to be convinced that racism persists, despite their "race neutral" policies or pro-diversity statements.

Root-Cause Analysis

Understanding an ailment's roots is critical to choosing the best remedy. Racism can have many psychological sources—cognitive biases, personality characteristics, ideological worldviews, psychological insecurity, perceived threat, or a need for power and ego enhancement. But most racism is the result of structural factors—established laws, institutional practices, and cultural norms. Many of these causes do not involve malicious intent. Nonetheless, managers often misattribute workplace discrimination to the character of individual actors—the so-called bad apples—rather than to broader structural factors. As a result, they roll out trainings to "fix" employees while dedicating relatively little attention to what may be a toxic organizational culture, for example. It is much easier to pinpoint and blame individuals when problems arise. When police departments face crises related to racism, the knee-jerk response is to fire the officers involved or replace the police chief rather than examining how the culture licenses, or even encourages, discriminatory behavior.

Appealing to circumstances beyond one's control is another way to exonerate deeply embedded cultural or institutional practices that are responsible for racial disparities. For example, an oceanographic organization I worked with attributed its lack of racial diversity to an insurmountable pipeline problem. "There just aren't any Black people out there studying the migration patterns of the humpback whale," one leader commented. Most leaders were unaware of the National Association of Black Scuba Divers, an organization boasting thousands of members, or of Hampton University, a historically Black college on the Chesapeake Bay, which awards bachelor's degrees in marine and environmental science. Both were entities that could source Black candidates for the job, especially given that the organization only needed to fill dozens, not thousands, of openings.

A *Fortune* 500 company I worked with cited similar pipeline problems. Closer examination revealed, however, that the real culprit was the culture-based practice of promoting leaders from within the organization—which already had low diversity—rather than conducting a broader industrywide search when leadership positions became available. The larger lesson here is that an organization's lack of diversity is often tied to inadequate recruitment efforts rather than an empty pipeline. Progress requires a deeper diagnosis of the routine practices that drive the outcomes leaders wish to change.

To help managers and employees understand how being embedded within a biased system can unwittingly influence outcomes and behaviors, I like to ask them to imagine being fish in a stream. In that stream, a current exerts force on everything in the water, moving it downstream. That current is analogous to systemic racism. If you do nothing—just float—the current will carry you along with it, whether you're aware of it or not. If you actively discriminate by swimming with the current, you will be propelled faster. In both cases, the current takes you in the same direction. From this perspective, racism has less to do with what's in your heart or mind and more to do with how your actions or inactions amplify or enable the systemic dynamics already in place.

Workplace discrimination often comes from well-educated, well-intentioned, open-minded, kindhearted people who are just floating along, severely underestimating the tug of the prevailing current on their actions, positions, and outcomes. Anti-racism requires swimming against that current, like a salmon making its way upstream. It demands much more effort, courage, and determination than simply going with the flow.

In short, organizations must be mindful of the "current," or the structural dynamics that permeate the system, not just the "fish," or individual actors that operate within it.

Empathy

Once people are aware of the problem and its underlying causes, the next question is whether they care enough to do something about it. There is a difference between sympathy and empathy. Many White people experience sympathy, or pity, when they witness racism. But what's more likely to lead to action in confronting the problem is empathy—experiencing the same hurt and anger that people of color are feeling. People of color want solidarity—and social justice—not sympathy, which simply quiets the symptoms while perpetuating the disease.

One way to increase empathy is through exposure and education. The video of George Floyd's murder exposed people to the ugly reality of racism in a visceral, protracted, and undeniable way. Similarly, in the 1960s, northern Whites witnessed innocent Black protesters being beaten with batons and blasted with fire hoses on television. What best prompts people in an organization to register concern about racism in their midst, I've found, are the moments when their non-White coworkers share vivid, detailed accounts of the negative impact that racism has on their lives. Managers can raise awareness and empathy through psychologically safe listening sessions—for employees who want to share their experiences, without feeling obligated to do so—supplemented by education and experiences that provide historical and scientific evidence of the persistence of racism.

For example, I spoke with Mike Kaufmann, CEO of Cardinal Health—the 16th largest corporation in America—who credited a visit to the Equal Justice Initiative's National Memorial for Peace and Justice, in Montgomery, Alabama, as a pivotal moment for the company. While diversity and inclusion initiatives have been a priority for Mike and his leadership team for well over a decade, their focus and conversations related to racial inclusion increased significantly during 2019. As he expressed to me, "Some Americans think when slavery ended in the 1860s that African Americans have had an equal opportunity ever since. That's just not true. Institutional systemic racism is still very much alive today; it's never gone away." Kaufmann is planning a comprehensive education program, which will include a trip for executives and other employees to visit the museum, because he is convinced that the experience will change hearts, open eyes, and drive action and behavioral change.

Empathy is critical for making progress toward racial equity because it affects whether individuals or organizations take any action and if so, what kind of action they take. There are at least four ways to respond to racism: join in and add to the injury, ignore it and mind your own business, experience sympathy and bake cookies for the victim, or experience empathic outrage and take measures to promote equal justice. The personal values of individual employees and the core values of the organization are two factors that affect which actions are undertaken.

Strategy

After the foundation has been laid, it's finally time for the "what do we do about it" stage. Most actionable strategies for change address three distinct but interconnected categories: personal attitudes, informal cultural norms, and formal institutional policies.

To most effectively combat discrimination in the workplace, leaders should consider how they can run interventions on all three of these fronts simultaneously. Focusing only on one is likely to be ineffective and could even backfire. For example, implementing institutional diversity policies without any attempt to create buy-in from employees is likely to produce a backlash. Likewise, focusing just on changing attitudes without also establishing institutional policies that hold people accountable for their decisions and actions may generate little behavioral change among those who don't agree with the policies. Establishing an anti-racist organizational culture, tied to core values and modeled by behavior from the CEO and other top leaders at the company, can influence both individual attitudes and institutional policies.

Just as there is no shortage of effective strategies for losing weight or promoting environmental sustainability, there are ample strategies for reducing racial bias at the individual, cultural, and institutional levels. The hard part is getting people to actually adopt them. Even the best strategies are worthless without implementation.

I'll discuss how to increase commitment to execution in the final section. But before I do, I want to give a specific example of an institutional strategy that works. It comes from Massport, a public organization that owns Boston Logan International Airport and commercial lots worth billions of dollars. When its leaders decided they wanted to increase diversity and inclusion in real estate development in Boston's booming Seaport District, they decided to leverage their land to do it. Massport's leaders made formal changes to the selection criteria determining who is awarded lucrative contracts to build and operate hotels and other large commercial buildings on their parcels. In addition to evaluating three traditional criteria—the developer's experience and financial capital, Massport's revenue potential, and the project's architectural design—they added a fourth criterion called "comprehensive diversity and inclusion," which accounted for 25% of the proposal's overall score, the same as the other three. This forced developers not only to think more deeply about how to create diversity but also to go out and do it. Similarly, organizations can integrate diversity and inclusion into managers' scorecards for raises and promotions—if they think it's important enough. I've found that the real barrier to diversity is not figuring out "What can we do?" but rather "Are we willing to do it?"

Sacrifice

Many organizations that desire greater diversity, equity, and inclusion may not be willing to invest the time, energy, resources, and commitment necessary to make it happen. Actions are often inhibited by the assumption that achieving one desired goal requires sacrificing another desired goal. But that's not always the case. Although nothing worth having is completely free, racial equity often costs less than people may assume. Seemingly conflicting goals or competing commitments are often relatively easy to reconcile—once the underlying assumptions have been identified.

As a society, are we sacrificing public safety and social order when police routinely treat people of color with compassion and respect? No. In fact, it's possible that kinder policing will actually increase public safety. Famously, the city of Camden, New Jersey, witnessed a 40% drop in violent crime after it reformed its police department, in 2012, and put a much greater emphasis on community policing.

The assumptions of sacrifice have enormous implications for the hiring and promotion of diverse talent, for at least two reasons. First, people often assume that increasing diversity means sacrificing principles of fairness and merit, because it requires giving "special" favors to people of color rather than treating everyone the same. But take a look at the scene in figure 14-2. Which of the two scenarios appears more "fair," the one on the left or the one on the right?

People often assume that fairness means treating everyone *equally,* or exactly the same—in this case, giving each person one crate of the same size. In reality, fairness requires treating people *equitably*—which may entail treating people differently, but in a way that makes sense. If you chose the scenario on the right, then you subscribe to the notion that fairness can require treating people differently in a sensible way.

Of course, what is "sensible" depends on the context and the perceiver. Does it make sense for someone with a physical disability to have a parking space closer to a building? Is it fair for new parents to have six weeks of paid leave to be able to care for their baby? Is it right to allow active-duty military personnel to board an airplane early to express gratitude for their service? My answer is yes to all three questions, but not everyone will agree. For this reason, equity

FIGURE 14-2

presents a greater challenge to gaining consensus than equality. In the first panel of the fence scenario, everybody gets the same number of crates. That's a simple solution. But is it fair?

In thinking about fairness in the context of American society, leaders must consider the unlevel playing fields and other barriers that exist—provided they are aware of systemic racism. They must also have the courage to make difficult or controversial calls. For example, it might make sense to have an employee resource group for Black employees but not White employees. Fair outcomes may require a process of treating people differently. To be clear, different treatment is not the same as "special" treatment—the latter is tied to favoritism, not equity.

One leader who understands the difference is Maria Klawe, the president of Harvey Mudd College. She concluded that the only way to increase the representation of women in computer science was to treat men and women differently. Men and women tended to have different levels of computing experience prior to entering college—different levels of *experience,* not intelligence or potential. Society treats boys and girls differently throughout secondary school—encouraging STEM subjects for boys but liberal arts subjects for girls, creating gaps in experience. To compensate for this gap created by bias in society, the college designed two introductory computer-science tracks—one for students with no computing experience and one for students with some computing experience in high school. The no-experience course tended to be 50% women whereas the some-experience course was predominantly men. By the end of the semester, the students in both courses were on par with one another. Through this and other equity-based interventions, Klawe and her team were able to dramatically increase the representation of women and minority computer-science majors and graduates.

The second assumption many people have is that increasing diversity requires sacrificing high quality and standards. Consider again the fence scenario. All three people have the same height or "potential." What varies is the level of the field and the fence—apt metaphors for privilege and discrimination, respectively. Because the person on the far left has lower barriers to access, does it make sense to treat the other two people differently to compensate? Do we have an obligation to do so when differences in outcomes are caused by the field and the fence, not someone's height? Maria Klawe sure thought so. How much human potential is left unrealized within organizations because we do not recognize the barriers that exist?

Finally, it's important to understand that quality is difficult to measure with precision. There is no test, instrument, survey, or interviewing technique that will enable you to invariably predict who the "best candidate" will be. The NFL draft illustrates the difficulty in predicting future job performance: Despite large scouting departments, plentiful video of prior performance, and extensive tryouts, almost half of first round picks turn out to be busts. This may be true for organizations as well. Research by Sheldon Zedeck and colleagues on corporate hiring processes has found that even the best screening or aptitude tests predict only 25% of intended outcomes, and that candidate quality is better reflected by "statistical bands" rather than a strict rank ordering. This means that there may be absolutely no difference in quality between the candidate who scored first out of 50 people and the candidate who scored eighth.

The big takeaway here is that "sacrifice" may actually involve giving up very little. If we look at people within a band of potential and choose the diverse candidate (for example, number eight) over the top scorer, we haven't sacrificed quality at all—statistically speaking—even if people's intuitions lead them to conclude otherwise.

Managers should abandon the notion that a "best candidate" must be found. That kind of search amounts to chasing unicorns. Instead, they should focus on hiring well-qualified people who show good promise, and then should invest time, effort, and resources into helping them reach their potential.

The tragedies and protests we have witnessed this year across the United States have increased public awareness and concern about racism as a persistent problem in our society. The question we now must confront is whether, as a nation, we are willing to do the hard work necessary to change widespread attitudes, assumptions, policies, and practices. Unlike society at large, the workplace very often requires contact and cooperation among people from different racial, ethnic, and cultural backgrounds. Therefore, leaders should host open and candid conversations about how their organizations are doing at each of the five stages of the model—and use their power to press for profound and perennial progress.

Reprinted from *Harvard Business Review*,
September–October 2020 (product #R2005D).

— 2001 —

CHAPTER FIFTEEN

Harnessing the Science of Persuasion

by Robert B. Cialdini

A lucky few have it; most of us do not. A handful of gifted "naturals" simply know how to capture an audience, sway the undecided, and convert the opposition. Watching these masters of persuasion work their magic is at once impressive and frustrating. What's impressive is not just the easy way they use charisma and eloquence to convince others to do as they ask. It's also how eager those others are to do what's requested of them, as if the persuasion itself were a favor they couldn't wait to repay.

The frustrating part of the experience is that these born persuaders are often unable to account for their remarkable skill or pass it on to others. Their way with people is an art, and artists as a rule are far better at doing than at explaining. Most of them can't offer much help to those of us who possess no more than the ordinary quotient of charisma and eloquence but who still have to wrestle with leadership's fundamental challenge: getting things done through others. That challenge is painfully familiar to corporate executives, who every day have to figure out how to motivate and direct a highly individualistic work force. Playing the "Because I'm the boss" card is out. Even if it weren't demeaning and demoralizing for all concerned, it would be out of place in a world where cross-functional teams, joint ventures, and intercompany partnerships have blurred the lines of authority. In such an environment, persuasion skills exert far greater influence over others' behavior than formal power structures do.

Which brings us back to where we started. Persuasion skills may be more necessary than ever, but how can executives acquire them if the most talented practitioners can't pass them along? By looking to science. For the past five decades, behavioral scientists have conducted experiments that shed considerable light on the way certain interactions lead people to concede, comply, or change. This research shows that persuasion works by appealing to a limited set of deeply rooted human drives and needs, and it does so in predictable ways. Persuasion, in other words, is governed by basic principles that can be taught, learned, and applied. By mastering these principles, executives can bring scientific rigor to the business of securing consensus, cutting deals, and winning concessions. In the pages that follow, I describe six fundamental principles of persuasion and suggest a few ways that executives can apply them in their own organizations.

The Principle of Liking

People like those who like them.

The application

Uncover real similarities and offer genuine praise.

The retailing phenomenon known as the Tupperware party is a vivid illustration of this principle in action. The demonstration party for Tupperware products is hosted by an individual, almost always a woman, who invites to her home an array of friends, neighbors, and relatives. The guests' affection for their hostess predisposes them to buy from her, a dynamic that was confirmed by a 1990 study of purchase decisions made at demonstration parties. The researchers, Jonathan Frenzen and Harry Davis, writing in the *Journal of Consumer Research*, found that the guests' fondness for their hostess weighed twice as heavily in their purchase decisions as their regard for the products they bought. So when guests at a Tupperware party buy something, they aren't just buying to please themselves. They're buying to please their hostess as well.

What's true at Tupperware parties is true for business in general: If you want to influence people, win friends. How? Controlled research has identified several factors that reliably increase liking, but two stand out as especially compelling—similarity and praise. Similarity literally draws people together. In one experiment, reported in a 1968 article in the *Journal of Personality,* participants stood physically closer to one another after learning that they shared political beliefs and social values. And in a 1963 article in *American Behavioral Scientists,* researcher F. B. Evans used demographic data from insurance company records to demonstrate that prospects were more willing to purchase a policy from a salesperson who was akin to them in age, religion, politics, or even cigarette-smoking habits.

Managers can use similarities to create bonds with a recent hire, the head of another department, or even a new boss. Informal conversations during the workday create an ideal opportunity to discover at least one common area of enjoyment, be it a hobby, a college basketball team, or reruns of *Seinfeld.* The important thing is to establish the bond early because it creates a presumption of goodwill and trustworthiness in every subsequent encounter. It's much easier to build support for a new project when the people you're trying to persuade are already inclined in your favor.

Praise, the other reliable generator of affection, both charms and disarms. Sometimes the praise doesn't even have to be merited. Researchers at the University of North Carolina writing in the *Journal of Experimental Social Psychology* found that men felt the greatest regard for an individual who flattered them unstintingly even if the comments were untrue. And in their book *Interpersonal Attraction* (Addison-Wesley, 1978), Ellen Berscheid and Elaine Hatfield Walster presented experimental data showing that positive remarks about another person's traits, attitude, or performance reliably generates liking in return, as well as willing compliance with the wishes of the person offering the praise.

Along with cultivating a fruitful relationship, adroit managers can also use praise to repair one that's damaged or unproductive. Imagine you're the manager of a good-sized unit within your organization. Your work frequently brings you into contact with another manager—call him Dan—whom you have come to dislike. No matter how much you do for him, it's not enough. Worse, he never seems to believe that you're doing the best you can for him. Resenting his attitude and his obvious lack of trust in your abilities and in your good faith, you don't spend as much time with him as you know you should; in consequence, the performance of both his unit and yours is deteriorating.

The research on praise points toward a strategy for fixing the relationship. It may be hard to find, but there has to be something about Dan you can sincerely admire, whether it's his concern for the people in his department, his devotion to his family, or simply his work ethic. In your next encounter with him, make an appreciative comment about that trait. Make it clear that in this case at least, you value what he values. I predict that Dan will relax his relentless negativity and give you an opening to convince him of your competence and good intentions.

The Principle of Reciprocity

People repay in kind.

The application

Give what you want to receive.

Praise is likely to have a warming and softening effect on Dan because, ornery as he is, he is still human and subject to the universal human tendency to treat people the way they treat him. If you have ever caught yourself smiling at a coworker just because he or she smiled first, you know how this principle works.

Charities rely on reciprocity to help them raise funds. For years, for instance, the Disabled American Veterans organization, using only a well-crafted fundraising letter, garnered a very respectable 18% rate of response to its appeals. But when the group started enclosing a small gift in the envelope, the response rate nearly doubled to 35%. The gift—personalized address labels—was extremely modest, but it wasn't what prospective donors received that made the difference. It was that they had gotten anything at all.

What works in that letter works at the office, too. It's more than an effusion of seasonal spirit, of course, that impels suppliers to shower gifts on purchasing departments at holiday time. In 1996, purchasing managers admitted to an interviewer from *Inc.* magazine that after having accepted a gift from a supplier, they were willing to purchase products and services they would have otherwise declined. Gifts also have a startling effect on retention. I have encouraged readers of my book to send me examples of the principles of influence at work in their own lives. One reader, an employee of the State of Oregon, sent a letter in which she offered these reasons for her commitment to her supervisor:

> He gives me and my son gifts for Christmas and gives me presents on my birthday. There is no promotion for the type of job I have, and my only choice for one is to move to another department. But I find myself resisting trying to move. My boss is reaching retirement age, and I am thinking I will be able to move out after he retires. . . . [F]or now, I feel obligated to stay since he has been so nice to me.

Ultimately, though, gift giving is one of the cruder applications of the rule of reciprocity. In its more sophisticated uses, it confers a genuine first-mover advantage on any manager who is trying to foster positive attitudes and productive personal relationships in the office: Managers can elicit the desired behavior from coworkers and employees by displaying it first. Whether it's a sense of trust, a spirit of cooperation, or a pleasant demeanor, leaders should model the behavior they want to see from others.

The same holds true for managers faced with issues of information delivery and resource allocation. If you lend a member of your staff to a colleague who is shorthanded and staring at a fast-approaching deadline, you will significantly increase your chances of getting help when you need it. Your odds will improve even more if you say, when your colleague thanks you for the assistance, something like, "Sure, glad to help. I know how important it is for me to count on your help when I need it."

The Principle of Social Proof

People follow the lead of similar others.

The application

Use peer power whenever it's available.

Social creatures that they are, human beings rely heavily on the people around them for cues on how to think, feel, and act. We know this intuitively, but intuition has also been confirmed by experiments, such as the one first described in 1982 in the *Journal of Applied Psychology*. A group of researchers went door-to-door in Columbia, South Carolina, soliciting donations for a charity campaign and displaying a list of neighborhood residents who had already donated to the cause. The researchers found that the longer the donor list was, the more likely those solicited would be to donate as well.

To the people being solicited, the friends' and neighbors' names on the list were a form of social evidence about how they should respond. But the evidence would not have been nearly as compelling had the names been those of random strangers. In an experiment from the 1960s, first described in the *Journal of Personality and Social Psychology,* residents of New York City were asked to return a lost wallet to its owner. They were highly likely to attempt to return the wallet when they learned that another New Yorker had previously attempted to do so. But learning that someone from a foreign country had tried to return the wallet didn't sway their decision one way or the other.

The lesson for executives from these two experiments is that persuasion can be extremely effective when it comes from peers. The science supports what most sales professionals already know: Testimonials from satisfied customers work best when the satisfied customer and the prospective customer share similar circumstances. That lesson can help a manager faced with the task of selling a new corporate initiative. Imagine that you're trying to streamline your department's work processes. A group of veteran employees is resisting. Rather than try to convince the employees of the move's merits yourself, ask an old-timer who supports the initiative to speak up for it at a team meeting. The compatriot's testimony stands a much better chance of convincing the group than yet another speech from the boss. Stated simply, influence is often best exerted horizontally rather than vertically.

The Principle of Consistency

People align with their clear commitments.

The application

Make their commitments active, public, and voluntary.

Liking is a powerful force, but the work of persuasion involves more than simply making people feel warmly toward you, your idea, or your product. People need not only to like you but to feel committed to what you want them to do. Good turns are one reliable way to make people feel obligated to you. Another is to win a public commitment from them.

My own research has demonstrated that most people, once they take a stand or go on record in favor of a position, prefer to stick to it. Other studies reinforce that finding and go on to show how even a small, seemingly trivial commitment can have a powerful effect on future actions. Israeli researchers writing in 1983 in the *Personality and Social Psychology Bulletin* recounted how they asked half the residents of a large apartment complex to sign a petition favoring the establishment of a recreation center for the handicapped. The cause was good and the request was small, so almost everyone who was asked agreed to sign. Two weeks later, on National Collection Day for the Handicapped, all residents of the complex were approached at home and asked to give to the cause. A little more than half of those who were not asked to sign the petition made a contribution. But an astounding 92% of those who did sign donated money. The residents of the apartment complex felt obligated to live up to their commitments because those commitments were active, public, and voluntary. These three features are worth considering separately.

There's strong empirical evidence to show that a choice made actively—one that's spoken out loud or written down or otherwise made explicit—is considerably more likely to direct someone's future conduct than the same choice left unspoken. Writing in 1996 in the *Personality and Social Psychology Bulletin,* Delia Cioffi and Randy Garner described an experiment in which college students in one group were asked to fill out a printed form saying they wished to volunteer for an AIDS education project in the public schools. Students in another group volunteered for the same project by leaving blank a form stating that they didn't want to participate. A few days later, when the volunteers reported for duty, 74% of those who showed up were students from the group that signaled their commitment by filling out the form.

The implications are clear for a manager who wants to persuade a subordinate to follow some particular course of action: Get it in writing. Let's suppose you want your employee to submit reports in a more timely fashion. Once you believe you've won agreement, ask him to summarize the decision in a memo and send it to you. By doing so, you'll have greatly increased the odds that he'll fulfill the commitment because, as a rule, people live up to what they have written down.

Research into the social dimensions of commitment suggests that written statements become even more powerful when they're made public. In a classic experiment, described in 1955 in the *Journal of Abnormal and Social Psychology,* college students were asked to estimate the length of lines projected on a screen. Some students were asked to write down their choices on a piece of paper, sign it, and hand the paper to the experimenter. Others wrote their choices on an erasable slate, then erased the slate immediately. Still others were instructed to keep their decisions to themselves.

The experimenters then presented all three groups with evidence that their initial choices may have been wrong. Those who had merely kept their decisions in their heads were the most likely to reconsider their original estimates. More loyal to their first guesses were the students in the group that had written them down and immediately erased them. But by a wide margin, the ones most reluctant to shift from their original choices were those who had signed and handed them to the researcher.

This experiment highlights how much most people wish to appear consistent to others. Consider again the matter of the employee who has been submitting late reports. Recognizing the power of this desire, you should, once you've successfully convinced him of the need to be more timely, reinforce the commitment by making sure it gets a public airing. One way to do that would be to send the employee an e-mail that reads, "I think your plan is just what we need. I showed it to Diane in manufacturing and Phil in shipping, and they thought it was right on target, too." Whatever way such commitments are formalized, they should never be like the New Year's resolutions people privately make and then abandon with no one the wiser. They should be publicly made and visibly posted.

More than 300 years ago, Samuel Butler wrote a couplet that explains succinctly why commitments must be voluntary to be lasting and effective: "He that complies against his will/Is of his own opinion still." If an undertaking is forced, coerced, or imposed from the outside, it's not a commitment; it's an unwelcome burden. Think how you would react if your boss pressured you to donate to the campaign of a political candidate. Would that make you more apt to opt for that candidate in the privacy of a voting booth? Not likely. In fact, in their 1981 book *Psychological Reactance* (Academic Press), Sharon S. Brehm and Jack W. Brehm present data that suggest you'd vote the opposite way just to express your resentment of the boss's coercion.

This kind of backlash can occur in the office, too. Let's return again to that tardy employee. If you want to produce an enduring change in his behavior, you should avoid using threats or pressure tactics to gain his compliance. He'd likely view any change in his behavior as the result of intimidation rather than a personal commitment to change. A better approach would be to identify something that the employee genuinely values in the workplace—high-quality workmanship, perhaps, or team spirit—and then describe how timely reports are consistent with those values. That gives the employee reasons for improvement that he can own. And because he owns them, they'll continue to guide his behavior even when you're not watching.

The Principle of Authority

People defer to experts.

The application

Expose your expertise; don't assume it's self-evident.

Two thousand years ago, the Roman poet Virgil offered this simple counsel to those seeking to choose correctly: "Believe an expert." That may or may not be good advice, but as a description of what people actually do, it can't be beaten. For instance, when the news media present an acknowledged expert's views on a topic, the effect on public opinion is dramatic. A single expert-opinion news story in the *New York Times* is associated with a 2% shift in public opinion nationwide, according to a 1993 study described in the *Public Opinion Quarterly*. And researchers writing in the *American Political Science Review* in 1987 found that when the expert's view was aired on national television, public opinion shifted as much as 4%. A cynic might argue that these findings only illustrate the docile submissiveness of the public. But a fairer explanation is that, amid the teeming complexity of contemporary life, a well-selected expert offers a valuable and efficient shortcut to good decisions. Indeed,

Persuasion Experts, Safe at Last

Thanks to several decades of rigorous empirical research by behavioral scientists, our understanding of the how and why of persuasion has never been broader, deeper, or more detailed. But these scientists aren't the first students of the subject. The history of persuasion studies is an ancient and honorable one, and it has generated a long roster of heroes and martyrs.

A renowned student of social influence, William McGuire, contends in a chapter of the *Handbook of Social Psychology,* 3rd ed. (Oxford University Press, 1985) that scattered among the more than four millennia of recorded Western history are four centuries in which the study of persuasion flourished as a craft. The first was the Periclean Age of ancient Athens, the second occurred during the years of the Roman Republic, the next appeared in the time of the European Renaissance, and the last extended over the hundred years that have just ended, which witnessed the advent of large-scale advertising, information, and mass media campaigns. Each of the three previous centuries of systematic persuasion study was marked by a flowering of human achievement that was suddenly cut short when political authorities had the masters of persuasion killed. The philosopher Socrates is probably the best known of the persuasion experts to run afoul of the powers that be.

Information about the persuasion process is a threat because it creates a base of power entirely separate from the one controlled by political authorities. Faced with a rival source of influence, rulers in previous centuries had few qualms about eliminating those rare individuals who truly understood how to marshal forces that heads of state have never been able to monopolize, such as cleverly crafted language, strategically placed information, and, most important, psychological insight.

It would perhaps be expressing too much faith in human nature to claim that persuasion experts no longer face a threat from those who wield political power. But because the truth about persuasion is no longer the sole possession of a few brilliant, inspired individuals, experts in the field can presumably breathe a little easier. Indeed, since most people in power are interested in remaining in power, they're likely to be more interested in acquiring persuasion skills than abolishing them.

some questions, be they legal, financial, medical, or technological, require so much specialized knowledge to answer, we have no choice but to rely on experts.

Since there's good reason to defer to experts, executives should take pains to ensure that they establish their own expertise before they attempt to exert influence. Surprisingly often, people mistakenly assume that others recognize and appreciate their experience.

That's what happened at a hospital where some colleagues and I were consulting. The physical therapy staffers were frustrated because so many of their stroke patients abandoned their exercise routines as soon as they left the hospital. No matter how often the staff emphasized the importance of regular home exercise—it is, in fact, crucial to the process of regaining independent function—the message just didn't sink in.

Interviews with some of the patients helped us pinpoint the problem. They were familiar with the background and training of their physicians, but the patients knew little about the credentials of the physical therapists who were urging them to exercise. It was a simple matter to remedy that lack of information: We merely asked the therapy director to display all the awards, diplomas, and certifications of her staff on the walls of the therapy rooms. The result was startling: Exercise compliance jumped 34% and has never dropped since.

What we found immensely gratifying was not just how much we increased compliance, but how. We didn't fool or browbeat any of the patients. We *informed* them into compliance. Nothing had to be invented; no time or resources had to be spent in the process. The staff's expertise was real—all we had to do was make it more visible.

The task for managers who want to establish their claims to expertise is somewhat more difficult. They can't simply nail their diplomas to the wall and wait for everyone to notice. A little subtlety is called for. Outside the United States, it is customary for people to spend time interacting socially before getting down to business for the first time. Frequently they gather for dinner the night before their meeting or negotiation. These get-togethers can make discussions easier and help blunt disagreements—remember the findings about liking and similarity—and they can also provide an opportunity to establish expertise. Perhaps it's a matter of telling an anecdote about successfully solving a problem similar to the one that's on the agenda at the next day's meeting. Or perhaps dinner is the time to describe years spent mastering a complex discipline—not in a boastful way but as part of the ordinary give-and-take of conversation.

Granted, there's not always time for lengthy introductory sessions. But even in the course of the preliminary conversation that precedes most meetings, there is almost always an opportunity to touch lightly on your relevant background and experience as a natural part of a sociable exchange. This initial disclosure of personal information gives you a chance to establish expertise early in the game, so that when the discussion turns to the business at hand, what you have to say will be accorded the respect it deserves.

The Principle of Scarcity

People want more of what they can have less of.

The application

Highlight unique benefits and exclusive information.

Study after study shows that items and opportunities are seen to be more valuable as they become less available. That's a tremendously useful piece of information for managers. They can harness the scarcity principle with the organizational equivalents of limited-time, limited-supply, and one-of-a-kind offers. Honestly informing a coworker of a closing window of opportunity—the chance to get the boss's ear before she leaves for an extended vacation, perhaps—can mobilize action dramatically.

Managers can learn from retailers how to frame their offers not in terms of what people stand to gain but in terms of what they stand to lose if they don't act on the information. The power of "loss language" was demonstrated in a 1988 study of California home owners written up in the *Journal of Applied Psychology*. Half were told that if they fully insulated their homes, they would save a certain amount of money each day. The other half were told that if they failed to insulate, they would lose that amount each day. Significantly more people insulated their homes when exposed to the loss language. The same phenomenon occurs in business. According to a 1994 study in the journal *Organizational Behavior and Human Decision Processes,* potential losses figure far more heavily in managers' decision making than potential gains.

In framing their offers, executives should also remember that exclusive information is more persuasive than widely available data. A doctoral student of mine, Amram Knishinsky, wrote his 1982 dissertation on the purchase decisions of wholesale beef buyers. He observed that they more than doubled their orders when they were told that, because of certain weather conditions overseas, there was likely to be a scarcity of foreign beef in the near future. But their orders increased 600% when they were informed that no one else had that information yet.

The persuasive power of exclusivity can be harnessed by any manager who comes into possession of information that's not broadly available and that supports an idea or initiative he or she would like the organization to adopt. The next time that kind of information crosses your desk, round up your organization's key players. The information itself may seem dull, but exclusivity will give it a special sheen. Push it across your desk and say, "I just got this report today. It won't be distributed until next week, but I want to give you an early look at what it shows." Then watch your listeners lean forward.

Allow me to stress here a point that should be obvious. No offer of exclusive information, no exhortation to act now or miss this opportunity forever should be made unless it is genuine. Deceiving colleagues into compliance is not only ethically objectionable, it's foolhardy. If the deception is detected—and it certainly will be—it will snuff out any enthusiasm the offer originally kindled. It will also invite dishonesty toward the deceiver. Remember the rule of reciprocity.

Putting It All Together

There's nothing abstruse or obscure about these six principles of persuasion. Indeed, they neatly codify our intuitive understanding of the ways people evaluate information and form decisions. As a result, the principles are easy for most people to grasp, even those with no formal education in psychology. But in the seminars and workshops I conduct, I have learned that two points bear repeated emphasis.

First, although the six principles and their applications can be discussed separately for the sake of clarity, they should be applied in combination to compound their impact. For instance, in discussing the importance of expertise, I suggested that managers use informal, social conversations to establish their credentials. But that conversation affords an opportunity to gain information as well as convey it. While you're showing your dinner companion that you have the skills and experience your business problem demands, you can also learn about your companion's background, likes, and dislikes—information that will help you locate genuine similarities and give sincere compliments. By letting your expertise surface and also establishing rapport, you double your persuasive power. And if you succeed in bringing your dinner partner on board, you may encourage other people to sign on as well, thanks to the persuasive power of social evidence.

The other point I wish to emphasize is that the rules of ethics apply to the science of social influence just as they do to any other technology. Not only is it ethically wrong to trick or trap others into assent, it's ill-advised in practical terms. Dishonest or high-pressure tactics work only in the short run, if at all. Their long-term effects are malignant, especially within an organization, which can't function properly without a bedrock level of trust and cooperation.

That point is made vividly in the following account, which a department head for a large textile manufacturer related at a training workshop I conducted. She described a vice president in her company who wrung public commitments from department heads in a highly manipulative manner. Instead of giving his subordinates time to talk or think through his proposals carefully, he would approach them individually at the busiest moment of their workday and describe the benefits of his plan in exhaustive, patience-straining detail. Then he would move in for the kill. "It's very important for me to see you as being on my team on this," he would say. "Can I count on your support?" Intimidated, frazzled, eager to chase the man from their offices so they could get back to work, the department heads would invariably go along with his request. But because the commitments never felt voluntary, the department heads never followed through, and as a result the vice president's initiatives all blew up or petered out.

This story had a deep impact on the other participants in the workshop. Some gulped in shock as they recognized their own manipulative behavior. But what stopped everyone cold was the expression on the department head's face as she recounted the damaging collapse of her superior's proposals. She was smiling.

Nothing I could say would more effectively make the point that the deceptive or coercive use of the principles of social influence is ethically wrong and pragmatically wrongheaded. Yet the same principles, if applied appropriately, can steer decisions correctly. Legitimate expertise, genuine obligations, authentic similarities, real social proof, exclusive news, and freely made commitments can produce choices that are likely to benefit both parties. And any approach that works to everyone's mutual benefit is good business, don't you think? Of course, I don't want to press you into it, but, if you agree, I would love it if you could just jot me a memo to that effect.

Reprinted from *Harvard Business Review*,
October 2001 (product #R0109D).

CHAPTER SIXTEEN

Barriers and Gateways to Communication

by Carl R. Rogers and F. J. Roethlisberger

Part I: Carl R. Rogers

It may seem curious that someone like me, a psychotherapist, should be interested in problems of communication. But, in fact, the whole task of psychotherapy is to deal with a failure in communication. In emotionally maladjusted people, communication within themselves has broken down, and as a result, their communication with others has been damaged. To put it another way, their unconscious, repressed, or denied desires have created distortions in the way they communicate with others. Thus they suffer both within themselves and in their interpersonal relationships.

The goal of psychotherapy is to help an individual achieve, through a special relationship with a therapist, good communication within himself or herself. Once this is achieved, that person can communicate more freely and effectively with others. So we may say that psychotherapy is good communication within and between people. We can turn that statement around and it will still be true. Good communication, or free communication, within or between people is always therapeutic.

Through my experience in counseling and psychotherapy, I've found that there is one main obstacle to communication: people's tendency to evaluate. Fortunately, I've also discovered that if people can learn to *listen* with understanding, they can mitigate their evaluative impulses and greatly improve their communication with others.

Barrier: The tendency to evaluate

We all have a natural urge to judge, evaluate, and approve (or disapprove) another person's statement. Suppose someone, commenting on what I've just stated, says, "I didn't like what that man said." How will you respond? Almost invariably your reply will be either approval or disapproval of the attitude expressed. Either you respond, "I didn't either; I thought it was terrible," or else you say, "Oh, I thought it was really good." In other words, your first reaction is to evaluate it from *your* point of view.

Or suppose I say with some feeling, "I think the Democrats are showing a lot of good sound sense these days." What is your first reaction? Most likely, it will be evaluative. You will find yourself agreeing or disagreeing, perhaps making some judgment about me such as, "He must be a liberal," or "He seems solid in his thinking." Although making evaluations is common in almost all conversation, this reaction is heightened in situations where feelings and emotions are deeply involved. So the stronger the feelings, the less likely it is that there will be a mutual element in the communication. There will be just two ideas, two feelings, or two judgments missing each other in psychological space.

If you've ever been a bystander at a heated discussion—one in which you were not emotionally involved—you've probably gone away thinking, "Well, they actually weren't talking about the same thing." And because it was heated, you were probably right. Each person was making a judgment, an evaluation, from a personal frame of reference. There was nothing that could be called communication in any real sense. And this impulse to evaluate any emotionally meaningful statement from our own viewpoint is what blocks interpersonal communication.

Gateway: Listening with understanding

We can achieve real communication and avoid this evaluative tendency when we listen with understanding. This means seeing the expressed idea and attitude from the other person's point of view, sensing how it feels to the person, achieving his or her frame of reference about the subject being discussed.

This may sound absurdly simple, but it is not. In fact, it is an extremely potent approach in psychotherapy. It is the most effective way we've found to alter a person's basic personality structure and to improve the person's relationships and communications with others. If I can listen to what a person can tell me and really understand how she hates her father or hates the company or hates conservatives, or if I can catch the essence of her fear of insanity or fear of nuclear bombs, I will be better able to help her alter those hatreds and fears and establish realistic and harmonious relationships with the people and situations that roused such emotions. We know from research that such empathic understanding—understanding *with* a person, not *about* her—is so effective that it can bring about significant changes in personality.

If you think that you listen well and yet have never seen such results, your listening probably has not been of the type I am describing. Here's one way to test the quality of your understanding. The next time you get into an argument with your spouse, friend, or small group of friends, stop the discussion for a moment and suggest this rule: "Before each person speaks up, he or she must *first* restate the ideas and feelings of the previous speaker accurately and to that speaker's satisfaction."

You see what this would mean. Before presenting your own point of view, you would first have to achieve the other speaker's frame of reference. Sounds simple, doesn't it? But if you try it, you will find it one of the most difficult things you have ever attempted to do. And even when you have been able to do it, your comments will have to be drastically revised. But you will also find that the emotion is dissipating—the differences are reduced, and those that remain are rational and understandable.

Can you imagine what this kind of approach could accomplish in larger arenas? What would happen to a labor-management dispute if labor, without necessarily conceding agreement, could accurately state management's point of view in a way that management could accept; and if management, without approving labor's stand, could state labor's case so that labor agreed it was accurate? It would mean that real communication was established and that some reasonable solution almost surely would be reached.

So why is this "listening" approach not more widely used? There are several reasons.

Lack of courage. Listening with understanding means taking a very real risk. If you really understand another person in this way, if you are willing to enter his private world and see the way life appears to him, without any attempt to make evaluative judgments, you run the risk of being changed yourself. You might see things his way; you might find that he has influenced your attitudes or your personality.

Most of us are afraid to take that risk. So instead we *cannot listen;* we find ourselves compelled to *evaluate* because listening seems too dangerous.

Heightened emotions. In heated discussions, emotions are strongest, so it is especially hard to achieve the frame of reference of another person or group. Yet it is precisely then that good listening is required if communication is to be established.

One solution is to use a third party, who is able to lay aside her own feelings and evaluations, to listen with understanding to each person or group and then clarify the views and attitudes each holds.

This has been effective in small groups in which contradictory or antagonistic attitudes exist. When the parties to a dispute realize they are being understood, that someone sees how the situation seems to them, the statements grow less exaggerated and less defensive, and it is no longer necessary to maintain the attitude, "I am 100% right, and you are 100% wrong."

The influence of such an understanding catalyst in the group permits the members to come closer to seeing the objective truth of the situation. This leads to improved communication, to greater acceptance of each other, and to attitudes that are more positive and more problem-solving in nature. There is a decrease in defensiveness, in exaggerated statements, in evaluative and critical behavior.

Mutual communication is established, and some type of agreement becomes much more possible.

Too large a group. Thus far, psychotherapists have been able to observe only small, face-to-face groups that are working to resolve religious, racial, or industrial tensions—or the personal tensions that are present in many therapy groups. What about trying to achieve understanding between larger groups that are geographically remote, for example, or between face-to-face groups that are speaking not for themselves but simply as representatives of others? Frankly, we do not know the answer. Based on our limited knowledge, however, there are some steps that even large groups can take to increase the amount of listening *with* and decrease the amount of evaluation *about*.

To be imaginative for a moment, suppose that a therapeutically oriented international group went to each of two countries involved in a dispute and said, "We want to achieve a genuine understanding of your views and, even more important, of your attitudes and feelings toward X country. We will summarize and resummarize these views and feelings if necessary, until you agree that our description represents the situation as it seems to you."

If they then widely distributed descriptions of these two views, might not the effect be very great? It would not guarantee the type of understanding I have been describing, but it would make it much more possible. We can understand the feelings of people who hate us much more readily when their attitudes are accurately described to us by a neutral third party than we can when they are shaking their fists at us.

Communication through a moderator who listens nonevaluatively and with understanding has proven effective, even when feelings run high. This procedure can be initiated by one party, without waiting for the other to be ready. It can even be initiated by a neutral third person, provided the person can gain a minimum of cooperation from one of the parties. The moderator can deal with the insincerities, the defensive exaggerations, the lies, and the "false fronts" that characterize almost every failure in communication. These defensive distortions drop away with astonishing speed as people find that the person's intention is to understand, not to judge. And when one party begins to drop its defenses, the other usually responds in kind, and together they begin to uncover the facts of a situation.

Gradually, mutual communication grows. It leads to a situation in which I see how the problem appears to you as well as to me, and you see how it appears to me as well as to you. Thus accurately and realistically defined, the problem is almost certain to yield to intelligent attack; or if it is in part insoluble, it will be comfortably accepted as such.

Part II: F. J. Roethlisberger

When we think about the many barriers to personal communication, particularly those due to differences in background, experience, and motivation, it seems extraordinary that any two people can ever understand each other. The potential for problems seems especially heightened in the context of a boss-subordinate relationship. How is communication possible when people do not see and assume the same things or share the same values?

On this question, there are two schools of thought. One school assumes that communication between A and B has failed when B does not accept what A has to say as being factual, true, or valid; and that the goal of communication is to get B to agree with A's opinions, ideas, facts, or information.

The other school of thought is quite different. It assumes that communication has failed when B does not feel free to express his feelings to A because B fears they will not be accepted by A. Communication is facilitated when A or B or both are willing to express and accept differences.

To illustrate, suppose Bill, an employee, is in his boss's office. The boss says, "I think, Bill, that this is the best way to do your job." And to that, Bill says, "Oh yeah?"

According to the first school of thought, this reply would be a sign of poor communication. Bill does not understand the best way of doing his work. To improve communication, therefore, it is up to the boss to explain to Bill why the boss's, not Bill's, way is the best.

From the second school's point of view, Bill's reply is a sign of neither good nor bad communication; it is indeterminate. But the boss can take the opportunity to find out what Bill means. Let us assume that this is what she chooses to do. So this boss tries to get Bill to talk more about his job.

We'll call the boss representing the first school of thought "Smith" and the boss subscribing to the second school "Jones." Given identical situations, each behaves differently. Smith chooses to *explain*; Jones chooses to *listen*. In my experience, Jones's response works better than Smith's, because Jones is making a more proper evaluation of what is taking place between her and Bill than Smith is.

"Oh yeah?"

Smith assumes that he understands what Bill means when Bill says, "Oh yeah?" so there is no need to find out. Smith is sure that Bill does not understand why this is the best way to do his job, so Smith has to tell him.

In this process, let us assume Smith is logical, lucid, and clear. He presents his facts and evidence well. But, alas, Bill remains unconvinced. What does Smith do? Operating under the assumption that what is taking place between him and Bill is something essentially logical, Smith can draw only one of two conclusions: either (1) he has not been clear enough or (2) Bill is too stupid to understand. So he has to either "spell out" his case in words of fewer and fewer syllables or give up. Smith is reluctant to give up, so he continues to explain. What happens?

The more Smith cannot get Bill to understand him, the more frustrated and emotional Smith becomes—and the more Smith's ability to reason logically is diminished. Since Smith sees himself as a reasonable, logical chap, this is a difficult thing for him to accept. It is much easier to perceive Bill as uncooperative or stupid. This perception will affect what Smith says and does.

— 1991 —

Retrospective Commentary

by John J. Gabarro

Reading "Barriers and Gateways" today, it is hard to understand the stir the article created when it was first published. But in 1952, Rogers's and Roethlisberger's ideas about the importance of listening were indeed radical. Not only did they stake out new territory that was anathema to the gray-flannel ethic—namely, the idea that people's feelings mattered. But they also challenged the sanctity of hierarchical relationships by suggesting that managers take their subordinates' thoughts and feelings seriously.

Today, however, these insights are so basic as to be obvious, which shows how much impact their ideas have had and how far management communication has come. Or has it? Contemporary managers do have a better grasp of how important listening is to good communication. Nonetheless, most still have a hard time putting this lesson into practice. One reason could be their own sophistication: simple lessons can be easily forgotten. Another reason, however, could be that this lesson is not so simple after all, that what the authors told us 40 years ago is more difficult to do than it appears and is really only half the story. The benefit of revisiting R&R, then, is both to remind ourselves of still-relevant, indeed powerful, insights and to find, from the vantage point of 40 years later, what R&R might have overlooked.

What speaks loudest to business today are three insights that in fact transcend institutional and social boundaries: They are the communication barriers and gateways that, as the authors show, can occur between two nations as well as between two individuals. These insights have endured because they are basic truths about human interaction.

The greatest barrier to effective communication is the tendency to evaluate what another person is saying and therefore to misunderstand or to not really "hear." The Bill and Smith scenario, which vividly illustrates this process, rings true today because such communication breakdowns still happen routinely. In fact, in today's arguably more complex business environment, they may be more likely to happen.

Greater work force diversity, for example, can complicate communication, as a common language of shared assumptions and experiences becomes harder to establish. Indeed, if in 1952 Roethlisberger thought it "extraordinary" that any two people could communicate, given their "differences in background, experience, and motivation," he would surely have thought it a miracle today.

Checking the natural tendency to judge yields a better understanding of the person with whom you are communicating. Of course, greater diversity also makes disciplined listening all the more important—because the potential for misunderstanding is greater. This gateway, then, is more vital than ever. By suspending assumptions and judgments, a manager can get to the heart of an employee's feelings, a better signpost to what the employee is saying than his or her words alone.

A better understanding of the other person's point of view in turn helps you communicate better. Effective communication is equal parts listening and expression; the clarity of one depends on the clarity of another. A manager with a clearer picture of whom he's talking to is able to express himself more accurately.

These insights have been the impetus behind a number of progressive practices—corporate efforts to empower employees, for example. When a manager shows a willingness to listen to an employee, she is more likely to engender trust and thus honesty. And by encouraging the employee to talk straight, without fear of reprisal, she boosts his self-confidence because he sees that the organization values his input. What's more, the manager stays tapped into a vital information source—the front lines.

Or consider the technique of "active listening," developed in the 1970s and still widely used in many management- and sales-training programs. A salesperson applying active listening, for example, reacts nonjudgmentally to what a prospect is saying, rephrasing it to make sure he truly understands the customer's point of view. The benefits are twofold. First, this process minimizes the likelihood that the salesperson is laying his biases on the customer's needs. Second, the prospect feels listened to and understood.

Ultimately, though, R&R may have had too much faith in nonevaluative listening. Researchers doing work in this field, and, for that matter, managers trying to apply these lessons, now realize how overly optimistic the authors were. First, a fundamental but unarticulated premise is that understanding equals resolution, but this is not the case. While understanding can improve the negotiation process—as various research, from Richard Walton's work in labor relations to Roger Fisher's in international negotiations, has shown—it cannot by itself resolve conflict.

Second, the process of establishing trust is not as one-dimensional as R&R imply. Jones would probably not be able to secure Bill's trust merely by showing a commitment to nonevaluative listening. Bill will assess many other aspects of Jones's behavior and character in deciding whether to talk openly with her: her motives, her discretion, the consistency of her behavior, even her managerial competence. Only if this assessment is positive will Bill respond candidly to

(continued)

Retrospective Commentary *(continued)*

Jones's overtures. Thus, as a rule, a minimum baseline of confidence is needed to evoke the kind of trust that honest communication requires. This is especially true where there is a power imbalance, which tends to foster greater initial distrust. (This dynamic works both ways: an employee may distrust her manager for fear of reprisal; but a manager may distrust his employee for fear that she'll say only what he wants to hear.)

Finally, managers today come up against a few more communication barriers than R&R envisioned. One is the pressure of time. Listening carefully takes time, and managers have little of that to spare. In today's business culture especially, with its emphasis on speed (overnight mail, faster computers, time-based competition), already pressed managers may give short shrift to the slower art of one-on-one communication.

Another barrier in this era of mergers, acquisitions, and delayering is insecurity and the fear that it breeds. When downsizing and layoffs loom, both the Bills and the Joneses of this world have good reason for not opening up, especially when people believe that their true feelings of beliefs may get them fired.

Even so, these limitations don't entirely explain why, some 40 years later, a salesperson can win over clients with active listening but a manager fails to have the slightest idea what makes his employees tick. This is because managers face still another, more significant, barrier, one I call the managerial paradox: while it is crucial that managers be able to listen nonjudgmentally (to understand other points of view and get valid information), the essence of management is to do just the opposite—to make judgments. Managers are called on daily to evaluate product lines, markets, numbers, and, of course, people. And in turn, they are evaluated on how well they do this. The danger, then, is that this bias for judging will subvert a manager's inclination to listen carefully and, in doing so, sabotage his or her ability to make accurate business and people judgments.

Managers may be tempted to resolve this paradox as an either/or. And for good reason: Rarely in their training have the two mindsets been reconciled. Business schools, for the most part, still reinforce evaluative listening; they teach students to defend their own positions while scoring points against others'. And those behavioral experts who do focus on nonevaluative listening tend to focus almost exclusively on the importance of empathy. But if one thing has made itself clear in the past 40 years, it is that managers must have the capacity to do both. They must recognize that to make judgments, you must suspend judgment.

Under these pressures, Smith evaluates Bill more and more in terms of his own values and tends to treat Bill's as unimportant, essentially denying Bill's uniqueness and difference. He treats Bill as if he had little capacity for self-direction.

Let us be clear. Smith does not see that he is doing these things. When he is feverishly scratching hieroglyphics on the back of an envelope, trying to explain to Bill why this is the best way to do his job, Smith is trying to be helpful. He is a man of goodwill, and he wants to set Bill straight. This is the way Smith sees himself and his behavior. But it is for this very reason that Bill's "Oh yeah?" is getting under Smith's skin.

"How dumb can a guy be?" is Smith's attitude, and unfortunately Bill will hear that more than Smith's good intentions. Bill will feel misunderstood. He will not see Smith as a man of goodwill trying to be helpful. Rather he will perceive him as a threat to his self-esteem and personal integrity. Against this threat Bill will feel the need to defend himself at all cost. Not being so logically articulate as Smith, Bill expresses this need by saying, again, "Oh yeah?"

Let us leave this sad scene between Smith and Bill, which I fear is going to end with Bill either leaving in a huff or being kicked out of Smith's office. Let us turn for a moment to Jones and see how she is interacting with Bill.

Jones, remember, does not assume that she knows what Bill means when he says, "Oh yeah?" so she has to find out. Moreover, she assumes that when Bill said this, he had not exhausted his vocabulary or his feelings. Bill may mean not just one thing but several different things. So Jones decides to listen.

In this process, Jones is not under any illusion that what will happen will be a purely logical exchange. Rather she is assuming that what happens will be primarily an interaction of feelings. Therefore, she cannot ignore Bill's feelings, the effect of Bill's feelings on her, or the effect of her feelings on Bill. In other words, she cannot ignore her relationship to Bill; she cannot assume that it will make no difference to what Bill will hear or accept.

Therefore, Jones will be paying strict attention to all of the things Smith has ignored. She will be addressing herself to Bill's feelings, her own feelings, and the interaction between them.

Jones will therefore realize that she has ruffled Bill's feelings with her comment, "I think, Bill, this is the best way to do your job." So instead of trying to get Bill to understand her, she decides to try to understand Bill. She does this by encouraging Bill to speak. Instead of telling Bill how he should feel or think, she asks Bill such questions as, "Is this what you feel?" "Is this what you see?" "Is this what you assume?" Instead of ignoring Bill's evaluations as irrelevant, not valid, inconsequential, or false, she tries to understand Bill's reality as he feels it, perceives it, and assumes it to be. As Bill begins to open up, Jones's curiosity is piqued by this process.

"Bill isn't so dumb; he's quite an interesting guy" becomes Jones's attitude. And that is what Bill hears. Therefore Bill feels understood and accepted as a person. He becomes less defensive. He is in a better frame of mind to explore and reexamine his perceptions, feelings, and assumptions. Bill feels free to express his differences. In this process, he sees Jones as a source of help and feels that Jones respects his capacity for self-direction. These positive feelings toward Jones make Bill more inclined to say, "Well, Jones, I don't quite agree with you that this is the best way to do my job, but I'll tell you what I'll do. I'll try to do it that way for a few days, and then I'll tell you what I think."

I grant that my two orientations do not work in practice quite so neatly as I have worked them out on paper. There are many other ways in which Bill could have responded to Smith in the first place. He might even have said, "OK, boss, I agree that your way of doing my job is better." But Smith still would not have known how Bill felt when he made this statement or whether Bill was actually going to do his job differently. Likewise, Bill could have responded to Jones differently. In spite of Jones's attitude, Bill might still have been reluctant to express himself freely to his boss.

Nevertheless, these examples give me something concrete to point to in making the following generalizations.

1. Smith represents a very common pattern of misunderstanding. The misunderstanding does not arise because Smith is not clear enough in expressing himself. Rather, Smith misevaluates what takes place when two people are talking together.

2. Smith's misunderstanding of the process of personal communication is based on common assumptions: (a) that what is taking place is something logical; (b) that words mean something in and of themselves, apart from the people speaking them; and (c) that the purpose of the interaction is to get Bill to see things from Smith's point of view.

3. These assumptions set off a chain reaction of perceptions and negative feelings, which blocks communication. By ignoring Bill's feelings and rationalizing his own, Smith ignores his relationship to Bill as an important determinant of their communication. As a result, Bill hears Smith's *attitude* more clearly than the logical content of Smith's words. Bill feels that his uniqueness is being denied. Since his personal integrity is at stake, he becomes defensive and belligerent. And this frustrates Smith. He perceives Bill as stupid, so he says and does things that make Bill still more defensive.

4. Jones makes a different set of assumptions: (a) that what is taking place between her and Bill is an interaction of sentiments; (b) that Bill—not his words in themselves—means something; and (c) that the object of the interaction is to give Bill a chance to express himself.

5. Because of these assumptions, there is a psychological chain reaction of reinforcing feelings and perceptions that eases communication between Bill and Jones. When Jones addresses Bill's feelings and perceptions from Bill's point of view, Bill feels understood and accepted as a person; he feels free to express his differences. Bill sees Jones as a source of help; Jones sees Bill as an interesting person. Bill, in turn, becomes more cooperative.

If I have identified correctly these very common patterns of personal communication, then we can infer some interesting hypotheses:

- Jones's method works better than Smith's not because of any magic but because Jones has a better map of the process of personal communication.

- Jones's method, however, is not merely an intellectual exercise. It depends on Jones's capacity and willingness to see and accept points of view that are different from her own and to practice this orientation in a face-to-face relationship. This is an emotional and intellectual achievement. It depends in part on Jones's awareness of herself, in part on the practice of a skill.

- Although universities try to get students to appreciate, at least intellectually, points of view different from their own, little is done to help them learn to apply this intellectual appreciation to simple, face-to-face relationships. Students are trained to be logical and clear—but no one helps them learn to *listen* skillfully. As a result, our educated world contains too many Smiths and too few Joneses.

The biggest block between two people is their inability to listen to each other intelligently, understandingly, and skillfully. This deficiency in the modern world is widespread and appalling. We need to make greater efforts to educate people in effective communication—which means, essentially, teaching people how to listen.

Reprinted from *Harvard Business Review*, November–December 1991 (product #91610). Originally published July–August 1952.

CHAPTER SEVENTEEN

The Business of Artificial Intelligence

by Erik Brynjolfsson and Andrew McAfee

For more than 250 years the fundamental drivers of economic growth have been technological innovations. The most important of these are what economists call general-purpose technologies—a category that includes the steam engine, electricity, and the internal combustion engine. Each one catalyzed waves of complementary innovations and opportunities. The internal combustion engine, for example, gave rise to cars, trucks, airplanes, chain saws, and lawnmowers, along with big-box retailers, shopping centers, cross-docking warehouses, new supply chains, and, when you think about it, suburbs. Companies as diverse as Walmart, UPS, and Uber found ways to leverage the technology to create profitable new business models.

The most important general-purpose technology of our era is artificial intelligence, particularly machine learning (ML)—that is, the machine's ability to keep improving its performance without humans having to explain exactly how to accomplish all the tasks it's given. Within just the past few years machine learning has become far more effective and widely available. We can now build systems that learn how to perform tasks on their own.

Why is this such a big deal? Two reasons. First, we humans know more than we can tell: We can't explain exactly how we're able to do a lot of things—from recognizing a face to making a smart move in the ancient Asian strategy game of Go. Prior to ML, this inability to articulate our own knowledge meant that we couldn't automate many tasks. Now we can.

Second, ML systems are often excellent learners. They can achieve superhuman performance in a wide range of activities, including detecting fraud and diagnosing disease. Excellent digital learners are being deployed across the economy, and their impact will be profound.

In the sphere of business, AI is poised to have a transformational impact, on the scale of earlier general-purpose technologies. Although it is already in use in thousands of companies around the world, most big opportunities have not yet been tapped. The effects of AI will be magnified in the coming decade, as manufacturing, retailing, transportation, finance, health care, law, advertising, insurance, entertainment, education, and virtually every other industry transform their core processes and business models to take advantage of machine learning. The bottleneck now is in management, implementation, and business imagination.

Like so many other new technologies, however, AI has generated lots of unrealistic expectations. We see business plans liberally sprinkled with references to machine learning, neural nets, and other forms of the technology, with little connection to its real capabilities. Simply calling a dating site "AI-powered," for example doesn't make it any more effective, but it might help with fundraising. This article will cut through the noise to describe the real potential of AI, its practical implications, and the barriers to its adoption.

What Can AI Do Today?

The term *artificial intelligence* was coined in 1955 by John McCarthy, a math professor at Dartmouth who organized the seminal conference on the topic the following year. Ever since, perhaps in part because of its evocative name, the field has given rise to more than its share of fantastic claims and promises. In 1957 the economist Herbert Simon predicted that computers would beat humans at chess within 10 years. (It took 40.) In 1967 the cognitive scientist Marvin Minsky said, "Within a generation the problem of creating 'artificial intelligence' will be substantially solved." Simon and Minsky were both intellectual giants, but they erred badly. Thus it's understandable that dramatic claims about future breakthroughs meet with a certain amount of skepticism.

Let's start by exploring what AI is already doing and how quickly it is improving. The biggest advances have been in two broad areas: perception and cognition. In the former category some of the most practical advances have been made in relation to speech. Voice recognition is still far from perfect, but millions of people are now using it—think Siri, Alexa, and Google Assistant. The text you are now reading was originally dictated to a computer and transcribed with sufficient accuracy to make it faster than typing. A study by the Stanford computer scientist James Landay and colleagues found that speech recognition is now about three times as fast, on average, as typing on a cell phone. The error rate, once 8.5%, has dropped to 4.9%. What's striking is that this substantial improvement has come not over the past 10 years but just since the summer of 2016.

Image recognition, too, has improved dramatically. You may have noticed that Facebook and other apps now recognize many of your friends' faces in posted photos and prompt you to tag them with their names. An app running on your smartphone will recognize virtually any bird in the wild. Image recognition is even replacing ID cards at corporate headquarters. Vision systems, such as those used in self-driving cars, formerly made a mistake when identifying a pedestrian as often as once in 30 frames (the cameras in these systems record about 30 frames a second); now they err less often than once in 30 million frames. The error rate for recognizing images from a large database called ImageNet, with several million photographs of common, obscure, or downright weird images, fell from higher than 30% in 2010 to about 4% in 2016 for the best systems. (See figure 17-1.)

FIGURE 17-1

Puppy or muffin? Progress in image recognition

Machines have made real strides in distinguishing among similar-looking categories of images.

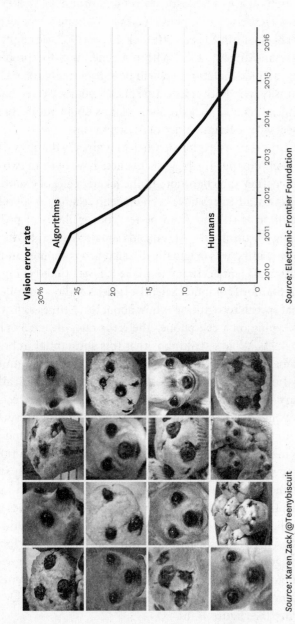

Vision error rate

Algorithms

Humans

Source: Karen Zack/ @Teenybiscuit

Source: Electronic Frontier Foundation

The speed of improvement has accelerated rapidly in recent years as a new approach, based on very large or "deep" neural nets, was adopted. The ML approach for vision systems is still far from flawless—but even people have trouble quickly recognizing puppies' faces or, more embarrassingly, see their cute faces where none exist.

The second type of major improvement has been in cognition and problem solving. Machines have already beaten the finest (human) players of poker and Go—achievements that experts had predicted would take at least another decade. Google's DeepMind team has used ML systems to improve the cooling efficiency at data centers by more than 15%, even after they were optimized by human experts. Intelligent agents are being used by the cybersecurity company Deep Instinct to detect malware, and by PayPal to prevent money laundering. A system using IBM technology automates the claims process at an insurance company in Singapore, and a system from Lumidatum, a data science platform firm, offers timely advice to improve customer support. Dozens of companies are using ML to decide which trades to execute on Wall Street, and more and more credit decisions are made with its help. Amazon employs ML to optimize inventory and improve product recommendations to customers. Infinite Analytics developed one ML system to predict whether a user would click on a particular ad, improving online ad placement for a global consumer packaged goods company, and another to improve customers' search and discovery process at a Brazilian online retailer. The first system increased advertising ROI threefold, and the second resulted in a $125 million increase in annual revenue.

Machine learning systems are not only replacing older algorithms in many applications, but are now superior at many tasks that were once done best by humans. Although the systems are far from perfect, their error rate—about 5%—on the ImageNet database is at or better than human-level performance. Voice recognition, too, even in noisy environments, is now nearly equal to human performance. Reaching this threshold opens up vast new possibilities for transforming the workplace and the economy. Once AI-based systems surpass human performance at a given task, they are much likelier to spread quickly. For instance, Aptonomy and San-bot, makers respectively of drones and robots, are using improved vision systems to automate much of the work of security guards. The software company Affectiva, among others, is using them to recognize emotions such as joy, surprise, and anger in focus groups. And Enlitic is one of several deep-learning start-ups that use them to scan medical images to help diagnose cancer.

These are impressive achievements, but the applicability of AI-based systems is still quite narrow. For instance, their remarkable performance on the ImageNet database, even with its millions of images, doesn't always translate into similar success "in the wild," where lighting conditions, angles, image resolution, and context may be very different. More fundamentally, we can marvel at a system that understands Chinese speech and translates it into English, but we don't expect such a system to know what a particular Chinese character means—let alone where to eat in Beijing. If some-one performs a task well, it's natural to assume that the person has some competence in related tasks. But ML systems are trained to do specific tasks, and typically their knowledge does not general-ize. The fallacy that a computer's narrow understanding implies broader understanding is perhaps the biggest source of confusion, and exaggerated claims, about AI's progress. We are far from ma-chines that exhibit general intelligence across diverse domains.

Understanding Machine Learning

The most important thing to understand about ML is that it rep-resents a fundamentally different approach to creating software: The machine learns from examples, rather than being explicitly programmed for a particular outcome. This is an important break from previous practice. For most of the past 50 years, advances in information technology and its applications have focused on codi-fying existing knowledge and procedures and embedding them in machines. Indeed, the term "coding" denotes the painstaking pro-cess of transferring knowledge from developers' heads into a form that machines can understand and execute. This approach has a fundamental weakness: Much of the knowledge we all have is tacit, meaning that we can't fully explain it. It's nearly impossible for us to write down instructions that would enable another person to learn how to ride a bike or to recognize a friend's face.

In other words, we all know more than we can tell. This fact is so important that it has a name: Polanyi's Paradox, for the philosopher and polymath Michael Polanyi, who described it in 1964. Polanyi's Paradox not only limits what we can tell one another but has historically placed a fundamental restriction on our ability to endow machines with intelligence. For a long time that limited the activities that machines could productively perform in the economy.

Machine learning is overcoming those limits. In this second wave of the second machine age, machines built by humans are learning from examples and using structured feedback to solve on their own problems such as Polanyi's classic one of recognizing a face.

Different Flavors of Machine Learning

Artificial intelligence and machine learning come in many flavors, but most of the successes in recent years have been in one category: supervised learning systems, in which the machine is given lots of examples of the correct answer to a particular problem. This process almost always involves mapping from a set of inputs, X, to a set of outputs, Y. For instance, the inputs might be pictures of various animals, and the correct outputs might be labels for those animals: dog, cat, horse. The inputs could also be waveforms from a sound recording and the outputs could be words: "yes," "no," "hello," "good-bye." (See table 17-1.)

Successful systems often use a training set of data with thousands or even millions of examples, each of which has been labeled with the correct answer. The system can then be let loose to look at new examples. If the training has gone well, the system will predict answers with a high rate of accuracy.

The algorithms that have driven much of this success depend on an approach called *deep learning,* which uses neural networks. Deep learning algorithms have a significant advantage over earlier generations of ML algorithms: They can make better use of much larger data sets. The old systems would improve as the number of examples in the training data grew, but only up to a point, after which additional data didn't lead to better predictions. According to Andrew Ng, one of the giants of the field, deep neural nets don't seem to level off in this way: More data leads to better and better predictions. Some very large systems are trained by using 36 million examples or more. Of course, working with extremely large data sets requires more and more processing power, which is one reason the very big systems are often run on supercomputers or specialized computer architectures.

Any situation in which you have a lot of data on behavior and are trying to predict an outcome is a potential application for supervised learning systems. Jeff Wilke, who leads Amazon's consumer business, says that supervised learning systems have largely

TABLE 17-1

Supervised learning systems

As two pioneers in the field, Tom Mitchell and Michael I. Jordan, have noted, most of the recent progress in machine learning involves mapping from a set of inputs to a set of outputs. Some examples:

Input X	Output Y	Application
Voice recording	Transcript	Speech recognition
Historical market data	Future market data	Trading bots
Photograph	Caption	Image tagging
Drug chemical properties	Treatment efficacy	Pharma R&D
Store transaction details	Is the transaction fraudulent?	Fraud detection
Recipe ingredients	Customer reviews	Food recommendations
Purchase histories	Future purchase behavior	Customer retention
Car locations and speed	Traffic flow	Traffic lights
Faces	Names	Face recognition

replaced the memory-based filtering algorithms that were used to make personalized recommendations to customers. In other cases, classic algorithms for setting inventory levels and optimizing supply chains have been replaced by more efficient and robust systems based on machine learning. JPMorgan Chase introduced a system for reviewing commercial loan contracts; work that used to take loan officers 360,000 hours can now be done in a few seconds. And supervised learning systems are now being used to diagnose skin cancer. These are just a few examples.

It's comparatively straightforward to label a body of data and use it to train a supervised learner; that's why supervised ML systems are more common than *un*supervised ones, at least for now. Unsupervised learning systems seek to learn on their own. We humans are excellent unsupervised learners: We pick up most of our knowledge of the world (such as how to recognize a tree) with little or no labeled data. But it is exceedingly difficult to develop a successful machine learning system that works this way.

If and when we learn to build robust unsupervised learners, exciting possibilities will open up. These machines could look at complex problems in fresh ways to help us discover patterns—in the spread of diseases, in price moves across securities in a market, in customers' purchase behaviors, and so on—that we are currently unaware of. Such possibilities lead Yann LeCun, the head of AI research at Facebook and a professor at NYU, to compare supervised learning systems to the frosting on the cake and unsupervised learning to the cake itself.

Another small but growing area within the field is *reinforcement learning*. This approach is embedded in systems that have mastered Atari video games and board games like Go. It is also helping to optimize data center power usage and to develop trading strategies for the stock market. Robots created by Kindred use machine learning to identify and sort objects they've never encountered before, speeding up the "pick and place" process in distribution centers for consumer goods. In reinforcement learning systems the programmer specifies the current state of the system and the goal, lists allowable actions, and describes the elements of the environment that constrain the outcomes for each of those actions. Using the allowable actions, the system has to figure out how to get as close to the goal as possible. These systems work well when humans can specify the goal but not necessarily how to get there. For instance, Microsoft used reinforcement learning to select headlines for MSN.com news stories by "rewarding" the system with a higher score when more visitors clicked on the link. The system tried to maximize its score on the basis of the rules its designers gave it. Of course, this means that a reinforcement learning system will optimize for the goal you explicitly reward, not necessarily the goal you really care about (such as lifetime customer value), so specifying the goal correctly and clearly is critical.

Putting Machine Learning to Work

There are three pieces of good news for organizations looking to put ML to use today. First, AI skills are spreading quickly. The world still has not nearly enough data scientists and machine learning experts, but the demand for them is being met by online educational resources as well as by universities. The best of these, including Udacity, Coursera, and fast.ai, do much more than teach introductory concepts; they can actually get smart, motivated students to the point of being able to create industrial-grade ML deployments. In addition to training their own people, interested companies can use online talent platforms such as Upwork, Topcoder, and Kaggle to find ML experts with verifiable expertise.

The second welcome development is that the necessary algorithms and hardware for modern AI can be bought or rented as needed. Google, Amazon, Microsoft, Salesforce, and other companies are making powerful ML infrastructure available via the cloud. The cutthroat competition among these rivals means that companies that want to experiment with or deploy ML will see more and more capabilities available at ever-lower prices over time.

The final piece of good news, and probably the most underappreciated, is that you may not need all that much data to start making productive use of ML. The performance of most machine learning systems improves as they're given more data to work with, so it seems logical to conclude that the company with the most data will win. That might be the case if "win" means "dominate the global market for a single application such as ad targeting or speech recognition." But if success is defined instead as significantly improving performance, then sufficient data is often surprisingly easy to obtain.

For example, Udacity cofounder Sebastian Thrun noticed that some of his salespeople were much more effective than others when replying to inbound queries in a chat room. Thrun and his graduate student Zayd Enam realized that their chat room logs were essentially a set of labeled training data—exactly what a supervised learning system needs. Interactions that led to a sale were labeled successes, and all others were labeled failures. Zayd used the data to predict what answers successful salespeople were likely to give in response to certain very common inquiries and then shared those predictions with the other salespeople to nudge them toward better performance. After 1,000 training cycles, the salespeople had increased their effectiveness by 54% and were able to serve twice as many customers at a time.

The AI start-up WorkFusion takes a similar approach. It works with companies to bring higher levels of automation to back-office processes such as paying international invoices and settling large trades between financial institutions. The reason these processes haven't been automated yet is that they're complicated; relevant information isn't always presented the same way every time ("How do we know what currency they're talking about?"), and some interpretation and judgment are necessary. WorkFusion's software watches in the background as people do their work and uses their actions as training data for the cognitive task of classification ("This invoice is in dollars. This one is in yen. This one is in euros . . ."). Once the system is confident enough in its classifications, it takes over the process.

Machine learning is driving changes at three levels: tasks and occupations, business processes, and business models. An example of task-and-occupation redesign is the use of machine vision systems to identify potential cancer cells—freeing up radiologists to focus on truly critical cases, to communicate with patients, and to coordinate with other physicians. An example of process redesign

is the reinvention of the workflow and layout of Amazon fulfill-
ment centers after the introduction of robots and optimization
algorithms based on machine learning. Similarly, business models need to be rethought to take advantage of ML systems that can
intelligently recommend music or movies in a personalized way.
Instead of selling songs à la carte on the basis of consumer choices,
a better model might offer a subscription to a personalized station
that predicted and played music a particular customer would like,
even if the person had never heard it before.

Note that machine learning systems hardly ever replace the entire job, process, or business model. Most often they complement
human activities, which can make their work ever more valuable.
The most effective rule for the new division of labor is rarely, if ever,
"give all tasks to the machine." Instead, if the successful comple-
tion of a process requires 10 steps, one or two of them may become
automated while the rest become more valuable for humans to do.
For instance, the chat room sales support system at Udacity didn't
try to build a bot that could take over all the conversations; rather,
it advised human salespeople about how to improve their performance. The humans remained in charge but became vastly more
effective and efficient. This approach is usually much more feasible
than trying to design machines that can do everything humans can
do. It often leads to better, more satisfying work for the people involved and ultimately to a better outcome for customers.

Designing and implementing new combinations of technologies,
human skills, and capital assets to meet customers' needs requires
large-scale creativity and planning. It is a task that machines are
not very good at. That makes being an entrepreneur or a business
manager one of society's most rewarding jobs in the age of ML.

Risks and Limits

The second wave of the second machine age brings with it new risks.
In particular, machine learning systems often have low "interpret-
ability," meaning that humans have difficulty figuring out how the

systems reached their decisions. Deep neural networks may have hundreds of millions of connections, each of which contributes a small amount to the ultimate decision. As a result, these systems' predictions tend to resist simple, clear explanation. Unlike humans, machines are not (yet!) good storytellers. They can't always give a rationale for why a particular applicant was accepted or rejected for a job, or a particular medicine was recommended. Ironically, even as we have begun to overcome Polanyi's Paradox, we're facing a kind of reverse version: Machines know more than they can tell us.

This creates three risks. First, the machines may have hidden biases, derived not from any intent of the designer but from the data provided to train the system. For instance, if a system learns which job applicants to accept for an interview by using a data set of decisions made by human recruiters in the past, it may inadvertently learn to perpetuate their racial, gender, ethnic, or other biases. Moreover, these biases may not appear as an explicit rule but, rather, be embedded in subtle interactions among the thousands of factors considered.

A second risk is that, unlike traditional systems built on explicit logic rules, neural network systems deal with statistical truths rather than literal truths. That can make it difficult, if not impossible, to prove with complete certainty that the system will work in all cases—especially in situations that weren't represented in the training data. Lack of verifiability can be a concern in mission-critical applications, such as controlling a nuclear power plant, or when life-or-death decisions are involved.

Third, when the ML system does make errors, as it almost inevitably will, diagnosing and correcting exactly what's going wrong can be difficult. The underlying structure that led to the solution can be unimaginably complex, and the solution maybe far from optimal if the conditions under which the system was trained change.

While all these risks are very real, the appropriate benchmark is not perfection but the best available alternative. After all, we humans, too, have biases, make mistakes, and have trouble explaining truthfully how we arrived at a particular decision. The advantage of machine-based systems is that they can be improved over time and will give consistent answers when presented with the same data.

Does that mean there is no limit to what artificial intelligence and machine learning can do? Perception and cognition cover a great deal of territory—from driving a car to forecasting sales to deciding whom to hire or promote. We believe the chances are excellent that AI will soon reach superhuman levels of performance in most or all of these areas. So what *won't* AI and ML be able to do?

We sometimes hear "Artificial intelligence will never be good at assessing emotional, crafty, sly, inconsistent human beings—it's too rigid and impersonal for that." We don't agree. ML systems like those at Affectiva are already at or beyond human-level performance in discerning a person's emotional state on the basis of tone of voice or facial expression. Other systems can infer when even the world's best poker players are bluffing well enough to beat them at the amazingly complex game Heads-up No-Limit Texas Hold'em. Reading people accurately is subtle work, but it's not magic. It requires perception and cognition—exactly the areas in which ML is currently strong and getting stronger all the time.

A great place to start a discussion of the limits of AI is with Pablo Picasso's observation about computers: "But they are useless. They can only give you answers." They're actually far from useless, as ML'S recent triumphs show, but Picasso's observation still provides insight. Computers are devices for answering questions, not for posing them. That means entrepreneurs, innovators, scientists, creators, and other kinds of people who figure out what problem or opportunity to tackle next, or what new territory to explore, will continue to be essential.

Similarly, there's a huge difference between passively assessing someone's mental state or morale and actively working to change it. ML systems are getting quite good at the former but remain well behind us at the latter. We humans are a deeply social species; other humans, not machines, are best at tapping into social drives such as compassion, pride, solidarity, and shame in order to persuade, motivate, and inspire. In 2014 the TED Conference and the XPRIZE Foundation announced an award for "the first artificial intelligence to come to this stage and give a TED Talk compelling enough to win a standing ovation from the audience." We doubt the award will be claimed anytime soon.

We think the biggest and most important opportunities for human smarts in this new age of superpowerful ML lie at the intersection of two areas: figuring out what problems to work on next, and persuading a lot of people to tackle them and go along with the solutions. This is a decent definition of leadership, which is becoming much more important in the second machine age.

The status quo of dividing up work between minds and machines is falling apart very quickly. Companies that stick with it are going to find themselves at an ever-greater competitive disadvantage compared with rivals who are willing and able to put ML to use in all the places where it is appropriate and who can figure out how to effectively integrate its capabilities with humanity's.

A time of tectonic change in the business world has begun, brought on by technological progress. As was the case with steam power and electricity, it's not access to the new technologies themselves, or even to the best technologists, that separates winners from losers. Instead, it's innovators who are open-minded enough to see past the status quo and envision very different approaches, and savvy enough to put them into place. One of machine learning's greatest legacies may well be the creation of a new generation of business leaders.

In our view, artificial intelligence, especially machine learning, is the most important general-purpose technology of our era. The impact of these innovations on business and the economy will be reflected not only in their direct contributions but also in their ability to enable and inspire complementary innovations. New products and processes are being made possible by better vision systems, speech recognition, intelligent problem solving, and many other capabilities that machine learning delivers.

Some experts have gone even further. Gil Pratt, who now heads the Toyota Research Institute, has compared the current wave of AI technology to the Cambrian explosion 500 million years ago that birthed a tremendous variety of new life forms. Then as now, one of the key new capabilities was vision. When animals first gained this capability, it allowed them to explore the environment far more effectively; that catalyzed an enormous increase in the number of species, both predators and prey, and in the range of ecological niches that were filled. Today as well we expect to see a variety of new products, services, processes, and organizational forms and also numerous extinctions. There will certainly be some weird failures along with unexpected successes.

Although it is hard to predict exactly which companies will dominate in the new environment, a general principle is clear: The most nimble and adaptable companies and executives will thrive. Organizations that can rapidly sense and respond to opportunities will seize the advantage in the AI-enabled landscape. So the successful strategy is to be willing to experiment and learn quickly. If managers aren't ramping up experiments in the area of machine learning, they aren't doing their job. Over the next decade, AI won't replace managers, but managers who use AI will replace those who don't.

Reprinted from hbr.org,
originally published July 18, 2017 (product #H03QXY).

CHAPTER EIGHTEEN

Data Scientist: The Sexiest Job of the 21st Century

by Thomas H. Davenport and D.J. Patil

When Jonathan Goldman arrived for work in June 2006 at LinkedIn, the business networking site, the place still felt like a start-up. The company had just under 8 million accounts, and the number was growing quickly as existing members invited their friends and colleagues to join. But users weren't seeking out connections with the people who were already on the site at the rate executives had expected. Something was apparently missing in the social experience. As one LinkedIn manager put it, "It was like arriving at a conference reception and realizing you don't know anyone. So you just stand in the corner sipping your drink—and you probably leave early."

Goldman, a PhD in physics from Stanford, was intrigued by the linking he did see going on and by the richness of the user profiles. It all made for messy data and unwieldy analysis, but as he began exploring people's connections, he started to see possibilities. He began forming theories, testing hunches, and finding patterns that allowed him to predict whose networks a given profile would land in. He could imagine that new features capitalizing on the heuristics he was developing might provide value to users. But LinkedIn's engineering team, caught up in the challenges of scaling up the site, seemed uninterested. Some colleagues were openly dismissive of Goldman's ideas. Why would users need LinkedIn to figure out their networks for them? The site already had an address book importer that could pull in all a member's connections.

Luckily, Reid Hoffman, LinkedIn's cofounder and CEO at the time (now its executive chairman), had faith in the power of analytics because of his experiences at PayPal, and he had granted Goldman a high degree of autonomy. For one thing, he had given Goldman a way to circumvent the traditional product release cycle by publishing small modules in the form of ads on the site's most popular pages.

Through one such module, Goldman started to test what would happen if you presented users with names of people they hadn't yet connected with but seemed likely to know—for example, people who had shared their tenures at schools and workplaces. He did this by ginning up a custom ad that displayed the three best new matches for each user based on the background entered in his or her LinkedIn profile. Within days it was obvious that something remarkable was taking place. The click-through rate on those ads was the highest ever seen. Goldman continued to refine how the suggestions were generated, incorporating networking ideas such as "triangle closing"—the notion that if you know Larry and Sue, there's a good chance that Larry and Sue know each other. Goldman and his team also got the action required to respond to a suggestion down to one click.

It didn't take long for LinkedIn's top managers to recognize a good idea and make it a standard feature. That's when things really took off. "People You May Know" ads achieved a click-through rate 30% higher than the rate obtained by other prompts to visit more pages on the site. They generated millions of new page views. Thanks to this one feature, LinkedIn's growth trajectory shifted significantly upward.

A New Breed

Goldman is a good example of a new key player in organizations: the "data scientist." It's a high-ranking professional with the training and curiosity to make discoveries in the world of big data. The title has been around for only a few years. (It was coined in 2008 by one of us, D.J. Patil, and Jeff Hammerbacher, then the respective leads of data and analytics efforts at LinkedIn and Facebook.) But thousands of data scientists are already working at both start-ups and well-established companies. Their sudden appearance on the business scene reflects the fact that companies are now wrestling with information that comes in varieties and volumes never encountered before. If your organization stores multiple petabytes of data, if the information most critical to your business resides in forms other than rows and columns of numbers, or if answering your biggest question would involve a "mashup" of several analytical efforts, you've got a big data opportunity.

Much of the current enthusiasm for big data focuses on technologies that make taming it possible, including Hadoop (the most widely used framework for distributed file system processing) and related open-source tools, cloud computing, and data visualization. While those are important breakthroughs, at least as important are the people with the skill set (and the mindset) to put them to good use. On this front, demand has raced ahead of supply. Indeed, the shortage of data scientists is becoming a serious constraint in some sectors. Greylock Partners, an early-stage venture firm that has backed companies such as Facebook, LinkedIn, Palo Alto Networks, and Workday, is worried enough about the tight labor pool that it has built its own specialized recruiting team to channel talent to businesses in its portfolio. "Once they have data," says Dan Portillo, who leads that team, "they really need people who can manage it and find insights in it."

Who Are These People?

If capitalizing on big data depends on hiring scarce data scientists, then the challenge for managers is to learn how to identify that talent, attract it to an enterprise, and make it productive. None of those tasks is as straightforward as it is with other, established organizational roles. Start with the fact that there are no university programs offering degrees in data science. There is also little consensus on where the role fits in an organization, how data scientists can add the most value, and how their performance should be measured.

The first step in filling the need for data scientists, therefore, is to understand what they do in businesses. Then ask, What skills do they need? And what fields are those skills most readily found in?

More than anything, what data scientists do is make discoveries while swimming in data. It's their preferred method of navigating the world around them. At ease in the digital realm, they are able to bring structure to large quantities of formless data and make analysis possible. They identify rich data sources, join them with other, potentially incomplete data sources, and clean the resulting set. In a competitive landscape where challenges keep changing and data never stop flowing, data scientists help decision makers shift from ad hoc analysis to an ongoing conversation with data.

Data scientists realize that they face technical limitations, but they don't allow that to bog down their search for novel solutions. As they make discoveries, they communicate what they've learned and suggest its implications for new business directions. Often they are creative in displaying information visually and making the patterns they find clear and compelling. They advise executives and product managers on the implications of the data for products, processes, and decisions.

Given the nascent state of their trade, it often falls to data scientists to fashion their own tools and even conduct academic-style research. Yahoo, one of the firms that employed a group of data scientists early on, was instrumental in developing Hadoop. Facebook's data team created the language Hive for programming Hadoop projects. Many other data scientists, especially at data-driven companies such as Google, Amazon, Microsoft, Walmart, eBay, LinkedIn, and Twitter, have added to and refined the tool kit.

What kind of person does all this? What abilities make a data scientist successful? Think of him or her as a hybrid of data hacker, analyst, communicator, and trusted adviser. The combination is extremely powerful—and rare.

Data scientists' most basic, universal skill is the ability to write code. This may be less true in five years' time, when many more people will have the title "data scientist" on their business cards. More enduring will be the need for data scientists to communicate in language that all their stakeholders understand—and to demonstrate the special skills involved in storytelling with data, whether verbally, visually, or—ideally—both.

But we would say the dominant trait among data scientists is an intense curiosity—a desire to go beneath the surface of a problem, find the questions at its heart, and distill them into a very clear set of hypotheses that can be tested. This often entails the associative thinking that characterizes the most creative scientists in any field. For example, we know of a data scientist studying a fraud problem who realized that it was analogous to a type of DNA sequencing problem. By bringing together those disparate worlds, he and his team were able to craft a solution that dramatically reduced fraud losses.

Perhaps it's becoming clear why the word "scientist" fits this emerging role. Experimental physicists, for example, also have to design equipment, gather data, conduct multiple experiments, and communicate their results. Thus, companies looking for people who can work with complex data have had good luck recruiting among those with educational and work backgrounds in the physical or social sciences. Some of the best and brightest data scientists are PhDs in esoteric fields like ecology and systems biology. George Roumeliotis, the head of a data science team at Intuit in Silicon Valley, holds a doctorate in astrophysics. A little less surprisingly, many of the data scientists working in business today were formally trained in computer science, math, or economics. They can emerge from any field that has a strong data and computational focus.

It's important to keep that image of the scientist in mind—because the word "data" might easily send a search for talent down the wrong path. As Portillo told us, "The traditional backgrounds of people you saw 10 to 15 years ago just don't cut it these days." A quantitative analyst can be great at analyzing data but not at subduing a mass of unstructured data and getting it into a form in which it can be analyzed. A data management expert might be great at generating and organizing data in structured form but not at turning unstructured data into structured data—and also not at actually analyzing the data. And while people without strong social skills might thrive in traditional data professions, data scientists must have such skills to be effective.

Roumeliotis was clear with us that he doesn't hire on the basis of statistical or analytical capabilities. He begins his search for data scientists by asking candidates if they can develop prototypes in a mainstream programming language such as Java. Roumeliotis seeks both a skill set—a solid foundation in math, statistics, probability, and computer science—and certain habits of mind. He wants people with a feel for business issues and empathy for customers. Then, he says, he builds on all that with on-the-job training and an occasional course in a particular technology.

Several universities are planning to launch data science programs, and existing programs in analytics, such as the Master of Science in Analytics program at North Carolina State, are busy adding big data exercises and coursework. Some companies are also trying to develop their own data scientists. After acquiring the big data firm Greenplum, EMC decided that the availability of data scientists would be a gating factor in its own—and customers'—exploitation of big data. So its Education Services division launched a data science and big data analytics training and certification program. EMC makes the program available to both employees and customers, and some of its graduates are already working on internal big data initiatives.

As educational offerings proliferate, the pipeline of talent should expand. Vendors of big data technologies are also working to make them easier to use. In the meantime one data scientist has come up with a creative approach to closing the gap. The Insight Data Science Fellows Program, a postdoctoral fellowship designed by Jake Klamka (a high-energy physicist by training), takes scientists from academia and in six weeks prepares them to succeed as data scientists. The program combines mentoring by data experts from local companies (such as Facebook, Twitter, Google, and LinkedIn)

How to Find the Data Scientists You Need

1. Focus recruiting at the "usual suspect" universities (Stanford, MIT, Berkeley, Harvard, Carnegie Mellon) and also at a few others with proven strengths: North Carolina State, UC Santa Cruz, the University of Maryland, the University of Washington, and UT Austin.

2. Scan the membership rolls of user groups devoted to data science tools. The R User Groups (for an open-source statistical tool favored by data scientists) and Python Interest Groups (for PIGgies) are good places to start.

3. Search for data scientists on LinkedIn—they're almost all on there, and you can see if they have the skills you want.

4. Hang out with data scientists at the Strata, Structure: Data, and Hadoop World conferences and similar gatherings (there is almost one a week now) or at informal data scientist "meet-ups" in the Bay Area; Boston; New York; Washington, DC; London; Singapore; and Sydney.

5. Make friends with a local venture capitalist, who is likely to have gotten a variety of big data proposals over the past year.

6. Host a competition on Kaggle or TopCoder, the analytics and coding competition sites. Follow up with the most-creative entrants.

7. Don't bother with any candidate who can't code. Coding skills don't have to be at a world-class level but should be good enough to get by. Look for evidence, too, that candidates learn rapidly about new technologies and methods.

8. Make sure a candidate can find a story in a data set and provide a coherent narrative about a key data insight. Test whether he or she can communicate with numbers, visually and verbally.

9. Be wary of candidates who are too detached from the business world. When you ask how their work might apply to your management challenges, are they stuck for answers?

10. Ask candidates about their favorite analysis or insight and how they are keeping their skills sharp. Have they gotten a certificate in the advanced track of Stanford's online Machine Learning course, contributed to open-source projects, or built an online repository of code to share (for example, on GitHub)?

with exposure to actual big data challenges. Originally aiming for 10 fellows, Klamka wound up accepting 30, from an applicant pool numbering more than 200. More organizations are now lining up to participate. "The demand from companies has been phenomenal," Klamka told us. "They just can't get this kind of high-quality talent."

Why Would a Data Scientist Want to Work Here?

Even as the ranks of data scientists swell, competition for top talent will remain fierce. Expect candidates to size up employment opportunities on the basis of how interesting the big data challenges are. As one of them commented, "If we wanted to work with structured data, we'd be on Wall Street." Given that today's most qualified prospects come from nonbusiness backgrounds, hiring managers may need to figure out how to paint an exciting picture of the potential for breakthroughs that their problems offer.

Pay will of course be a factor. A good data scientist will have many doors open to him or her, and salaries will be bid upward. Several data scientists working at start-ups commented that they'd demanded and got large stock option packages. Even for someone accepting a position for other reasons, compensation signals a level of respect and the value the role is expected to add to the business. But our informal survey of the priorities of data scientists revealed something more fundamentally important. They want to be "on the bridge." The reference is to the 1960s television show *Star Trek*, in which the starship captain James Kirk relies heavily on data supplied by Mr. Spock. Data scientists want to be in the thick of a developing situation, with real-time awareness of the evolving set of choices it presents.

Considering the difficulty of finding and keeping data scientists, one would think that a good strategy would involve hiring them as consultants. Most consulting firms have yet to assemble many of them. Even the largest firms, such as Accenture, Deloitte, and IBM Global Services, are in the early stages of leading big data projects for their clients. The skills of the data scientists they do have on staff are mainly being applied to more-conventional quantitative analysis problems. Offshore analytics services firms, such as Mu Sigma, might be the ones to make the first major inroads with data scientists.

But the data scientists we've spoken with say they want to build things, not just give advice to a decision maker. One described being a consultant as "the dead zone—all you get to do is tell someone else what the analyses say they should do." By creating solutions that work, they can have more impact and leave their marks as pioneers of their profession.

Care and Feeding

Data scientists don't do well on a short leash. They should have the freedom to experiment and explore possibilities. That said, they need close relationships with the rest of the business. The most important ties for them to forge are with executives in charge of products and services rather than with people overseeing business functions. As the story of Jonathan Goldman illustrates, their greatest opportunity to add value is not in creating reports or presentations for senior executives but in innovating with customer-facing products and processes.

LinkedIn isn't the only company to use data scientists to generate ideas for products, features, and value-adding services. At Intuit data scientists are asked to develop insights for small-business customers and consumers and report to a new senior vice president of big data, social design, and marketing. GE is already using data science to optimize the service contracts and maintenance intervals for industrial products. Google, of course, uses data scientists to refine its core search and ad-serving algorithms. Zynga uses data scientists to optimize the game experience for both long-term engagement and revenue. Netflix created the well-known Netflix Prize, given to the data science team that developed the best way to improve the company's movie recommendation system. The test-preparation firm Kaplan uses its data scientists to uncover effective learning strategies.

There is, however, a potential downside to having people with sophisticated skills in a fast-evolving field spend their time among general management colleagues. They'll have less interaction with similar specialists, which they need to keep their skills sharp and their tool kit state-of-the-art. Data scientists have to connect with communities of practice, either within large firms or externally. New conferences and informal associations are springing up to support collaboration and technology sharing, and companies should encourage scientists to become involved in them with the understanding that "more water in the harbor floats all boats."

Data scientists tend to be more motivated, too, when more is expected of them. The challenges of accessing and structuring big data sometimes leave little time or energy for sophisticated analytics involving prediction or optimization. Yet if executives make it clear that simple reports are not enough, data scientists will devote more effort to advanced analytics. Big data shouldn't equal "small math."

The Hot Job of the Decade

Hal Varian, the chief economist at Google, is known to have said, "The sexy job in the next 10 years will be statisticians. People think I'm joking, but who would've guessed that computer engineers would've been the sexy job of the 1990s?"

If "sexy" means having rare qualities that are much in demand, data scientists are already there. They are difficult and expensive to hire and, given the very competitive market for their services, difficult to retain. There simply aren't a lot of people with their combination of scientific background and computational and analytical skills.

Data scientists today are akin to Wall Street "quants" of the 1980s and 1990s. In those days people with backgrounds in physics and math streamed to investment banks and hedge funds, where they could devise entirely new algorithms and data strategies. Then a variety of universities developed master's programs in financial engineering, which churned out a second generation of talent that was more accessible to mainstream firms. The pattern was repeated later in the 1990s with search engineers, whose rarefied skills soon came to be taught in computer science programs.

One question raised by this is whether some firms would be wise to wait until that second generation of data scientists emerges, and the candidates are more numerous, less expensive, and easier to vet and assimilate in a business setting. Why not leave the trouble of hunting down and domesticating exotic talent to the big data start-ups and to firms like GE and Walmart, whose aggressive strategies require them to be at the forefront?

The problem with that reasoning is that the advance of big data shows no signs of slowing. If companies sit out this trend's early days for lack of talent, they risk falling behind as competitors and channel partners gain nearly unassailable advantages. Think of big data as an epic wave gathering now, starting to crest. If you want to catch it, you need people who can surf.

Reprinted from *Harvard Business Review*,
October 2012 (product #R1210D).

CHAPTER NINETEEN

Nine Things Successful People Do Differently

by Heidi Grant

Why have you been so successful in reaching some of your goals but not others? If you aren't sure, you are far from alone in your confusion. It turns out that even brilliant, highly accomplished people are pretty lousy when it comes to understanding why they succeed or fail. The intuitive answer—that you are born predisposed to certain talents and lacking in others—is really just one small piece of the puzzle. In fact, decades of research on achievement suggest that successful people reach their goals not simply because of who they are but more often because of what they do.

Get specific

When you set yourself a goal, try to be as specific as possible. "Lose five pounds" is a better goal than "lose some weight," because it gives you a clear idea of what success looks like. Knowing exactly what you want to achieve keeps you motivated until you get there. Also, think about the specific actions that need to be taken to reach your goal. Just promising you'll "eat less" or "sleep more" is too vague—be clear and precise. "I'll be in bed by 10 p.m. on weeknights" leaves no room for doubt about what you need to do and whether or not you've actually done it.

Seize the moment to act on your goals

Given how busy most of us are, and how many goals we are juggling at once, it's not surprising that we routinely miss opportunities to act on a goal because we simply fail to notice them. Did you really have no time to work out today? No chance at any point to return that phone call? Achieving your goal means grabbing hold of these opportunities before they slip through your fingers.

To seize the moment, decide when and where you will take each action you want to take, in advance. Again, be as specific as possible (for example, "If it's Monday, Wednesday, or Friday, I'll work out for 30 minutes before work"). Studies show that this kind of planning will help your brain to detect and seize the opportunity when it arises, increasing your chances of success by roughly 300%.

Know exactly how far you have left to go

Achieving any goal also requires honest and regular monitoring of your progress—if not by others, then by you yourself. If you don't know how well you are doing, you can't adjust your behavior or your strategies accordingly. Check your progress frequently—weekly, or even daily, depending on the goal.

Be a realistic optimist

When you are setting a goal, by all means engage in lots of positive thinking about how likely you are to achieve it. Believing in your ability to succeed is enormously helpful for creating and sustaining your motivation. But whatever you do, don't underestimate how difficult it will be to reach your goal. Most goals worth achieving require time, planning, effort, and persistence. Studies show that thinking things will come to you easily and effortlessly leaves you ill-prepared for the journey ahead and significantly increases the odds of failure.

Focus on getting better rather than being good

Believing you have the ability to reach your goals is important, but so is believing you can *get* the ability. Many of us believe that our intelligence, our personality, and our physical aptitudes are fixed— that no matter what we do, we won't improve. As a result, we focus on goals that are all about proving ourselves, rather than developing and acquiring new skills.

Fortunately, decades of research suggest that the belief in fixed ability is completely wrong—abilities of all kinds are profoundly malleable. Embracing the fact that you can change will allow you to make better choices and reach your fullest potential. People whose goals are about getting better, rather than being good, take difficulty in stride and appreciate the journey as much as the destination.

Have grit

Grit is a willingness to commit to long-term goals and to persist in the face of difficulty. Studies show that gritty people obtain more education in their lifetime and earn higher college GPAs. Grit predicts which cadets will stick out their first grueling year at West Point. In fact, grit even predicts which round contestants will make it to at the Scripps National Spelling Bee.

The good news is that if you aren't particularly gritty now, there is something you can do about it. People who lack grit more often than not believe that they just don't have the innate abilities successful people have. If that describes your own thinking . . . well, there's no way to put this nicely: You are wrong. As I mentioned earlier, effort, planning, persistence, and good strategies are what it really takes to succeed. Embracing this knowledge will not only help you see yourself and your goals more accurately but also do wonders for your grit.

Build your willpower muscle

Your self-control "muscle" is just like the other muscles in your body—when it doesn't get much exercise, it becomes weaker over time. But when you give it regular workouts by putting it to good use, it will grow stronger and stronger, and better able to help you successfully reach your goals.

To build willpower, take on a challenge that requires you to do something you'd honestly rather not do. Give up high-fat snacks, do 100 sit-ups a day, stand up straight when you catch yourself slouching, try to learn a new skill. When you find yourself wanting to give in, give up, or just not bother—don't. Start with just one activity, and make a plan for how you will deal with troubles when they occur ("If I have a craving for a snack, I will eat one piece of fresh or three pieces of dried fruit"). It will be hard in the beginning, but it will get easier, and that's the whole point. As your strength grows, you can take on more challenges and step up your self-control workout.

Don't tempt fate

No matter how strong your willpower muscle becomes, it's important to always respect the fact that it is limited, and if you overtax it, you will temporarily run out of steam. Don't try to take on two challenging tasks at once, if you can help it (like quitting smoking and starting a diet at the same time). And don't put yourself in harm's way—many people are overconfident in their ability to resist temptation, and as a result they put themselves in situations where temptations abound. Successful people know not to make reaching a goal harder than it already is.

Focus on what you *will* do, not what you *won't* do

Do you want to successfully lose weight, quit smoking, or put a lid on your bad temper? Then plan how you will replace bad habits with good ones, rather than focusing only on the bad habits themselves. Research on thought suppression ("Don't think about white bears!") has shown that trying to avoid a thought makes it even more active in your mind. The same holds true when it comes to behavior—by trying not to engage in a bad habit, our habits get strengthened rather than broken.

If you want to change your ways, ask yourself, "What will I do instead?" For example, if you are trying to gain control of your temper and stop flying off the handle, you might make a plan like, "If I am starting to feel angry, then I will take three deep breaths to calm down." By using deep breathing as a replacement for giving in to your anger, your bad habit will get worn away over time until it disappears completely.

It is my hope that, after reading about the nine things successful people do differently, you have gained some insight into all the things you have been doing right all along. Even more important, I hope you are able to identify the mistakes that have derailed you and use that knowledge to your advantage from now on. Remember, you don't need to become a different person to become a more successful one. It's never what you are—it's what you do.

Adapted from content posted on hbr.org,
February 25, 2011 (product #H006W2).

— 1974 —

CHAPTER TWENTY

Management Time: Who's Got the Monkey?

by William Oncken, Jr., and Donald L. Wass

EDITOR'S NOTE: *This article was originally published in the November–December 1974 issue of HBR and has been one of the publication's best-selling reprints ever. The practical advice it shares about empowering employees in problem-solving are just as relevant now as they were when it was originally printed. But in these almost 50 years, we've realized the metaphor used in the article can be read as offensive. While this is not the intent of the article, we want to acknowledge this concern, and note that it is meant solely as an example of someone carrying the weight of decision-making, nothing more.*

Why is it that managers are typically running out of time while their subordinates are typically running out of work? Here we shall explore the meaning of management time as it relates to the interaction between managers and their bosses, their peers, and their subordinates.

Specifically, we shall deal with three kinds of management time:

Boss-imposed time, used to accomplish those activities that the boss requires and that the manager cannot disregard without direct and swift penalty.

System-imposed time, used to accommodate requests from peers for active support. Neglecting these requests will also result in penalties, though not always as direct or swift.

Self-imposed time, used to do those things that the manager originates or agrees to do. A certain portion of this kind of time, however, will be taken by subordinates and is called *subordinate-imposed time.* The remaining portion will be the manager's own and is called *discretionary time.* Self-imposed time is not subject to penalty since neither the boss nor the system can discipline the manager for not doing what they didn't know he had intended to do in the first place.

To accommodate those demands, managers need to control the timing and the content of what they do. Since what their bosses and the system impose on them are subject to penalty, managers cannot tamper with those requirements. Thus their self-imposed time becomes their major area of concern.

Managers should try to increase the discretionary component of their self-imposed time by minimizing or doing away with the subordinate component. They will then use the added increment to get better control over their boss-imposed and system-imposed activities. Most managers spend much more time dealing with subordinates' problems than they even faintly realize. Hence we shall use the monkey-on-the-back metaphor to examine how subordinate-imposed time comes into being and what the superior can do about it.

Where Is the Monkey?

Let us imagine that a manager is walking down the hall and that he notices one of his subordinates, Jones, coming his way. When the two meet, Jones greets the manager with, "Good morning. By the way, we've got a problem. You see. . . ." As Jones continues, the manager recognizes in this problem the two characteristics common to all the problems his subordinates gratuitously bring to his attention. Namely, the manager knows (a) enough to get involved, but (b) not enough to make the on-the-spot decision expected of him. Eventually, the manager says, "So glad you brought this up. I'm in a rush right now. Meanwhile, let me think about it, and I'll let you know." Then he and Jones part company.

Let us analyze what just happened. Before the two of them met, on whose back was the "monkey"? The subordinate's. After they parted, on whose back was it? The manager's. Subordinate-imposed time begins the moment a monkey successfully leaps from the back of a subordinate to the back of his or her superior and does not end until the monkey is returned to its proper owner for care and feeding. In accepting the monkey, the manager has voluntarily assumed a position subordinate to his subordinate. That is, he has allowed Jones to make him subordinate by doing two things a subordinate is generally expected to do for a boss—the manager has accepted a responsibility from his subordinate, and the manager has promised her a progress report.

The subordinate, to make sure the manager does not miss this point, will later stick her head in the manager's office and cheerily query, "How's it coming?" (This is called supervision.)

Or let us imagine in concluding a conference with Johnson, another subordinate, the manager's parting words are, "Fine. Send me a memo on that."

Let us analyze this one. The monkey is now on the subordinate's back because the next move is his, but it is poised for a leap. Watch that monkey. Johnson dutifully writes the requested memo and drops it in his out-basket. Shortly thereafter, the manager plucks it from his in-basket and reads it. Whose move is it now? The manager's. If he does not make that move soon, he will get a follow-up memo from the subordinate. (This is another form of supervision.) The longer the manager delays, the more frustrated the subordinate will become (he'll be spinning his wheels) and the more guilty the manager will feel (his backlog of subordinate-imposed time will be mounting).

Or suppose once again that at a meeting with a third subordinate, Smith, the manager agrees to provide all the necessary backing for a public relations proposal he has just asked Smith to develop. The manager's parting words to her are, "Just let me know how I can help."

Now let us analyze this. Again the monkey is initially on the subordinate's back. But for how long? Smith realizes that she cannot let the manager know until her proposal has the manager's approval. And from experience, she also realizes that her proposal will likely be sitting in the manager's briefcase for weeks before he eventually gets to it. Who's really got the monkey? Who will be checking up on whom? Wheel spinning and bottlenecking are well on their way again.

A fourth subordinate, Reed, has just been transferred from another part of the company so that he can launch and eventually manage a newly created business venture. The manager has said they should get together soon to hammer out a set of objectives for the new job, adding, "I will draw up an initial draft for discussion with you."

Let us analyze this one, too. The subordinate has the new job (by formal assignment) and the full responsibility (by formal delegation), but the manager has the next move. Until he makes it, he will have the monkey, and the subordinate will be immobilized.

Why does all of this happen? Because in each instance the manager and the subordinate assume at the outset, wittingly or unwittingly, that the matter under consideration is a joint problem. The monkey in each case begins its career astride both their backs. All it has to do is move the wrong leg, and—presto!—the subordinate deftly disappears. The manager is thus left with another acquisition for his menagerie. Of course, monkeys can be trained not to move the wrong leg. But it is easier to prevent them from straddling backs in the first place.

Who Is Working for Whom?

Let us suppose that these same four subordinates are so thoughtful and considerate of their superior's time that they take pains to allow no more than three monkeys to leap from each of their backs to his in any one day. In a five-day week, the manager will have picked up 60 screaming monkeys—far too many to do anything about them individually. So he spends his subordinate-imposed time juggling his priorities.

Late Friday afternoon, the manager is in his office with the door closed for privacy so he can contemplate the situation, while his subordinates are waiting outside to get their last chance before the weekend to remind him that he will have to fish or cut bait. Imagine what they are saying to one another about the manager as they wait: "What a bottleneck. He just can't make up his mind. How anyone ever got that high up in our company without being able to make a decision we'll never know."

Worst of all, the reason the manager cannot make any of these next moves is that his time is almost entirely eaten up by meeting his own boss-imposed and system-imposed requirements. To control those tasks, he needs discretionary time that is in turn denied him when he is preoccupied with all these monkeys. The manager is caught in a vicious circle. But time is a-wasting (an understatement). The manager calls his secretary on the intercom and instructs her to tell his subordinates that he won't be able to see them until Monday morning. At 7 p.m., he drives home, intending with firm resolve to return to the office tomorrow to get caught up over the weekend. He returns bright and early the next day only to see, on the nearest green of the golf course across from his office window, a foursome. Guess who?

That does it. He now knows who is really working for whom. Moreover, he now sees that if he actually accomplishes during this weekend what he came to accomplish, his subordinates' morale will go up so sharply that they will each raise the limit on the number of monkeys they will let jump from their backs to his. In short, he now sees, with the clarity of a revelation on a mountaintop, that the more he gets caught up, the more he will fall behind.

He leaves the office with the speed of a person running away from a plague. His plan? To get caught up on something else he hasn't had time for in years: a weekend with his family. (This is one of the many varieties of discretionary time.)

— 1999 —

Making Time for Gorillas

by Stephen R. Covey

When Bill Oncken wrote this article in 1974, managers were in a terrible bind. They were desperate for a way to free up their time, but command and control was the status quo. Managers felt they weren't allowed to empower their subordinates to make decisions. Too dangerous. Too risky. That's why Oncken's message—give the monkey back to its rightful owner—involved a critically important paradigm shift. Many managers working today owe him a debt of gratitude.

It is something of an understatement, however, to observe that much has changed since Oncken's radical recommendation. Command and control as a management philosophy is all but dead, and "empowerment" is the word of the day in most organizations trying to thrive in global, intensely competitive markets. But command and control stubbornly remains a common practice. Management thinkers and executives have discovered in the last decade that bosses cannot just give a monkey back to their subordinates and then merrily get on with their own business. Empowering subordinates is hard and complicated work.

The reason: When you give problems back to subordinates to solve themselves, you have to be sure that they have both the desire and the ability to do so. As every executive knows, that isn't always the case. Enter a whole new set of problems. Empowerment often means you have to develop people, which is initially much more time consuming than solving the problem on your own.

Just as important, empowerment can only thrive when the whole organization buys into it—when formal systems and the informal culture support it. Managers need to be rewarded for delegating decisions and developing people. Otherwise, the degree of real empowerment in an organization will vary according to the beliefs and practices of individual managers.

But perhaps the most important lesson about empowerment is that effective delegation—the kind Oncken advocated—depends on a trusting relationship between a manager and his subordinate. Oncken's message may have been ahead of his time, but what he suggested was still a fairly dictatorial solution. He basically told bosses, "Give the problem back!" Today, we know that this approach by itself is too authoritarian. To delegate effectively, executives need to establish a running dialogue with subordinates. They need to establish a partnership. After all, if subordinates are afraid of failing in front of their boss, they'll keep coming back for help rather than truly take initiative.

Oncken's article also doesn't address an aspect of delegation that has greatly interested me during the past two decades—that many managers are actually *eager* to take on their subordinates' monkeys. Nearly all the managers I talk with agree that their people are underutilized in their present jobs. But even some of the most successful, seemingly self-assured executives have talked about how hard it is to give up control to their subordinates.

I've come to attribute that eagerness for control to a common, deep-seated belief that rewards in life are scarce and fragile. Whether they learn it from their family, school, or athletics, many people establish an identity by comparing themselves with others. When they see others gain power, information, money, or recognition, for instance, they experience what the psychologist Abraham Maslow called "a feeling of deficiency"—a sense that something is being taken from them. That makes it hard for them to be genuinely happy about the success of others—even of their loved ones. Oncken implies that managers can easily give back or refuse monkeys, but many managers may subconsciously fear that a subordinate taking the initiative will make them appear a little less strong and a little more vulnerable.

How, then, do managers develop the inward security, the mentality of "abundance," that would enable them to relinquish control and seek the growth and development of those around them? The work I've done with numerous organizations suggests that managers who live with integrity according to a principle-based value system are most likely to sustain an empowering style of leadership.

Given the times in which he wrote, it was no wonder that Oncken's message resonated with managers. But it was reinforced by Oncken's wonderful gift for storytelling. I got to know Oncken on the speaker's circuit in the 1970s, and I was always impressed by how he dramatized his ideas in colorful detail. Like the Dilbert comic strip, Oncken had a tongue-in-cheek style that got to the core of managers' frustrations and made them want to take back control of their time. And the monkey on your back wasn't just a metaphor for Oncken—it was his personal symbol. I saw him several times walking through airports with a stuffed monkey on his shoulder.

I'm not surprised that his article is one of the two best-selling HBR articles ever. Even with all we know about empowerment, its vivid message is even more important and relevant now than it was 25 years ago. Indeed, Oncken's insight is a basis for my own work on time management, in which I have people categorize their activities according to urgency and importance. I've heard from executives again and again that half or more of their time is spent on matters that are urgent but not important. They're trapped in an endless cycle of dealing with other people's monkeys, yet they're reluctant to help those people take their own initiative. As a result, they're often too busy to spend the time they need on the real gorillas in their organization. Oncken's article remains a powerful wake-up call for managers who need to delegate effectively.

Sunday night he enjoys ten hours of sweet, untroubled slumber, because he has clear-cut plans for Monday. He is going to get rid of his subordinate-imposed time. In exchange, he will get an equal amount of discretionary time, part of which he will spend with his subordinates to make sure that they learn the difficult but rewarding managerial art called "the care and feeding of monkeys."

The manager will also have plenty of discretionary time left over for getting control of the timing and the content not only of his boss-imposed time but also of his system-imposed time. It may take months, but compared with the way things have been, the rewards will be enormous. His ultimate objective is to manage his time.

Getting Rid of the Monkeys

The manager returns to the office Monday morning just late enough so that his four subordinates have collected outside his office waiting to see him about their monkeys. He calls them in one by one. The purpose of each interview is to take a monkey, place it on the desk between them, and figure out together how the next move might conceivably be the subordinate's. For certain monkeys, that will take some doing. The subordinate's next move may be so elusive that the manager may decide—just for now—merely to let the monkey sleep on the subordinate's back overnight and have him or her return with it at an appointed time the next morning to continue the joint quest for a more substantive move by the subordinate. (Monkeys sleep just as soundly overnight on subordinates' backs as they do on superiors'.)

As each subordinate leaves the office, the manager is rewarded by the sight of a monkey leaving his office on the subordinate's back. For the next 24 hours, the subordinate will not be waiting for the manager; instead, the manager will be waiting for the subordinate.

Later, as if to remind himself that there is no law against his engaging in a constructive exercise in the interim, the manager strolls by the subordinate's office, sticks his head in the door, and cheerily asks, "How's it coming?" (The time consumed in doing this is discretionary for the manager and boss imposed for the subordinate.)

When the subordinate (with the monkey on his or her back) and the manager meet at the appointed hour the next day, the manager explains the ground rules in words to this effect:

"At no time while I am helping you with this or any other problem will your problem become my problem. The instant your problem becomes mine, you no longer have a problem. I cannot help a person who hasn't got a problem.

"When this meeting is over, the problem will leave this office exactly the way it came in—on your back. You may ask my help at any appointed time, and we will make a joint determination of what the next move will be and which of us will make it.

"In those rare instances where the next move turns out to be mine, you and I will determine it together. I will not make any move alone."

The manager follows this same line of thought with each subordinate until about 11 p.m., when he realizes that he doesn't have to close his door. His monkeys are gone. They will return—but by appointment only. His calendar will assure this.

Transferring the Initiative

What we have been driving at in this monkey-on-the-back analogy is that managers can transfer initiative back to their subordinates and keep it there. We have tried to highlight a truism as obvious as it is subtle: namely, before developing initiative in subordinates, the manager must see to it that they *have* the initiative. Once the manager takes it back, he will no longer have it and he can kiss his discretionary time good-bye. It will all revert to subordinate-imposed time.

Nor can the manager and the subordinate effectively have the same initiative at the same time. The opener, "Boss, we've got a problem," implies this duality and represents, as noted earlier, a monkey astride two backs, which is a very bad way to start a monkey on its career. Let us, therefore, take a few moments to examine what we call "the anatomy of managerial initiative."

There are five degrees of initiative that the manager can exercise in relation to the boss and to the system:

1. wait until told (lowest initiative);

2. ask what to do;

3. recommend, then take resulting action;

4. act, but advise at once;

5. and act on own, then routinely report (highest initiative).

Clearly, the manager should be professional enough not to indulge in initiatives 1 and 2 in relation either to the boss or to the system. A manager who uses initiative 1 has no control over either the timing or the content of boss-imposed or system-imposed time and thereby forfeits any right to complain about what he or she is told to do or when. The manager who uses initiative 2 has control over the timing but not over the content. Initiatives 3, 4, and 5 leave the manager in control of both, with the greatest amount of control being exercised at level 5.

In relation to subordinates, the manager's job is twofold. First, to outlaw the use of initiatives 1 and 2, thus giving subordinates no choice but to learn and master "completed staff work." Second, to see that for each problem leaving his or her office there is an agreed-upon level of initiative assigned to it, in addition to an agreed-upon time and place for the next manager-subordinate conference. The latter should be duly noted on the manager's calendar.

The Care and Feeding of Monkeys

To further clarify our analogy between the monkey on the back and the processes of assigning and controlling, we shall refer briefly to the manager's appointment schedule, which calls for five hard-

and-fast rules governing the care and feeding of monkeys. (Violation of these rules will cost discretionary time.)

Rule 1

Monkeys should be fed or shot. Otherwise, they will starve to death, and the manager will waste valuable time on postmortems or attempted resurrections.

Rule 2

The monkey population should be kept below the maximum number the manager has time to feed. Subordinates will find time to work as many monkeys as he or she finds time to feed, but no more. It shouldn't take more than five to 15 minutes to feed a properly maintained monkey.

Rule 3

Monkeys should be fed by appointment only. The manager should not have to hunt down starving monkeys and feed them on a catch-as-catch-can basis.

Rule 4

Monkeys should be fed face-to-face or by telephone, but never by mail. (Remember—with mail, the next move will be the manager's.) Documentation may add to the feeding process, but it cannot take the place of feeding.

Rule 5

Every monkey should have an assigned next feeding time and degree of initiative. These may be revised at any time by mutual consent but never allowed to become vague or indefinite.

Otherwise, the monkey will either starve to death or wind up on the manager's back.

———————

"Get control over the timing and content of what you do" is appropriate advice for managing time. The first order of business is for the manager to enlarge his or her discretionary time by eliminating subordinate-imposed time. The second is for the manager to use a portion of this newfound discretionary time to see to it that each subordinate actually has the initiative and applies it. The third is for the manager to use another portion of the increased discretionary time to get and keep control of the timing and content of both boss-imposed and system-imposed time. All these steps will increase the manager's leverage and enable the value of each hour spent in managing management time to multiply without theoretical limit.

———————

Reprinted from *Harvard Business Review*,
November–December 1999 (product #99609).
Originally published November–December 1974.

— 2013 —

CHAPTER TWENTY-ONE

Why the Lean Start-Up Changes Everything

by Steve Blank

Launching a new enterprise—whether it's a tech start-up, a small business, or an initiative within a large corporation—has always been a hit-or-miss proposition. According to the decades-old formula, you write a business plan, pitch it to investors, assemble a team, introduce a product, and start selling as hard as you can. And somewhere in this sequence of events, you'll probably suffer a fatal setback. The odds are not with you: As new research by Harvard Business School's Shikhar Ghosh shows, 75% of all start-ups fail.

But recently an important countervailing force has emerged, one that can make the process of starting a company less risky. It's a methodology called the "lean start-up," and it favors experimentation over elaborate planning, customer feedback over intuition, and iterative design over traditional "big design up front" development. Although the methodology is just a few years old, its concepts—such as "minimum viable product" and "pivoting"—have quickly taken root in the start-up world, and business schools have already begun adapting their curricula to teach them.

The lean start-up movement hasn't gone totally mainstream, however, and we have yet to feel its full impact. In many ways it is roughly where the big data movement was five years ago—consisting mainly of a buzzword that's not yet widely understood, whose implications companies are just beginning to grasp. But as its practices spread, they're turning the conventional wisdom about entrepreneurship on its head. New ventures of all kinds are attempting to improve their chances of success by following its principles of failing fast and continually learning. And despite the methodology's name, in the long term some of its biggest payoffs may be gained by the *large* companies that embrace it.

In this article I'll offer a brief overview of lean start-up techniques and how they've evolved. Most important, I'll explain how, in combination with other business trends, they could ignite a new entrepreneurial economy.

The Fallacy of the Perfect Business Plan

According to conventional wisdom, the first thing every founder must do is create a business plan—a static document that describes the size of an opportunity, the problem to be solved, and the solution that the new venture will provide. Typically it includes a five-year forecast for income, profits, and cash flow. A business plan is essentially a research exercise written in isolation at a desk before an entrepreneur has even begun to build a product. The assumption is that it's possible to figure out most of the unknowns of a business in advance, before you raise money and actually execute the idea.

Once an entrepreneur with a convincing business plan obtains money from investors, he or she begins developing the product in a similarly insular fashion. Developers invest thousands of man-hours to get it ready for launch, with little if any customer input. Only after building and launching the product does the venture get substantial feedback from customers—when the sales force attempts to sell it. And too often, after months or even years of development, entrepreneurs learn the hard way that customers do not need or want most of the product's features.

After decades of watching thousands of start-ups follow this standard regimen, we've now learned at least three things:

1. Business plans rarely survive first contact with customers. As the boxer Mike Tyson once said about his opponents'

prefight strategies: "Everybody has a plan until they get punched in the mouth."

2. No one besides venture capitalists and the late Soviet Union requires five-year plans to forecast complete unknowns. These plans are generally fiction, and dreaming them up is almost always a waste of time.

3. Start-ups are not smaller versions of large companies. They do not unfold in accordance with master plans. The ones that ultimately succeed go quickly from failure to failure, all the while adapting, iterating on, and improving their initial ideas as they continually learn from customers.

One of the critical differences is that while existing companies *execute* a business model, start-ups *look* for one. This distinction is at the heart of the lean start-up approach. It shapes the lean definition of a start-up: a temporary organization designed to search for a repeatable and scalable business model.

The lean method has three key principles:

First, rather than engaging in months of planning and research, entrepreneurs accept that all they have on day one is a series of untested hypotheses—basically, good guesses. So instead of writing an intricate business plan, founders summarize their hypotheses in a framework called a *business model canvas*. Essentially, this is a diagram of how a company creates value for itself and its customers. (See table 21-1.)

Second, lean start-ups use a "get out of the building" approach called *customer development* to test their hypotheses. They go out and ask potential users, purchasers, and partners for feedback on all elements of the business model, including product features, pricing, distribution channels, and affordable customer acquisition strategies. The emphasis is on nimbleness and speed: New ventures rapidly assemble minimum viable products and immediately elicit customer feedback. Then, using customers' input to revise their assumptions, they start the cycle over again, testing redesigned offerings and making further small adjustments (iterations) or

TABLE 21-1

Sketch out your hypotheses

The business model canvas lets you look at all nine building blocks of your business on one page. Each component of the business model contains a series of hypotheses that you need to test.

Key partners	Key activities	Value propositions	Customer relationships	Customer segments
Who are our key partners? Who are our key suppliers? Which key resources are we acquiring from our partners? Which key activities do partners perform?	What key activities do our value propositions require? Our distribution channels? Customer relationships? Revenue streams?	What value do we deliver to the customer? Which one of our customers' problems are we helping to solve? What bundles of products and services are we offering to each segment? Which customer needs are we satisfying? What is the minimum viable product?	How do we get, keep, and grow customers? Which customer relationships have we established? How are they integrated with the rest of our business model? How costly are they?	For whom are we creating value? Who are our most important customers? What are the customer archetypes?
	Key resources		**Channels**	
	What key resources do our value propositions require? Our distribution channels? Customer relationships? Revenue streams?		Through which channels do our customer segments want to be reached? How do other companies reach them now? Which ones work best? Which ones are most cost-efficient? How are we integrating them with customer routines?	

Cost structure			Revenue streams	
What are the most important costs inherent to our business model? Which key resources are most expensive? Which key activities are most expensive?			For what value are our customers really willing to pay? For what do they currently pay? What is the revenue model? What are the pricing tactics?	

Source: See www.businessmodelgeneration.com/canvas. Canvas concept developed by Alexander Osterwalder and Yves Pigneur.

FIGURE 21-1

Listen to customers

During customer development, a start-up searches for a business model that works. If customer feedback reveals that its business hypotheses are wrong, it either revises them or "pivots" to new hypotheses. Once a model is proven, the start-up starts executing, building a formal organization. Each stage of customer development is iterative: A start-up will probably fail several times before finding the right approach.

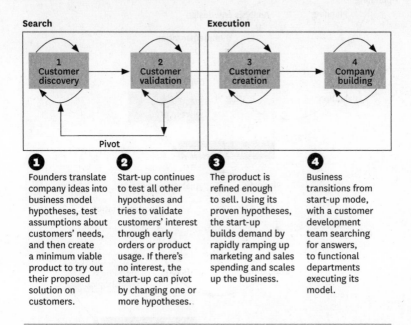

Search

Execution

| 1 Customer discovery | 2 Customer validation | 3 Customer creation | 4 Company building |

Pivot

1 Founders translate company ideas into business model hypotheses, test assumptions about customers' needs, and then create a minimum viable product to try out their proposed solution on customers.

2 Start-up continues to test all other hypotheses and tries to validate customers' interest through early orders or product usage. If there's no interest, the start-up can pivot by changing one or more hypotheses.

3 The product is refined enough to sell. Using its proven hypotheses, the start-up builds demand by rapidly ramping up marketing and sales spending and scales up the business.

4 Business transitions from start-up mode, with a customer development team searching for answers, to functional departments executing its model.

more substantive ones (pivots) to ideas that aren't working. (See figure 21-1.)

Third, lean start-ups practice something called *agile development,* which originated in the software industry. Agile development works hand-in-hand with customer development. Unlike typical yearlong product development cycles that presuppose knowledge of customers' problems and product needs, agile development eliminates wasted time and resources by developing the product

FIGURE 21-2

Quick, responsive development

In contrast to traditional product development, in which each stage occurs in linear order and lasts for months, agile development builds products in short, repeated cycles. A start-up produces a minimum viable product—containing only critical features—gathers feedback on it from customers, and then starts over with a revised minimum viable product.

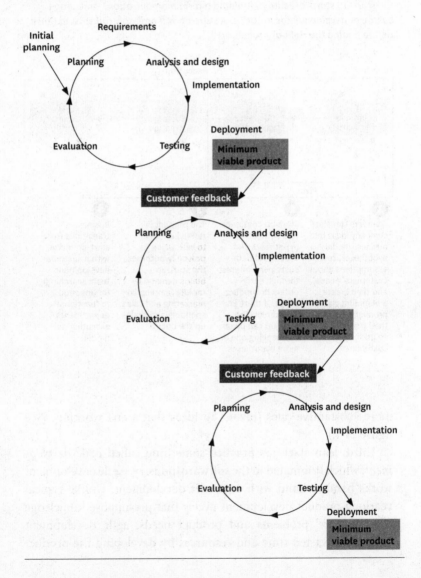

iteratively and incrementally. It's the process by which start-ups create the minimum viable products they test. (See figure 21-2.)

When Jorge Heraud and Lee Redden started Blue River Technology, they were students in my class at Stanford. They had a vision of building robotic lawn mowers for commercial spaces. After talking to over 100 customers in 10 weeks, they learned their initial customer target—golf courses—didn't value their solution. But then they began to talk to farmers and found a huge demand for an automated way to kill weeds without chemicals. Filling it became their new product focus, and within 10 weeks Blue River had built and tested a prototype. Nine months later the start-up had obtained more than $3 million in venture funding. The team expected to have a commercial product ready just nine months after that.

Stealth Mode's Declining Popularity

Lean methods are changing the language start-ups use to describe their work. During the dot-com boom, start-ups often operated in "stealth mode" (to avoid alerting potential competitors to a market opportunity), exposing prototypes to customers only during highly orchestrated "beta" tests. The lean start-up methodology makes those concepts obsolete because it holds that in most industries customer feedback matters more than secrecy and that constant feedback yields better results than cadenced unveilings.

Those two fundamental precepts crystallized for me during my career as an entrepreneur. (I've been involved with eight high-tech start-ups, as either a founder or an early employee.) When I shifted into teaching, a decade ago, I came up with the formula for customer development described earlier. By 2003 I was outlining this process in a course at the Haas School of Business at the University of California at Berkeley.

In 2004, I invested in a start-up founded by Eric Ries and Will Harvey and, as a condition of my investment, insisted that they take my course. Eric quickly recognized that waterfall development, the tech industry's traditional, linear product development approach, should be replaced by iterative agile techniques. He also saw similarities between this emerging set of start-up disciplines and the Toyota Production System, which had become known as "lean manufacturing." Eric dubbed the combination of customer development and agile practices the "lean start-up."

The tools were popularized by a series of successful books. In 2003, I wrote *The Four Steps to the Epiphany,* articulating for the first time that start-ups were not smaller versions of large companies and laying out the customer development process in detail. In 2010, Alexander Osterwalder and Yves Pigneur gave entrepreneurs the standard framework for business model canvases in *Business Model Generation.* In 2011 Eric published an overview in *The Lean Startup.* And in 2012 Bob Dorf and I summarized what we'd learned about lean techniques in a step-by-step handbook called *The Startup Owner's Manual.*

The lean start-up method is now being taught at more than 25 universities and through a popular online course at Udacity.com. In addition, in almost every city around the world, you'll find organizations like Startup Weekend introducing the lean method to hundreds of prospective entrepreneurs at a time. At such gatherings a roomful of start-up teams can cycle through half a dozen potential product ideas in a matter of hours. Although it sounds incredible to people who haven't been to one, at these events some businesses are formed on a Friday evening and are generating actual revenue by Sunday afternoon.

Creating an Entrepreneurial, Innovation-Based Economy

While some adherents claim that the lean process can make individual start-ups more successful, I believe that claim is too grandiose. Success is predicated on too many factors for one methodology to guarantee that any single start-up will be a winner. But on the basis of what I've seen at hundreds of start-ups, at programs that teach lean principles, and at established companies that practice them, I can make a more important claim: Using lean methods across a portfolio of start-ups will result in fewer failures than using traditional methods.

A lower start-up failure rate could have profound economic consequences. Today the forces of disruption, globalization, and regulation are buffeting the economies of every country. Established industries are rapidly shedding jobs, many of which will never return. Employment growth in the 21st century will have to come from new ventures, so we all have a vested interest in fostering an environment that helps them succeed, grow, and hire more workers. The creation of an innovation economy that's driven by the rapid expansion of start-ups has never been more imperative.

In the past, growth in the number of start-ups was constrained by five factors in addition to the failure rate:

1. The high cost of getting the first customer and the even higher cost of getting the product wrong

2. Long technology development cycles

3. The limited number of people with an appetite for the risks inherent in founding or working at a start-up

4. The structure of the venture capital industry, in which a small number of firms each needed to invest big sums in a handful of start-ups to have a chance at significant returns

5. The concentration of real expertise in how to build start-ups, which in the United States was mostly found in pockets on the East and West coasts. (This is less of an issue in Europe and other parts of the world, but even overseas there are geographic entrepreneurial hot spots.)

The lean approach reduces the first two constraints by helping new ventures launch products that customers actually want, far more quickly and cheaply than traditional methods, and the third by making start-ups less risky. And it has emerged at a time when

What Lean Start-Ups Do Differently

The founders of lean start-ups don't begin with a business plan; they begin with the search for a business model. Only after quick rounds of experimentation and feedback reveal a model that works do lean founders focus on execution.

Lean	Traditional
STRATEGY	
Business model Hypothesis-driven	**Business plan** Implementation-driven
NEW-PRODUCT PROCESS	
Customer development Get out of the office and test hypotheses	**Product management** Prepare the offering for market following a linear, step-by-step plan
ENGINEERING	
Agile development Build the product iteratively and incrementally	**Agile or waterfall development** Build the product iteratively or fully specify the product before building it
ORGANIZATION	
Customer and agile development teams Hire for learning, nimbleness, and speed	**Departments by function** Hire for experience and ability to execute
FINANCIAL REPORTING	
Metrics that matter Customer acquisition cost, lifetime customer value, churn, viralness	**Accounting** Income statement, balance sheet, cash flow statement
FAILURE	
Expected Fix by iterating on ideas and pivoting away from ones that don't work	**Exception** Fix by firing executives
SPEED	
Rapid Operates on good-enough data	**Measured** Operates on complete data

other business and technology trends are likewise breaking down the barriers to start-up formation. The combination of all these forces is altering the entrepreneurial landscape.

Today open source software, like GitHub, and cloud services, such as Amazon Web Services, have slashed the cost of software development from millions of dollars to thousands. Hardware start-ups no longer have to build their own factories, since offshore manufacturers are so easily accessible. Indeed, it's become quite common to see young tech companies that practice the lean start-up methodology offer software products that are simply "bits" delivered over the web or hardware that's built in China within weeks of being formed. Consider Roominate, a start-up designed to inspire girls' confidence and interest in science, technology, engineering, and math. Once its founders had finished testing and iterating on the design of their wired dollhouse kit, they sent the specs off to a contract manufacturer in China. Three weeks later the first products arrived.

Another important trend is the decentralization of access to financing. Venture capital used to be a tight club of formal firms clustered near Silicon Valley, Boston, and New York. In today's entrepreneurial ecosystem, new super angel funds, smaller than the traditional hundred-million-dollar-sized VC fund, can make early-stage investments. Worldwide, hundreds of accelerators, like Y Combinator and TechStars, have begun to formalize seed investments. And crowdsourcing sites like Kickstarter provide another, more democratic method of financing start-ups.

The instantaneous availability of information is also a boon to today's new ventures. Before the internet, new company founders got advice only as often as they could have coffee with experienced investors or entrepreneurs. Today the biggest challenge is sorting through the overwhelming amount of start-up advice they get. The lean concepts provide a framework that helps you differentiate the good from the bad.

Lean start-up techniques were initially designed to create fast-growing tech ventures. But I believe the concepts are equally valid for creating the Main Street small businesses that make up the bulk of the economy. If the entire universe of small business embraced them, I strongly suspect it would increase growth and efficiency, and have a direct and immediate impact on GDP and employment.

There are signs that this may in fact happen. In 2011 the U.S. National Science Foundation began using lean methods to commercialize basic science research in a program called the Innovation Corps. Eleven universities now teach the methods to hundreds of teams of senior research scientists across the United States.

MBA programs are adopting these techniques, too. For years they taught students to apply large-company approaches—such as accounting methods for tracking revenue and cash flow, and organizational theories about managing—to start-ups. Yet start-ups face completely different issues. Now business schools are realizing that new ventures need their own management tools.

As business schools embrace the distinction between management execution and searching for a business model, they're abandoning the business plan as the template for entrepreneurial education. And the business plan competitions that have been a celebrated part of the MBA experience for over a decade are being replaced by business model competitions. (Harvard Business School became the latest to make this switch, in 2012.) Stanford, Harvard, Berkeley, and Columbia are leading the charge and embracing the lean start-up curriculum. My Lean LaunchPad course for educators is now training over 250 college and university instructors a year.

A New Strategy for the 21st-Century Corporation

It's already becoming clear that lean start-up practices are not just for young tech ventures.

Corporations have spent the past 20 years increasing their efficiency by driving down costs. But simply focusing on improving existing business models is not enough anymore. Almost every large company understands that it also needs to deal with ever-increasing external threats by continually innovating. To ensure their survival and growth, corporations need to keep inventing new business models. This challenge requires entirely new organizational structures and skills.

Over the years managerial experts such as Clayton Christensen, Rita McGrath, Vijay Govindarajan, Henry Chesbrough, Ian Mac-Millan, Alexander Osterwalder, and Eric von Hippel have advanced the thinking on how large companies can improve their innovation processes. During the past three years, however, we have seen large companies, including General Electric, Qualcomm, and Intuit, begin to implement the lean start-up methodology.

GE's Energy Storage division, for instance, is using the approach to transform the way it innovates. In 2010 Prescott Logan, the general manager of the division, recognized that a new battery developed by the unit had the potential to disrupt the industry. Instead of preparing to build a factory, scale up production, and launch the new offering (ultimately named Durathon) as a traditional product extension, Logan applied lean techniques. He started searching for a business model and engaging in customer discovery. He and his team met face-to-face with dozens of global prospects to explore potential new markets and applications. These weren't sales calls: The team members left their PowerPoint slides behind and listened to customers' issues and frustrations with the battery status quo. They dug deep to learn how customers bought industrial batteries, how often they used them, and the operating conditions. With this feedback, they made a major shift in their customer focus. They eliminated one of their initial target segments, data centers, and discovered a new one—utilities. In addition, they narrowed the broad customer segment of "telecom" to cell phone providers in developing countries with unreliable electric grids. Eventually GE invested $100 million to build a world-class battery manufacturing facility in Schenectady, New York, which it opened in 2012. According to press reports, demand for the new batteries is so high that GE is already running a backlog of orders.

The first hundred years of management education focused on building strategies and tools that formalized execution and efficiency for existing businesses. Now, we have the first set of tools for searching for new business models as we launch start-up ventures. It also happens to have arrived just in time to help existing companies deal with the forces of continual disruption. In the 21st century those forces will make people in every kind of organization—start-ups, small businesses, corporations, and government—feel the pressure of rapid change. The lean start-up approach will help them meet it head-on, innovate rapidly, and transform business as we know it.

Reprinted from *Harvard Business Review*,
May 2013 (product #R1305C).

CHAPTER TWENTY-TWO

Bring Agile to the Whole Organization

by Jeff Gothelf

Software has eaten the world. And as it continues to consume new and diverse industries, it's transforming the way business is done. We are all in the "software business" now, regardless of the product or service we provide, forcing us to reexamine how we structure and manage our organizations.

When I ask managers if their organizations practice "agile," they almost always say yes. Probing a bit deeper reveals that most of this agility starts and ends with the product development teams—specifically software engineering. There is rarely a mention of "agile in the HR group" or "continuous improvement in finance." And yet, it is in these infrastructural disciplines that agility must take root to support software-driven businesses.

As the nature of software continues to shift toward continuous delivery, we are able to create a new type of conversation with the marketplace—a continuous one. We deploy products, observe, measure, interview, learn, and optimize in hours, not months. Decisions are made quickly. Directions shift overnight. To support this rapid, iterative optimization of our business, the internal organizations that staff, fund, manage, and reward our people need to exhibit that same level of agility. "The way we've always done it" starts to put the management tier in direct conflict with the potential of the execution teams.

Let's take a look at HR first. The object around which most HR organizations operate is the job requisition. A traditional job requisition is usually nothing more than a list of tools and capabilities buffered by ambiguous language about "self-starters" and "team players." These job descriptions are written to fill a gap in a discipline-specific silo (for example, the software engineering team or the design team). Recruiters, incentivized to fill roles quickly, scour résumés for these skill sets, ensuring that anything that makes it through to the next round has "ticked all the boxes." Three years of Rails? Check. GitHub? Check. Candidates are passed on to hiring managers, who are then pressured to make a decision—ensuring the HR teams hit their time-to-fill quotas.

This style of hiring doesn't build organizational agility. Quite the contrary, it reinforces the barriers between disciplines and minimizes cooperation. Instead, HR teams need to start hiring for creativity, collaboration, and curiosity. They need to seek out the nonconformists—the candidates that don't easily fit into a box. These are the generalists with an entrepreneurial spirit. They're the multifaceted tinkerers who have specialized in a discipline like design but turn out to be pretty good coders. They're the skeptical members of the team. The ones always pushing back on the status quo and forcing the business to rethink the way it presents itself to its customers. New hiring practices must be put in place to attract these candidates. Interview structures and exercises have to be completely rethought. It's nearly impossible to assess a candidate's collaboration skills in a one-hour Q&A. What do we need to change in order to learn if this new candidate is the innovator that will push our company forward? How do we ensure that our hiring practices continue to improve as the nature of our business evolves?

If we're hiring ever-curious, entrepreneurial team members, the next logical question is, How do we incentivize and retain them? In the past, we'd just assign them to a team, give them a project to build, and if they shipped on time and on budget (or at least close enough to it), they got rewarded in some way. That's not enough anymore. Financial compensation is not the main motivator for these folks. Building something meaningful, something they can call their own, holds much more value. Is there a way for us to re-think compensation structures to include equity (or at least upside) for the ideas our collaborative teams create?

Project funding is another monolith that must conform to our new reality. CFOs want to know what will ship in return for fund-ing an initiative. While there is never a shortage of answers (you are trying to get funded, after all), the true answer—we really don't know—is rarely given. There is an ambiguity in software develop-ment that renders the end state unknowable. Unpredictable levels of complexity, market turmoil, and shifts in customer behavior put any product road map longer than four to six weeks at a high risk of quickly becoming an outdated artifact.

Taking a cue from the startup world, the CFO's office needs to start treating each team as an in-house startup—a group of people tasked with solving a business problem. That business problem has an objective, measurable goal that ultimately determines the team's success. At the end of each funding period, the teams must present their cases to the finance office for re-funding. This builds a ca-denced resilience into the way the organization makes decisions, allowing it to make short commitments and then further those commitments or not, based on real-time, market-based realities as opposed to lofty predictions of a future state that may never come.

Lastly, decision-making hierarchies need to change. Tradition-ally decisions are run past layers of management, ensuring buy-in from everyone before direction shifts. These processes are slow. They provide cover in the event that someone makes a mistake. Agility in the organization requires decision-making to be done as close to the customer feedback as possible. The teams working on the products need to be able to quickly decide how to move forward based on the continuous inbound stream of market insight. Mak-ing mistakes shouldn't be a capital crime. Instead, mistakes should be quickly analyzed and any new information should be incorpo-rated into the next set of tactics.

Incentives should support measuring outcomes, making evi-dence-based decisions, and learning. The culture of software devel-opment allows all of this, but without organizational support, the teams can't take full advantage of it. Ultimately, the day-to-day tactical decisions the teams make should not be the concern of managers. Instead, managers should focus on the teams' progress toward the strategic business objectives. To allay managerial anxiety and ensure broader strategic cohesion, the onus falls on the teams to communicate back to the organization as much as possible. They must proactively report on their tactics, learnings, progress, and next steps. However, without the safety to report the whole process, warts and all, most teams will opt for security and predictability—effectively undermining their agility.

As our companies turn into highly focused software organizations, we must change the way we manage them. A continuous-learning environment fueled by around-the-clock customer insight and feedback demands teams, environments, decision-making structures, and funding models that exhibit the true meaning of the word "agility"—resilience, responsiveness, and learning.

Adapted from content posted on hbr.org,
November 14, 2014 (product #H01P9M).

CHAPTER TWENTY-THREE

The Three Types of Leaders of Innovative Companies

An interview with Deborah Ancona
and Kate Isaacs by Curt Nickisch

Command and control has lost its mojo. Nowadays, if you want to create an innovative organization, no one would tell you to build a rigid bureaucracy. But what *should* you build? How can you have creativity without chaos?

That's a question that grabbed Deborah Ancona, professor at MIT Sloan School of Management and founder of the MIT Leadership Center, and Kate Isaacs, a research fellow at the center. They wanted a clearer picture of the ideal company, so they looked at two organizations: PARC, the R&D division of Xerox; and W. L. Gore & Associates, the materials science company best known for GORE-TEX.

In this interview, they describe how three different kinds of leaders at these organizations work in conjunction, flexibly, within a set of prescribed rules—what they refer to as nimble leadership.

CURT NICKISCH: *Why did you choose these two companies?*

DEBORAH ANCONA: We were interested in this idea of what we used to call *distributed leadership*—what we're now calling *nimble leadership*. We wanted to look at companies that were at the forefront of leading innovation and had entrepreneurial behavior inside of them, but ones that did not do so with a lot of bureaucracy and rules.

They were also not startups. They had been around for a long time and were a proven concept, if you will, of an organization that could continuously adapt to a changing environment, continue at high levels of innovation over time, and continue to have employees who are very engaged and excited about the work they were doing. The companies we picked were the prototypes of this kind of organization.

Do you feel right away that you're in a different sort of company when you visit these places?

DA: Absolutely. I do a lot of interviews with employees in many different kinds of organizations, and some of those interviews are fairly scary. People are disengaged from their work. They don't like coming to work. We had some interviews where people were actually crying.

It's a completely different experience to go back every couple of months, let's say, to Gore, and people are so excited. "We just invented this." "This is a new thing that we're working on." "We just created a new idea of a business model that will reshape the way the organization operates." There was a lot of energy, excitement, and movement all the time, without being frenzied. People were doing a lot, and they were satisfied with what they were doing.

If you hear about a company where people can be creative without being chaotic, some people would think, "Well, there's a CEO who really knows what they're doing." What do you think is the secret sauce of Gore and this sort of company?

KATE ISAACS: At Gore there are certainly leaders; there's a CEO. But it's the culture that really embodies the principles that keep it running like it does. The individual leadership, the culture of the place, and the structures they have—that's what makes the whole system work. The principles that make it operate that way have been there since the beginning and have been refined over time.

One thing that struck me reading your HBR article "Nimble Leadership" is that you said that a high proportion of people at these firms describe themselves as leaders. This is the idea of distributed leadership. Why do you think nimble leadership is a better way to describe what's happening?

KI: I have always disliked the term "distributed leadership." It makes me think of a glass of water that you put a drop of red food coloring in. Everything turns slightly pink. To me, "distributed" evokes this idea of everything being diluted a bit. That's not what we mean by "distributed."

What we mean is that in these sorts of organizations, everyone feels they are empowered. They step up and lead in their domain of expertise, and they even step out of their domain of expertise and stretch into new areas of experience—and they're supported in doing so. There's a constant developmental process going on at these organizations that's supported by the culture, their peers, and other sponsors of their development.

So, when we use the term "nimble," we mean that the leadership itself is appropriate for whatever needs to happen in the moment inside the organization, and the organization as a whole is able to quickly adapt to changing market conditions and what they're sensing from their customers. If a customer is unhappy, they're able to quickly respond, because everyone is empowered to do what's needed to execute according to their strategy and what their customers need and want.

It sounds like everybody there is in tune with the company strategy.

DA: Yes, and the strategy is not just some esoteric set of terms that people have learned. It's really in-depth: *Here are the kinds of products we make. This is how we make money.* It's amazing to me when you go to other organizations and they're working on projects—they don't necessarily even think about whether it's going to win in the marketplace. Whereas, in these organizations, you have people who really understand what the business model is and how the organization can be successful with the inputs they are creating.

KI: And it's broken down into pieces that people can understand in their domain, wherever they are in the organization. For instance, at Gore there is a simple rule called "fit for use." Whatever you do, whatever product you're creating, has to be fit for the use that you're intending it. They don't want to send a cable up into space that's going to fail. They don't want to send somebody to the top of Mt. Everest with a jacket that's going to leak.

That drives the extensive testing, constant attention to quality, and constant communication with customers about how the product is performing in the field. It's a simple rule that's true both at the organizational strategy level and the product development level. These simple rules knit together the high-level strategy with what people are doing on the ground everywhere and throughout the organization.

You came up with taxonomy for different types of leaders, at different levels of the organization. Entrepreneurial leaders *at the lower levels, at project levels;* enabling leaders *a little higher up; and then* architecting leaders *above that. Tell us more about these three different classifications.*

DA: Entrepreneurial leaders are the folks that are creating that frothy, bubble-up innovation for the organization, and they do so because they're constantly coming up with new product ideas, new business models, and new ways of organizing in the firm. It can be enticing others to follow them, to come and work with them on a particular idea. They're the ones who create teams, and those teams bring new ideas through the organization. It's not just coming up with an idea; it's also seizing the opportunity and moving it through the organization.

There is also a lot of freedom for people to leave projects and join other ones.

DA: What that does is create a kind of prediction market in the organization, because people are free to go and join a product that they think is a better bet for success in the environment. People are orchestrating what the next projects will be by voting with their feet. Managers aren't sitting in a room making these decisions; people are actively choosing what projects will be the best. So, managers beware.

KI: This also puts demands on the leaders of project teams to be willing to let talented people move around to other teams instead of trying to hoard talent. By and large, we found that managers knew that *OK, over there is a cool project that has a lot of potential for the organization* and *Gee, I'd rather keep this person on my team because they're very talented, but I know that while they'd be able to contribute a lot over here, they want to contribute over there. Far be it for me to keep them here against their wishes and against the greater organizational good.* They were constantly paying attention to what would be best for the whole organization and what would be best for the individual.

Deborah, you just said "managers beware." Is this the point where people are afraid of losing control?

DA: I do a lot of executive education, and almost every company we see wants to make this move from command, control, and bureaucracy to a more nimble, distributed-learning network—whatever word you want to use—kind of organization. This is in keeping with a lot of research being done now: that executives feel like there are going to be major changes in their industries and their environment in the next three years—76% of executives believe this, compared to 26% last year. The sense that there's an increase in change is going to require a different kind of organization.

But with that comes incredible anxiety and inertia in making the move, because of a fear of not knowing what to do. *I don't know how to create this system. It's going to mean that I lose my power as an executive. What's going to happen if I let go of the reins?* This is a big fear that we see in these leaders. It's scary.

You describe enabling leaders as those who direct and manage resources—that sounds like middle management. What makes that different?

DA: The enabling leader is helping the entrepreneurial leaders. Often the entrepreneurial leaders are a bit less experienced. They aren't always able to do everything that needs to be done, so enabling leaders step in to help them, not by ordering them around but by guiding and asking questions. That's a very different approach to leadership.

Are the questions like, "Which way do you think you should go?" "Where do you think the opportunity is?" or "Have you thought about talking to this person in this other department?"—that kind of stuff?

DA: Absolutely. It's not "do this" or "do that." It's "Have you thought about this?" or "Have you thought about that?" It's a much more open-ended approach that helps people develop their own independent way of thinking through a problem. Their jobs are not rigidly specified.

We often depict organizations as little boxes, where people inhabit a box that says you can do this, this, this, and this but nothing else, whereas enabling leaders are more fluid. They help in whatever way is needed. If they need to reinforce something about the culture, they can reinforce something about the culture. If they have to be more of an explainer of the organizational strategy, they can do that. If they have to roll up their sleeves and help out with what the team is doing, they can do that. It's a flexible, moving, emergent kind of relationship.

They are also connectors. Very often the enabling leaders have broad networks, and they travel. They know lots of different people. So, they're connecting the team—the entrepreneurial leaders and those teams to others in the organization to create what we call *creative collisions*, collisions with other forms of expertise that help innovation to grow.

KI: I would add to that: Imagine a traditional hierarchy that has the folks at the top and senior leadership. Then you've got middle management, which is like a layer of clay through which all the resources, approvals, and everything has to come up and down to the people who are doing the real work on the ground.

I've heard somebody describe that layer as permafrost.

KI: Permafrost. Beautiful. I love it. You get stuck at that layer of permafrost, and if you do drill through finally and get your message to senior management, then maybe your initiative and bright idea will get some play at some point. But by the time you get some budget or some attention, the moment may have passed, and your competitor has already moved.

We chose the name "enabling leaders" specifically because, as Deborah was describing, it's their job to make sure that the people who are on the front line have what they need to move forward with their ideas, to respond to customer concerns and problems and manufacturing issues. They are enabling the work of the front line to happen. It's not their job to restrict anything. They are to make sure that the flow of resources, attention, coaching, networking, and connections that those frontline leaders need happens.

Let's talk about the architecting leaders, which other places would call senior leaders or the executive suite. What makes these leaders special and different?

DA: First and foremost, the architecting leaders are creating the game board—the structures and culture necessary for the entrepreneurial leaders to be able to create and follow through on their ideas and for the enabling leaders to be able to do their jobs. They're the keepers of the culture. They are very mindful of what the values of the organization are and what the rules of engagement are.

Ironically, the architecting leaders are the ones who are designing change, yet they're in an organization where they're not dictating, because that's not how these organizations are run. So, first, before they're able to make change, they must have a reputation for being a great leader and caring about the company.

Second, they do a huge amount of consultation with members of the community to make sure that they understand why this change is necessary and why it's a good idea. They have to listen to people who don't agree with the change and respond. One funny example is a CEO who was so nervous about making a change from on high that it was taking a very long time. People in the organization were complaining, *OK, enough already. Just rip the Band-Aid off and let's get to it*, because of that necessary process.

KI: One of their functions is to knit together the emergent product ideas and new innovative ideas into a coherent organizational strategy. Architecting leaders have to be good "sense makers," to use a term that Deborah has been developing for a long time, in that the people who are at a more senior level have their eye on global, market, technological, and economic trends.

These aren't things that everybody in the organization is paying attention to. That information resides in their heads, and then they're watching all the innovative ideas that are bubbling up throughout the organization, and they're knitting all that together into an emergent, strategic process.

It can sound loosey-goosey to some people, but there's actually a lot of discipline in the way things are structured.

KI: Yeah, there is a lot of discipline. However, it's a different kind of discipline than the top people deciding. It's much more collective. It's much more inculcated in people's view of the strategic and culturally appropriate moves to make inside these organizations. And, because people have such high degrees of autonomy, good talent sticks to good ideas.

We've talked about this idea of prediction markets. If you have a good idea, that's going to attract talent. It goes along through the organization, and as you continue to talk about it—if you're a champion of a project and it's a good idea—people will flock to it.

If it's a bad idea, you're not going to be able to attract the kind of talent that you need to move it forward, because eventually people are going to see that it's not going to work for one reason or another. That's another way that this control happens through the process. Does talent stick to it, or not? Do people make autonomous choices to sign on to what you're selling or not?

So instead of deciding what the market forces are and then coming up with commands to respond to them, these architecting leaders are essentially letting the market forces work throughout the organization.

KI: Yes. That's the difference.

DA: This type of organization is not for the faint of heart. It's complicated and complex. One of the things that I've done, though, to help people navigate changing in this direction, is a little card exercise. There are 21 cards with one attribute of a nimble organization on every card. I ask people, "Pick the cards. What do you have now in your organization? What do you wish you had? And, of the things you wish you had, what are the top three things that you can do right now to get change started?"

Results of that exercise have been really fun. Sometimes people in an organization agree on what they have. Sometimes they don't. People from Google think they have everything, although not everything is as strong as they'd like it to be. Other people think they have none of those attributes. But the exercise is a way of getting people to think about what this whole system looks like and how they can start with small steps to make the changes needed to move in a new direction.

Is nimble leadership possible anywhere?

KI: A number of organizations are experimenting with this way of working. A successful Dutch bank called ING has shifted to "an agile way of working," which looks very similar to what we've described in our piece. They reorganized themselves into 350 nine-person interdisciplinary teams, and they have mechanisms to make the connections across those teams. Leaders there say, "Yeah, I was kind of a control freak and I'm finding this way of working is challenging me, because I have to let go and give people more autonomy."

But the reports from this bank are that it's a lot more fun to work there. They're much faster at solving customer problems. It's a bank. They're dealing in mortgage securities and things like that. So, if a bank can do it, it's probably transferrable to a lot of other industries beyond the product innovation space.

DA: In the HBR article, we also talk about Satya Nadella and the change at Microsoft. That's a company of 125,000 people, and it is an example of where you don't have to take on the entire system that we're talking about, but there are ways to move your organization in that direction.

Nadella did somewhat of a turnaround at Microsoft. He came in, in 2014, and the organization was kind of a hierarchy and pecking order, where different groups were at each other all the time. That was stifling collaboration, creativity, and innovation. In his mind, this was not how the organization was going to grow and develop. So, he came in with some of the similar kinds of steps that we saw in the companies we've been describing. He brought in a new game board, a new senior leadership team. They got rid of a stacked-ranking performance-management system, and instead moved toward more of a coaching and developing approach like you would find at Gore or at PARC.

It also gave more authority to managers below to change compensation and a lot of those things that had been more centralized.

DA: Absolutely. They were giving people more freedom to do the things they needed to do to keep that innovation flowing. They also refocused the culture on something called the *growth mindset*, which is built off the research of Carol Dweck, a psychologist at Stanford. She had the idea that people are not fixed in what they can learn and how they can develop; rather, they can grow. They can always learn more. They can pick themselves up from failure and say, *What can I learn from this and how can I do it better the next time?* as opposed to stopping right there.

There's not a culture of blame. It's a culture of, *How do we do it better? How can we innovate next time?* Nadella has worked hard to inculcate that notion of a growth mindset within the entire company. He's taken a number of steps that bring this closer to the model we've identified.

———————

Adapted from "The 3 Types of Leaders of Innovative Companies" on
HBR IdeaCast (podcast), July 9, 2019.

CHAPTER TWENTY-FOUR

Is Your Company Ready for a Zero-Carbon Future?

by Nigel Topping

There is growing public demand for a rapid transition to a zero-carbon economy. But global protests and youth climate strikes are not enough to create change alone. Companies need to take action. Beyond the very serious threats the current crisis poses to our planet, organizations are increasingly seeing the material risks it poses to their business.

U.S. financial regulator Rostin Behnam likened the financial risks from climate change to those caused by the mortgage meltdown that led to the financial crisis of 2008.[1] And recently, AT&T—which has already lost $847 million to climate disasters—announced that they will be paying the U.S. Department of Energy to track climate-related events that could damage their infrastructure in coming years.

Businesses that bake carbon reduction into their strategies will not only reduce these kinds of risks from affecting their organizations, they will see significant benefits as well: increased innovation, competitiveness, risk management, and growth.

More than 900 global companies representing over $17.6 trillion in market cap are already ensuring that their business strategies are built for growth and emissions reductions through the We Mean Business Take Action campaign. (We Mean Business is a nonprofit coalition of which I am CEO.) This includes over 560 companies that have committed to set ambitious science-based emission reduction targets, and over 175 that have committed to switching to 100% renewable electricity. Beyond that, companies are beginning to use their influence to speed an economy-wide transition by supporting climate policies targeting net-zero emissions by 2050. Others are demanding climate action throughout their supply chains.

Your organization also has a responsibility to become a part of the solution. Failing to do so will impact your ability to attract talent, manage risk, and innovate for growth. Below are a few critical steps you can take to set your business up for success in a zero-carbon future.

Align Your Company with the Paris Agreement

The science has never been clearer. The 2018 IPCC special report on the impacts of global warming of 1.5°C highlights the importance of aligning emission reductions with the goals of the Paris Agreement and striving for net-zero emissions by 2050—at the latest.[2]

Science-based greenhouse gas emission reduction targets are the gold standard for companies setting emissions reduction goals, both in their direct operations and across their value chains. It is now possible for organizations to set targets that are in line with the level of decarbonization required to limit global warming to 1.5°C. These targets, as ambitious as they are, are vital to reaching net-zero emissions by 2050 and should be the ultimate goal for all companies.

If you're hesitant, consider the risks of not acting: The world's largest sovereign wealth fund—Norway's $1 trillion Government Pension Fund—confirmed it will divest some $13 billion of fossil fuel–related investments. This is one of many signals that there will continue to be a global move away from fossil fuels, indicating the need for companies to incorporate the emissions impact of their assets into their investment plans, or be left with assets that will rapidly lose value. Science-based targets will provide you with a way to future-proof your business plans by ensuring that all strategic decisions incorporate climate risk and opportunity analysis. This will simultaneously drive zero-carbon innovation and help you guard against stranded assets.

To date, the majority of the 560+ companies that have jumped on board report improvements to brand reputation and investor confidence. Consumers and investors are increasingly aware of the effects their choices have on the environment. Companies that commit to these targets, then, are gaining a competitive advantage in multiple areas of their business.

Join a Transformative Initiative

Committing to achieving net-zero emissions by 2050 is no doubt an ambitious goal. There are several initiatives companies can turn to for support.

The Climate Group's global EP100 initiative is a good place to start. It brings together a growing group of energy-smart companies committed to using energy more productively with the goal of lowering greenhouse gas emissions and accelerating a clean economy. As part of the EP100 initiative, companies can commit to doubling energy productivity and to net-zero carbon buildings through the Net Zero Carbon Buildings Commitment.

Companies engaged in this initiative report cost savings as well as emissions reductions. For example, energy productivity improvements at Wisconsin-based Johnson Controls contributed to a 41% reduction in the company's greenhouse gas emissions intensity and over $100 million in annual energy savings.

In addition, collaborative initiatives, like the Low Carbon Technology Partnerships (LCTPi), led by the World Business Council for Sustainable Development, bring companies together to generate shared natural climate solutions across the value chains in specific business sectors. LCTPi focuses primarily on the agricultural, energy, and transport industries. These kinds of initiatives provide businesses with greater access to resources and innovations that can help them develop new markets.

Commit to 100%

Committing to doing something completely, to doing it 100%, leaves no room for excuses and will send a powerful signal to your stakeholders. If you commit to switch 100% of your electricity consumption to renewable sources, as opposed to 20% or even 50%, your objective will be clear to everyone inside and outside of your organization.

Over 175 of the world's most influential companies have already made this commitment through the global corporate leadership initiative, RE100. When they have made the full switch to 100% renewable electricity, these RE100 companies will be generating demand for over 184 Terawatt-hours (TWh) of renewable electricity annually, more than enough to power Argentina and Portugal. This is driving up demand for renewable electricity and creating a shift in demand patterns away from fossil fuels across the global power system.

Google, Autodesk, Elopak, and Interface are just a few of the companies that have already achieved their goal and are now powered by 100% renewable energy. Not only are these organizations creating change, they are saving money as the price of wind and solar continues to drop, and they are demonstrating to their stakeholders—including investors, customers, and policy makers—that they see a future in which businesses are powered by renewables.

The same efforts are being made in the transportation sector. With air quality legislation expected to increasingly restrict polluting vehicles in cities around the world, companies are realizing that it pays to get ahead and make the transition to electric vehicles (EVs). More and more businesses are committing to transition their auto fleets through the global initiative, EV100. LeasePlan, a car leasing company with 1.8 million vehicles on the road, is aiming to transition its employee fleet to 100% EVs by 2021—one step toward their larger goal of reaching net-zero emissions by 2030. In addition to the environmental benefits, their EV integration could dramatically reduce the costs of fleets as charging an electric vehicle is cheaper than buying gas, and maintenance costs are also lower. Deutsche Post DHL is already seeing 60%–70% savings on fuel costs and 60%–80% savings on maintenance from its StreetScooter EVs.

Review Your Industry Groups

Industry groups look out for companies' strategic interests and are based on common lines of business. If the groups that your company is a member of are not taking serious action to address the climate crisis, whole industries are at risk of getting left behind once we do reach net-zero emissions. Don't let outdated lobbying positions hold your company back.

The time has come for businesses to review their membership of trade groups and make sure that their climate action goals are aligned. If they aren't, use your company's influence to help change the group's position, or leave the group to show policy makers where you stand. You won't be alone in doing so.

Volkswagen put VDA, the German carmaker lobby group, on notice that it will leave unless it adjusts its position on the auto-sector transition and starts supporting EVs. In addition, Shell is walking away from the American Fuel and Petrochemical Manufacturers association over its lack of support for the Paris Agreement. Finally, Unilever CEO Alan Jope has requested that all trade bodies the company is associated with confirm that their lobbying positions on climate are consistent with Unilever's own goals.

Get Smart on Climate Governance

Your plans to tackle climate change will only work if your company has the right governance in place to support it. This includes equipping board and management teams with knowledge and skills that will help them recognize the risks and opportunities posed by the climate crisis.

If you are running a global food company, for example, ask: Is my organization up to date with the findings of the EAT Lancet report? Do we have board expertise on the societal shift away from meat, and is our corporate venturing aligned with this shift? Can we explain to staff and customers how our business model is evolving to protect nature rather than harm it?

To help in this effort, Ceres and The B Team have published a primer on climate competent boards, which also focuses on the adaptability and relevance of the Task Force on Climate-related Financial Disclosure (TCFD) recommendations. These guidelines emphasize the financial risks associated with climate as well as how this informs all business strategy.

Speak Up in Support of Climate Policy

Your company can inspire legislators to create more drastic and ambitious climate policies through face-to-face dialogue. This was highly effective during the negotiations of the Paris Agreement in 2015, when representatives from leading organizations were able to sit down with policy makers and talk openly about the challenges and opportunities different policies would bring to their businesses. The conversation needs to continue.

Many businesses are well-positioned to help inform ongoing policy discussions based on their experience with emissions reduction plans. Those that have acted to help improve the state of the climate emergency have the unique ability to point to the progress made through their efforts, demonstrating that climate action is feasible and that inaction is costly.

In Japan, 93 businesses—representing sales of approximately $670 billion and electricity consumption of 36 TWh—called upon the Japanese government to include a goal of net-zero emissions domestically by 2050. Since then, Japan's cabinet has outlined its emissions reduction strategy, which aims to transition the economy to being "carbon neutral" close to that time frame. Hundreds of businesses also called upon the EU to commit to net-zero GHG emissions by 2050, at the latest. The UK government has already announced it is legislating for net-zero emissions by 2050, and pressure is mounting on the EU to follow suit.

Communicate Your Purpose

The more businesses that share the efforts they are making through their reporting and external communications, the more visible they will be to policy makers, customers, and employees. Setting this example can help give those people the confidence they need to increase their own climate ambition and help drive the market shift required to spark competition and innovation.

Perhaps the largest benefit of this is that it has the potential to help put into action long-term climate policies that provide businesses with the clarity they need to decarbonize products and services in faster and smarter ways.

Making your efforts visible to the public will also help your company attract and retain new generations of talent. Some 75% of millennials expect employers to address the climate crisis, and recent research suggests that Generation Z takes an equally strong stance on climate issues.[3]

Companies looking to harness the benefits of climate action need to step up and commit to taking these crucial steps—and don't forget to shout about it when you do. Inspiring others to work toward a zero-carbon future is the best way to drive innovation and ensure that you succeed while others fall by the wayside. We all have a responsibility to tackle the climate crisis and to help drive toward a solution that works for our economies and our planet.

NOTES

1. Coral Davenport, "Climate Change Poses Major Risks to Financial Markets, Regulator Warns," *New York Times,* June 11, 2019, https://www.nytimes.com/2019/06/11/climate/climate-financial-market-risk.html.

2. Intergovernmental Panel on Climate Change, "Special Report: Global Warming of 1.5°C," 2019, https://www.ipcc.ch/sr15/.

3. Glassdoor Team, "New Survey Reveals 75% of Millennials Expect Employers to Take a Stand on Social Issues," Glassdoor, September 25, 2017, https://www.glassdoor.com/blog/corporate-social-responsibility/; Kim Parker, Nikki Graf, and Ruth Igielnik, "Generation Z Looks a Lot Like Millennials on Key Social and Political Issues," Pew Research Center, January 17, 2019, https://www.pewsocialtrends.org/2019/01/17/generation-z-looks-a-lot-like-millennials-on-key-social-and-political-issues/.

Adapted from content posted on hbr.org,
June 21, 2019 (product #H050QH).

— 2008 —

CHAPTER TWENTY-FIVE

Design Thinking

by Tim Brown

Thomas Edison created the electric light bulb and then wrapped an entire industry around it. The light bulb is most often thought of as his signature invention, but Edison understood that the bulb was little more than a parlor trick without a system of electric power generation and transmission to make it truly useful. So he created that, too.

Thus Edison's genius lay in his ability to conceive of a fully developed marketplace, not simply a discrete device. He was able to envision how people would want to use what he made, and he engineered toward that insight. He wasn't always prescient (he originally believed the phonograph would be used mainly as a business machine for recording and replaying dictation), but he invariably gave great consideration to users' needs and preferences.

Edison's approach was an early example of what is now called "design thinking"—a methodology that imbues the full spectrum of innovation activities with a human-centered design ethos. By this I mean that innovation is powered by a thorough understanding, through direct observation, of what people want and need in their lives and what they like or dislike about the way particular products are made, packaged, marketed, sold, and supported.

Many people believe that Edison's greatest invention was the modern R&D laboratory and methods of experimental investigation. Edison wasn't a narrowly specialized scientist but a broad generalist with a shrewd business sense. In his Menlo Park, New Jersey, laboratory he surrounded himself with gifted tinkerers, improvisers, and experimenters. Indeed, he broke the mold of the "lone genius inventor" by creating a team-based approach to innovation. Although Edison biographers write of the camaraderie enjoyed by this merry band, the process also featured endless rounds of trial and error—the "99% perspiration" in Edison's famous definition of genius. His approach was intended not to validate preconceived hypotheses but to help experimenters learn something new from each iterative stab. Innovation is hard work; Edison made it a profession that blended art, craft, science, business savvy, and an astute understanding of customers and markets.

Design thinking is a lineal descendant of that tradition. Put simply, it is a discipline that uses the designer's sensibility and methods to match people's needs with what is technologically feasible and what a viable business strategy can convert into customer value and market opportunity. Like Edison's painstaking innovation process, it often entails a great deal of perspiration.

I believe that design thinking has much to offer a business world in which most management ideas and best practices are freely available to be copied and exploited. Leaders now look to innovation as a principal source of differentiation and competitive advantage; they would do well to incorporate design thinking into all phases of the process.

Getting Beneath the Surface

Historically, design has been treated as a downstream step in the development process—the point where designers, who have played no earlier role in the substantive work of innovation, come along and put a beautiful wrapper around the idea. To be sure, this approach has stimulated market growth in many areas by making new products and technologies aesthetically attractive and therefore more desirable to consumers or by enhancing brand perception through smart, evocative advertising and communication strategies. During the latter half of the twentieth century design became an increasingly valuable competitive asset in, for example, the consumer electronics, automotive, and consumer packaged goods industries. But in most others it remained a late-stage add-on.

Now, however, rather than asking designers to make an already developed idea more attractive to consumers, companies are asking them to create ideas that better meet consumers' needs and desires. The former role is tactical, and results in limited value creation; the latter is strategic, and leads to dramatic new forms of value.

Moreover, as economies in the developed world shift from industrial manufacturing to knowledge work and service delivery, innovation's terrain is expanding. Its objectives are no longer just physical products; they are new sorts of processes, services, IT-powered interactions, entertainments, and ways of communicating and collaborating—exactly the kinds of human-centered activities in which design thinking can make a decisive difference. (See the sidebar "A Design Thinker's Personality Profile.")

Consider the large health care provider Kaiser Permanente, which sought to improve the overall quality of both patients' and medical practitioners' experiences. Businesses in the service sector can often make significant innovations on the front lines of service creation and delivery. By teaching design-thinking techniques to nurses, doctors, and administrators, Kaiser hoped to inspire its practitioners to contribute new ideas. Over the course of several months Kaiser teams participated in workshops with the help of my firm, IDEO, and a group of Kaiser coaches. These workshops led to a portfolio of innovations, many of which are being rolled out across the company.

One of them—a project to reengineer nursing-staff shift changes at four Kaiser hospitals—perfectly illustrates both the broader nature of innovation "products" and the value of a holistic design approach. The core project team included a strategist (formerly a nurse), an organizational-development specialist, a technology expert, a process designer, a union representative, and designers from IDEO. This group worked with innovation teams of frontline practitioners in each of the four hospitals.

A Design Thinker's Personality Profile

Contrary to popular opinion, you don't need weird shoes or a black turtleneck to be a design thinker. Nor are design thinkers necessarily created only by design schools, even though most professionals have had some kind of design training. My experience is that many people outside professional design have a natural aptitude for design thinking, which the right development and experiences can unlock. Here, as a starting point, are some of the characteristics to look for in design thinkers:

Empathy

They can imagine the world from multiple perspectives—those of colleagues, clients, end users, and customers (current and prospective). By taking a "people first" approach, design thinkers can imagine solutions that are inherently desirable and meet explicit or latent needs. Great design thinkers observe the world in minute detail. They notice things that others do not and use their insights to inspire innovation.

Integrative Thinking

They not only rely on analytical processes (those that produce either/or choices) but also exhibit the ability to see all of the salient—and sometimes contradictory—

During the earliest phase of the project, the core team collaborated with nurses to identify a number of problems in the way shift changes occurred. Chief among these was the fact that nurses routinely spent the first 45 minutes of each shift at the nurses' station debriefing the departing shift about the status of patients. Their methods of information exchange were different in every hospital, ranging from recorded dictation to face-to-face conversations. And they compiled the information they needed to serve patients in a variety of ways—scrawling quick notes on the back of any available scrap of paper, for example, or even on their scrubs. Despite a significant investment of time, the nurses often failed to learn some of the things that mattered most to patients, such as how they had fared during the previous shift, which family members were with them, and whether or not certain tests or therapies had been administered. For many patients, the team learned, each shift change aspects of a confounding problem and create novel solutions that go beyond and dramatically improve on existing alternatives. (See Roger Martin's *The Opposable Mind: How Successful Leaders Win Through Integrative Thinking*.)

Optimism

They assume that no matter how challenging the constraints of a given problem, at least one potential solution is better than the existing alternatives.

Experimentalism

Significant innovations don't come from incremental tweaks. Design thinkers pose questions and explore constraints in creative ways that proceed in entirely new directions.

Collaboration

The increasing complexity of products, services, and experiences has replaced the myth of the lone creative genius with the reality of the enthusiastic interdisciplinary collaborator. The best design thinkers don't simply work alongside other disciplines; many of them have significant experience in more than one. At IDEO we employ people who are engineers *and* marketers, anthropologists *and* industrial designers, architects *and* psychologists.

felt like a hole in their care. Using the insights gleaned from observing these important times of transition, the innovation teams explored potential solutions through brainstorming and rapid prototyping. (Prototypes of a service innovation will of course not be physical, but they must be tangible. Because pictures help us understand what is learned through prototyping, we often videotape the performance of prototyped services, as we did at Kaiser.)

Prototyping doesn't have to be complex and expensive. In another health care project, IDEO helped a group of surgeons develop a new device for sinus surgery. As the surgeons described the ideal physical characteristics of the instrument, one of the designers grabbed a whiteboard marker, a film canister, and a clothespin and taped them together. "Do you mean like this?" he asked. With his rudimentary prototype in hand, the surgeons were able to be much more precise about what the ultimate design should accomplish.

— 2015 —

How Indra Nooyi Turned Design Thinking into Strategy

An interview with Indra K. Nooyi by Adi Ignatius

Just a few years ago, it wasn't clear whether Indra Nooyi would survive as Pepsi-Co's CEO. Many investors saw Pepsi as a bloated giant whose top brands were losing market share. And they were critical of Nooyi's shift toward a more health-oriented overall product line. Prominent activist investor Nelson Peltz fought hard to split the company in two.

These days Nooyi exudes confidence. The company has enjoyed steady revenue growth during her nine years in the top job, and Pepsi's stock price is rising again after several flat years. Peltz even agreed to a truce in return for a board seat for one of his allies.

All of this frees Nooyi to focus on what she says is now driving innovation in the company: design thinking. In 2012 she brought in Mauro Porcini as Pepsi's first-ever chief design officer. Now, Nooyi says, "design" has a voice in nearly every important decision that the company makes.

ADI IGNATIUS: *What problem were you trying to solve by making PepsiCo more design-driven?*

INDRA NOOYI: As CEO, I visit a market every week to see what we look like on the shelves. I always ask myself—not as a CEO but as a mom—"What products really speak to me?" The shelves just seem more and more cluttered, so I thought we had to rethink our innovation process and design experiences for our consumers—from conception to what's on the shelf.

How did you begin to drive that change?

First, I gave each of my direct reports an empty photo album and a camera. I asked them to take pictures of anything they thought represented good design.

After six weeks, only a few people returned the albums. Some had their wives take pictures. Many did nothing at all. They didn't know what design was. Every time I tried to talk about design within the company, people would refer to packaging: "Should we go to a different blue?" It was like putting lipstick on a pig, as opposed to redesigning the pig itself. I realized we needed to bring a designer into the company.

How easy was it to find Mauro Porcini?

We did a search, and we saw that he'd achieved this kind of success at 3M. So we brought him in to talk about our vision. He said he wanted resources, a design studio, and a seat at the table. We gave him all of that. Now our teams are pushing design through the entire system, from product creation, to packaging and labeling, to how a product looks on the shelf, to how consumers interact with it.

What's your definition of good design?

For me, a well-designed product is one you fall in love with. Or you hate. It may be polarizing, but it has to provoke a real reaction. Ideally, it's a product you want to engage with in the future, rather than just "Yeah, I bought it, and I ate it."

You say it's not just about packaging, but a lot of what you're talking about seems to be that.

It's much more than packaging. We had to rethink the entire experience, from conception to what's on the shelf to the postproduct experience. Let's take Pepsi Spire, our new touchscreen fountain machine. Other companies with dispensing machines have focused on adding a few more buttons and combinations of flavors. Our design guys essentially said that we're talking about a fundamentally different interaction between consumer and machine. We basically have a gigantic iPad on a futuristic machine that talks to you and invites you to interact with it. It tracks what you buy so that in the future, when you swipe your ID, it reminds you of the flavor combinations you tried last time and suggests new ones. It displays beautiful shots of the product, so when you add lime or cranberry, it actually shows those flavors being added—you *experience* the infusion of the flavor, as opposed to merely hitting a button and out comes the finished product.

Have you developed other notable design-led innovations?

We're working on new products for women. Our old approach was "shrink it or pink it." We'd put Doritos, say, in a pink Susan G. Komen bag and say it's for women. That's fine, but there's more to how women like to snack.

OK, how do women like to snack?

When men finish a snack bag, they pour what's left into their mouths. Women don't do that. And they worry about how much the product may stain—they

(continued)

How Indra Nooyi Turned Design
Thinking into Strategy (*continued*)

won't rub it on a chair, which a lot of guys do. In China, we've introduced a stacked chip that comes in a plastic tray inside a canister. When a woman wants to snack, she can open her drawer and eat from the tray. When she's done, she can push it back in. The chip is also less noisy to eat: Women don't want people to hear them crunching away.

Basically, you're paying a lot more attention to user experience.

Definitely. In the past, user experience wasn't part of our lexicon. Focusing on crunch, taste, and everything else now pushes us to rethink shape, packaging, form, and function. All of that has consequences for what machinery we put in place—to produce, say, a plastic tray instead of a flex bag. We're forcing the design thinking way back in the supply chain.

When I picture design thinking, I think about rapid prototyping and testing. Is that part of what you're trying to do?

Not so much in the U.S., but China and Japan are lead horses for that process—test, prove, launch. If you launch quickly, you have more failures, but that's OK because the cost of failure in those markets is low. In the U.S., we tend to follow very organized processes and then launch. The China-Japan model may have to come to the U.S. at some point.

Isn't this model already established in the U.S., or at least in Silicon Valley?

Lots of small companies take this approach, and for them the cost of failure is acceptable. We're more cautious, especially when playing with big brands. Line extensions are fine: If you launch a flavor of Doritos that doesn't work, you just pull it. But if you launch a new product, you want to make sure you've tested it enough. In Japan, we launch a new version of Pepsi every three months—green, pink, blue. We just launched cucumber-flavored Pepsi. In three months it either works or we pull it and go to the next product.

Is your design approach giving Pepsi competitive advantage?

We have to do two things as a company: Keep our top line growing in the mid-single digits and grow our bottom line faster than the top. Line extensions keep the base growing. And then we're always looking for hero products—the two or three big products that will drive the top line significantly in a particular country or segment. Mountain Dew Kickstart is one of those. It's a completely different product: higher juice content, fewer calories, new flavors. We thought about this innovation differently. In the past we just would have created new flavors of Mountain Dew. But Kickstart comes in a slim can and doesn't look or taste like the old Mountain Dew. It's bringing new users into the franchise: women who say, "Hey, this is an 80-calorie product with juice in a package I can walk around with." It has generated more than $200 million in two years, which in our business is hard to do.

Is this an example of design thinking, or just part of the innovation process?

There's a fine line between innovation and design. Ideally, design leads to innovation and innovation demands design. We're just getting started. Innovation accounted for 9% of our net revenue last year. I'd like to raise that to the mid-teens, because I think the marketplace is getting more creative. To get there, we'll have to be willing to tolerate more failure and shorter cycles of adaptation.

Excerpted from "How Indra Nooyi Turned Design
Thinking into Strategy," from *Harvard Business Review*,
September 2015 (product #R1509F).

Prototypes should command only as much time, effort, and investment as are needed to generate useful feedback and evolve an idea. The more "finished" a prototype seems, the less likely its creators will be to pay attention to and profit from feedback. The goal of prototyping isn't to finish. It is to learn about the strengths and weaknesses of the idea and to identify new directions that further prototypes might take.

The design that emerged for shift changes had nurses passing on information in front of the patient rather than at the nurses' station. In only a week the team built a working prototype that included new procedures and some simple software with which nurses could call up previous shift-change notes and add new ones. They could input patient information throughout a shift rather than scrambling at the end to pass it on. The software collated the data in a simple format customized for each nurse at the start of a shift. The result was both higher-quality knowledge transfer and reduced prep time, permitting much earlier and better-informed contact with patients.

As Kaiser measured the impact of this change over time, it learned that the mean interval between a nurse's arrival and first interaction with a patient had been more than halved, adding a huge amount of nursing time across the four hospitals. Perhaps just as important was the effect on the quality of the nurses' work experience. One nurse commented, "I'm an hour ahead, and I've only been here 45 minutes." Another said, "[This is the] first time I've ever made it out of here at the end of my shift."

Thus did a group of nurses significantly improve their patients' experience while also improving their own job satisfaction and productivity. By applying a human-centered design methodology, they were able to create a relatively small process innovation that produced an outsize impact. The new shift changes are being rolled out across the Kaiser system, and the capacity to reliably record critical patient information is being integrated into an electronic medical records initiative at the company.

What might happen at Kaiser if every nurse, doctor, and administrator in every hospital felt empowered to tackle problems the way this group did? To find out, Kaiser has created the Garfield Innovation Center, which is run by Kaiser's original core team and acts as a consultancy to the entire organization. The center's mission is to pursue innovation that enhances the patient experience and, more broadly, to envision Kaiser's "hospital of the future." It is introducing tools for design thinking across the Kaiser system.

How Design Thinking Happens

The myth of creative genius is resilient: We believe that great ideas pop fully formed out of brilliant minds, in feats of imagination well beyond the abilities of mere mortals. But what the Kaiser nursing team accomplished was neither a sudden breakthrough nor the lightning strike of genius; it was the result of hard work augmented by a creative human-centered discovery process and followed by iterative cycles of prototyping, testing, and refinement.

The design process is best described metaphorically as a system of spaces rather than a predefined series of orderly steps. The spaces demarcate different sorts of related activities that together form the continuum of innovation. Design thinking can feel chaotic to those experiencing it for the first time. But over the life of a project participants come to see—as they did at Kaiser—that the process makes sense and achieves results, even though its architecture differs from the linear, milestone-based processes typical of other kinds of business activities.

Design projects must ultimately pass through three spaces (see figure 25-1). We label these "inspiration," for the circumstances (be they a problem, an opportunity, or both) that motivate the search for solutions; "ideation," for the process of generating, developing, and testing ideas that may lead to solutions; and "implementation," for the charting of a path to market. Projects will loop back through these spaces—particularly the first two—more than once as ideas are refined and new directions taken.

Sometimes the trigger for a project is leadership's recognition of a serious change in business fortunes. In 2004 Shimano, a Japanese manufacturer of bicycle components, faced flattening growth in its traditional high-end road-racing and mountain-bike segments in the United States. The company had always relied on technology innovations to drive its growth and naturally tried to predict where the next one might come from. This time Shimano thought a high-end casual bike that appealed to boomers would be an interesting area to explore. IDEO was invited to collaborate on the project.

During the inspiration phase, an interdisciplinary team of IDEO and Shimano people—designers, behavioral scientists, marketers, and engineers—worked to identify appropriate constraints for the project. The team began with a hunch that it should focus more broadly than on the high-end market, which might prove to be neither the only nor even the best source of new growth. So it set out to learn why 90% of American adults don't ride bikes. Looking

FIGURE 25-1

Inspiration, ideation, implementation

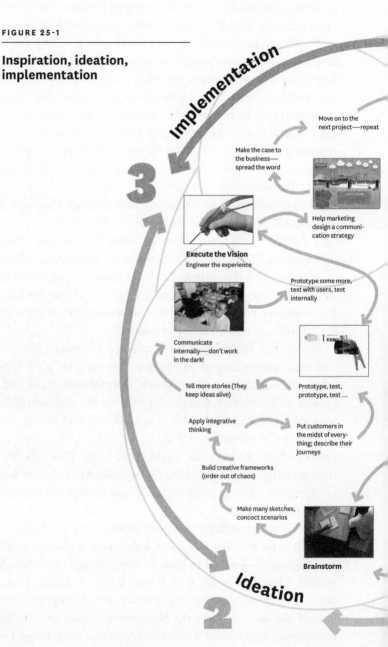

Implementation

3

Move on to the
next project—repeat

Make the case to
the business—
spread the word

Help marketing
design a communi-
cation strategy

Execute the Vision
Engineer the experience

Prototype some more,
test with users, test
internally

Communicate
internally—don't work
in the dark!

Tell more stories (They
keep ideas alive)

Prototype, test,
prototype, test ...

Apply integrative
thinking

Put customers in
the midst of every-
thing; describe their
journeys

Build creative frameworks
(order out of chaos)

Make many sketches,
concoct scenarios

Brainstorm

Ideation

2

Inspiration

Expect Success
Build implementation
resources into your plan

What's the business prob-
lem? Where's the oppor-
tunity? What has changed
(or soon may change)?

Look at the world:
Observe what people do,
how they think, what they
need and want

Involve many disciplines
from the start (e.g., engineering and marketing)

What are the business constraints (time, lack of resources,
impoverished customer base,
shrinking market)?

Pay close attention to
"extreme" users such as
children or the elderly

Have a project room
where you can share
insights, tell stories

How can new
technology help?

Are valuable ideas, as-
sets, and expertise hiding
inside the business?

Organize information and
synthesize possibilities
(Tell more stories!)

for new ways to think about the problem, the team members spent time with all kinds of consumers. They discovered that nearly everyone they met rode a bike as a child and had happy memories of doing so. They also discovered that many Americans are intimidated by cycling today—by the retail experience (including the young, Lycra-clad athletes who serve as sales staff in most independent bike stores); by the complexity and cost of the bikes, accessories, and specialized clothing; by the danger of cycling on roads not designed for bicycles; and by the demands of maintaining a technically sophisticated bike that is ridden infrequently.

This human-centered exploration—which took its insights from people outside Shimano's core customer base—led to the realization that a whole new category of bicycling might be able to reconnect American consumers to their experiences as children while also dealing with the root causes of their feelings of intimidation—thus revealing a large untapped market.

The design team, responsible for every aspect of what was envisioned as a holistic experience, came up with the concept of "Coasting" (see figure 25-2). Coasting would aim to entice lapsed bikers into an activity that was simple, straightforward, and fun. Coasting bikes, built more for pleasure than for sport, would have no controls on the handlebars, no cables snaking along the frame. As on the earliest bikes many of us rode, the brakes would be applied by backpedaling. With the help of an onboard computer, a minimalist three gears would shift automatically as the bicycle gained speed or slowed. The bikes would feature comfortably padded seats, be easy to operate, and require relatively little maintenance.

Three major manufacturers—Trek, Raleigh, and Giant—developed new bikes incorporating innovative components from Shimano. But the design team didn't stop with the bike itself. In-store retailing strategies were created for independent bike dealers, in part to alleviate the discomfort that biking novices felt in stores designed to serve enthusiasts. The team developed a brand that identified Coasting as a way to enjoy life. ("Chill. Explore. Dawdle. Lollygag. First one there's a rotten egg.") And it designed a public

FIGURE 25-2

Coasting

*A **sketch** (top, seat plus helmet storage) and a **prototype** (middle) show elements of Coasting bicycles. Shimano's Coasting **website** (bottom) points users to safe bike paths.*

relations campaign—in collaboration with local governments and cycling organizations—that identified safe places to ride.

Although many others became involved in the project when it reached the implementation phase, the application of design thinking in the earliest stages of innovation is what led to this complete solution. Indeed, the single thing one would have expected the design team to be responsible for—the look of the bikes—was intentionally deferred to later in the development process, when the team created a reference design to inspire the bike companies' own design teams. After a successful launch in 2007, seven more bicycle manufacturers signed up to produce Coasting bikes in 2008.

Taking a Systems View

Many of the world's most successful brands create breakthrough ideas that are inspired by a deep understanding of consumers' lives and use the principles of design to innovate and build value. Sometimes innovation has to account for vast differences in cultural and socioeconomic conditions. In such cases design thinking can suggest creative alternatives to the assumptions made in developed societies.

India's Aravind Eye Care System is probably the world's largest provider of eye care. From April 2006 to March 2007 Aravind served more than 2.3 million patients and performed more than 270,000 surgeries. Founded in 1976 by Dr. G. Venkataswamy, Aravind has as its mission nothing less than the eradication of needless blindness among India's population, including the rural poor, through the effective delivery of superior ophthalmic care (see figure 25-3). (One of the company's slogans is "Quality is for everyone.") From 11 beds in Dr. Venkataswamy's home, Aravind has grown to encompass five hospitals (three others are under Aravind management), a plant that manufactures ophthalmic products, a research foundation, and a training center.

Aravind's execution of its mission and model is in some respects reminiscent of Edison's holistic concept of electric power delivery.

FIGURE 25-3

Aravind

*Aravind's outreach to rural patients frequently brings basic **diagnostic tools** (top and center) and an advanced satellite-linked **telemedicine truck** (bottom) to remote areas of India.*

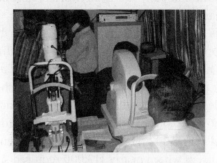

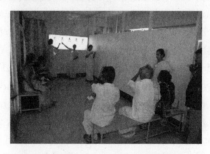

The challenge the company faces is logistic: how best to deliver eye care to populations far removed from the urban centers where Aravind's hospitals are located. Aravind calls itself an "eye care system" for a reason: Its business goes beyond ophthalmic care per se to transmit expert practice to populations that have historically lacked access. The company saw its network of hospitals as a beginning rather than an end.

Much of its innovative energy has focused on bringing both preventive care and diagnostic screening to the countryside. Since 1990 Aravind has held "eye camps" in India's rural areas, in an effort to register patients, administer eye exams, teach eye care, and identify people who may require surgery or advanced diagnostic services or who have conditions that warrant monitoring.

In 2006 and early 2007 Aravind eye camps screened more than 500,000 patients, of whom nearly 113,000 required surgery. Access to transportation is a common problem in rural areas, so the company provides buses that take patients needing further treatment to one of its urban facilities and then home again. Over the years it has bolstered its diagnostic capabilities in the field with telemedicine trucks, which enable doctors back at Aravind's hospitals to participate in care decisions. In recent years Aravind's analysis of its screening data has led to specialized eye camps for certain demographic groups, such as school-age children and industrial and government workers; the company also holds camps specifically to screen for eye diseases associated with diabetes. All these services are free for the roughly 60% of patients who cannot afford to pay.

In developing its system of care, Aravind has consistently exhibited many characteristics of design thinking. It has used as a creative springboard two constraints: the poverty and remoteness of its clientele and its own lack of access to expensive solutions. For example, a pair of intraocular lenses made in the West costs $200, which severely limited the number of patients Aravind could help. Rather than try to persuade suppliers to change the way they did things, Aravind built its own solution: a manufacturing plant in the basement of one of its hospitals. It eventually discovered that it could use relatively inexpensive technology to produce lenses for $4 a pair.

Throughout its history—defined by the constraints of poverty, ignorance, and an enormous unmet need—Aravind has built a systemic solution to a complex social and medical problem.

Getting Back to the Surface

I argued earlier that design thinking can lead to innovation that goes beyond aesthetics, but that doesn't mean that form and aesthetics are unimportant. Magazines like to publish photographs of the newest, coolest products for a reason: They are sexy and appeal to our emotions. Great design satisfies both our needs and our desires. Often the emotional connection to a product or an image is what engages us in the first place. Time and again we see successful products that were not necessarily the first to market but were the first to appeal to us emotionally *and* functionally. In other words, they do the job and we love them. The iPod was not the first MP3 player, but it was the first to be delightful. Target's products appeal emotionally through design and functionally through price—simultaneously.

This idea will grow ever more important in the future. As Daniel Pink writes in his book *A Whole New Mind,* "Abundance has satisfied, and even over-satisfied, the material needs of millions—boosting the significance of beauty and emotion and accelerating individuals' search for meaning." As more of our basic needs are met, we increasingly expect sophisticated experiences that are emotionally satisfying and meaningful. These experiences will not be simple products. They will be complex combinations of products, services, spaces, and information. They will be the ways we get educated, the ways we are entertained, the ways we stay healthy, the ways we share and communicate. Design thinking is a tool for imagining these experiences as well as giving them a desirable form.

How to Make Design Thinking
Part of the Innovation Drill

- **Begin at the beginning.** Involve design thinkers at the very start of the innovation process, before any direction has been set. Design thinking will help you explore more ideas more quickly than you could otherwise.

- **Take a human-centered approach.** Along with business and technology considerations, innovation should factor in human behavior, needs, and preferences. Human-centered design thinking—especially when it includes research based on direct observation—will capture unexpected insights and produce innovation that more precisely reflects what consumers want.

- **Try early and often.** Create an expectation of rapid experimentation and prototyping. Encourage teams to create a prototype in the first week of a project. Measure progress with a metric such as average time to first prototype or number of consumers exposed to prototypes during the life of a program.

- **Seek outside help.** Expand the innovation ecosystem by looking for opportunities to cocreate with customers and consumers. Exploit Web 2.0 networks to enlarge the effective scale of your innovation team.

- **Blend big and small projects.** Manage a portfolio of innovation that stretches from shorter-term incremental ideas to longer-term revolutionary ones. Expect business units to drive and fund incremental innovation, but be willing to initiate revolutionary innovation from the top.

- **Budget to the pace of innovation.** Design thinking happens quickly, yet the route to market can be unpredictable. Don't constrain the pace at which you can innovate by relying on cumbersome budgeting cycles. Be prepared to rethink your funding approach as projects proceed and teams learn more about opportunities.

- **Find talent any way you can.** Look to hire from interdisciplinary programs like the new Institute of Design at Stanford and progressive business schools like Rotman, in Toronto. People with more-conventional design backgrounds can push solutions far beyond your expectations. You may even be able to train nondesigners with the right attributes to excel in design-thinking roles.

- **Design for the cycle.** In many businesses people move every 12 to 18 months. But design projects may take longer than that to get from day one through implementation. Plan assignments so that design thinkers go from inspiration to ideation to implementation. Experiencing the full cycle builds better judgment and creates great long-term benefits for the organization.

One example of experiential innovation comes from a financial services company. In late 2005 Bank of America launched a new savings account service called "Keep the Change." IDEO, working with a team from the bank, helped identify a consumer behavior that many people will recognize: After paying cash for something, we put the coins we received in change into a jar at home. Once the jar is full, we take the coins to the bank and deposit them in a savings account. For many people, it's an easy way of saving. Bank of America's innovation was to build this behavior into a debit card account. Customers who use their debit cards to make purchases can now choose to have the total rounded up to the nearest dollar and the difference deposited in their savings accounts.

The success of this innovation lay in its appeal to an instinctive desire we have to put money aside in a painless and invisible way. Keep the Change creates an experience that feels natural because it models behavior that many of us already exhibit. To be sure, Bank of America sweetens the deal by matching 100% of the change saved in the first three months and 5% of annual totals (up to $250) thereafter. This encourages customers to try it out. But the real payoff is emotional: the gratification that comes with monthly statements showing customers they've saved money without even trying.

In less than a year the program attracted 2.5 million customers. It is credited with 700,000 new checking accounts and a million new savings accounts. Enrollment now totals more than 5 million people who together have saved more than $500 million. Keep the Change demonstrates that design thinking can identify an aspect of human behavior and then convert it into both a customer benefit and a business value.

Thomas Edison represents what many of us think of as a golden age of American innovation—a time when new ideas transformed every aspect of our lives. The need for transformation is, if anything, greater now than ever before. No matter where we look, we see problems that can be solved only through innovation: unaffordable or unavailable health care, billions of people trying to live on just a few dollars a day, energy usage that outpaces the planet's ability to support it, education systems that fail many students, companies whose traditional markets are disrupted by new technologies or demographic shifts. These problems all have people at their heart. They require a human-centered, creative, iterative, and practical approach to finding the best ideas and ultimate solutions. Design thinking is just such an approach to innovation.

Reprinted from *Harvard Business Review*,
June 2008 (product #R0806E).

CHAPTER TWENTY-SIX

Marketing Myopia

by Theodore Levitt

Every major industry was once a growth industry. But some that are now riding a wave of growth enthusiasm are very much in the shadow of decline. Others that are thought of as seasoned growth industries have actually stopped growing. In every case, the reason growth is threatened, slowed, or stopped is *not* because the market is saturated. It is because there has been a failure of management.

Fateful Purposes

The failure is at the top. The executives responsible for it, in the last analysis, are those who deal with broad aims and policies. Thus:

- The railroads did not stop growing because the need for passenger and freight transportation declined. That grew. The railroads are in trouble today not because that need was filled by others (cars, trucks, airplanes, and even telephones) but because it was *not* filled by the railroads themselves. They let others take customers away from them because they assumed themselves to be in the railroad business rather than in the transportation business. The reason they defined their industry incorrectly was that they were railroad-oriented instead of transportation-oriented; they were product-oriented instead of customer-oriented.

- Hollywood barely escaped being totally ravished by television. Actually, all the established film companies went through drastic reorganizations. Some simply disappeared. All of them got into trouble not because of TV's inroads but because of their own myopia. As with the railroads, Hollywood defined its business incorrectly. It thought it was in the movie business when it was actually in the entertainment business. "Movies" implied a specific, limited product. This produced a fatuous contentment that from the beginning led producers to view TV as a threat. Hollywood scorned and rejected TV when it should have welcomed it as an opportunity—an opportunity to expand the entertainment business.

Today, TV is a bigger business than the old narrowly defined movie business ever was. Had Hollywood been customer-oriented (providing entertainment) rather than product-oriented (making movies), would it have gone through the fiscal purgatory that it did? I doubt it. What ultimately saved Hollywood and accounted for its resurgence was the wave of new young writers, producers, and directors whose previous successes in television had decimated the old movie companies and toppled the big movie moguls.

There are other, less obvious examples of industries that have been and are now endangering their futures by improperly defining their purposes. I shall discuss some of them in detail later and analyze the kind of policies that lead to trouble. Right now, it may help to show what a thoroughly customer-oriented management can do to keep a growth industry growing, even after the obvious opportunities have been exhausted, and here there are two examples that have been around for a long time. They are nylon and glass—specifically, E. I. du Pont de Nemours and Company and Corning Glass Works.

Both companies have great technical competence. Their product orientation is unquestioned. But this alone does not explain their success. After all, who was more pridefully product-oriented and product-conscious than the erstwhile New England textile companies that have been so thoroughly massacred? The DuPonts and the Cornings have succeeded not primarily because of their product or research orientation but because they have been thoroughly customer-oriented also. It is constant watchfulness for opportunities to apply their technical know-how to the creation of customer-satisfying uses that accounts for their prodigious output of successful new products. Without a very sophisticated eye on the customer, most of their new products might have been wrong, their sales methods useless.

Aluminum has also continued to be a growth industry, thanks to the efforts of two wartime-created companies that deliberately set about inventing new customer-satisfying uses. Without Kaiser Aluminum & Chemical Corporation and Reynolds Metals Company, the total demand for aluminum today would be vastly less.

Error of analysis

Some may argue that it is foolish to set the railroads off against aluminum or the movies off against glass. Are not aluminum and glass naturally so versatile that the industries are bound to have more growth opportunities than the railroads and the movies? This view commits precisely the error I have been talking about. It defines an industry or a product or a cluster of know-how so narrowly as to guarantee its premature senescence. When we mention "railroads," we should make sure we mean "transportation." As transporters, the railroads still have a good chance for very considerable growth. They are not limited to the railroad business as such (though in my opinion, rail transportation is potentially a much stronger transportation medium than is generally believed).

What the railroads lack is not opportunity but some of the managerial imaginativeness and audacity that made them great. Even an amateur like Jacques Barzun can see what is lacking when he says, "I grieve to see the most advanced physical and social organization of the last century go down in shabby disgrace for lack of the same comprehensive imagination that built it up. [What is lacking is] the will of the companies to survive and to satisfy the public by inventiveness and skill."[1]

Shadow of Obsolescence

It is impossible to mention a single major industry that did not at one time qualify for the magic appellation of "growth industry." In each case, the industry's assumed strength lay in the apparently unchallenged superiority of its product. There appeared to be no effective substitute for it. It was itself a runaway substitute for the product it so triumphantly replaced. Yet one after another of these celebrated industries has come under a shadow. Let us look briefly at a few more of them, this time taking examples that have so far received a little less attention.

Dry cleaning

This was once a growth industry with lavish prospects. In an age of wool garments, imagine being finally able to get them clean safely and easily. The boom was on. Yet here we are 30 years after the boom started, and the industry is in trouble. Where has the competition come from? From a better way of cleaning? No. It has come from synthetic fibers and chemical additives that have cut the need for dry cleaning. But this is only the beginning. Lurking in the wings and ready to make chemical dry cleaning totally obsolete is that powerful magician, ultrasonics.

Electric utilities

This is another one of those supposedly "no substitute" products that has been enthroned on a pedestal of invincible growth. When the incandescent lamp came along, kerosene lights were finished. Later, the waterwheel and the steam engine were cut to ribbons by the flexibility, reliability, simplicity, and just plain easy availability of electric motors. The prosperity of electric utilities continues to wax extravagant as the home is converted into a museum of electric gadgetry. How can anybody miss by investing in utilities, with no competition, nothing but growth ahead?

But a second look is not quite so comforting. A score of nonutility companies are well advanced toward developing a powerful chemical fuel cell, which could sit in some hidden closet of every home silently ticking off electric power. The electric lines that vulgarize so many neighborhoods would be eliminated. So would the endless demolition of streets and service interruptions during storms. Also on the horizon is solar energy, again pioneered by nonutility companies.

Who says that the utilities have no competition? They may be natural monopolies now, but tomorrow they may be natural deaths. To avoid this prospect, they too will have to develop fuel cells, solar energy, and other power sources. To survive, they themselves will have to plot the obsolescence of what now produces their livelihood.

Grocery stores

Many people find it hard to realize that there ever was a thriving establishment known as the "corner store." The supermarket took over with a powerful effectiveness. Yet the big food chains of the 1930s narrowly escaped being completely wiped out by the aggressive expansion of independent supermarkets. The first genuine supermarket was opened in 1930, in Jamaica, Long Island. By 1933, supermarkets were thriving in California, Ohio, Pennsylvania, and elsewhere. Yet the established chains pompously ignored them. When they chose to notice them, it was with such derisive descriptions as "cheapy," "horse-and-buggy," "cracker-barrel storekeeping," and "unethical opportunists."

The executive of one big chain announced at the time that he found it "hard to believe that people will drive for miles to shop for foods and sacrifice the personal service chains have perfected and to which [the consumer] is accustomed."[2] As late as 1936, the National Wholesale Grocers convention and the New Jersey Retail Grocers Association said there was nothing to fear. They said that the supers' narrow appeal to the price buyer limited the size of their market. They had to draw from miles around. When imitators came, there would be wholesale liquidations as volume fell. The high sales of the supers were said to be partly due to their novelty. People wanted convenient neighborhood grocers. If the neighborhood stores would "cooperate with their suppliers, pay attention to their costs, and improve their service," they would be able to weather the competition until it blew over.[3]

It never blew over. The chains discovered that survival required going into the supermarket business. This meant the wholesale destruction of their huge investments in corner store sites and in established distribution and merchandising methods. The companies with "the courage of their convictions" resolutely stuck to the corner store philosophy. They kept their pride but lost their shirts.

A self-deceiving cycle

But memories are short. For example, it is hard for people who today confidently hail the twin messiahs of electronics and chemicals to see how things could possibly go wrong with these galloping industries. They probably also cannot see how a reasonably sensible businessperson could have been as myopic as the famous Boston millionaire who early in the twentieth century unintentionally sentenced his heirs to poverty by stipulating that his entire estate be forever invested exclusively in electric streetcar securities. His posthumous declaration, "There will always be a big demand for efficient urban transportation" is no consolation to his heirs, who sustain life by pumping gasoline at automobile filling stations.

Yet, in a casual survey I took among a group of intelligent business executives, nearly half agreed that it would be hard to hurt their heirs by tying their estates forever to the electronics industry. When I then confronted them with the Boston streetcar example, they chorused unanimously, "That's different!" But is it? Is not the basic situation identical?

In truth, *there is no such thing as a growth industry,* I believe. There are only companies organized and operated to create and capitalize on growth opportunities. Industries that assume themselves to be riding some automatic growth escalator invariably descend into stagnation. The history of every dead and dying "growth" industry shows a self-deceiving cycle of bountiful expansion and undetected decay. There are four conditions that usually guarantee this cycle:

1. The belief that growth is assured by an expanding and more affluent population;

2. The belief that there is no competitive substitute for the industry's major product;

3. Too much faith in mass production and in the advantages of rapidly declining unit costs as output rises;

4. Preoccupation with a product that lends itself to carefully controlled scientific experimentation, improvement, and manufacturing cost reduction.

I should like now to examine each of these conditions in some detail. To build my case as boldly as possible, I shall illustrate the points with reference to three industries: petroleum, automobiles, and electronics. I'll focus on petroleum in particular, because it spans more years and more vicissitudes. Not only do these three industries have excellent reputations with the general public and also enjoy the confidence of sophisticated investors, but their managements have become known for progressive thinking in areas like financial control, product research, and management training. If obsolescence can cripple even these industries, it can happen anywhere.

Population Myth

The belief that profits are assured by an expanding and more affluent population is dear to the heart of every industry. It takes the edge off the apprehensions everybody understandably feels about the future. If consumers are multiplying and also buying more of your product or service, you can face the future with considerably more comfort than if the market were shrinking. An expanding market keeps the manufacturer from having to think very hard or imaginatively. If thinking is an intellectual response to a problem, then the absence of a problem leads to the absence of thinking. If your product has an automatically expanding market, then you will not give much thought to how to expand it.

One of the most interesting examples of this is provided by the petroleum industry. Probably our oldest growth industry, it has an enviable record. While there are some current concerns about its growth rate, the industry itself tends to be optimistic.

But I believe it can be demonstrated that it is undergoing a fundamental yet typical change. It is not only ceasing to be a growth industry but may actually be a declining one, relative to other businesses. Although there is widespread unawareness of this fact, it is conceivable that in time, the oil industry may find itself in much the same position of retrospective glory that the railroads are now in. Despite its pioneering work in developing and applying the present-value method of investment evaluation, in employee relations, and in working with developing countries, the petroleum business is a distressing example of how complacency and wrongheadedness can stubbornly convert opportunity into near disaster.

One of the characteristics of this and other industries that have believed very strongly in the beneficial consequences of an expanding population, while at the same time having a generic product for which there has appeared to be no competitive substitute, is that the individual companies have sought to outdo their competitors by improving on what they are already doing. This makes sense, of course, if one assumes that sales are tied to the country's population strings, because the customer can compare products only on a feature-by-feature basis. I believe it is significant, for example, that not since John D. Rockefeller sent free kerosene lamps to China has the oil industry done anything really outstanding to create a demand for its product. Not even in product improvement has it showered itself with eminence. The greatest single improvement—the development of tetraethyl lead—came from outside the industry, specifically from General Motors and DuPont. The big contributions made by the industry itself are confined to the technology of oil exploration, oil production, and oil refining.

Asking for trouble

In other words, the petroleum industry's efforts have focused on improving the *efficiency* of getting and making its product, not really on improving the generic product or its marketing. Moreover, its chief product has continually been defined in the narrowest possible terms—namely, gasoline, not energy, fuel, or transportation. This attitude has helped assure that:

- Major improvements in gasoline quality tend not to originate in the oil industry. The development of superior alternative fuels also comes from outside the oil industry, as will be shown later.

- Major innovations in automobile fuel marketing come from small, new oil companies that are not primarily preoccupied with production or refining. These are the companies that have been responsible for the rapidly expanding multipump gasoline stations, with their successful emphasis on large and clean layouts, rapid and efficient driveway service, and quality gasoline at low prices.

Thus, the oil industry is asking for trouble from outsiders. Sooner or later, in this land of hungry investors and entrepreneurs, a threat is sure to come. The possibility of this will become more apparent when we turn to the next dangerous belief of many managements. For the sake of continuity, because this second belief is tied closely to the first, I shall continue with the same example.

The idea of indispensability

The petroleum industry is pretty much convinced that there is no competitive substitute for its major product, gasoline—or, if there is, that it will continue to be a derivative of crude oil, such as diesel fuel or kerosene jet fuel.

There is a lot of automatic wishful thinking in this assumption. The trouble is that most refining companies own huge amounts of crude oil reserves. These have value only if there is a market for products into which oil can be converted. Hence the tenacious belief in the continuing competitive superiority of automobile fuels made from crude oil.

This idea persists despite all historic evidence against it. The evidence not only shows that oil has never been a superior product for any purpose for very long but also that the oil industry has never really been a growth industry. Rather, it has been a succession of different businesses that have gone through the usual historic cycles of growth, maturity, and decay. The industry's overall survival is owed to a series of miraculous escapes from total obsolescence, of last-minute and unexpected reprieves from total disaster reminiscent of the perils of Pauline.

The perils of petroleum

To illustrate, I shall sketch in only the main episodes. First, crude oil was largely a patent medicine. But even before that fad ran out, demand was greatly expanded by the use of oil in kerosene lamps. The prospect of lighting the world's lamps gave rise to an extravagant promise of growth. The prospects were similar to those the industry now holds for gasoline in other parts of the world. It can hardly wait for the underdeveloped nations to get a car in every garage.

In the days of the kerosene lamp, the oil companies competed with each other and against gaslight by trying to improve the illuminating characteristics of kerosene. Then suddenly the impossible happened. Edison invented a light that was totally nondependent on crude oil. Had it not been for the growing use of kerosene in space heaters, the incandescent lamp would have completely finished oil as a growth industry at that time. Oil would have been good for little else than axle grease.

Then disaster and reprieve struck again. Two great innovations occurred, neither originating in the oil industry. First, the successful development of coal-burning domestic central-heating systems made the space heater obsolete. While the industry reeled, along came its most magnificent boost yet: the internal combustion engine, also invented by outsiders. Then, when the prodigious expansion for gasoline finally began to level off in the 1920s, along came the miraculous escape of the central oil heater. Once again, the escape was provided by an outsider's invention and development. And when that market weakened, wartime demand for aviation fuel came to the rescue. After the war, the expansion of civilian aviation, the dieselization of railroads, and the explosive demand for cars and trucks kept the industry's growth in high gear.

Meanwhile, centralized oil heating—whose boom potential had only recently been proclaimed—ran into severe competition from natural gas. While the oil companies themselves owned the gas that now competed with their oil, the industry did not originate the natural gas revolution, nor has it to this day greatly profited from its gas ownership. The gas revolution was made by newly formed transmission companies that marketed the product with an aggressive ardor. They started a magnificent new industry, first against the advice and then against the resistance of the oil companies.

By all the logic of the situation, the oil companies themselves should have made the gas revolution. They not only owned the gas, they also were the only people experienced in handling, scrubbing, and using it and the only people experienced in pipeline technology and transmission. They also understood heating problems. But, partly because they knew that natural gas would compete with their own sale of heating oil, the oil companies pooh-poohed the potential of gas. The revolution was finally started by oil pipeline executives who, unable to persuade their own companies to go into gas, quit and organized the spectacularly successful gas transmission companies. Even after their success became painfully evident to the oil companies, the latter did not go into gas transmission. The multibillion-dollar business that should have been theirs went to others. As in the past, the industry was blinded by its narrow preoccupation with a specific product and the value of its reserves. It paid little or no attention to its customers' basic needs and preferences.

The postwar years have not witnessed any change. Immediately after World War II, the oil industry was greatly encouraged about its future by the rapid increase in demand for its traditional line of products. In 1950, most companies projected annual rates of domestic expansion of around 6% through at least 1975. Though the ratio of crude oil reserves to demand in the free world was about 20 to 1, with 10 to 1 being usually considered a reasonable working ratio in the United States, booming demand sent oil explorers searching for more without sufficient regard to what the future really promised. In 1952, they "hit" in the Middle East; the ratio skyrocketed to 42 to 1. If gross additions to reserves continue at the average rate of the past five years (37 billion barrels annually), then by 1970, the reserve ratio will be up to 45 to 1. This abundance of oil has weakened crude and product prices all over the world.

An uncertain future

Management cannot find much consolation today in the rapidly expanding petrochemical industry, another oil-using idea that did not originate in the leading firms. The total U.S. production of petrochemicals is equivalent to about 2% (by volume) of the demand for all petroleum products. Although the petrochemical industry is now expected to grow by about 10% per year, this will not offset other drains on the growth of crude oil consumption. Furthermore, while petrochemical products are many and growing, it is important to remember that there are nonpetroleum sources of the basic raw material, such as coal. Besides, a lot of plastics can be produced with relatively little oil. A 50,000-barrel-per-day oil refinery is now considered the absolute minimum size for efficiency. But a 5,000-barrel-per-day chemical plant is a giant operation.

Oil has never been a continuously strong growth industry. It has grown by fits and starts, always miraculously saved by innovations and developments not of its own making. The reason it has not grown in a smooth progression is that each time it thought it had a superior product safe from the possibility of competitive substitutes, the product turned out to be inferior and notoriously subject to obsolescence. Until now, gasoline (for motor fuel, anyhow) has escaped this fate. But, as we shall see later, it too may be on its last legs.

The point of all this is that there is no guarantee against product obsolescence. If a company's own research does not make a product obsolete, another's will. Unless an industry is especially lucky, as oil has been until now, it can easily go down in a sea of red figures—just as the railroads have, as the buggy whip manufacturers have, as the corner grocery chains have, as most of the big movie companies have, and, indeed, as many other industries have.

The best way for a firm to be lucky is to make its own luck. That requires knowing what makes a business successful. One of the greatest enemies of this knowledge is mass production.

Production Pressures

Mass production industries are impelled by a great drive to produce all they can. The prospect of steeply declining unit costs as output rises is more than most companies can usually resist. The profit possibilities look spectacular. All effort focuses on production. The result is that marketing gets neglected.

John Kenneth Galbraith contends that just the opposite occurs.[4] Output is so prodigious that all effort concentrates on trying to get rid of it. He says this accounts for singing commercials, the desecration of the countryside with advertising signs, and other wasteful and vulgar practices. Galbraith has a finger on something real, but he misses the strategic point. Mass production does indeed generate great pressure to "move" the product. But what usually gets emphasized is selling, not marketing. Marketing, a more sophisticated and complex process, gets ignored.

The difference between marketing and selling is more than semantic. Selling focuses on the needs of the seller, marketing on the needs of the buyer. Selling is preoccupied with the seller's need to convert the product into cash, marketing with the idea of satisfying the needs of the customer by means of the product and the whole cluster of things associated with creating, delivering, and, finally, consuming it.

In some industries, the enticements of full mass production have been so powerful that top management in effect has told the sales department, "You get rid of it; we'll worry about profits." By contrast, a truly marketing-minded firm tries to create value-satisfying goods and services that consumers will want to buy. What it offers for sale includes not only the generic product or service but also how it is made available to the customer, in what form, when, under what conditions, and at what terms of trade. Most important, what it offers for sale is determined not by the seller but by the buyer. The seller takes cues from the buyer in such a way that the product becomes a consequence of the marketing effort, not vice versa.

A lag in Detroit

This may sound like an elementary rule of business, but that does not keep it from being violated wholesale. It is certainly more violated than honored. Take the automobile industry.

Here mass production is most famous, most honored, and has the greatest impact on the entire society. The industry has hitched its fortune to the relentless requirements of the annual model change, a policy that makes customer orientation an especially urgent necessity. Consequently, the auto companies annually spend millions of dollars on consumer research. But the fact that the new compact cars are selling so well in their first year indicates that Detroit's vast researches have for a long time failed to reveal what customers really wanted. Detroit was not convinced that people wanted anything different from what they had been getting until it lost millions of customers to other small-car manufacturers.

How could this unbelievable lag behind consumer wants have been perpetuated for so long? Why didn't research reveal consumer preferences before consumers' buying decisions themselves revealed the facts? Isn't that what consumer research is for—to find out before the fact what is going to happen? The answer is that Detroit never really researched customers' wants. It only researched their preferences between the kinds of things it had already decided to offer them. For Detroit is mainly product-oriented, not customer-oriented. To the extent that the customer is recognized as having needs that the manufacturer should try to satisfy, Detroit usually acts as if the job can be done entirely by product changes. Occasionally, attention gets paid to financing, too, but that is done more in order to sell than to enable the customer to buy.

As for taking care of other customer needs, there is not enough being done to write about. The areas of the greatest unsatisfied needs are ignored or, at best, get stepchild attention. These are at the point of sale and on the matter of automotive repair and maintenance. Detroit views these problem areas as being of secondary importance. That is underscored by the fact that the retailing and servicing ends of this industry are neither owned and operated nor controlled by the manufacturers. Once the car is produced, things are pretty much in the dealer's inadequate hands. Illustrative of Detroit's arm's-length attitude is the fact that, while servicing holds enormous sales-stimulating, profit-building opportunities, only 57 of Chevrolet's 7,000 dealers provide night maintenance service.

Motorists repeatedly express their dissatisfaction with servicing and their apprehensions about buying cars under the present selling setup. The anxieties and problems they encounter during the auto buying and maintenance processes are probably more intense and widespread today than many years ago. Yet the automobile companies do not seem to listen to or take their cues from the anguished consumer. If they do listen, it must be through the filter of their own preoccupation with production. The marketing effort is still viewed as a necessary consequence of the product—not vice versa, as it should be. That is the legacy of mass production, with its parochial view that profit resides essentially in low-cost full production.

What Ford put first

The profit lure of mass production obviously has a place in the plans and strategy of business management, but it must always *follow* hard thinking about the customer. This is one of the most important lessons we can learn from the contradictory behavior of Henry Ford. In a sense, Ford was both the most brilliant and the most senseless marketer in American history. He was senseless because he refused to give the customer anything but a black car. He was brilliant because he fashioned a production system designed to fit market needs. We habitually celebrate him for the wrong reason: for his production genius. His real genius was marketing. We think he was able to cut his selling price and therefore sell millions of $500 cars because his invention of the assembly line had reduced the costs. Actually, he invented the assembly line because he had concluded that at $500 he could sell millions of cars. Mass production was the *result,* not the cause, of his low prices.

Ford emphasized this point repeatedly, but a nation of production-oriented business managers refuses to hear the great lesson he taught. Here is his operating philosophy as he expressed it succinctly:

> Our policy is to reduce the price, extend the operations, and improve the article. You will notice that the reduction of price comes first. We have never considered any costs as fixed. Therefore we first reduce the price to the point where we believe more sales will result. Then we go ahead and try to make the prices. We do not bother about the costs. The new price forces the costs down. The more usual way is to take the costs and then determine the price; and although that method may be scientific in the narrow sense, it is not scientific in the broad sense, because what earthly use is it to know the cost if it tells you that you cannot manufacture at a price at which the article can be sold? But more to the point is the fact that, although one may calculate what a cost is, and of course all of our costs are carefully calculated, no one knows what a cost ought to be. One of the ways of discovering . . . is to name a price so low as to force everybody in the place to the highest point of efficiency. The low price makes everybody dig for profits. We make more discoveries concerning manufacturing and selling under this forced method than by any method of leisurely investigation.[5]

Product provincialism

The tantalizing profit possibilities of low unit production costs may be the most seriously self-deceiving attitude that can afflict a company, particularly a "growth" company, where an apparently assured expansion of demand already tends to undermine a proper concern for the importance of marketing and the customer.

The usual result of this narrow preoccupation with so-called concrete matters is that instead of growing, the industry declines. It usually means that the product fails to adapt to the constantly changing patterns of consumer needs and tastes, to new and modified marketing institutions and practices, or to product developments in competing or complementary industries. The industry has its eyes so firmly on its own specific product that it does not see how it is being made obsolete.

The classic example of this is the buggy whip industry. No amount of product improvement could stave off its death sentence. But had the industry defined itself as being in the transportation business rather than in the buggy whip business, it might have survived. It would have done what survival always entails—that is, change. Even if it had only defined its business as providing a stimulant or catalyst to an energy source, it might have survived by becoming a manufacturer of, say, fan belts or air cleaners.

What may someday be a still more classic example is, again, the oil industry. Having let others steal marvelous opportunities from it (including natural gas, as already mentioned; missile fuels; and jet engine lubricants), one would expect it to have taken steps never to let that happen again. But this is not the case. We are now seeing extraordinary new developments in fuel systems specifically designed to power automobiles. Not only are these developments concentrated in firms outside the petroleum industry, but petroleum is almost systematically ignoring them, securely content in its wedded bliss to oil. It is the story of the kerosene lamp versus the incandescent lamp all over again. Oil is trying to improve hydrocarbon fuels rather than develop *any* fuels best suited to the needs of their users, whether or not made in different ways and with different raw materials from oil.

Here are some things that nonpetroleum companies are working on:

- More than a dozen such firms now have advanced working models of energy systems, which, when perfected, will replace the internal combustion engine and eliminate the demand for gasoline. The superior merit of each of these systems is their elimination of frequent, time-consuming, and irritating refueling stops. Most of these systems are fuel cells designed to create electrical energy directly from chemicals without combustion. Most of them use chemicals that are not derived from oil—generally, hydrogen and oxygen.

- Several other companies have advanced models of electric storage batteries designed to power automobiles. One of these is an aircraft producer that is working jointly with several electric utility companies. The latter hope to use off-peak generating capacity to supply overnight plug-in battery regeneration. Another company, also using the battery approach, is a medium-sized electronics firm with extensive small-battery experience that it developed in connection with its work on hearing aids. It is collaborating with an automobile manufacturer. Recent improvements arising from the need for high-powered miniature power storage plants in rockets have put us within reach of a relatively small battery capable of withstanding great overloads or surges of power. Germanium diode applications and batteries using sintered plate and nickel cadmium techniques promise to make a revolution in our energy sources.

- Solar energy conversion systems are also getting increasing attention. One usually cautious Detroit auto executive recently ventured that solar-powered cars might be common by 1980.

As for the oil companies, they are more or less "watching developments," as one research director put it to me. A few are doing a bit of research on fuel cells, but this research is almost always confined to developing cells powered by hydrocarbon chemicals. None of them is enthusiastically researching fuel cells, batteries, or solar power plants. None of them is spending a fraction as much on research in these profoundly important areas as it is on the usual run-of-the-mill things like reducing combustion chamber deposits in gasoline engines. One major integrated petroleum company recently took a tentative look at the fuel cell and concluded that although "the companies actively working on it indicate a belief in ultimate success . . . the timing and magnitude of its impact are too remote to warrant recognition in our forecasts."

One might, of course, ask, Why should the oil companies do anything different? Would not chemical fuel cells, batteries, or solar energy kill the present product lines? The answer is that they would indeed, and that is precisely the reason for the oil firms' having to develop these power units before their competitors do, so they will not be companies without an industry.

Management might be more likely to do what is needed for its own preservation if it thought of itself as being in the energy business. But even that will not be enough if it persists in imprisoning itself in the narrow grip of its tight product orientation. It has to think of itself as taking care of customer needs, not finding, refining, or even selling oil. Once it genuinely thinks of its business as taking care of people's transportation needs, nothing can stop it from creating its own extravagantly profitable growth.

Creative destruction

Since words are cheap and deeds are dear, it may be appropriate to indicate what this kind of thinking involves and leads to. Let us start at the beginning: the customer. It can be shown that motorists strongly dislike the bother, delay, and experience of buying gasoline. People actually do not buy gasoline. They cannot see it, taste it, feel it, appreciate it, or really test it. What they buy is the right to continue driving their cars. The gas station is like a tax collector to whom people are compelled to pay a periodic toll as the price of using their cars. This makes the gas station a basically unpopular institution. It can never be made popular or pleasant, only less unpopular, less unpleasant.

Reducing its unpopularity completely means eliminating it. Nobody likes a tax collector, not even a pleasantly cheerful one. Nobody likes to interrupt a trip to buy a phantom product, not even from a handsome Adonis or a seductive Venus. Hence, companies that are working on exotic fuel substitutes that will eliminate the need for frequent refueling are heading directly into the outstretched arms of the irritated motorist. They are riding a wave of inevitability, not because they are creating something that is technologically superior or more sophisticated but because they are satisfying a powerful customer need. They are also eliminating noxious odors and air pollution.

Once the petroleum companies recognize the customer-satisfying logic of what another power system can do, they will see that they have no more choice about working on an efficient, long-lasting fuel (or some way of delivering present fuels without bothering the motorist) than the big food chains had a choice about going into the supermarket business or the vacuum tube companies had a choice about making semiconductors. For their own good, the oil firms will have to destroy their own highly profitable assets. No amount of wishful thinking can save them from the necessity of engaging in this form of "creative destruction."

I phrase the need as strongly as this because I think management must make quite an effort to break itself loose from conventional ways. It is all too easy in this day and age for a company or industry to let its sense of purpose become dominated by the economies of full production and to develop a dangerously lopsided product orientation. In short, if management lets itself drift, it invariably drifts in the direction of thinking of itself as producing goods and services, not customer satisfactions. While it probably will not descend to the depths of telling its salespeople, "You get rid of it; we'll worry about profits," it can, without knowing it, be practicing precisely that formula for withering decay. The historic fate of one growth industry after another has been its suicidal product provincialism.

Dangers of R&D

Another big danger to a firm's continued growth arises when top management is wholly transfixed by the profit possibilities of technical research and development. To illustrate, I shall turn first to a new industry—electronics—and then return once more to the oil companies. By comparing a fresh example with a familiar one, I hope to emphasize the prevalence and insidiousness of a hazardous way of thinking.

Marketing shortchanged

In the case of electronics, the greatest danger that faces the glamorous new companies in this field is not that they do not pay enough attention to research and development but that they pay too much attention to it. And the fact that the fastest-growing electronics firms owe their eminence to their heavy emphasis on technical research is completely beside the point. They have vaulted to affluence on a sudden crest of unusually strong general receptiveness to new technical ideas. Also, their success has been shaped in the virtually guaranteed market of military subsidies and by military orders that in many cases actually preceded the existence of facilities to make the products. Their expansion has, in other words, been almost totally devoid of marketing effort.

Thus, they are growing up under conditions that come dangerously close to creating the illusion that a superior product will sell itself. It is not surprising that, having created a successful company by making a superior product, management continues to be oriented toward the product rather than the people who consume it. It develops the philosophy that continued growth is a matter of continued product innovation and improvement.

A number of other factors tend to strengthen and sustain this belief:

1. Because electronic products are highly complex and sophisticated, managements become top-heavy with engineers and

scientists. This creates a selective bias in favor of research and production at the expense of marketing. The organization tends to view itself as making things rather than as satisfying customer needs. Marketing gets treated as a residual activity, "something else" that must be done once the vital job of product creation and production is completed.

2. To this bias in favor of product research, development, and production is added the bias in favor of dealing with controllable variables. Engineers and scientists are at home in the world of concrete things like machines, test tubes, production lines, and even balance sheets. The abstractions to which they feel kindly are those that are testable or manipulatable in the laboratory or, if not testable, then functional, such as Euclid's axioms. In short, the managements of the new glamour-growth companies tend to favor business activities that lend themselves to careful study, experimentation, and control—the hard, practical realities of the lab, the shop, and the books.

What gets shortchanged are the realities of the *market*. Consumers are unpredictable, varied, fickle, stupid, shortsighted, stubborn, and generally bothersome. This is not what the engineer managers say, but deep down in their consciousness, it is what they believe. And this accounts for their concentration on what they know and what they can control—namely, product research, engineering, and production. The emphasis on production becomes particularly attractive when the product can be made at declining unit costs. There is no more inviting way of making money than by running the plant full blast.

The top-heavy science-engineering-production orientation of so many electronics companies works reasonably well today because they are pushing into new frontiers in which the armed services have pioneered virtually assured markets. The companies are in the felicitous position of having to fill, not find, markets, of not having to discover what the customer needs and wants but of having the customer voluntarily come forward with specific new product demands. If a team of consultants had been assigned specifically to design a business situation calculated to prevent the emergence and development of a customer-oriented marketing viewpoint, it could not have produced anything better than the conditions just described.

Stepchild treatment

The oil industry is a stunning example of how science, technology, and mass production can divert an entire group of companies from their main task. To the extent the consumer is studied at all (which is not much), the focus is forever on getting information that is designed to help the oil companies improve what they are now doing. They try to discover more convincing advertising themes, more effective sales promotional drives, what the market shares of the various companies are, what people like or dislike about service station dealers and oil companies, and so forth. Nobody seems as interested in probing deeply into the basic human needs that the industry might be trying to satisfy as in probing into the basic properties of the raw material that the companies work with in trying to deliver customer satisfactions.

Basic questions about customers and markets seldom get asked. The latter occupy a stepchild status. They are recognized as existing, as having to be taken care of, but not worth very much real thought or dedicated attention. No oil company gets as excited about the customers in its own backyard as about the oil in the Sahara Desert. Nothing illustrates better the neglect of marketing than its treatment in the industry press.

The centennial issue of the *American Petroleum Institute Quarterly,* published in 1959 to celebrate the discovery of oil in Titusville, Pennsylvania, contained 21 feature articles proclaiming the industry's greatness. Only one of these talked about its achievements in marketing, and that was only a pictorial record of how service station architecture has changed. The issue also contained a special section on "New Horizons," which was devoted to showing the magnificent role oil would play in America's future. Every reference was ebulliently optimistic, never implying once that oil might have some hard competition. Even the reference to atomic energy was a cheerful catalog of how oil would help make atomic energy a success. There was not a single apprehension that the oil industry's affluence might be threatened or a suggestion that one "new horizon" might include new and better ways of serving oil's present customers.

But the most revealing example of the stepchild treatment that marketing gets is still another special series of short articles on "The Revolutionary Potential of Electronics." Under that heading, this list of articles appeared in the table of contents:

- "In the Search for Oil"
- "In Production Operations"
- "In Refinery Processes"
- "In Pipeline Operations"

Significantly, every one of the industry's major functional areas is listed, *except* marketing. Why? Either it is believed that electronics holds no revolutionary potential for petroleum marketing (which is palpably wrong), or the editors forgot to discuss marketing (which is more likely and illustrates its stepchild status).

The order in which the four functional areas are listed also betrays the alienation of the oil industry from the consumer. The industry is implicitly defined as beginning with the search for oil and ending with its distribution from the refinery. But the truth is, it seems to me, that the industry begins with the needs of the customer for its products. From that primal position its definition moves steadily back stream to areas of progressively lesser importance until it finally comes to rest at the search for oil.

The beginning and end

The view that an industry is a customer-satisfying process, not a goods-producing process, is vital for all businesspeople to understand. An industry begins with the customer and his or her needs, not with a patent, a raw material, or a selling skill. Given the customer's needs, the industry develops backwards, first concerning itself with the physical *delivery* of customer satisfactions. Then it moves back further to *creating* the things by which these satisfactions are in part achieved. How these materials are created is a matter of indifference to the customer, hence the particular form of manufacturing, processing, or what have you cannot be considered as a vital aspect of the industry. Finally, the industry moves back still further to *finding* the raw materials necessary for making its products.

The irony of some industries oriented toward technical research and development is that the scientists who occupy the high executive positions are totally unscientific when it comes to defining their companies' overall needs and purposes. They violate the first two rules of the scientific method: being aware of and defining their companies' problems and then developing testable hypotheses about solving them. They are scientific only about the convenient things, such as laboratory and product experiments.

The customer (and the satisfaction of his or her deepest needs) is not considered to be "the problem"—not because there is any certain belief that no such problem exists but because an organizational lifetime has conditioned management to look in the opposite direction. Marketing is a stepchild.

I do not mean that selling is ignored. Far from it. But selling, again, is not marketing. As already pointed out, selling concerns itself with the tricks and techniques of getting people to exchange their cash for your product. It is not concerned with the values that the exchange is all about. And it does not, as marketing invariably does, view the entire business process as consisting of a tightly integrated effort to discover, create, arouse, and satisfy customer needs. The customer is somebody "out there" who, with proper cunning, can be separated from his or her loose change.

Actually, not even selling gets much attention in some technologically minded firms. Because there is a virtually guaranteed market for the abundant flow of their new products, they do not actually know what a real market is. It is as if they lived in a planned economy, moving their products routinely from factory to retail outlet. Their successful concentration on products tends to convince them of the soundness of what they have been doing, and they fail to see the gathering clouds over the market.

———————

Less than 75 years ago, American railroads enjoyed a fierce loyalty among astute Wall Streeters. European monarchs invested in them heavily. Eternal wealth was thought to be the benediction for anybody who could scrape together a few thousand dollars to put into rail stocks. No other form of transportation could compete with the railroads in speed, flexibility, durability, economy, and growth potentials.

As Jacques Barzun put it, "By the turn of the century it was an institution, an image of man, a tradition, a code of honor, a source of poetry, a nursery of boyhood desires, a sublimest of toys, and the most solemn machine—next to the funeral hearse—that marks the epochs in man's life."[6]

Even after the advent of automobiles, trucks, and airplanes, the railroad tycoons remained imperturbably self-confident. If you had told them 60 years ago that in 30 years they would be flat on their backs, broke, and pleading for government subsidies, they would have thought you totally demented. Such a future was simply not considered possible. It was not even a discussable subject, or an askable question, or a matter that any sane person would consider worth speculating about. Yet a lot of "insane" notions now have matter-of-fact acceptance—for example, the idea of 100-ton tubes of metal moving smoothly through the air 20,000 feet above the earth, loaded with 100 sane and solid citizens casually drinking martinis—and they have dealt cruel blows to the railroads.

What specifically must other companies do to avoid this fate? What does customer orientation involve? These questions have in part been answered by the preceding examples and analysis. It would take another article to show in detail what is required for specific industries. In any case, it should be obvious that building an effective customer-oriented company involves far more than good intentions or promotional tricks; it involves profound matters of human organization and leadership. For the present, let me merely suggest what appear to be some general requirements.

The visceral feel of greatness

Obviously, the company has to do what survival demands. It has to adapt to the requirements of the market, and it has to do it sooner rather than later. But mere survival is a so-so aspiration. Anybody can survive in some way or other, even the skid row bum. The trick is to survive gallantly, to feel the surging impulse of commercial mastery: not just to experience the sweet smell of success but to have the visceral feel of entrepreneurial greatness.

No organization can achieve greatness without a vigorous leader who is driven onward by a pulsating *will to succeed*. A leader has to have a vision of grandeur, a vision that can produce eager followers in vast numbers. In business, the followers are the customers.

In order to produce these customers, the entire corporation must be viewed as a customer-creating and customer-satisfying organism. Management must think of itself not as producing products but as providing customer-creating value satisfactions. It must push this idea (and everything it means and requires) into every nook and cranny of the organization. It has to do this continuously and with the kind of flair that excites and stimulates the people in it. Otherwise, the company will be merely a series of pigeonholed parts, with no consolidating sense of purpose or direction.

In short, the organization must learn to think of itself not as producing goods or services but as *buying customers,* as doing the things that will make people *want* to do business with it. And the chief executive has the inescapable responsibility for creating this environment, this viewpoint, this attitude, this aspiration. The chief executive must set the company's style, its direction, and its goals. This means knowing precisely where he or she wants to go and making sure the whole organization is enthusiastically aware of where that is. This is a first requisite of leadership, for *unless a leader knows where he is going, any road will take him there.*

If any road is okay, the chief executive might as well pack his attaché case and go fishing. If an organization does not know or care where it is going, it does not need to advertise that fact with a ceremonial figurehead. Everybody will notice it soon enough.

NOTES

1. Jacques Barzun, "Trains and the Mind of Man," *Holiday,* February 1960.

2. For more details, see M.M. Zimmerman, *The Super Market: A Revolution in Distribution* (McGraw-Hill, 1955).

3. Ibid., pp. 45–47.

4. John Kenneth Galbraith, *The Affluent Society* (Houghton Mifflin, 1958).

5. Henry Ford, *My Life and Work* (Doubleday, 1923).

6. Barzun, "Trains and the Mind of Man."

Reprinted from *Harvard Business Review,*
July–August 2004 (product #R0407L).
Originally published July–August 1960.

— 2021 —

CHAPTER TWENTY-SEVEN

The Commercial Space Age Is Here

by Matt Weinzierl and Mehak Sarang

There's no shortage of hype surrounding the commercial space industry. But while tech leaders promise us moon bases and settlements on Mars, the space economy has thus far remained distinctly local—at least in a cosmic sense. In 2020, however, we crossed an important threshold: For the first time in human history, humans accessed space via a vehicle built and owned not by any government but by a private corporation with its sights set on affordable space settlement. It was the first significant step toward building an economy both *in* space and *for* space. The implications—for business, policy, and society at large—are hard to overstate.

In 2019, 95% of the estimated $366 billion in revenue earned in the space sector was from the *space-for-earth* economy: that is, goods or services produced in space for use on Earth. The space-for-earth economy includes telecommunications and internet infrastructure, earth observation capabilities, national security satellites, and more. This economy is booming, and though research shows that it faces the challenges of overcrowding and monopolization that tend to arise whenever companies compete for a scarce natural resource, projections for its future are optimistic.[1] Decreasing costs for launch and space hardware in general have enticed new entrants into this market, and companies in a variety of industries have already begun leveraging satellite technology and access to space to drive innovation and efficiency in their bound-for-earth products and services.

In contrast, the *space-for-space* economy—that is, goods and services produced in space for use in space, such as mining the moon or asteroids for material with which to construct in-space habitats or supply refueling depots—has struggled to get off the ground. As far back as the 1970s, research commissioned by NASA predicted the rise of a space-based economy that would supply the demands of hundreds, thousands, even millions of humans living in space, dwarfing the space-for-earth economy (and eventually the entire terrestrial economy as well).[2] The realization of such a vision would change how all of us do business, live our lives, and govern our societies—but to date, we've never even had more than 13 people in space at one time, leaving that dream as little more than science fiction.

Today, however, there is reason to think that we may finally be reaching the first stages of a true space-for-space economy. SpaceX's recent achievements (in cooperation with NASA), as well as upcoming efforts by Boeing, Blue Origin, and Virgin Galactic to put people in space sustainably and at scale, mark the opening of a new chapter of spaceflight led by private firms. These firms have both the intention and capability to bring private citizens to space as passengers, tourists, and—eventually—settlers, opening the door for businesses to start meeting the demand those people create over the next several decades with an array of space-for-space goods and services.

Welcome to the (Commercial) Space Age

In our research, we examined how the model of centralized, government-directed human space activity born in the 1960s has, over the last two decades, made way for a new model, in which public initiatives in space increasingly share the stage with private priorities.[3] Centralized, government-led space programs will inevitably focus on space-for-earth activities that are in the public interest, such as national security, basic science, and national pride. This is only natural, as expenditures for these programs must be justified by demonstrating benefits for citizens—and the citizens these governments represent are (nearly) all on Earth.

In contrast to governments, the private sector is eager to put people in space to pursue their own personal interests, not the state's—and then supply the demand they create. This is the vision driving SpaceX, which in its first 20 years has entirely upended the rocket launch industry, securing 60% of the global commercial launch market and building ever-larger spacecraft designed to ferry passengers not just to the International Space Station (ISS) but also to its own promised settlement on Mars.

Today, the space-for-space market is limited to supplying the people who are already in space: that is, the handful of astronauts employed by NASA and other government programs. While SpaceX has grand visions of supporting large numbers of private space travelers, their current space-for-space activities have all been in response to demand from government customers (i.e., NASA). But as decreasing launch costs enable companies like SpaceX to leverage economies of scale and put more people into space, growing private-sector demand (that is, tourists and settlers, rather than government employees) could turn these proof-of-concept initiatives into a sustainable, large-scale industry.

This model—of selling to NASA with the hopes of eventually creating and expanding into a larger private market—is exemplified by SpaceX, but the company is by no means the only player taking this approach. For instance, while SpaceX is focused on space-for-space transportation, another key component of this burgeoning industry will be manufacturing.

Made In Space has been at the forefront of manufacturing "in space, for space" since 2014, when it 3D-printed a wrench on board the ISS. Today, the company is exploring other products, such as high-quality fiber-optic cable, that terrestrial customers may be willing to pay to have manufactured in zero gravity. But the company also recently received a $74 million contract to 3D-print large metal beams in space for use on NASA spacecraft, and future private-sector spacecraft will certainly have similar manufacturing needs, which Made In Space hopes to be well positioned to fulfill. Just as SpaceX has begun by supplying NASA but hopes to eventually serve a much larger, private-sector market, Made In Space's current work with NASA could be the first step along a path toward supporting a variety of private-sector manufacturing applications for which the costs of manufacturing on Earth and transporting into space would be prohibitive.

Another major area of space-for-space investment is in building and operating space infrastructure such as habitats, laboratories, and factories. Axiom Space, a current leader in this field, recently announced that it would be flying the "first fully private commercial mission to space" in 2022 on board SpaceX's Crew Dragon capsule. Axiom was also awarded a contract for exclusive access to a module of the ISS, facilitating its plans to develop modules for commercial activity on the station (and eventually, beyond it).

This infrastructure is likely to spur investment in a wide array of complementary services to supply the demand of the people living and working within it. For example, in February 2020, Maxar Technologies was awarded a $142 million contract from NASA to develop a robotic construction tool that would be assembled in space for use on low-Earth-orbit spacecraft. Private-sector spacecraft or settlements will no doubt have need for a variety of similar construction and repair tools.

And of course, the private sector isn't just about industrial products. Creature comforts also promise to be an area of rapid growth, as companies endeavor to support the human side of life in the harsh environment of space. In 2015, for example, Argotec and Lavazza collaborated to build an espresso machine that could function in the zero-gravity environment of the ISS, delivering a bit of everyday luxury to the crew.

To be sure, for half a century people have dreamt of using the vacuum and weightlessness of space to source or make things that cannot be made on Earth, and time and again the business case has failed to pan out. Skepticism is natural. Those failures, however, have been in space-for-earth applications. For example, two startups of the 2010s, Planetary Resources and Deep Space Industries, recognized the potential of space mining early on. But for both companies, the lack of a space-for-space economy meant that their near-term survival depended on selling mined material—precious metals or rare elements—to Earth-bound customers. When it became clear that demand was insufficient to justify the high costs, funding dried up, and both companies pivoted to other ventures.

These were failures of space-for-earth business models—but the demand for in-space mining of raw building material, metals, and water will be enormous once humans are living in space (and therefore far cheaper to supply). In other words, when people are living and working in space, we are likely to look back on these early asteroid-mining companies less as failures and more as simply ahead of their time.

Seizing the Space-for-Space Opportunity

The opportunity presented by the space-for-space economy is huge—but it could easily be missed. To seize this moment, policy makers must provide regulatory and institutional frameworks that will enable the risk-taking and innovation necessary for a decentralized, private-sector-driven space economy. We believe three specific policy areas will be especially important:

Enabling private individuals to take on greater risk than would be tolerable for government-employed astronauts. First, as part of a general shift to that more decentralized, market-oriented space sector, policy makers should consider allowing private space tourists and settlers to voluntarily take on more risk than states would tolerate for government-employed astronauts. In the long run, ensuring high safety levels will be essential to convince larger numbers of people to travel or live in space, but in the early years of exploration, too great an aversion to risk will stop progress before it starts.

An instructive analogy can be found in how NASA works with its contractors: In the mid-2000s, NASA shifted from using cost-plus contracts (in which NASA shouldered all the economic risk of investing in space) to fixed-price contracts (in which risk was distributed between NASA and their contractors). Because of private companies' greater tolerance for risk, this shift catalyzed a burst of activity in the sector—sometimes referred to as "New Space." A similar shift in how we approach voluntary risk-taking by private-sector astronauts may be necessary in order to launch the space-for-space economy.

Judiciously implementing government regulation and support. Second, as with most markets, developing a stable space economy will depend on judicious government regulation and support. NASA and the U.S. Commerce and State Departments' recommitment to "create a regulatory environment in [low-Earth orbit] that enables American commercial activities to thrive" is a good sign that the government is on a path of continued collaboration with industry, but there's still a long way to go.[4]

Governments should start by clarifying how property rights over limited resources such as water on Mars, ice on the moon, or orbital slots (i.e., "parking spots" in space) will be governed. Recent steps—including NASA's offer to purchase lunar soil and rocks, the April 2020 executive order on the governance of space resources, and the 2015 Commercial Space Launch Competitiveness Act—indicate that the U.S. government is interested in establishing some form of regulatory framework to support the economic development of space.

In 2017, Luxembourg became the first European country to establish a legal framework securing private rights over resources mined in space, and similar steps have been taken at the domestic level in Japan and the United Arab Emirates. Moreover, nine countries (though Russia and China are notably missing) have signed the Artemis Accords, which lay out a vision for the sustainable, international development of the moon, Mars, and asteroids. These are important first steps, but they have yet to be clearly translated into comprehensive treaties that govern the fair use and allocation of scarce space resources among all major spacefaring nations.

In addition, governments should continue to fill the financial gaps in the still-maturing space-for-space economic ecosystem by funding basic scientific research in support of sending humans to space and by providing contracts to space startups. Similarly, while excessive regulation will stifle the industry, some government incentives, such as policies to reduce space debris, can help reduce the costs of operating in space for everyone in ways that would be difficult to coordinate independently.

Moving beyond geopolitical rivalries. Finally, the development of the space-for-space economy must not be undermined by earthly geopolitical rivalries, such as that between the United States and China. These conflicts will unavoidably extend into space at least to some extent, and military demand has long been an important source of funding for aerospace companies. But if not kept in check, such rivalries will not only distract attention and resources from borderless commercial pursuits but also create barriers and risks that hamper private investment.

On Earth, private economic activity has long tied together people whose states are at odds. The growing space-for-space economy offers exceptional potential to be such a force for unity—but it's the job of the world's governments not to get in the way. A collaborative, international approach to establishing—and enforcing—the rule of law in space will be essential to encouraging a healthy space-for-space economy.

Visions of a space-for-space economy have been around since the dawn of the Space Age, in the 1960s. Thus far, those hopes have gone largely unfulfilled—but this moment is different. For the first time in history, the private sector's capital, risk tolerance, and profit motive are being channeled into putting people in space. If we seize this opportunity, we will look back on this as the moment when we started the truly transformational project of building an economy and a society in space, for space.

NOTES

1. Matthew C. Weinzierl, Angela Acocella, and Mayuka Yamazaki, "Astroscale, Space Debris, and Earth's Orbital Commons," Harvard Business School, February 25, 2016, https://hbsp.harvard.edu/product/716037-PDF-ENG; and Matthew C. Weinzierl, Kylie Lucas, and Mehak Sarang, "SpaceX, Economies of Scale, and a Revolution in Space Access," Harvard Business School, April 9, 2020, https://hbsp.harvard.edu/product/720027-PDF-ENG.

2. William M. Brown and Herman Kahn, "Long-Term Prospects for Developments in Space: A Scenario Approach," NASA Technical Reports Server, October 30, 1977, https://ntrs.nasa.gov/citations/19780004167.

3. Matthew C. Weinzierl, "Space, the Final Economic Frontier," *Journal of Economic Perspectives* 32, no. 2 (Spring 2018), 173–192, https://www.hbs.edu/ris/Publication%20Files/jep.32.2.173_Space,%20the%20Final%20Economic%20Frontier_413bf24d-42e6-4cea-8cc5-a0d2f6fc6a70.pdf.

4. Marcia Smith, "Space Council Gets Human Spaceflight Strategy Report," SpacePolicyOnline.com, November 19, 2018, https://spacepolicyonline.com/news/space-council-gets-human-spaceflight-strategy-report/.

Adapted from content posted on hbr.org,
February 12, 2021 (product #H066NH).

CHAPTER TWENTY-EIGHT

That Discomfort You're Feeling Is Grief

An interview with David Kessler by Scott Berinato

Some of the HBR edit staff met virtually the other day—a screen full of faces in a scene becoming more common everywhere. We talked about the content we're commissioning in this harrowing time of a pandemic and how we can help people. But we also talked about how we were feeling. One colleague mentioned that what she felt was grief. Heads nodded in all the panes.

If we can name it, perhaps we can manage it. We turned to David Kessler for ideas on how to do that. Kessler is the world's foremost expert on grief. He cowrote with Elisabeth Kübler-Ross *On Grief and Grieving: Finding the Meaning of Grief through the Five Stages of Loss*. His new book adds another stage to the process, *Finding Meaning: The Sixth Stage of Grief*. Kessler also has worked for a decade in a three-hospital system in Los Angeles. He served on their biohazards team. His volunteer work includes being an LAPD Specialist Reserve for traumatic events as well as having served on the Red Cross's disaster services team. He is the founder of www.grief.com, which has over 5 million visits yearly from 167 countries.

Kessler shared his thoughts on why it's important to acknowledge the grief you may be feeling, how to manage it, and how he believes we will find meaning in it. The conversation is lightly edited for clarity.

People are feeling any number of things right now. Is it right to call some of what they're feeling grief?

Yes, and we're feeling a number of different griefs. We feel the world has changed, and it has. We know this is temporary, but it doesn't feel that way, and we realize things will be different. Just as going to the airport is forever different from how it was before 9/11, things will change and this is the point at which they changed. The loss of normalcy; the fear of economic toll; the loss of connection. This is hitting us and we're grieving. Collectively. We are not used to this kind of collective grief in the air.

You said we're feeling more than one kind of grief?

Yes, we're also feeling anticipatory grief. Anticipatory grief is that feeling we get about what the future holds when we're uncertain. Usually it centers on death. We feel it when someone gets a dire diagnosis or when we have the normal thought that we'll lose a parent someday. Anticipatory grief is also more broadly imagined futures. There is a storm coming. There's something bad out there. With a virus, this kind of grief is so confusing for people. Our primitive mind knows something bad is happening, but you can't see it. This breaks our sense of safety. We're feeling that loss of safety. I don't think we've collectively lost our sense of general safety like this. Individually or as smaller groups, people have felt this. But all together, this is new. We are grieving on a micro and a macro level.

What can individuals do to manage all this grief?

Understanding the stages of grief is a start. But whenever I talk about the stages of grief, I have to remind people that the stages aren't linear and may not happen in this order. It's not a map, but it provides some scaffolding for this unknown world. There's denial, which we say a lot of early on: *This virus won't affect us.* There's anger: *You're making me stay home and taking away my activities.* There's bargaining: *Okay, if I social distance for two weeks, everything will be better, right?* There's sadness: *I don't know when this will end.* And finally there's acceptance. *This is happening; I have to figure out how to proceed.*

Acceptance, as you might imagine, is where the power lies. We find control in acceptance. *I can wash my hands. I can keep a safe distance. I can learn how to work virtually.*

When we're feeling grief, there's that physical pain. And the racing mind. Are there techniques to deal with that to make it less intense?

Let's go back to anticipatory grief. Unhealthy anticipatory grief is really anxiety, and that's the feeling you're talking about. Our mind begins to show us images. My parents getting sick. We see the worst scenarios. That's our minds being protective. Our goal is not to ignore those images or to try to make them go away—your mind won't let you do that, and it can be painful to try to force it. The goal is to find balance in the things you're thinking. If you feel the worst image taking shape, make yourself think of the best image. We all get a little sick and the world continues. Not everyone I love dies. Maybe no one does because we're all taking the right steps. Neither scenario should be ignored, but neither should dominate either.

Anticipatory grief is the mind going to the future and imagining the worst. To calm yourself, you want to come into the present. This will be familiar advice to anyone who has meditated or practiced mindfulness, but people are always surprised at how prosaic this can be. You can name five things in the room. There's a computer, a chair, a picture of the dog, an old rug, and a coffee mug. It's that simple. Breathe. Realize that in the present moment, nothing you've anticipated has happened. In this moment, you're okay. You have food. You are not sick. Use your senses and think about what they feel. The desk is hard. The blanket is soft. I can feel the breath coming into my nose. This really will work to dampen some of that pain.

You can also think about how to let go of what you can't control. What your neighbor is doing is out of your control. What is in your control is staying six feet away from them and washing your hands. Focus on that.

Finally, it's a good time to stock up on compassion. Everyone will have different levels of fear and grief, and it manifests in different ways. A coworker got very snippy with me the other day, and I thought, *That's not like this person; that's how they're dealing with this. I'm seeing their fear and anxiety.* So be patient. Think about who someone usually is and not who they seem to be in this moment.

One particularly troubling aspect of this pandemic is the open-endedness of it.

This is a temporary state. It helps to say it. I worked for 10 years in the hospital system. I've been trained for situations like this. I've also studied the 1918 flu pandemic. The precautions we're taking are the right ones. History tells us that. This is survivable. We will survive. This is a time to overprotect but not overreact.

And, I believe we will find meaning in it. I've been honored that Elisabeth Kübler-Ross's family has given me permission to add a sixth stage to grief: meaning. I had talked to Elisabeth quite a bit about what came after acceptance. I did not want to stop at acceptance when I experienced some personal grief. I wanted meaning in those darkest hours. And I do believe we find light in those times. Even now people are realizing they can connect through technology. They are not as remote as they thought. They are realizing they can use their phones for long conversations. They're appreciating walks. I believe we will continue to find meaning now and when this is over.

What do you say to someone who's read all this and is still feeling overwhelmed with grief?

Keep trying. There is something powerful about naming this as grief. It helps us feel what's inside of us. So many have told me in the past week, "I'm telling my coworkers I'm having a hard time," or "I cried last night." When you name it, you feel it and it moves through you. Emotions need motion. It's important we acknowledge what we go through. One unfortunate by-product of the self-help movement is we're the first generation to have feelings about our feelings. We tell ourselves things like, *I feel sad, but I shouldn't feel that; other people have it worse.* We can—we should—stop at the first feeling. *I feel sad. Let me go for five minutes to feel sad.* Your work is to feel your sadness and fear and anger whether or not someone else is feeling something. Fighting it doesn't help because your body is producing the feeling. If we allow the feelings to happen, they'll happen in an orderly way, and it empowers us. Then we're not victims.

In an orderly way?

Yes. Sometimes we try not to feel what we're feeling because we have this image of a "gang of feelings." If I feel sad and let that in, it'll never go away. The gang of bad feelings will overrun me. The truth is a feeling that moves through us. We feel it and it goes and then we go to the next feeling. There's no gang out to get us. It's absurd to think we shouldn't feel grief right now. Let yourself feel the grief and keep going.

———————

Adapted from content posted on hbr.org, March 23, 2020 (product #H05HVE).

CHAPTER TWENTY-NINE

What Psychological Safety Looks Like in a Hybrid Workplace

by Amy C. Edmondson and Mark Mortensen

"Our office policy is that people should come into the office once per week. Now they are organizing a team meeting with 15 people. I guess some people seem to feel comfortable with that, but I'm not; I have a young family at home and we have been very careful. I can't say that though."

—Executive at a global food brand, shared privately

[To a colleague working from home] "We miss having you here with us in the office. We are seeing more people in the office these days, and it's really nice to have more people around."

—Comments made in a virtual team coffee chat

Since the Covid-19 pandemic changed the landscape of work, much attention has been given to the more visible aspects of working from home (WFH), including the challenges of managing people from a distance (including reduced trust and new power dynamics). But a far less visible factor may dramatically influence the effectiveness of hybrid workplaces. As suggested by the above quotes, sorting out future work arrangements, and attending to employees' inevitable anxieties about those arrangements, will require managers to rethink and expand one of strongest proven predictors of team effectiveness: psychological safety.

How New Forms of Work Affect Psychological Safety

Psychological safety—the belief that one can speak up without risk of punishment or humiliation—has been well established as a critical driver of high-quality decision-making, healthy group dynamics and interpersonal relationships, greater innovation, and more-effective execution in organizations.[1] Simple as it may be to understand, Amy's work has shown how hard it is to establish and maintain psychological safety even in the most straightforward, factual, and critical contexts—for example, ensuring that operating room staff speak up to avoid a wrong-side surgery, or that a CEO is corrected before sharing inaccurate data in a public meeting (both are real-life examples of psychological safety failures reported in interviews). Unfortunately, WFH and hybrid working make psychological safety anything but straightforward.

When it comes to psychological safety, managers have traditionally focused on enabling candor and dissent with respect to work content. The problem is, as the boundary between work and life becomes increasingly blurry, managers must make staffing, scheduling, and coordination decisions that take into account employees' personal circumstances—a categorically different domain.

For one employee, the decision of when to work from home may be driven by a need to spend time with a widowed parent or to help a child struggling at school. For another, it may be influenced by undisclosed health issues (something Covid-19 brought into stark relief) or a nonwork passion, as was the case with a young professional who trained as an Olympic-level athlete on the side. It's worth noting that we've both heard from employees who feel marginalized, penalized, or excluded from this dialogue around work-life balance because they're single or have no children, often being told they're lucky they don't have to deal with those challenges.

Having psychologically safe discussions around work-life balance issues is challenging because these topics are more likely to touch on deep-seated aspects of employees' identity, values, and choices. This makes them both more personal and riskier from legal and ethical standpoints with respect to bias.

We Can't Just Keep Doing What We're Doing

In the past, we've approached "work" and "nonwork" discussions as separable, allowing managers to keep the latter off the table. Over the past year, however, many managers have found that previously off-limits topics like childcare, health-risk comfort levels, or challenges faced by spouses or other family members are increasingly required for joint (manager and employee) decisions about how to structure and schedule hybrid work.

While it may be tempting to think we can reseparate the two once we return to the office, the shift to a higher proportion of WFH means that's neither a realistic nor a sustainable long-term solution. Organizations that don't update their approach going forward will find themselves trying to optimize extremely complicated scheduling and coordination challenges with incomplete—if not incorrect—information. Keep in mind that hybrid working arrangements present a parallel increase in managerial complexity; managers face the same workflow coordination challenges they've managed in the past, now with the added challenge of coordinating among people who can't be counted on to be present at predictable times.

Strategies for Managers

Let's start with the fact that the reasons why managers have avoided seeking personal details remain just as relevant and critical today as they've always been. Sharing personal information carries real and significant risks, given legal restrictions related to asking personal questions, the potential for bias, and a desire to respect employee privacy. The solution thus cannot be to demand greater disclosure of personal details. Instead, managers must create an environment that encourages employees to share aspects of their personal situations as relevant to their work scheduling or location and/or to trust employees to make the right choices for themselves and their families, balanced against the needs of their teams. Management's responsibility is to expand the domain of which work-life issues are safe to raise. Psychological safety is needed today to enable productive conversations in new, challenging (and potentially fraught) territory.

Obviously, simply saying "just trust me" won't work. Instead, we suggest a series of five steps to create a culture of psychological safety that extends beyond the work content to include broader aspects of employees' experiences.

Step 1: Set the scene

Trite as it sounds, the first step is having a discussion with your team to help them recognize not only their challenges but yours as well. The objective of this discussion is to share ownership of the problem.

We suggest framing this as a need for the group to problem-solve to develop new ways to work effectively. Clarify what's at stake. Employees must understand that getting the work done (for customers, for the mission, for their careers) matters just as much as it always has, but that it won't be done exactly as it was in the past—they'll need to play a (creative and responsible) role in that. As a group, you and your employees must come to recognize that everyone has to be clear and transparent about the needs of the work and of the team and jointly own responsibility for succeeding, despite the many hurdles that lie ahead.

Step 2: Lead the way

Words are cheap, and when it comes to psychological safety, there are far too many stories of managers who demand candor of their employees—particularly around mistakes or other potentially embarrassing topics—without demonstrating it themselves or without protecting it when others do share.

The best way to show you're serious is to expose your own vulnerability by sharing your own WFH/hybrid-work personal challenges and constraints. Remember, managers have to go first in taking these kinds of risks. Be vulnerable and humble about not having a clear plan, and be open about how you're thinking about managing your own challenges. If you're not willing to be candid with your employees, why should you expect them to be candid with you?

Step 3: Take baby steps

Don't expect your employees to share their most personal and risky challenges right away. It takes time to build trust, and even if you have a healthy culture of psychological safety established around work, remember that this is a new domain, and speaking up about buggy code is different from sharing struggles at home.

Start by making small disclosures yourself, and then make sure to welcome others' disclosures to help your employees build confidence that sharing is not penalized.

Step 4: Share positive examples

Don't assume that your employees will immediately have access to all the information that you have that supports the benefits of sharing these challenges and needs.

Put your marketing hat on and promote psychological safety by sharing your conviction that increased transparency is happening and is helping the team design new arrangements that serve both individual needs and organizational goals. The goal here isn't to share information that was disclosed to you privately but rather to explain that disclosure has allowed you to collaboratively come up with solutions that were better not just for the team but also for the employees. This needs to be done with tact and skill to avoid creating pressure to conform—the goal here is to provide employees with the evidence they need to buy in voluntarily.

Step 5: Be a watchdog

Most people recognize that psychological safety takes time to build but just moments to destroy. The default is for people to hold back, to fail to share even their most relevant thoughts at work if they're not sure they'll be well received. When they do take the risk of speaking up but get shot down, they—and everyone else—will be less likely to do it the next time.

As a team leader, you need to be vigilant and push back when you notice employees making seemingly innocent comments like "We want to see more of you" or "We could really use you," which may leave employees feeling they're letting their teammates down. This is a really hard thing to do and requires skill. The idea isn't to become thought police or punish those who genuinely do miss their WFH colleagues or need their help but rather to help employees frame these remarks in a more positive and understanding way—for example, "We miss your thoughtful perspective, and understand you face constraints. Let us know if there is any way we can help . . ." Be open about your intentions to be inclusive and helpful so that people don't see requests for their presence as a rebuke. At the same time, be ready to firmly censure those who inappropriately take advantage of shared personal information.

It's important that managers view (and discuss) these conversations as a work in progress. As with all group dynamics, they're emergent processes that develop and shift over time. This is a first step; the journey ahead comes without a road map and will have to be navigated iteratively. You may overstep and need to correct, but it's better to err on the side of trying and testing the waters than assuming topics are off-limits. View this as a learning or problem-solving undertaking that may never reach a steady state. The more you maintain that perspective—rather than declaring victory and moving on—the more successful you and your team will be at developing and maintaining true, expanded psychological safety.

NOTE

1. Amy C. Edmondson, *The Fearless Organization: Creating Psychological Safety in the Workplace for Learning, Innovation, and Growth* (Hoboken, NJ: John Wiley & Sons, 2018).

Adapted from content posted on hbr.org,
April 19, 2021 (product #H06AWX).

CHAPTER THIRTY

Strategic Intent

by Gary Hamel and C.K. Prahalad

Today managers in many industries are working hard to match the competitive advantages of their new global rivals. They are moving manufacturing offshore in search of lower labor costs, rationalizing product lines to capture global scale economies, instituting quality circles and just-in-time production, and adopting Japanese human resource practices. When competitiveness still seems out of reach, they form strategic alliances—often with the very companies that upset the competitive balance in the first place.

Important as these initiatives are, few of them go beyond mere imitation. Too many companies are expending enormous energy simply to reproduce the cost and quality advantages their global competitors already enjoy. Imitation may be the sincerest form of flattery, but it will not lead to competitive revitalization. Strategies based on imitation are transparent to competitors who have already mastered them. Moreover, successful competitors rarely stand still. So it is not surprising that many executives feel trapped in a seemingly endless game of catch-up, regularly surprised by the new accomplishments of their rivals.

For these executives and their companies, regaining competitiveness will mean rethinking many of the basic concepts of strategy.[1] As "strategy" has blossomed, the competitiveness of Western companies has withered. This may be coincidence, but we think not. We believe that the application of concepts such as "strategic fit" (between resources and opportunities), "generic strategies" (low cost versus differentiation versus focus), and the "strategy hierarchy" (goals, strategies, and tactics) has often abetted the process of competitive decline. The new global competitors approach strategy from a perspective that is fundamentally different from that which underpins Western management thought. Against such competitors, marginal adjustments to current orthodoxies are no more likely to produce competitive revitalization than are marginal improvements in operating efficiency. (The sidebar "Remaking Strategy" describes our research and summarizes the two contrasting approaches to strategy we see in large multinational companies.)

Few Western companies have an enviable track record anticipating the moves of new global competitors. Why? The explanation begins with the way most companies have approached competitor analysis. Typically, competitor analysis focuses on the existing resources (human, technical, and financial) of present competitors. The only companies seen as a threat are those with the resources to erode margins and market share in the next planning period. Resourcefulness, the pace at which new competitive advantages are being built, rarely enters in.

In this respect, traditional competitor analysis is like a snapshot of a moving car. By itself, the photograph yields little information about the car's speed or direction—whether the driver is out for a quiet Sunday drive or warming up for the Grand Prix. Yet many managers have learned through painful experience that a business's initial resource endowment (whether bountiful or meager) is an unreliable predictor of future global success.

Think back: In 1970, few Japanese companies possessed the resource base, manufacturing volume, or technical prowess of U.S. and European industry leaders. Komatsu was less than 35% as large as Caterpillar (measured by sales), was scarcely represented outside Japan, and relied on just one product line—small bulldozers—for most of its revenue. Honda was smaller than American Motors and had not yet begun to export cars to the United States. Canon's first halting steps in the reprographics business looked pitifully small compared with the $4 billion Xerox powerhouse.

Remaking Strategy

Over the last ten years, our research on global competition, international alliances, and multinational management has brought us into close contact with senior managers in the United States, Europe, and Japan. As we tried to unravel the reasons for success and surrender in global markets, we became more and more suspicious that executives in Western and Far Eastern companies often operated with very different conceptions of competitive strategy. Understanding these differences, we thought, might help explain the conduct and outcome of competitive battles as well as supplement traditional explanations for Japan's ascendance and the West's decline.

We began by mapping the implicit strategy models of managers who had participated in our research. Then we built detailed histories of selected competitive battles. We searched for evidence of divergent views of strategy, competitive advantage, and the role of top management.

Two contrasting models of strategy emerged. One, which most Western managers will recognize, centers on the problem of maintaining strategic fit. The other centers on the problem of leveraging resources. The two are not mutually exclusive, but they represent a significant difference in emphasis—an emphasis that deeply affects how competitive battles get played out over time.

Both models recognize the problem of competing in a hostile environment with limited resources. But while the emphasis in the first is on trimming ambitions to match available resources, the emphasis in the second is on leveraging resources to reach seemingly unattainable goals.

Both models recognize that relative competitive advantage determines relative profitability. The first emphasizes the search for advantages that are inherently sustainable; the second emphasizes the need to accelerate organizational learning to outpace competitors in building new advantages.

Both models recognize the difficulty of competing against larger competitors. But while the first leads to a search for niches (or simply dissuades the company from challenging an entrenched competitor), the second produces a quest for new rules that can devalue the incumbent's advantages.

Both models recognize that balance in the scope of an organization's activities reduces risk. The first seeks to reduce financial risk by building a balanced portfolio of cash-generating and cash-consuming businesses. The second seeks to reduce competitive risk by ensuring a well-balanced and sufficiently broad portfolio of advantages.

Both models recognize the need to disaggregate the organization in a way that allows top management to differentiate among the investment needs of various planning units. In the first model, resources are allocated to product-market units in which relatedness is defined by common products, channels,

(continued)

and customers. Each business is assumed to own all the critical skills it needs to execute its strategy successfully. In the second, investments are made in core competences (microprocessor controls or electronic imaging, for example) as well as in product-market units. By tracking these investments across businesses, top management works to assure that the plans of individual strategic units don't undermine future developments by default.

Both models recognize the need for consistency in action across organizational levels. In the first, consistency between corporate and business levels is largely a matter of conforming to financial objectives. Consistency between business and functional levels comes by tightly restricting the means the business uses to achieve its strategy—establishing standard operating procedures, defining the served market, adhering to accepted industry practices. In the second model, business-corporate consistency comes from allegiance to a particular strategic intent. Business-functional consistency comes from allegiance to intermediate-term goals or challenges with lower-level employees encouraged to invent how those goals will be achieved.

If Western managers had extended their competitor analysis to include these companies, it would merely have underlined how dramatic the resource discrepancies between them were. Yet by 1985, Komatsu was a $2.8 billion company with a product scope encompassing a broad range of earth-moving equipment, industrial robots, and semiconductors. Honda manufactured almost as many cars worldwide in 1987 as Chrysler. Canon had matched Xerox's global unit market share.

The lesson is clear: Assessing the current tactical advantages of known competitors will not help you understand the resolution, stamina, or inventiveness of potential competitors. Sun-tzu, a Chinese military strategist, made the point 3,000 years ago: "All men can see the tactics whereby I conquer," he wrote, "but what none can see is the strategy out of which great victory is evolved."

Companies that have risen to global leadership over the past 20 years invariably began with ambitions that were out of all proportion to their resources and capabilities. But they created an obsession with winning at all levels of the organization and then sustained that obsession over the 10- to 20-year quest for global leadership. We term this obsession "strategic intent."

On the one hand, strategic intent envisions a desired leadership position and establishes the criterion the organization will use to chart its progress. Komatsu set out to "encircle Caterpillar." Canon sought to "beat Xerox." Honda strove to become a second Ford—an automotive pioneer. All are expressions of strategic intent.

At the same time, strategic intent is more than simply unfettered ambition. (Many companies possess an ambitious strategic intent yet fall short of their goals.) The concept also encompasses an active management process that includes focusing the organization's attention on the essence of winning, motivating people by communicating the value of the target, leaving room for individual and team contributions, sustaining enthusiasm by providing new operational definitions as circumstances change, and using intent consistently to guide resource allocations.

Strategic intent captures the essence of winning

The Apollo program—landing a man on the moon ahead of the Soviets—was as competitively focused as Komatsu's drive against Caterpillar. The space program became the scorecard for America's technology race with the USSR. In the turbulent information technology industry, it was hard to pick a single competitor as a target, so NEC's strategic intent, set in the early 1970s, was to acquire the technologies that would put it in the best position to exploit the convergence of computing and telecommunications. Other industry observers foresaw this convergence, but only NEC made convergence the guiding theme for subsequent strategic decisions by adopting "computing and communications" as its intent. For Coca-Cola, strategic intent has been to put a Coke within "arm's reach" of every consumer in the world.

Strategic intent is stable over time

In battles for global leadership, one of the most critical tasks is to lengthen the organization's attention span. Strategic intent provides consistency to short-term action, while leaving room for reinterpretation as new opportunities emerge. At Komatsu, encircling

Caterpillar encompassed a succession of medium-term programs aimed at exploiting specific weaknesses in Caterpillar or building particular competitive advantages. When Caterpillar threatened Komatsu in Japan, for example, Komatsu responded by first improving quality, then driving down costs, then cultivating export markets, and then underwriting new product development.

Strategic intent sets a target that deserves personal effort and commitment

Ask the CEOs of many American corporations how they measure their contributions to their companies' success, and you're likely to get an answer expressed in terms of shareholder wealth. In a company that possesses a strategic intent, top management is more likely to talk in terms of global market leadership. Market share leadership typically yields shareholder wealth, to be sure. But the two goals do not have the same motivational impact. It is hard to imagine middle managers, let alone blue-collar employees, waking up each day with the sole thought of creating more shareholder wealth. But mightn't they feel different given the challenge to "beat Benz"—the rallying cry at one Japanese auto producer? Strategic intent gives employees the only goal that is worthy of commitment: to unseat the best or remain the best, worldwide.

Many companies are more familiar with strategic planning than they are with strategic intent. The planning process typically acts as a "feasibility sieve." Strategies are accepted or rejected on the basis of whether managers can be precise about the "how" as well as the "what" of their plans. Are the milestones clear? Do we have the necessary skills and resources? How will competitors react? Has the market been thoroughly researched? In one form or another, the admonition "Be realistic!" is given to line managers at almost every turn.

But can you *plan* for global leadership? Did Komatsu, Canon, and Honda have detailed 20-year strategies for attacking Western markets? Are Japanese and Korean managers better planners than their Western counterparts? No. As valuable as strategic planning is, global leadership is an objective that lies outside the range of planning. We know of few companies with highly developed planning systems that have managed to set a strategic intent. As tests of strategic fit become more stringent, goals that cannot be planned for fall by the wayside. Yet companies that are afraid to commit to goals that lie outside the range of planning are unlikely to become global leaders.

Although strategic planning is billed as a way of becoming more future-oriented, most managers, when pressed, will admit that their strategic plans reveal more about today's problems than tomorrow's opportunities. With a fresh set of problems confronting managers at the beginning of every planning cycle, focus often shifts dramatically from year to year. And with the pace of change accelerating in most industries, the predictive horizon is becoming shorter and shorter. So plans do little more than project the present forward incrementally. The goal of strategic intent is to fold the future back into the present. The important question is not "How will next year be different from this year?" but "What must we do differently next year to get closer to our strategic intent?" Only with a carefully articulated and adhered to strategic intent will a succession of year-on-year plans sum up to global leadership.

Just as you cannot plan a ten- to 20-year quest for global leadership, the chance of falling into a leadership position by accident is also remote. We don't believe that global leadership comes from an undirected process of intrapreneurship. Nor is it the product of a skunkworks or other technique for internal venturing. Behind such programs lies a nihilistic assumption: that the organization is so hidebound, so orthodox-ridden, the only way to innovate is to put a few bright people in a dark room, pour in some money, and hope that something wonderful will happen. In this Silicon Valley approach to innovation, the only role for top managers is to retrofit their corporate strategy to the entrepreneurial successes that emerge from below. Here the value added of top management is low indeed.

Sadly, this view of innovation may be consistent with reality in many large companies.[2] On the one hand, top management lacks any particular point of view about desirable ends beyond satisfying shareholders and keeping raiders at bay. On the other, the planning format, reward criteria, definition of served market, and belief in accepted industry practice all work together to tightly constrain the range of available means. As a result, innovation is necessarily an isolated activity. Growth depends more on the inventive capacity of individuals and small teams than on the ability of top management to aggregate the efforts of multiple teams toward an ambitious strategic intent.

In companies that have overcome resource constraints to build leadership positions, we see a different relationship between means and ends. While strategic intent is clear about ends, it is flexible as to means—it leaves room for improvisation. Achieving strategic intent requires enormous creativity with respect to means: Witness Fujitsu's use of strategic alliances in Europe to attack IBM. But this creativity comes in the service of a clearly prescribed end. Creativity is unbridled but not uncorralled, because top management establishes the criterion against which employees can pretest the logic of their initiatives. Middle managers must do more than deliver on promised financial targets; they must also deliver on the broad direction implicit in their organization's strategic intent.

Strategic intent implies a sizable stretch for an organization. Current capabilities and resources will not suffice. This forces the organization to be more inventive, to make the most of limited resources. Whereas the traditional view of strategy focuses on the degree of fit between existing resources and current opportunities, strategic intent creates an extreme misfit between resources and ambitions. Top management then challenges the organization to close the gap by systematically building new advantages. For Canon, this meant first understanding Xerox's patents, then licensing technology to create a product that would yield early market experience, then gearing up internal R&D efforts, then licensing its own technology to other manufacturers to fund further R&D, then entering market segments in Japan and Europe where Xerox was weak, and so on.

In this respect, strategic intent is like a marathon run in 400-meter sprints. No one knows what the terrain will look like at mile 26, so the role of top management is to focus the organization's attention on the ground to be covered in the next 400 meters. In several companies, management did this by presenting the organization with a series of corporate challenges, each specifying the next hill in the race to achieve strategic intent. One year the challenge might be quality, the next it might be total customer care, the next, entry into new markets, and the next, a rejuvenated product line. As this example indicates, corporate challenges are a way to stage the acquisition of new competitive advantages, a way to identify the focal point for employees' efforts in the near to medium term. As with strategic intent, top management is specific about the ends (reducing product development times by 75%, for example) but less prescriptive about the means.

Like strategic intent, challenges stretch the organization. To preempt Xerox in the personal copier business, Canon set its engineers a target price of $1,000 for a home copier. At the time, Canon's least expensive copier sold for several thousand dollars. Trying to reduce the cost of existing models would not have given Canon the radical price-performance improvement it needed to delay or deter Xerox's entry into personal copiers. Instead, Canon engineers were challenged to reinvent the copier—a challenge they met by substituting a disposable cartridge for the complex image-transfer mechanism used in other copiers.

Corporate challenges come from analyzing competitors as well as from the foreseeable pattern of industry evolution. Together these reveal potential competitive openings and identify the new skills the organization will need to take the initiative away from better-positioned players. (The table "Building competitive advantage at Komatsu" illustrates the way challenges helped Komatsu achieve its intent.)

For a challenge to be effective, individuals and teams throughout the organization must understand it and see its implications for their own jobs. Companies that set corporate challenges to create new competitive advantages (as Ford and IBM did with quality

Building competitive advantage at Komatsu

Corporate challenge	Protect Komatsu's home market against Caterpillar	Reduce costs while maintaining quality
Programs	**Early 1960s** Licensing deals with Cummins Engine, International Harvester, and Bucyrus-Erie to acquire technology and establish benchmarks	**1965** Cost Down (CD) program
		1966 Total CD program
	1961 Project A (for Ace) to advance the product quality of Komatsu's small and midsize bulldozers above Caterpillar's	
	1962 Quality circles company-wide to provide training for all employees	

improvement) quickly discover that engaging the entire organization requires top management to do the following:

- *Create a sense of urgency,* or quasi crisis, by amplifying weak signals in the environment that point up the need to improve, instead of allowing inaction to precipitate a real crisis. Komatsu, for example, budgeted on the basis of worst-case exchange rates that overvalued the yen.

- *Develop a competitor focus at every level through widespread use of competitive intelligence.* Every employee should be able to benchmark his or her efforts against best-in-class competitors so that the challenge becomes personal. For in-

Make Komatsu an international enterprise and build export markets	Respond to external shocks that threaten markets	Create new products and markets
Early 1960s Develop Eastern bloc countries	**1975** V-10 program to reduce costs by 10% while maintaining quality, reduce parts by 20%, and rationalize manufacturing system	**Late 1970s** Accelerate product development to expand line
1967 Komatsu Europe marketing subsidiary established		**1979** Future and Frontiers program to identify new businesses based on society's needs and company's know-how
1970 Komatsu America established	**1977** ¥180 program to budget companywide for 180 yen to the dollar when the exchange rate was 240	**1981** EPOCHS program to reconcile greater product variety with improved production efficiencies
1972 Project B to improve the durability and reliability and to reduce costs of large bulldozers	**1979** Project E to establish teams to redouble cost and quality efforts in response to oil crisis	
1972 Project C to improve payloaders		
1972 Project D to improve hydraulic excavators		
1974 Establish presales and service departments to assist newly industrializing countries in construction projects		

stance, Ford showed production-line workers videotapes of operations at Mazda's most efficient plant.

- *Provide employees with the skills they need to work effectively*—training in statistical tools, problem-solving, value engineering, and team building, for example.

- *Give the organization time to digest one challenge before launching another.* When competing initiatives overload the organization, middle managers often try to protect their people from the whipsaw of shifting priorities. But this "wait and see if they're serious this time" attitude ultimately destroys the credibility of corporate challenges.

- *Establish clear milestones and review mechanisms* to track progress, and ensure that internal recognition and rewards reinforce desired behaviors. The goal is to make the challenge inescapable for everyone in the company.

It is important to distinguish between the process of managing corporate challenges and the advantages that the process creates. Whatever the actual challenge may be—quality, cost, value engineering, or something else—there is the same need to engage employees intellectually and emotionally in the development of new skills. In each case, the challenge will take root only if senior executives and lower-level employees feel a reciprocal responsibility for competitiveness.

We believe workers in many companies have been asked to take a disproportionate share of the blame for competitive failure. In one U.S. company, for example, management had sought a 40% wage-package concession from hourly employees to bring labor costs into line with Far Eastern competitors. The result was a long strike and, ultimately, a 10% wage concession from employees on the line. However, direct labor costs in manufacturing accounted for less than 15% of total value added. The company thus succeeded in demoralizing its entire blue-collar workforce for the sake of a 1.5% reduction in total costs. Ironically, further analysis showed that their competitors' most significant costs savings came not from lower hourly wages but from better work methods invented by employees. You can imagine how eager the U.S. workers were to make similar contributions after the strike and concessions. Contrast this situation with what happened at Nissan when the yen strengthened: Top management took a big pay cut and then asked middle managers and line employees to sacrifice relatively less.

Reciprocal responsibility means shared gain and shared pain. In too many companies, the pain of revitalization falls almost exclusively on the employees least responsible for the enterprise's decline. Too often, workers are asked to commit to corporate goals without any matching commitment from top management—be it employment security, gain sharing, or an ability to influence the direction of the business. This one-sided approach to regaining competitiveness keeps many companies from harnessing the intellectual horsepower of their employees.

Creating a sense of reciprocal responsibility is crucial because competitiveness ultimately depends on the pace at which a company embeds new advantages deep within its organization, not on its stock of advantages at any given time. Thus, the concept of competitive advantage must be expanded beyond the scorecard many managers now use: Are my costs lower? Will my product command a price premium?

Few competitive advantages are long lasting. Uncovering a new competitive advantage is a bit like getting a hot tip on a stock: The first person to act on the insight makes more money than the last. When the experience curve was young, a company that built capacity ahead of competitors, dropped prices to fill plants, and reduced costs as volume rose went to the bank. The first mover traded on the fact that competitors undervalued market share—they didn't price to capture additional share because they didn't understand how market share leadership could be translated into lower costs and better margins. But there is no more undervalued market share when each of 20 semiconductor companies builds enough capacity to serve 10% of the world market.

Keeping score of existing advantages is not the same as building new advantages. The essence of strategy lies in creating tomorrow's competitive advantages faster than competitors mimic the ones you possess today. In the 1960s, Japanese producers relied on labor and capital cost advantages. As Western manufacturers began to move production offshore, Japanese companies accelerated their investment in process technology and created scale and quality advantages. Then, as their U.S. and European competitors rationalized manufacturing, they added another string to their bow by accelerating the rate of product development. Then they built global brands. Then they deskilled competitors through alliances and outsourcing deals. The moral? An organization's capacity to improve existing skills and learn new ones is the most defensible competitive advantage of all.

To achieve a strategic intent, a company must usually take on larger, better-financed competitors. That means carefully managing competitive engagements so that scarce resources are conserved. Managers cannot do that simply by playing the same game better—making marginal improvements to competitors' technology and business practices. Instead, they must fundamentally change the game in ways that disadvantage incumbents: devising novel approaches to market entry, advantage building, and competitive warfare. For smart competitors, the goal is not competitive imitation but competitive innovation, the art of containing competitive risks within manageable proportions.

Four approaches to competitive innovation are evident in the global expansion of Japanese companies. These are: building layers of advantage, searching for loose bricks, changing the terms of engagement, and competing through collaboration.

The wider a company's portfolio of advantages, the less risk it faces in competitive battles. New global competitors have built such portfolios by steadily expanding their arsenals of competitive weapons. They have moved inexorably from less defensible advantages such as low wage costs to more defensible advantages such as global brands. The Japanese color television industry illustrates this layering process.

By 1967, Japan had become the largest producer of black-and-white television sets. By 1970, it was closing the gap in color televisions. Japanese manufacturers used their competitive advantage—at that time, primarily, low labor costs—to build a base in the private-label business, then moved quickly to establish world-scale plants. This investment gave them additional layers of advantage—quality and reliability—as well as further cost reductions from process improvements. At the same time, they recognized that these cost-based advantages were vulnerable to changes in labor costs, process and product technology, exchange rates, and trade policy. So throughout the 1970s, they also invested heavily in building channels and brands, thus creating another layer of advantage: a global franchise. In the late 1970s, they enlarged the scope of their products and businesses to amortize these grand investments, and by

1980 all the major players—Matsushita, Sharp, Toshiba, Hitachi, Sanyo—had established related sets of businesses that could support global marketing investments. More recently, they have been investing in regional manufacturing and design centers to tailor their products more closely to national markets.

These manufacturers thought of the various sources of competitive advantage as mutually desirable layers, not mutually exclusive choices. What some call competitive suicide—pursuing both cost and differentiation—is exactly what many competitors strive for.[3] Using flexible manufacturing technologies and better marketing intelligence, they are moving away from standardized "world products" to products like Mazda's minivan, developed in California expressly for the U.S. market.

Another approach to competitive innovation, searching for loose bricks, exploits the benefits of surprise, which is just as useful in business battles as it is in war. Particularly in the early stages of a war for global markets, successful new competitors work to stay below the response threshold of their larger, more powerful rivals. Staking out underdefended territory is one way to do this.

To find loose bricks, managers must have few orthodoxies about how to break into a market or challenge a competitor. For example, in one large U.S. multinational, we asked several country managers to describe what a Japanese competitor was doing in the local market. The first executive said, "They're coming at us in the low end. Japanese companies always come in at the bottom." The second speaker found the comment interesting but disagreed: "They don't offer any low-end products in my market, but they have some exciting stuff at the top end. We really should reverse engineer that thing." Another colleague told still another story. "They haven't taken any business away from me," he said, "but they've just made me a great offer to supply components." In each country, the Japanese competitor had found a different loose brick.

The search for loose bricks begins with a careful analysis of the competitor's conventional wisdom: How does the company define its "served market"? What activities are most profitable? Which geographic markets are too troublesome to enter? The objective is not to find a corner of the industry (or niche) where larger competitors seldom tread but to build a base of attack just outside the market territory that industry leaders currently occupy. The goal is an uncontested profit sanctuary, which could be a particular product segment (the "low end" in motorcycles), a slice of the value chain (components in the computer industry), or a particular geographic market (Eastern Europe).

When Honda took on leaders in the motorcycle industry, for example, it began with products that were just outside the conventional definition of the leaders' product-market domains. As a result, it could build a base of operations in underdefended territory and then use that base to launch an expanded attack. What many competitors failed to see was Honda's strategic intent and its growing competence in engines and power trains. Yet even as Honda was selling 50cc motorcycles in the United States, it was already racing larger bikes in Europe—assembling the design skills and technology it would need for a systematic expansion across the entire spectrum of motor-related businesses.

Honda's progress in creating a core competence in engines should have warned competitors that it might enter a series of seemingly unrelated industries—automobiles, lawn mowers, marine engines, generators. But with each company fixated on its own market, the threat of Honda's horizontal diversification went unnoticed. Today, companies like Matsushita and Toshiba are similarly poised to move in unexpected ways across industry boundaries. In protecting loose bricks, companies must extend their peripheral vision by tracking and anticipating the migration of global competitors across product segments, businesses, national markets, value-added stages, and distribution channels.

Changing the terms of engagement—refusing to accept the front-runner's definition of industry and segment boundaries—represents still another form of competitive innovation. Canon's entry into the copier business illustrates this approach.

During the 1970s, both Kodak and IBM tried to match Xerox's business system in terms of segmentation, products, distribution, service, and pricing. As a result, Xerox had no trouble decoding the new entrants' intentions and developing countermoves. IBM eventually withdrew from the copier business, while Kodak remains a distant second in the large copier market that Xerox still dominates.

Canon, on the other hand, changed the terms of competitive engagement. While Xerox built a wide range of copiers, Canon standardized machines and components to reduce costs. It chose to distribute through office product dealers rather than try to match Xerox's huge direct sales force. It also avoided the need to create a national service network by designing reliability and serviceability into its product and then delegating service responsibility to the dealers. Canon copiers were sold rather than leased, freeing Canon from the burden of financing the lease base. Finally, instead of selling to the heads of corporate duplicating departments, Canon appealed to secretaries and department managers who wanted distributed copying. At each stage, Canon neatly sidestepped a potential barrier to entry.

Canon's experience suggests that there is an important distinction between barriers to entry and barriers to imitation. Competitors that tried to match Xerox's business system had to pay the same entry costs—the barriers to imitation were high. But Canon dramatically reduced the barriers to entry by changing the rules of the game.

Changing the rules also short-circuited Xerox's ability to retaliate quickly against its new rival. Confronted with the need to rethink its business strategy and organization, Xerox was paralyzed for a time. Its managers realized that the faster they downsized the product line, developed new channels, and improved reliability, the faster they would erode the company's traditional profit base. What might have been seen as critical success factors—Xerox's national sales force and service network, its large installed base of leased machines, and its reliance on service revenues—instead became barriers to retaliation. In this sense, competitive innovation is like judo: The goal is to use a larger competitor's weight against it. And that happens not by matching the leader's capabilities but by developing contrasting capabilities of one's own.

Competitive innovation works on the premise that a successful competitor is likely to be wedded to a recipe for success. That's why the most effective weapon new competitors possess is probably a clean sheet of paper. And why an incumbent's greatest vulnerability is its belief in accepted practice.

Through licensing, outsourcing agreements, and joint ventures, it is sometimes possible to win without fighting. For example, Fujitsu's alliances in Europe with Siemens and STC (Britain's largest computer maker) and in the United States with Amdahl yield manufacturing volume and access to Western markets. In the early 1980s, Matsushita established a joint venture with Thorn (in the United Kingdom), Telefunken (in Germany), and Thomson (in France), which allowed it to quickly multiply the forces arrayed against Philips in the battle for leadership in the European VCR business. In fighting larger global rivals by proxy, Japanese companies have adopted a maxim as old as human conflict itself: My enemy's enemy is my friend.

Hijacking the development efforts of potential rivals is another goal of competitive collaboration. In the consumer electronics war, Japanese competitors attacked traditional businesses like TVs and hi-fis while volunteering to manufacture next generation products like VCRs, camcorders, and CD players for Western rivals. They hoped their rivals would ratchet down development spending, and, in most cases, that is precisely what happened. But companies that abandoned their own development efforts seldom reemerged as serious competitors in subsequent new product battles.

Collaboration can also be used to calibrate competitors' strengths and weaknesses. Toyota's joint venture with GM, and Mazda's with Ford, give these automakers an invaluable vantage point for assessing the progress their U.S. rivals have made in cost reduction, quality, and technology. They can also learn how GM and Ford compete—when they will fight and when they won't. Of course, the reverse is also true: Ford and GM have an equal opportunity to learn from their partner-competitors.

The route to competitive revitalization we have been mapping implies a new view of strategy. Strategic intent assures consistency in resource allocation over the long term. Clearly articulated corporate challenges focus the efforts of individuals in the medium term. Finally, competitive innovation helps reduce competitive risk in the short term. This consistency in the long term, focus in the medium term, and inventiveness and involvement in the short term provide the key to leveraging limited resources in pursuit of ambitious goals. But just as there is a process of winning, so there is a process of surrender. Revitalization requires understanding that process, too.

Given their technological leadership and access to large regional markets, how did U.S. and European countries lose their apparent birthright to dominate global industries? There is no simple answer. Few companies recognize the value of documenting failure. Fewer still search their own managerial orthodoxies for the seeds of competitive surrender. But we believe there is a pathology of surrender that gives some important clues. (See the sidebar "The Process of Surrender.")

It is not very comforting to think that the essence of Western strategic thought can be reduced to eight rules for excellence, seven S's, five competitive forces, four product life-cycle stages, three generic strategies, and innumerable two-by-two matrices.[4] Yet for the past 20 years, "advances" in strategy have taken the form of ever more typologies, heuristics, and laundry lists, often with dubious empirical bases. Moreover, even reasonable concepts like the product life cycle, experience curve, product portfolios, and generic strategies often have toxic side effects: They reduce the number of strategic options management is willing to consider. They create a preference for selling businesses rather than defending them. They yield predictable strategies that rivals easily decode.

Strategy recipes limit opportunities for competitive innovation. A company may have 40 businesses and only four strategies— invest, hold, harvest, or divest. Too often, strategy is seen as a positioning exercise in which options are tested by how they fit the existing industry structure. But current industry structure reflects the strengths of the industry leader, and playing by the leader's rules is usually competitive suicide.

Armed with concepts like segmentation, the value chain, competitor benchmarking, strategic groups, and mobility barriers,

The Process of Surrender

On the battles for global leadership that have taken place during the past two decades, we have seen a pattern of competitive attack and retrenchment that was remarkably similar across industries. We call this the process of surrender.

The process started with unseen intent. Not possessing long-term, competitor-focused goals themselves, Western companies did not ascribe such intentions to their rivals. They also calculated the threat posed by potential competitors in terms of their existing resources rather than their resourcefulness. This led to systematic underestimation of smaller rivals who were fast gaining technology through licensing arrangements, acquiring market understanding from downstream OEM partners, and improving product quality and manufacturing productivity through companywide employee involvement programs. Oblivious to the strategic intent and intangible advantages of their rivals, American and European businesses were caught off guard.

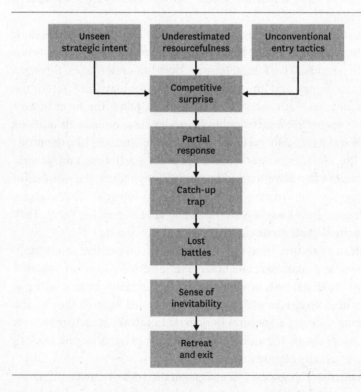

Adding to the competitive surprise was the fact that the new entrants typically attacked the periphery of a market (Honda in small motorcycles, Yamaha in grand pianos, Toshiba in small black-and-white televisions) before going head-to-head with incumbents. Incumbents often misread these attacks, seeing them as part of a niche strategy and not as a search for "loose bricks." Unconventional market entry strategies (minority holdings in less-developed countries, use of nontraditional channels, extensive corporate advertising) were ignored or dismissed as quirky. For example, managers we spoke with said Japanese companies' position in the European computer industry was nonexistent. In terms of brand share that's nearly true, but the Japanese control as much as one-third of the manufacturing value added in the hardware sales of European-based computer businesses. Similarly, German auto producers claimed to feel unconcerned over the proclivity of Japanese producers to move upmarket. But with its low-end models under tremendous pressure from Japanese producers, Porsche has now announced that it will no longer make "entry level" cars.

Western managers often misinterpreted their rivals' tactics. They believed that Japanese and Korean companies were competing solely on the basis of cost and quality. This typically produced a partial response to those competitors' initiatives: moving manufacturing offshore, outsourcing, or instituting a quality program. Seldom was the full extent of the competitive threat appreciated—the multiple layers of advantage, the expansion across related product segments, the development of global brand positions. Imitating the currently visible tactics of rivals put Western businesses into a perpetual catch-up trap. One by one, companies lost battles and came to see surrender as inevitable. Surrender was not inevitable, of course, but the attack was staged in a way that disguised ultimate intentions and sidestepped direct confrontation.

many managers have become better and better at drawing industry maps. But while they have been busy mapmaking, their competitors have been moving entire continents. The strategist's goal is not to find a niche within the existing industry space but to create new space that is uniquely suited to the company's own strengths—space that is off the map.

This is particularly true now that industry boundaries are becoming more and more unstable. In industries such as financial services and communications, rapidly changing technology, deregulation, and globalization have undermined the value of traditional industry analysis. Mapmaking skills are worth little in the epicenter of an earthquake. But an industry in upheaval presents opportunities for ambitious companies to redraw the map in their favor, so long as they can think outside traditional industry boundaries.

Concepts like "mature" and "declining" are largely definitional. What most executives mean when they label a business "mature" is that sales growth has stagnated in their current geographic markets for existing products sold through existing channels. In such cases, it's not the industry that is mature, but the executives' conception of the industry. Asked if the piano business was mature, a senior executive at Yamaha replied, "Only if we can't take any market share from anybody anywhere in the world and still make money. And anyway, we're not in the 'piano' business, we're in the 'keyboard' business." Year after year, Sony has revitalized its radio and tape recorder businesses, despite the fact that other manufacturers long ago abandoned these businesses as mature.

A narrow concept of maturity can foreclose a company from a broad stream of future opportunities. In the 1970s, several U.S. companies thought that consumer electronics had become a mature industry. What could possibly top the color TV? they asked themselves. RCA and GE, distracted by opportunities in more "attractive" industries like mainframe computers, left Japanese producers with a virtual monopoly in VCRs, camcorders, and CD players. Ironically, the TV business, once thought mature, is on the verge of a dramatic renaissance. A $20-billion-a-year business will be created when high-definition television is launched in the United States. But the pioneers of television may capture only a small part of this bonanza.

Most of the tools of strategic analysis are focused domestically. Few force managers to consider global opportunities and threats. For example, portfolio planning portrays top management's investment options as an array of businesses rather than as an array of geographic markets. The result is predictable: As businesses come under attack from foreign competitors, the company attempts to abandon them and enter other areas in which the forces of global competition are not yet so strong. In the short term, this may be an appropriate response to waning competitiveness, but there are fewer and fewer businesses in which a domestic-oriented company can find refuge. We seldom hear such companies asking, Can we move into emerging markets overseas ahead of our global rivals and prolong the profitability of this business? Can we counterattack in our global competitors' home market and slow the pace of their expansion? A senior executive in one successful global company made a telling comment: "We're glad to find a competitor managing by the portfolio concept—we can almost predict how much share we'll have to take away to put the business on the CEO's 'sell list.'"

Companies can also be overcommitted to organizational recipes, such as strategic business units (SBUs) and the decentralization an SBU structure implies. Decentralization is seductive because it places the responsibility for success or failure squarely on the shoulders of line managers. Each business is assumed to have all the resources it needs to execute its strategies successfully, and in this no-excuses environment, it is hard for top management to fail. But desirable as clear lines of responsibility and accountability are, competitive revitalization requires positive value added from top management.

Few companies with a strong SBU orientation have built successful global distribution and brand positions. Investments in a global brand franchise typically transcend the resources and risk propensity of a single business. While some Western companies have had global brand positions for 30 or 40 years or more (Heinz, Siemens, IBM, Ford, and Kodak, for example), it is hard to identify any American or European company that has created a new global brand franchise in the past ten to 15 years. Yet Japanese companies have created a score or more—NEC, Fujitsu, Panasonic (Matsushita), Toshiba, Sony, Seiko, Epson, Canon, Minolta, and Honda among them.

General Electric's situation is typical. In many of its businesses, this American giant has been almost unknown in Europe and Asia. GE made no coordinated effort to build a global corporate franchise. Any GE business with international ambitions had to bear the burden of establishing its credibility and credentials in the new market alone. Not surprisingly, some once-strong GE businesses opted out of the difficult task of building a global brand position. By contrast, smaller Korean companies like Samsung, Daewoo, and Lucky-Goldstar are busy building global-brand umbrellas that will ease market entry for a whole range of businesses. The underlying principle is simple: Economies of scope may be as important as economies of scale in entering global markets. But capturing economies of scope demands interbusiness coordination that only top management can provide.

We believe that inflexible SBU-type organizations have also contributed to the de-skilling of some companies. For a single SBU, incapable of sustaining an investment in a core competence such as semiconductors, optical media, or combustion engines, the only way to remain competitive is to purchase key components from potential (often Japanese or Korean) competitors. For an SBU defined in product market terms, competitiveness means offering an end product that is competitive in price and performance. But that gives an SBU manager little incentive to distinguish between external sourcing that achieves "product embodied" competitiveness and internal development that yields deeply embedded organizational competencies that can be exploited across multiple businesses. Where upstream component-manufacturing activities are seen as cost centers with cost-plus transfer pricing, additional investment in the core activity may seem a less profitable use of capital than investment in downstream activities. To make matters worse, internal accounting data may not reflect the competitive value of retaining control over a core competence.

Together, a shared global corporate brand franchise and a shared core competence act as mortar in many Japanese companies. Lacking this mortar, a company's businesses are truly loose bricks—easily knocked out by global competitors that steadily invest in core competences. Such competitors can co-opt domestically oriented companies into long-term sourcing dependence and capture the economies of scope of global brand investment through interbusiness coordination.

Last in decentralization's list of dangers is the standard of managerial performance typically used in SBU organizations. In many companies, business unit managers are rewarded solely on the basis of their performance against return on investment targets. Unfortunately, that often leads to denominator management because executives soon discover that reductions in investment and head count—the denominator—"improve" the financial ratios by which they are measured more easily than growth in the numerator: revenues. It also fosters a hair-trigger sensitivity to industry downturns that can be very costly. Managers who are quick to reduce investment and dismiss workers find it takes much longer to regain lost skills and catch up on investment when the industry turns upward again. As a result, they lose market share in every business cycle. Particularly in industries where there is fierce competition for the best people and where competitors invest relentlessly, denominator management creates a retrenchment ratchet.

The concept of the general manager as a movable peg reinforces the problem of denominator management. Business schools are guilty here because they have perpetuated the notion that a manager with net present value calculations in one hand and portfolio planning in the other can manage any business anywhere.

In many diversified companies, top management evaluates line managers on numbers alone because no other basis for dialogue exists. Managers move so many times as part of their "career development" that they often do not understand the nuances of the businesses they are managing. At GE, for example, one fast-track manager heading an important new venture had moved across five businesses in five years. His series of quick successes finally came to an end when he confronted a Japanese competitor whose managers had been plodding along in the same business for more than a decade.

Regardless of ability and effort, fast-track managers are unlikely to develop the deep business knowledge they need to discuss technology options, competitors' strategies, and global opportunities substantively. Invariably, therefore, discussions gravitate to "the numbers," while the value added of managers is limited to the financial and planning savvy they carry from job to job. Knowledge of the company's internal planning and accounting systems substitutes for substantive knowledge of the business, making competitive innovation unlikely.

When managers know that their assignments have a two- to three-year time frame, they feel great pressure to create a good track record fast. This pressure often takes one of two forms. Either the manager does not commit to goals whose time line extends beyond his or her expected tenure. Or ambitious goals are adopted and squeezed into an unrealistically short time frame. Aiming to be number one in a business is the essence of strategic intent; but imposing a three- to four-year horizon on the effort simply invites disaster. Acquisitions are made with little attention to the problems of integration. The organization becomes overloaded with initiatives. Collaborative ventures are formed without adequate attention to competitive consequences.

Almost every strategic management theory and nearly every corporate planning system is premised on a strategy hierarchy in which corporate goals guide business unit strategies and business unit strategies guide functional tactics.[5] In this hierarchy, senior management makes strategy and lower levels execute it. The dichotomy between formulation and implementation is familiar and widely accepted. But the strategy hierarchy undermines competitiveness by fostering an elitist view of management that tends to disenfranchise most of the organization. Employees fail to identify with corporate goals or involve themselves deeply in the work of becoming more competitive.

The strategy hierarchy isn't the only explanation for an elitist view of management, of course. The myths that grow up around successful top managers—"Lee Iacocca saved Chrysler," "Carlo De Benedetti rescued Olivetti," "John Sculley turned Apple around"— perpetuate it. So does the turbulent business environment. Middle managers buffeted by circumstances that seem to be beyond their control desperately want to believe that top management has all the answers. And top management, in turn, hesitates to admit it does not for fear of demoralizing lower-level employees.

The result of all this is often a code of silence in which the full extent of a company's competitiveness problem is not widely shared. We interviewed business unit managers in one company, for example, who were extremely anxious because top management wasn't talking openly about the competitive challenges the company faced. They assumed the lack of communication indicated a lack of awareness on their senior managers' part. But when asked whether they were open with their own employees, these same managers replied that while they could face up to the problems, the people below them could not. Indeed, the only time the workforce heard about the company's competitiveness problems was during wage negotiations when problems were used to extract concessions.

Unfortunately, a threat that everyone perceives but no one talks about creates more anxiety than a threat that has been clearly identified and made the focal point for the problem-solving efforts of the entire company. That is one reason honesty and humility on the part of top management may be the first prerequisite of revitalization. Another reason is the need to make "participation" more than a buzzword.

Programs such as quality circles and total customer service often fall short of expectations because management does not recognize that successful implementation requires more than administrative structures. Difficulties in embedding new capabilities are typically put down to "communication" problems, with the unstated assumption that if only downward communication were more effective—"if only middle management would get the message straight"—the new program would quickly take root. The need for upward communication is often ignored, or assumed to mean nothing more than feedback. In contrast, Japanese companies win not because they have smarter managers but because they have developed ways to harness the "wisdom of the anthill." They realize that top managers are a bit like the astronauts who circle the Earth in the space shuttle. It may be the astronauts who get all the glory, but everyone knows that the real intelligence behind the mission is located firmly on the ground.

Where strategy formulation is an elitist activity, it is also difficult to produce truly creative strategies. For one thing, there are not enough heads and points of view in divisional or corporate planning departments to challenge conventional wisdom. For another, creative strategies seldom emerge from the annual planning ritual. The starting point for next year's strategy is almost always this year's strategy. Improvements are incremental. The company sticks to the segments and territories it knows, even though the real opportunities may be elsewhere. The impetus for Canon's pioneering entry into the personal copier business came from an overseas sales subsidiary, not from planners in Japan.

The goal of the strategy hierarchy remains valid—to ensure consistency up and down the organization. But this consistency is better derived from a clearly articulated strategic intent than from inflexibly applied top-down plans. In the 1990s, the challenge will be to enfranchise employees to invent the means to accomplish ambitious ends.

We seldom found cautious administrators among the top managements of companies that came from behind to challenge incumbents for global leadership. But in studying organizations that had surrendered, we invariably found senior managers who, for whatever reason, lacked the courage to commit their companies to heroic goals—goals that lay beyond the reach of planning and existing resources. The conservative goals they set failed to generate pressure and enthusiasm for competitive innovation or give the organization much useful guidance. Financial targets and vague mission statements just cannot provide the consistent direction that is a prerequisite for winning a global competitive war.

This kind of conservatism is usually blamed on the financial markets. But we believe that in most cases, investors' so-called short-term orientation simply reflects a lack of confidence in the ability of senior managers to conceive and deliver stretch goals. The chairman of one company complained bitterly that even after improving return on capital employed to over 40% (by ruthlessly divesting lackluster businesses and downsizing others), the stock market held the company to an 8:1 price/earnings ratio. Of course, the market's message was clear: "We don't trust you. You've shown no ability to achieve profitable growth. Just cut out the slack, manage the denominators, and perhaps you'll be taken over by a company that can use your resources more creatively." Very little in the track record of most large Western companies warrants the confidence of the stock market. Investors aren't hopelessly short-term; they're justifiably skeptical.

We believe that top management's caution reflects a lack of confidence in its own ability to involve the entire organization in revitalization, as opposed to simply raising financial targets. Developing faith in the organization's ability to deliver on tough goals, motivating it to do so, focusing its attention long enough to internalize new capabilities—this is the real challenge for top management. Only by rising to this challenge will senior managers gain the courage they need to commit themselves and their companies to global leadership.

NOTES

1. Among the first to apply the concept of strategy to management were H. Igor Ansoff in *Corporate Strategy: An Analytic Approach to Business Policy for Growth and Expansion* (McGraw-Hill, 1965) and Kenneth R. Andrews in *The Concept of Corporate Strategy* (Dow Jones-Irwin, 1971).

2. Robert A. Burgelman, "A Process Model of Internal Corporate Venturing in the Diversified Major Firm," *Administrative Science Quarterly,* June 1983.

3. For example, see Michael E. Porter, *Competitive Strategy* (Free Press, 1980).

4. Strategic frameworks for resource allocation in diversified companies are summarized in Charles W. Hofer and Dan E. Schendel, *Strategy Formulation: Analytical Concepts* (West Publishing, 1978).

5. For example, see Peter Lorange and Richard F. Vancil, *Strategic Planning Systems* (Prentice-Hall, 1977).

Reprinted from *Harvard Business Review*,
July–August 2005 (product #R0507N).
Originally published May–June 1989.

ABOUT THE CONTRIBUTORS

TERESA M. AMABILE is a Baker Foundation Professor at Harvard Business School and a coauthor of *The Progress Principle* (Harvard Business Review Press, 2011). Her current research investigates how life inside organizations can influence people and their performance, as well as how people approach and experience the transition to retirement.

DEBORAH ANCONA is the Seley Distinguished Professor of Management, a professor of organization studies, and the founder of the MIT Leadership Center at the Massachusetts Institute of Technology Sloan School of Management. She is the coauthor, with Henrik Bresman, of *X-Teams* (Harvard Business School Press, 2007) and a coauthor of the *Harvard Business Review* article "In Praise of the Incomplete Leader."

SCOTT BERINATO is a senior editor at *Harvard Business Review* and the author of *Good Charts: The HBR Guide to Making Smarter, More Persuasive Data Visualizations* (Harvard Business Review Press, 2016) and *Good Charts Workbook: Tips, Tools, and Exercises for Making Better Data Visualizations* (Harvard Business Review Press, 2019).

AMY BERNSTEIN is the editor of *Harvard Business Review* and vice president and executive editorial director of Harvard Business Publishing. She is also a cohost of the *Women at Work* podcast. Follow her on Twitter @asbernstein2185.

STEVE BLANK is an adjunct professor at Stanford University, a senior fellow at Columbia University, and a lecturer at the University of California, Berkeley. He has been either a cofounder or an early employee at eight high-tech startups, and he helped start the National Science Foundation Innovation Corps and the Hacking for Defense and Hacking for Diplomacy programs. He blogs at www.steveblank.com.

JOSEPH L. BOWER is the Donald Kirk David Professor, Emeritus, at Harvard Business School and a coauthor of the HBR article "Global Capitalism at Risk: What Are You Doing About It?" and the book *Capitalism at Risk* (Harvard Business Review Press, 2011).

TIM BROWN is the executive chair of the international design consulting firm IDEO and the author of *Change by Design*.

ERIK BRYNJOLFSSON is a professor and senior fellow at the Stanford Institute for Human-Centered AI (HAI), the director of the Stanford Digital Economy Lab, and a research associate at the National Bureau of Economic Research. He is the author or coauthor of nine books, including *The Second Machine Age* and *Machine, Platform, Crowd*.

SARAH GREEN CARMICHAEL is an editor and columnist at Bloomberg Opinion and a former executive editor at *Harvard Business Review*. Follow her on Twitter @skgreen.

TOMAS CHAMORRO-PREMUZIC is the chief innovation officer at ManpowerGroup, a professor of business psychology at University College London and at Columbia University, and an associate at Harvard's Entrepreneurial Finance Lab. He is the author of *Why Do So Many Incompetent Men Become Leaders? (and How to Fix It)* (Harvard Business Review Press, 2019), upon which his TEDx talk was based. Follow him on Twitter @drtcp or find him at www.drtomas.com.

CLAYTON M. CHRISTENSEN was the Kim B. Clark Professor of Business Administration at Harvard Business School and a frequent contributor to *Harvard Business Review.*

ROBERT B. CIALDINI is the Regents' Professor of Psychology at Arizona State University and the author of *Influence: The Psychology of Persuasion.* Find regularly updated information about the influence process at www.influenceatwork.com.

STEPHEN R. COVEY was vice chairman of the Franklin Covey Company, a global provider of leadership development and productivity services and products, and the author of *The 7 Habits of Highly Effective People* and *First Things First.*

THOMAS H. DAVENPORT is the President's Distinguished Professor of Information Technology and Management at Babson College, a visiting professor at Oxford's Saïd School of Business, a research fellow at the MIT Initiative on the Digital Economy, and a senior adviser to Deloitte's AI practice.

SUSAN DAVID is a founder of the Harvard/McLean Institute of Coaching, is on faculty at Harvard Medical School, and is recognized as one of the world's leading management thinkers. She is the author of the *Wall Street Journal* number one bestseller *Emotional Agility,* based on the concept named by HBR as a Management Idea of the Year. An in-demand speaker and adviser, David has worked with the senior leadership of hundreds of major organizations, including the United Nations, Ernst & Young, and the World Economic Forum.

PETER F. DRUCKER was a management consultant, educator, and author whose writings contributed to the philosophical and practical foundations of the modern business corporation. He was a leader in the development of management education, invented the concept known as *management by objectives,* and has been described as "the founder of modern management."

AMY C. EDMONDSON is the Novartis Professor of Leadership and Management at Harvard Business School. She is the author of *The Fearless Organization*.

JOHN J. GABARRO is the UPS Foundation Professor of Human Resource Management, Emeritus, at Harvard Business School. He is the author or coauthor of five books, including *Interpersonal Behavior* with Anthony G. Athos and *The Dynamics of Taking Charge*, which won the 1988 New Directions in Leadership Award.

DANIEL GOLEMAN, best known for his writing on emotional intelligence, is codirector of the Consortium for Research on Emotional Intelligence in Organizations at Rutgers University. His latest book is *Building Blocks of Emotional Intelligence*, a 12-primer set on each of the emotional intelligence competencies, and he offers training on the competencies through an online learning platform, Emotional Intelligence Coaching and Training Programs. His other books include *Primal Leadership* (Harvard Business Review Press, 2016) and *Altered Traits*.

JEFF GOTHELF helps organizations build better products and executives build the cultures that build better products. He is a coauthor of the award-winning book *Lean UX* and the Harvard Business Review Press book *Sense and Respond* (2017), and the author of *Forever Employable*. He works as a coach, consultant, and keynote speaker helping companies bridge the gaps between business agility, digital transformation, product management, and human-centered design.

VIJAY GOVINDARAJAN is the Coxe Distinguished Professor of Management at Dartmouth College's Tuck School of Business. He is the author or coauthor of more than a dozen books, including *The Three-Box Solution* (Harvard Business Review Press, 2016) and *Reverse Innovation* (Harvard Business Review Press, 2012).

HEIDI GRANT is a social psychologist who researches, writes, and speaks about the science of motivation. She is the director of research and development for EY Americas Learning and serves as associate director of Columbia's Motivation Science Center. Her most recent book is *Reinforcements* (Harvard Business Review Press, 2018). She is also the author of *Nine Things Successful People Do Differently* (Harvard Business Review Press, 2012) and *No One Understands You and What to Do About It* (Harvard Business Review Press, 2015).

GARY HAMEL is a visiting professor at London Business School and the founder of the Management Lab. He is a coauthor of *Humanocracy* (Harvard Business Review Press, 2020).

FREDERICK HERZBERG was formerly Distinguished Professor of Management at the University of Utah, in Salt Lake City, and head of the department of psychology at Case Western Reserve University, in Cleveland. His writings include the book *Work and the Nature of Man*.

LINDA A. HILL is the Wallace Brett Donham Professor of Business Administration at Harvard Business School. She is the author of *Becoming a Manager* (Harvard Business School Press, 2019) and a coauthor of *Being the Boss* (Harvard Business Review Press, 2019) and *Collective Genius* (Harvard Business Review Press, 2014).

ADI IGNATIUS is the editor in chief of *Harvard Business Review*.

AMANTHA IMBER is the founder of behavioral science consultancy Inventium and the host of *How I Work*, a podcast about the habits and rituals of the world's most successful people.

KATE ISAACS is a research affiliate at the MIT Leadership Center, a partner at Dialogos Generative Capital, and an executive fellow at the Center for Higher Ambition Leadership. She helps companies and multistakeholder collaboratives create social and economic value through trust-based relationships.

DAVID KESSLER is the world's foremost expert on grief and a co-author, with Elisabeth Kübler-Ross, of *On Grief and Grieving*. His latest book is *Finding Meaning: The Sixth Stage of Grief*. He is the founder of Grief.com.

W. CHAN KIM is a professor of strategy and management at INSEAD and codirector of the INSEAD Blue Ocean Strategy Institute, in Fontainebleau, France. He is the coauthor, along with Renée Mauborgne, of the book *Blue Ocean Strategy, Expanded Edition* (Harvard Business Review Press, 2015). Find out more at www.blueoceanstrategy.com.

JOHN P. KOTTER is a bestselling author, award-winning business and management thought leader, business entrepreneur, and the Konosuke Matsushita Professor of Leadership, Emeritus, at Harvard Business School. His ideas, books, and company, Kotter, help people lead organizations in an era of increasingly rapid change. He is a coauthor of the book *Change*, which details how leaders can leverage challenges and opportunities to make sustainable workplace changes in a rapidly accelerating world.

STEVEN J. KRAMER is an independent researcher, writer, and consultant in Wayland, Massachusetts. He is a coauthor of the HBR articles "Creativity Under the Gun" and "Inner Work Life" and of the book *The Progress Principle* (Harvard Business Review Press, 2011).

THEODORE LEVITT was a longtime professor of marketing at Harvard Business School and later professor emeritus. He is the author of *Thinking About Management* and *The Marketing Imagination*.

ROBERT LIVINGSTON is the author of *The Conversation: How Seeking and Speaking the Truth About Racism Can Radically Trans-*

form Individuals and Organizations. He also serves on the faculty of the Harvard Kennedy School.

RENÉE MAUBORGNE is a professor of strategy and management at INSEAD and codirector of the INSEAD Blue Ocean Strategy Institute, in Fontainebleau, France. She is the coauthor, along with W. Chan Kim, of *Blue Ocean Strategy, Expanded Edition* (Harvard Business Review Press, 2015). Find out more at www .blueoceanstrategy.com.

ANDREW McAFEE is a cofounder of the Initiative on the Digital Economy in the MIT Sloan School of Management. He is the author of *Enterprise 2.0* (Harvard Business Review Press, 2009) and a coauthor of *The Second Machine Age*.

MARK MORTENSEN is an associate professor of organizational behavior at INSEAD. He researches, teaches, and consults on issues of collaboration, organizational design and new ways of working, and leadership.

CURT NICKISCH is a senior editor at *Harvard Business Review*, where he makes podcasts and cohosts *HBR IdeaCast*. He previously reported for NPR's *Marketplace*, WBUR, and *Fast Company*. He speaks *ausgezeichnet* German and binges history podcasts. Find him on Twitter @CurtNickisch.

INDRA K. NOOYI was the chairperson and CEO of PepsiCo from 2006 to 2018 and is now a member of the boards of directors of Amazon and Schlumberger.

WILLIAM ONCKEN, JR., was the chairman of the William Oncken Corporation until his death in 1988. His son, William Oncken III, now heads the company.

TINA OPIE is the founder of Opie Consulting Group LLC, where she advises large firms in the financial services, entertainment, media, beauty, educational, and health-care industries. She is an award-winning researcher, a consultant, an associate professor of management at Babson College, and a visiting scholar at Harvard Business School. Her work has appeared in such outlets as *O Magazine*, the *Washington Post*, the *Boston Globe*, and *Harvard Business Review*. She is also a regular commentator on HBR's *Women at Work* podcast and Greater Boston's PBS affiliate television station WGBH. She is a coauthor of the book *Shared Sisterhood* (Harvard Business Review Press, 2022).

ANDREA OVANS is a former senior editor at *Harvard Business Review*.

D.J. PATIL was appointed as the first U.S. chief data scientist and has led product development at LinkedIn, eBay, and PayPal. He is the author of *Data Jujitsu*.

MICHAEL E. PORTER is a university professor at Harvard, based at Harvard Business School, in Boston. He is a coauthor of *The Politics Industry* (Harvard Business Review Press, 2020).

C.K. PRAHALAD was the Paul and Ruth McCracken Distinguished University Professor of Strategy at the University of Michigan's Ross School of Business.

KATHLEEN REARDON is professor emerita at the University of Southern California Marshall School of Business and an expert in workplace politics, persuasion, and negotiation. She is the author of the Amazon bestsellers *The Secret Handshake*, *It's All Politics*, and *Comebacks at Work*. She is also the author of *Shadow Campus*, a crime mystery, and just completed writing a second crime mystery focusing on sexual misconduct, *Damned If She Does*. Her blog and art website is www.kathleenkelleyreardon.com.

F. J. ROETHLISBERGER was the Wallace Brett Donham Professor of Human Relations at the Harvard Business School. His writings include *Man-in-Organization* and other books and articles.

CARL R. ROGERS was a professor of psychology at the University of Chicago. His many books include the groundbreaking *Client-Centered Therapy*.

MEHAK SARANG is a research associate at Harvard Business School and the Lunar Exploration Projects Lead for the MIT Space Exploration Initiative.

KABIR SEHGAL is the *New York Times* and *Wall Street Journal* bestselling author of seven books, including *Coined: The Rich Life of Money and How Its History Has Shaped Us*. He works in corporate strategy at a *Fortune* 500 company and previously served as a vice president at J. P. Morgan. He is also a U.S. Navy veteran and a multiple Grammy and Latin Grammy Award–winning producer. You can follow him on Twitter @kabirsehgal or find him on Facebook.

NIGEL TOPPING serves as the CEO of We Mean Business coalition, which harnesses business leadership to drive the innovations and policies that accelerate action on climate change. Previously, he was the executive director of CDP (formerly the Carbon Disclosure Project), and he has 18 years of experience in the manufacturing sector.

NICOLE TORRES is an editor at Bloomberg Opinion, based in London, and a former senior editor at *Harvard Business Review*.

CHRIS TRIMBLE is on the faculties of the Tuck School of Business at Dartmouth and the Dartmouth Institute for Health Policy and Clinical Practice. He is the author of *How Physicians Can Fix Health Care*.

DONALD L. WASS was the president of the William Oncken Company of Texas. He later headed the Dallas–Fort Worth region of The Executive Committee (TEC), an international organization for presidents and CEOs.

MATT WEINZIERL is the Joseph and Jacqueline Elbling Professor of Business Administration at Harvard Business School and a research associate at the National Bureau of Economic Research. His research and teaching focus on the design of economic policy and the economics and business of space.

INDEX

Engage with HBR content the way you want, on any device.

With HBR's subscription plans, you can access world-renowned case studies from Harvard Business School and receive four **free eBooks**. Download and customize prebuilt **slide decks and graphics** from our **Data & Visuals** collection. With HBR's archive, top 50 best-selling articles, and five new articles every day, HBR is more than just a magazine.

Subscribe Today
HBR.org/success